THE PLACES TO KISS™

IN NORTHERN CALIFORNIA

A Romantic Travel Guide

COMPLETELY REVISED
4th EDITION
AND UPDATED

by

Stephanie Bell,
Elizabeth Janda & Laura Kraemer

BEGINNING
PRESS

OTHER BOOKS IN THE

BEST PLACES TO KISS™

SERIES:

The Best Places To Kiss In Southern California, 4th Edition $13.95

The Best Places To Kiss In The Northwest, 6th Edition $15.95

The Best Places To Kiss In Hawaii, 2nd Edition $12.95

ANY OF THESE BOOKS CAN BE ORDERED DIRECTLY FROM THE PUBLISHER.

Please send a check or money order for the total
amount of the books, plus shipping and handling
($3 for the first book, and $1 for each additional book) to:

Beginning Press
5418 South Brandon
Seattle, Washington 98118

All prices are listed in U.S. funds.
For information about ordering from Canada or to place
an order using Visa or MasterCard, call (206) 723-6300.

Art Direction and Production: Studio Pacific, Inc.
Cover Design: Studio Pacific, Inc., Deb McCarroll
Editors: Miriam Bulmer and Laura Kraemer
Printing: Publishers Press
Contributor: Kristin Folsom

Copyright 1990, 1992, 1994, 1996 by Paula Begoun

First Edition: June 1990
Second Edition: June 1992
Third Edition: June 1994
Fourth Edition: January 1997
  2 3 4 5 6 7 8 9 10

BEST PLACES TO KISS™

is a registered trademark of Beginning Press
ISBN 1-877988-19-7

This book is distributed to the U.S. book trade by:
Publisher's Group West
4065 Hollis Street
Emeryville, CA 94608
(800) 788-3123

This book is distributed to the Canadian book trade by:
Raincoast Books
8680 Cambie Street
Vancouver, B.C.
V6P-6M9
Canada
(800) 663-5714

"As usual with most lovers in the city, they were troubled by the lack of that essential need of love—a meeting place."

Thomas Wolfe

Publisher's Note

Travel books have many different criteria for the places they include. We would like the reader to know that this book is not an advertising vehicle. As is true in all *The Best Places To Kiss* books, the businesses included were not charged fees, nor did they pay us for their reviews. This book is a sincere, unbiased effort to highlight those special parts of the region that are filled with romance and splendor. Sometimes those places were created by people, such as restaurants, inns, lounges, lodges, hotels, and bed and breakfasts. Sometimes those places are untouched by people and simply created by God for us to enjoy. Wherever you go, be gentle with each other and with the earth.

The publisher made the final decision on the recommendations in this collection, but we would love to hear what you think of our suggestions. We strive to create a reliable guide for your amorous outings, and in this quest for blissful sojourns, your romantic feedback assists greatly in increasing our accuracy and our resources for information. If you have any additional comments, criticisms, or cherished memories of your own from a place we directed you to or a place you discovered on your own, feel free to write us at:

Beginning Press
5418 South Brandon Street
Seattle, WA 98118

We would love to hear from you!

" *What of soul was left, I wonder, when the kissing had to stop?*"

Robert Browning

Table of Contents

The Fine Art of Kissing

Why It's Still Best To Kiss In Northern California

It is no secret that Northern California is a splendid part of the world. For those of us who kiss and tell for a living, it is simply our favorite place to visit again and again. Every region is brimming with romantic potential. From the brilliant lights of San Francisco, it is only a short drive to mountains, forests, vineyards, rugged shorelines, and sandy beaches. Regardless of the season or the area, misty mornings, sultry afternoons, and cool evenings are standard. The seasons themselves are all exhilarating and temperate: mild winters, lush autumns, vivid springs, perfect summers. In short, there probably is not a more diverse, yet compact, place in the world in which to pucker up.

From the North Coast and South Coast to Wine Country, the Bay Area, Lake Tahoe, and the mesmerizing terrain of Yosemite National Park—all will ignite your imagination and your passions. If you've ever longed for a special place to share time together, you'll find it in Northern California. Charming wineries, elite bed and breakfasts, fanciful hot-air balloons, alluring restaurants, scenic hikes, lofty woods, city streets filled with extravagant shopping, expansive parks, not to mention the ocean and the bridges and the valleys and the entertainment and . . . in short, Northern California is an adult carnival. From the Sierras to the shore, the vitality and romance here are contagious, and when you're accompanied by the right someone, the only challenge will be to find the lovable niche that serves your hearts best.

You Call This Research?

This book was undertaken primarily as a journalistic effort and is the product of ongoing interviews, travel, thorough investigation, and critical observation. Although it would have been nice, even preferable, kissing was not the major research method used to select the locations listed in this book. If smooching had been the determining factor, several inescapable problems would have developed. First, we would still be researching, and this book would be just a good idea, some breathless moments, random notes, and nothing more. Second, depending on the mood of the moment, many kisses might have occurred in places that do not meet the requirements of this travel guide. Therefore, for both practical and physical reasons, more objective criteria had to be established.

You may be wondering how, if we did not kiss at every location during our research, we could be certain that a particular place was good for such an activity? The answer is that we employed our reporters' instincts to evaluate the heartfelt, magnetic pull of each place we visited. If, upon examining a place, we felt a longing inside to share what we had discovered with our special someone, we considered this to be as reliable as a kissing analysis. In the final evaluation, we can guarantee that when you visit any of the places listed, you will be assured of some degree of privacy, a beautiful setting, heart-stirring ambience, and romantic accommodations. What you do when you get there is up to you and your partner.

Rating Romance

The three major factors that determined whether or not we included a place were:

- Privacy
- Location/view/setting
- Ambience

Of these determining factors, "privacy" and "location" are fairly self-explanatory, but "ambience" can probably use some clarification. Wonderful, loving environments are not just four-poster beds covered with down quilts and lace pillows, or tables decorated with white tablecloths and nicely folded linen napkins. Instead, there must be other engaging features that encourage intimacy and allow for uninterrupted affectionate discourse. For the most part, ambience was rated according to degree of comfort and number of gracious appointments, as opposed to image and frills

If a place had all three factors going for it, inclusion was automatic. But if one or two of the criteria were weak or nonexistent, the other feature(s) had to be superior before the location would be included. For example, if a breathtakingly beautiful panoramic vista was in a spot that's inundated with tourists and children on field trips, the place was not included. If a fabulous bed and breakfast was set in a less than desirable location, it would be included if, and only if, its interior was so wonderfully inviting and cozy that the outside world no longer mattered. Extras like complimentary champagne, handmade truffles, or extraordinary service earned brownie points and frequently determined the difference between three-and-a-half and four-lip ratings.

Romantic Note: If you're planning to celebrate a special occasion, such as an anniversary or birthday, we highly recommend telling the proprietors about it when making your reservation. Many bed and breakfasts and hotels offer "special occasion packages," which can include a complimentary bottle of wine, breakfast in bed, fresh flowers, and special touches during turndown service, like dimmed lights and your beloved's favorite CD playing in the background to set the right romantic mood. Restaurants are also sometimes willing to accommodate special occasions by offering free desserts or helping you coordinate a surprise proposal.

Kiss Ratings

The lip rating following each entry is our way of indicating just how romantic we thought a place was and how contented we were during our visit. The number of lips awarded each location indicates:

No lips	=	Reputed to be a romantic destination, but we strongly disagree
💋	=	Romantic possibilities with potential drawbacks
💋💋	=	Can provide a satisfying experience
💋💋💋	=	Very desirable
💋💋💋💋	=	Simply sublime
Unrated	=	Not open at the time this edition went to print, but looks promising

Cost Ratings

We have included additional ratings to help you determine whether your lips can afford to kiss in a particular restaurant, hotel, or bed and breakfast. (Almost all of the outdoor places are free; some charge a small fee.) The price for overnight accommodations is always based on double occupancy; otherwise there wouldn't be anyone to kiss. Eating establishment prices are based on a full dinner for two, excluding liquor, unless otherwise indicated. Because prices and business hours change, it is always advisable to call each place you plan to visit, so your lips will not end up disappointed.

Restaurants

Inexpensive	Less than $30
Moderate	$30 to $50
Expensive	$50 to $80
Very Expensive	$80 to $110
Unbelievably Expensive	More than $110

Lodgings

Inexpensive	Less than $95
Moderate	$95 to $115
Expensive	$115 to $155
Very Expensive	$155 to $250
Unbelievably Expensive	More than $250

Wedding Bells

One of the most auspicious times to kiss is the moment after you've exchanged wedding vows. The setting for that magical moment can vary, from your own cozy living room to a lush garden perched at the ocean's edge to a grand ballroom at an elegant downtown hotel. As an added service to those of you in the midst of prenuptial arrangements, we have indicated which properties have impressive wedding facilities. For more specific information about the facilities and services offered, please call the establishments directly. They should be able to provide you with menus, prices, and all the details needed to make your wedding day as spectacular as you have ever imagined.

Romantic Note: If wedding bells aren't in your near future and you are going to an establishment that specializes in weddings and private parties, call ahead to ensure that a function isn't scheduled during your stay. Unless you hope that seeing a wedding will magically inspire your partner to "pop the question," you might feel like uninvited guests.

North Coast

If you've never witnessed the North Coast's indescribably dramatic and arresting scenery, be prepared for the visual experience of a lifetime. Unlike the developed coastline south of San Francisco, this rugged, breathtaking shoreline remains relatively pristine and unblemished. Much of the surrounding region consists of sprawling pastoral farmland, poised in direct contrast to the dynamic Northern California coast. In some areas, turbulent, foaming whitecaps thunder against the coast's tall, rocky cliffs; in other areas, waves lap gently at beaches or sand dunes overgrown with grass and wildflowers. Not surprisingly, the coast offers many superlative places to stay, eat, and hike, though not in such abundance that the region's natural beauty has been obstructed in any way. We can't think of a better setting for romance—kissing here seems inevitable.

Romantic Note: Many of the Hotel/Bed and Breakfast Kissing options in this chapter are situated on Highway 1. In some cases, traffic noise is a drawback, but a location on Highway 1 can also mean a remarkable ocean-front setting. Throughout this chapter, we have noted each establishment's relation to the highway and whether road noise is a problem or not.

Outdoor Kissing

HIGHWAY 1

Highway 1 breaks off from Highway 101 near the town of Leggett, about 80 miles south of Eureka, and extends south to the Golden Gate Bridge.

Northern California Coast Highway 1 is an exhilarating roller-coaster ride of a lifetime. A compact two-lane roadway writhes along terrain that would otherwise seem impassable. Hugging the ocean from atop towering cliffs, each turn capriciously switches back on itself, following the edge so closely that you may feel like you're hang-gliding instead of motoring. At other times, feeling the ocean mist on your face and hearing the surf's constant cry, you can imagine you're sailing.

Be sure to allow enough time to travel this highway at a leisurely, touring pace. With myriad coiled turns and a lack of passing lanes, maneuvering and speeding are impossible. Scads of turnoffs will demand your attention, so go slowly and stop at any intriguing point to take in the visual glory. Each corner and each turn has views so astonishing that a warning seems in order: driving and kissing don't mix! Before you indulge, pull over and park the car; you can return to negotiating the narrow turns later.

Romantic Warning: If you are in a hurry to get to points south, do yourselves and the rest of the traffic on Highway 1 a favor: take Highway 101.

Eureka

Eureka, the northernmost town included in this book, is located about five and a half hours from San Francisco via Highway 101 or about three hours from Mendocino if you are traveling up the coast on Highway 1.

Only 75 miles south of the Oregon border, the modern-day logging town of Eureka is considerably more than a hop, skip, and a jump from the coastal village of Mendocino, and it is hard to recommend a trip here just for the sights. Yes, the redwoods on the way are amazing, and yes, the town has a lot of Victorian buildings to look at and antique shops to look through. Still, we are hesitant to recommend that you make the three-hour drive up here from Mendocino. However, if you happen to be in this neck of the redwoods, you'll be glad to know we found some wonderful places to kiss.

Hotel/Bed and Breakfast Kissing

HOTEL CARTER, Eureka
301 L Street
(707) 444-8062, (800) 404-1390
Moderate to Expensive

Pick up this pale yellow Victorian and plant it in Wine Country or even just a bit farther south in Mendocino and this review would read like a dream come true. Comments like this have been driving the very dedicated owners of this inn crazy for years. No matter how hard they work to make their hotel lovely (and it truly is), the fact remains that Eureka is hardly a destination spot on its own, and Hotel Carter's location right in town is not exactly peaceful. Having said all this, let us explain why an overnight stay here can still be a thoroughly kissable experience.

Comfort and gracious service are immediately evident when you enter the comfortably plush lobby. Soft beige couches and chairs are placed around a crackling fireplace, and afternoon wine and hors' d'oeuvres are set out for all to enjoy. Twenty-three rooms, each with taupe walls, weathered pine furnishings, wooden shutters, antique pine armoires (holding entertainment centers), and Adirondack-style couches or chairs, are dispersed over three floors. The most luxurious rooms are on the third floor; they feature marble wood-burning fireplaces, jetted tubs for two, and double-headed showers, and some have massive pine four-poster beds. In addition to all this, the best restaurant in town is located on the hotel's main level (see Restaurant Kissing) and you should definitely reserve a table for dinner. If you don't splurge on dessert at dinnertime (or even if you do), venture to the lobby for warm homemade cookies and soothing herbal tea before bed.

A delicious gourmet breakfast, also included with your stay, is served in the restaurant each morning. Regardless of how we happen to feel about Eureka, the innkeepers' hometown enthusiasm is endearing, and the inn's warm hospitality welcomes you with open arms.

Romantic Alternative: Kitty-corner to the Hotel Carter, and under the same ownership, is the **CARTER HOUSE**, 1033 Third Street, (707) 445-1390, (800) 404-1390 (Moderate to Expensive). This is where the Carter family's hotel business started about 15 years ago, with the construction of an impressive dark brown Victorian with towering brick chimneys. There are five guest rooms here, in what is now called the Original Carter House, each with polished hardwood floors, antique headboards and furnishings, wooden shutters, and varying fabrics. Three more rooms are available in Bell Cottage, another Victorian just two doors down. These rooms have a modern edge, with halogen lamps, black leather furniture, parquet wood floors, and boldly printed fabrics in shades of gray and black. Rooms in the Original Carter House and Bell Cottage are not as luxurious as those across the street at Hotel Carter. They have more of a bed-and-breakfast feeling, but because the staff is also over at Hotel Carter, there isn't the hands-on attention that many bed-and-breakfast-goers appreciate. For the best of both worlds (luxury and service), we recommend that you stay in one of the rooms at the Hotel Carter.

Restaurant Kissing

RESTAURANT 301 AT THE HOTEL CARTER, Eureka
301 L Street
(707) 444-8062
Moderate to Expensive
Dinner Daily

Restaurant 301 at the Hotel Carter brings a whole new level of dining to Eureka, not only in terms of food but with its exquisitely sophisticated dining room. Stylish tapestries hang from the high ceiling, modern artwork dresses the warm beige walls, and candles and little lanterns flicker at every crisp white linen–covered table. Pale pine furnishings lend European flair, and tall windows look out to the street and the harbor in the distance. The regionally influenced menu, featuring local seafood, meat, and produce, changes weekly, and there is a different prix fixe meal nightly. Each entrée comes with homemade soup or salad; we're partial to the salad with mixed greens picked fresh from the hotel's own organic garden, just across the street. After your starting course and possibly a glass of wine (the wine list is extensive), consider the mushroom-stuffed chicken breast with tarragon cream or the sautéed scallops with sesame, ginger, and soy. The kitchen's focus is on keeping flavors clear and full, and the presentation is lovely. Top off your meal with an unforgettable dessert—perhaps the bread pudding drenched in warm caramel sauce—then call it a night (an exceptional night, we might add).

Ferndale

Several hours north of San Francisco (much longer if you drive up the coast instead of taking Interstate 5), the Victorian village of Ferndale hugs the hills of the Eel River Valley. Beautifully preserved Victorian homes line the residential streets, and dozens of boutiques, antique stores, coffee shops, and art galleries lure tourists from all over. Even if this small, out-of-the-way town, now a State Historic Landmark, weren't so affable, it would be well worth visiting for the infamous GINGERBREAD MANSION INN alone (see Hotel/Bed and Breakfast Kissing).

Hotel/Bed and Breakfast Kissing

GINGERBREAD MANSION INN, Ferndale   ❦ ❦ ❦ ❦
400 Berding Street
(707) 786-4000, (800) 952-4136
http://www.bbonline.com/ca/gingerbread/
Moderate to Very Expensive

With its elaborate trim and manicured shrubs, the peach and yellow Gingerbread Mansion Inn graces the covers of innumerable guidebooks. It's not surprising that this Victorian mansion is one of Northern California's most photographed homes—the Gingerbread is as pretty as a picture. Built in 1899 as a private residence, the expansive Victorian now operates as a ten-room bed and breakfast. From the gleaming hardwood floors in the downstairs common areas to the Battenburg lace comforters in every guest room, the owner of this marvelous home has attended to every detail with painstaking care.

Each elegant room has been lovingly decorated with old-fashioned wallpaper, beautiful antiques, luscious linens and fabrics, and romantic fireplaces. Two claw-foot tubs placed toe-to-toe in several of the spacious, sunlit bathrooms add a frolicking touch. Deciding among the different but equally gorgeous rooms can be difficult, but if a splurge is in your budget, the newly finished Empire Suite should be your first choice. Situated at the top of the house, this dramatic suite is actually a converted attic with peaked 12-foot ceilings, alcoves, and gables. Rich gold and black Regency Revival wallpaper has been artistically applied to the angular walls. White classical ionic columns frame an enormous king-size bed draped with luxurious, sexy black-and-gold Egyptian cotton linens. A claw-foot tub and an oversized glass-enclosed shower (with five massage jets and three shower heads) face a gas fireplace at one end of the suite. At the other end, a cozy love seat faces a second fireplace and a sumptuous reading chair (big enough for two) is tucked into a corner alcove under a softly lit reading lamp. You'll feel on top of the world in this spectacular room, especially when your gourmet breakfast arrives at your doorstep. (Other guests also have the option to have breakfast in bed.) In the afternoon you can enjoy a vast array of choice hors d'oeuvres served on hand-painted china in the formal sitting room, which brims with turn-of-the-century antiques.

Restaurant Kissing

CURLEY'S GRILL, Ferndale
460 Main Street
(707) 786-9696
Moderate
Lunch and Dinner Daily

Romantic restaurants are few and far between in this area, but Curley's excels even without competition. Casual but classy, this one-room restaurant has a handful of nicely spaced tables topped with handcrafted wood salt and pepper shakers; track lighting illuminates vivid local artwork. For the most privacy (and the best kissing), request one of the tables tucked into a window alcove. The menu is on the casual side, with an abundance of soups, sandwiches, and seafood, but everything is superbly prepared and graciously presented. At the end of the meal, desserts are showcased on a tray at your table—save room, because they are irresistible!

Garberville

Hotel/Bed and Breakfast Kissing

BENBOW INN, Garberville
445 Lake Benbow Drive
(707) 923-2124, (800) 355-3301
http://www.cdiguide.com

Moderate to Unbelievably Expensive
Minimum stay requirement on weekends
Closed January through mid-April

Mile after mile of ancient towering redwoods draws tourists north on Highway 101, but surprisingly few overnight accommodations in this region cater to the romantically-inclined. We wouldn't recommend the Benbow Inn as a destination unto itself, but this National Historic Landmark, set just off the highway and surrounded by stands of oak and redwood, makes a perfect stopover on your way through the redwoods. Built in 1926, the Tudor-style hotel hosted dignitaries such as Eleanor Roosevelt and Herbert Hoover in its glory days. Today, the Benbow is a little worn around the edges but still elegant, filled with a blend of old-world antiques and accents. Complimentary English tea with freshly baked scones is served every afternoon in the spacious rustic lobby, where Oriental carpets cloak hardwood floors, rocking chairs beckon near the hearth, and a life-size teddy bear lounges around in life-like positions.

Although the hotel's 55 small rooms have all been renovated, they retain a historic feeling, replete with antiques and old-fashioned wallpaper, red velvet lounge chairs, Oriental carpets, paisley linens, and nicely tiled but otherwise standard baths. We especially liked the Terrace rooms, with private patios that overlook the nicely landscaped grounds and nearby burbling river. A basket of mystery novels is provided to each guest room for added amusement, and bikes are available for those who want to explore the outlying grounds. There is even a film projector in the lobby showing favorite black-and-white flicks starring Charlie Chaplin and Clara Bow.

Romantic Suggestion: For lack of nearby alternatives, the **BENBOW INN RESTAURANT** (Moderate to Expensive) is a convenient and reasonably romantic option for breakfast, lunch, or dinner. Chandeliers and candle lanterns cast dim light across the Tudor-style dining room, where an abundance of two-person tables are arranged next to large windows with views of the trees. Whet your palate with appetizers such as an artichoke tart with sweet onions or grilled portobello mushrooms; the kitchen's pasta and seafood specialties are also excellent.

Mendocino

Exemplifying coastal life in Northern California, Mendocino offers the yin and yang of getaway spots. The streets of this quaint and serene (albeit popular) Cape Cod-style seaside town are lined with whitewashed storefronts that house small art galleries and specialty shops ripe for browsing. Its enviable bed and breakfasts are frequently booked on weekends, often months in advance. Of course, Mendocino's main attraction is its view of the tranquil bay and surrounding rugged bluffs. Unfortunately, the very elements that make Mendocino so alluring also make it very crowded, especially in the spring and summer. Still, there is the off-season, when the crowds and sun are less prevalent and fog shrouds the area in a veil of misty white. That's when you can best appreciate this area's plethora of cozy restaurants and bed and breakfasts.

Hotel/Bed and Breakfast Kissing

AGATE COVE INN, Mendocino
11201 North Lansing Street
(707) 937-0551, (800) 527-3111 (in California)
Moderate to Expensive
Minimum stay requirement on weekends

Oceanfront accommodations are wonderful, especially when the surf is close enough to serenade you all night long. This is the case at the Agate Cove Inn, ensconced on a bluff across the street from the ocean. The crashing surf also drowns out any road noise that might otherwise distract or annoy you. The small, antique-filled lobby and glass-enclosed dining room set in an 1880s historic farmhouse revel in ringside views of the potent, rugged shoreline. Here, guests can witness spectacular sunsets by the fireside hearth or glimpse reflections of sunrise over a scrumptious hot breakfast, prepared on a 100-year-old wood-burning stove.

Stone walkways ramble through resplendent gardens surrounding the property's ten cozy country-style cottages, many with their own mesmerizing view of the ocean. Although somewhat small and mismatched, every room has comfortable country furnishings and antiques, a four-poster or canopied bed covered with handmade patchwork quilts, and a gas-burning fireplace. The best bets for romance are the Emerald Room and the Obsidian Room, which have "companion" tubs for two, double-headed showers, king-size beds, fireplaces, and spectacular white-water panoramas.

Romantic Warning: When making reservations, steer clear of the cottages at the very back of the property; they have limited ocean views and are literally yards from an adjacent highway.

COAST RETREATS, Mendocino
(707) 937-1121, (800) 859-6260
Expensive to Very Expensive
Minimum stay requirement

Having traveled the world over looking for romantic retreats of their own, the owners of this impressive rental company finally found their slice of heaven in Mendocino. Fortunately, they're eager to share. Some of Mendocino's most dramatic ocean views are visible from the decks, porches, and front yards of Coast Retreat's six sensational, ultra-private rental properties. (Actually, two of Coastal Retreat's properties do not have ocean views, but they do offer stylish ambience and romance-oriented amenities that won't disappoint.)

Built as close to the ocean as possible, four of these rental homes are perched atop steep bluffs that jut out over the incoming tide. French doors open onto a spacious water-view deck at the Jameson House, showcasing sea gulls and osprey sailing at eye level. A large hot tub, a walk-in shower for two, a beautiful jade-colored tile kitchen, and even a telescope are other romantic features here. Just down the road, the artistically decorated Bungalow shares the same breathtaking oceanfront stage, plus a hot tub and a deck that wraps around three sides of the house. Copper countertops in the kitchen, mosaic tiles in the bathrooms, and other hand-worked details give the one-bedroom home added personality.

Two-level floor-to-ceiling windows in the nearby Tidepool House look out to the ocean, and decks enclose three sides of the house. This three-bedroom, weathered redwood home has a woodstove, a hot tub, a loft master bedroom that overlooks the dining room, and glorious water views. Cheryl's House, a two-bedroom home, roosts 600 feet above the Navarro River and features spectacular river and distant ocean views, a full kitchen, decks with more amazing views, and a spacious outdoor hot tub. You get the picture. No matter which property you decide on, you're in for a treat, with amenities and views designed to cater to your romantic sensibilities.

CYPRESS COVE, Mendocino   ❤❤❤❤
45200 Chapman Drive
(707) 937-1456, (800) 942-6300 (in California)
http://www.mcn.org/b/cypresscove/
Expensive; No Credit Cards
Minimum stay requirement on weekends

Once the word gets out about Cypress Cove, it will be nearly impossible to get reservations. It's hard enough as it is, and our four-lip review will only make matters worse. Still, believe us when we say that it is well worth the effort to plan your getaway around the availability of the two suites here. Perched on a rocky bluff, this two-story beach house has wraparound floor-to-ceiling windows that bring spectacular views of Mendocino and the bay practically inside. Both suites are simply decorated in contemporary style and have private decks, indoor whirlpool tubs for two, separate showers, wood-burning fireplaces, complete stereo systems, and sublime comfort. Pacifica, the second-floor suite, is accented with bright linens, colorful tiles, large bouquets of fresh flowers, and terra-cotta-tiled floors. Cove is decorated in a more subdued style, with shades of gray, black, and green. One particularly noteworthy aspect of the Cove Suite is the corner window seat with magnificent views—this has to be one of the absolute *best places to kiss* in all of California.

On top of all this, one of the best features of Cypress Cove is that you can hear the ocean, not just view it. This is something most of us do not have the pleasure of hearing at home, and there is something very special about being lulled to sleep by such a pure and powerful sound.

Romantic Note: Coffee, tea, brandy, and chocolates are provided; breakfast is not. Luckily, you're not far from Mendocino's many restaurants and bakeries, and each suite is equipped with a kitchenette so you can prepare your own meals. Maid service is every third day only.

THE HEADLANDS INN, Mendocino
Howard and Albion Streets
(707) 937-4431, (800) 354-4431
http://www.mcn.org/b/headlands/
Moderate to Expensive
Minimum stay requirement on weekends and holidays

Charm, comfort, and a cheerful atmosphere distinguish this pretty Cape Cod-style Victorian located in the heart of Mendocino, just a few blocks from the ocean. Most of the inn's five distinctive rooms have full views or glimpses of the surf. Down-filled comforters, handmade quilts, and overstuffed reading pillows cover sumptuous feather beds in every guest room, each warmed by a fireplace or parlor stove. Views of the Pacific's churning water are outstanding in the spacious Bessie Strauss Room, which features a large bay window. Arched ceilings and a cozy window seat add character to the George Switzer Room, situated at the top of the house. Even the W.J. Wilson Room has glimpses of the ocean from its large private deck embellished with potted plants. Designed for ultimate privacy, self-contained Casper Cottage is set behind the main house, with a four-poster queen-size bed, wood-burning fireplace, and large sunken soaking tub.

In the morning you can lounge in bed as you await an exceptional gourmet breakfast brought directly to your room. Be prepared for such delicacies as Florentine baked rolls with cheddar-sherry sauce, peach or blackberry crêpes in an amaretto sauce, and fresh pastries and fruits on your personalized tray.

REED MANOR, Mendocino
Palette Drive
(707) 937-5446
Expensive to Unbelievably Expensive
Minimum stay requirement on weekends

Who knew that such an elegant kissing locale could be found in down-to-earth Mendocino? Luckily, now *you* do. If opulent luxury is what you're looking for, check into stately, voluptuous Reed Manor. Upon entering you'll pass by glass cases full of the innkeepers' antique collections. The five palatial guest rooms all feature a gas log fireplace, two-person whirlpool tub, sumptuous decor, high beamed ceilings, mini-fridge, coffeemaker, teapot, stereo, and a television and VCR tucked away in cabinets. High-power telescopes are set up on some of the private decks for viewing the village below and the ocean beyond. Complimentary wine encourages you to make a toast to it all (and to each other). In the Napoleon Room, a double-sided fireplace warms both the bathroom, with its Jacuzzi tub and dual-headed shower, and the silvery French Provincial bedroom, with its romantic four-poster bed. Josephine's Garden Room opens to a delightful redwood patio laced with colorful blooms. Even Imperial Garden, the smallest, least expensive room (still in the Expensive category), is elegant and cozy.

A continental breakfast of nut breads, fruit, and locally made apple juice is wrapped and delivered to your room in the evening, so you can enjoy it at your own leisure the following morning.

SEA ROCK BED AND BREAKFAST INN, Mendocino
11101 Lansing Street
(707) 937-0926, (800) 906-0926
http://www.searock.com
Moderate to Expensive
Minimum stay requirement on weekends and holidays

Inspired innkeepers have spent the last couple of years improving these quaint cottages and guest rooms. Although the renovations are still underway, the romantic potential is already apparent. There are 14 rooms all together: ten small ones dispersed in six weathered gray cottages and another four in the two-story Stratton House. While the style and decor vary drastically, from old-fashioned to country to bohemian, every room offers down comforters, mini-patios, and televisions with VCRs, and many boast Franklin fireplaces and feather beds. The Stratton House rooms have the best views (particularly from the second story), with corner fireplaces in all but one room, better decor, and four-poster or carved bed frames. Although the options here aren't what we would call luxurious, they are comfortable, and the innkeepers are eager to help make your stay special.

An expanded continental breakfast is presented beside the reception area, and you can eat at tables set along windows that view the ocean beyond Lansing Street. If you prefer, you can take a tray back to your room or to one of the benches scattered around the grounds. One bench, set at the edge of a bluff across the street from the inn, is especially picturesque.

Romantic Warning: Although Sea Rock Bed and Breakfast Inn has a lot of charm, sounds from the highway behind the property and the busy road in front could interrupt the peace and quiet you may be searching for.

STANFORD INN BY THE SEA, Mendocino
Coast Highway and Comptche-Ukiah Road
(707) 937-5615, (800) 331-8884
http://www.stanfordinn.com
Expensive to Unbelievably Expensive
Minimum stay requirement on weekends

A perfect marriage of luxury and rustic elegance, this expansive redwood lodge takes advantage of its beautiful setting. All 24 rooms feature private decks where you can observe the sun setting on the distant horizon. Enjoy views of the Pacific (across the street), as well as the inn's sloping lawn, gardens, and llamas grazing in corralled pastures. If the evening is chilly, as it usually is in this region, cuddle by the fire in your knotty pine-paneled room, pop open the complimentary bottle of wine, and slide a mood-setting CD into your stereo. Even the smallest rooms have a fireplace, private balcony, stereo, television, VCR, and a sleigh or four-poster bed covered with richly colored, plush linens. If privacy is a priority, we recommend the rustic suite on the bottom floor of a converted barn filled with contemporary furnishings, or two similar suites in a nearby restored farmhouse.

In the morning, take a dip in the alluring greenhouse-enclosed pool, spa, and sauna. The warmth of this bright and humid solarium might make you think you're actually in the South Pacific. After you've warmed yourselves thoroughly, fill up on a communal champagne breakfast of cereals, yogurt, pastries, fruits, and more, served in a crowded but countrified firelit parlor.

Romantic Note: See the coast in style on one of the inn's state-of-the-art mountain bikes, available at no cost to guests. Or rent a canoe for a romantic paddle along the Big River, following it inland to secluded picnicking and kissing spots.

WHITEGATE INN, Mendocino
499 Howard Street
(707) 937-4892, (800) 531-7282
Moderate to Expensive
Minimum stay requirement seasonally

In some towns, Victorian-style bed and breakfasts are so abundant that they start to look like carbon copies of each other, but that's not the case in Mendocino. The Whitegate Inn, a gorgeous milky white Victorian with black trim, stands out as one of the few traditionally Victorian places to stay in town, with its elegant crystal chandeliers, antique furnishings, claw-foot tubs, and floral-and-textured wall coverings. It also stands out as an excellent example of why some people fall in love with the bed-and-breakfast experience. A warm greeting, friendly hospitality, and lavish breakfasts and snacks are just a few things you can expect from the very gracious hosts.

An expansive redwood deck, charming gazebo, and garden benches provide prime kissing spots, where you can smell the flowers, gaze at the clear blue sea, then roam to the parlor for afternoon wine and cheese. Six comfortably elegant guest rooms await in the main house, each with ocean or village views and cozy down comforters; five have fireplaces. A separate cottage with its own private garden deck, king-size bed, corner woodstove, and claw-foot tub, is set behind the house, and guests staying here can opt to have breakfast delivered. A sweet table for two can be arranged in advance for anyone else who wants some morning privacy. Otherwise, the multicourse breakfast is served family-style in the formal dining room; it may not be very intimate, but you might overhear some good ideas on how to spend your day (just in case you've already done everything we've suggested), and you will probably meet some nice people who are enjoying the Whitegate Inn as much as you are.

Restaurant Kissing

955 UKIAH STREET RESTAURANT, Mendocino
955 Ukiah Street
(707) 937-1955
Moderate to Expensive
Dinner Wednesday-Monday

When it comes to dinner recommendations in Mendocino, 955 Ukiah is on the tip of every local's tongue. A long boardwalk embroidered with greenery leads to the entrance of this popular restaurant, set overlooking a stand of trees draped with tiny white lights. A 20-foot vaulted ceiling in the split-level dining room absorbs some (but not all) of the sounds coming from the busy open kitchen located on the lower floor. Local artwork and trailing plants accentuate partially wood-paneled walls. Adequately spaced tables covered with white linens, fresh flowers, and votive candles create a comfortable atmosphere in which you can enjoy delicately flavored California cuisine. We were especially impressed with the steamed crisp vegetable medley on couscous and polenta, and "Grandma's secret" bread pudding with huckleberry compote for dessert.

CAFE BEAUJOLAIS, Mendocino
961 Ukiah Street
(707) 937-5614
Expensive
Dinner Daily

Some say Cafe Beaujolais is the most romantic restaurant in Mendocino. Others argue that the tables are too close together for comfort. In the end, everyone agrees that the candles at every table, warm oak paneling, and wood-burning stove do create a pretty cozy atmosphere. Even if you're closer to other diners than you prefer, the incredible cuisine and gracious service make up for the compact seating. A casual, glassed-in porch overlooking the gardens hold additional tables; it's nice on a pretty day, but the room can get too hot when the sun beats down.

Despite the French name, Cafe Beaujolais specializes in creative European-style cuisine with Mexican and Asian influences. Freshness and quality are the kitchen's top priorities, and the chefs' dedication is apparent in dishes like broiled tuna with avocado-corn salsa and roasted free-range chicken with saffron-chanterelle sauce. The desserts, say, blueberry brioche bread pudding with maple-whiskey sauce and house-made hazelnut ice cream profiteroles with warm chocolate sauce, are just as interesting and just as delicious.

MACCALLUM HOUSE RESTAURANT, Mendocino
45020 Albion Street
(707) 937-5763
Moderate
Dinner Friday-Tuesday

A substantial cobblestone fireplace fills the dining rooms here with a burnished light that flickers warmly against the redwood paneling. The romance of days past is the MacCallum House Restaurant's specialty, and its dark Victorian ambience is complemented by a seasonal menu of fresh regional fish, meats, and produce. If you bring a hearty appetite with you to dinner, consider the grilled pork chop with pear–dried cranberry marmalade, or the charred tuna served rare with a pinot noir sauce. On the lighter side, the roasted autumn vegetable fricassee in an acorn squash bowl with nasturtium butter is savory and unique. Whatever you do, try to save room for desert. A chocolate truffle parfait with mocha mousse or a praline cookie taco filled with samples of six different ice creams might be the perfect end to a perfect day.

Romantic Alternative: For a more casual meal or just for drinks, consider the **SUNPORCH CAFE AND DINING ROOM**, at the same address (Moderate). This charming window-framed sunporch at the front of the restaurant overlooks greenery and the nearby street scene.

Romantic Note: THE MACCALLUM HOUSE INN, (707) 937-0289 (Inexpensive to Very Expensive), under separate management from the restaurant, is one of the most unusual bed and breakfasts we've ever seen. The meandering array of rooms and suites ranges in style from overly rustic and run-down to somewhat romantic. For kissing purposes, the best units are the Barn and the Barn Apartment. The Barn has a massive stone fireplace, cozy sitting area, and a large picture window overlooking the bay. The Barn Apartment is similar, with the addition of a sensual, very large bathroom. For the most part, however, with all of the truly lip-worthy overnight options to choose from in Mendocino, this one should not be at the top of your list.

MENDOCINO HOTEL VICTORIAN
DINING ROOM, Mendocino
45080 Main Street
(707) 937-0511, (800) 548-0513
Expensive
Breakfast, Lunch, and Dinner Daily

Arrive early to ease yourselves back in time as you cuddle next to the fire in the Mendocino Hotel's elegant lobby, with its tapestried settees and Persian carpets. Candles flicker on tables in the adjacent dining room, casting a nostalgic glow on dark wood accents, deep red wall coverings, and faceted glass partitions. While the setting is authentic and lovely, we were disappointed with both the lackluster food and the neglectful service the evenings we dined here. Instead of dinner, we recommend savoring the ambience of the enchanting lobby as you sip an aperitif; simply cozy up in the plush wing-backed chairs tucked in window alcoves near the front of the lobby. Another option for lunch or early dinner is the hotel's Garden Room—a gloriously lush greenhouse setting, especially inviting when the sun streams in.

Romantic Suggestion: Although most of the rooms at this historic hostel-style hotel share bathrooms and are not the least bit conducive to romance, we do recommend the higher-priced suites, which range from Expensive to Unbelievably Expensive. Situated in self-contained buildings behind the original hotel and surrounded by beautiful rose gardens and sweet-scented walking paths, some of these suites have parlors, fireplaces, balconies, water views, private baths, and even whirlpool tubs.

THE MOOSSE CAFE, Mendocino
390 Kasten Street
(707) 937-4323
Inexpensive to Moderate; No Credit Cards
Breakfast, Lunch, and Dinner Daily

Plan on light romance at lunch in this cozy, casual cafe, especially on a chilly, foggy day when firelight warms the room. Daily specials are written on a blackboard and can range from salmon smoked over apple wood to a saucy lasagne and an inventive quiche. Gourmet coffees and decadent desserts, such as the irresistible Moose Puff, a cream puff filled with vanilla ice cream and topped with hot fudge and whipped cream, can make even a dreary day enjoyable when shared by two. The dinner menu offers similarly imaginative dishes, and sparkling white lights trim the windows, warming the night.

Romantic Alternative: If the sun is shining, choose a table on the casual patio of **THE MENDOCINO BAKERY**, Lansing at Ukiah, (707) 937-0836 (Inexpensive). Standard soups, salads, sandwiches, and light entrées are served along with a view of the crashing coastline.

Outdoor Kissing

MENDOCINO COAST BOTANICAL GARDENS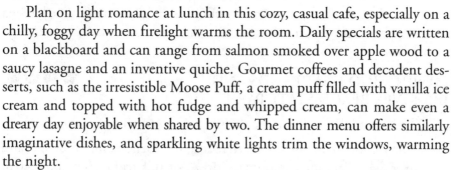
18220 North Highway 1
(707) 964-4352
$5 per adult

The garden is located on the west side of Highway 1, approximately eight miles north of Mendocino, in the town of Fort Bragg.

Fronted by a rustic garden shop and a roadside cafe, the garden's entrance gives little indication of the 47 beautiful acres of botanical wonders found inside. Natural gardens unfold with ever-expanding layers of brilliance, each one surprising and evocative. Follow walkways festooned with rhododendrons as you stroll hand-in-hand past formally landscaped colorful annuals, hillsides laced with hydrangeas, and meadows mellow with heather. No matter what time of year you visit, something will be in bloom. Wander to the farthest reaches of the garden to find a stunning seascape with welcoming benches perched high above the crashing surf. In the winter you may even see a whale pass by, its spout punctuating the vast horizon.

Romantic Suggestion: If you've worked up an appetite after exploring the nearly three miles of paths in this heavenly garden, consider eating lunch or dinner at the **GARDEN'S GRILL**, 18218 North Highway 1, (707) 964-7474 (Moderate). Located just off the highway and parking lot at the entrance of the gardens, the cafe is a very casual affair. Tables draped with white and floral tablecloths are arranged indoors under peaked wood ceilings and outside on a deck under umbrellas and shade trees. The kitchen serves up laid-back California cuisine, from pasta specials to burgers and tasty soups.

MENDOCINO HEADLANDS AND BIG RIVER BEACH STATE PARK

The coastal headlands and the park surround Mendocino on all sides.

Perhaps more than any other attraction, the Mendocino headlands and Big River State Park are the primary draws of this region. The protected, flawless curve of land is an easily accessible place to see, hear, and feel nature in all its magnitude and glory. On calm sunny days, the glistening ocean reveals hidden grottos, sea arches, and tide pools, as foamy white surf encircles the rock-etched boundary of Mendocino. If you happen to be here December through March, you may see a school of whales making its way down the coast. Even on days when the thick ocean fog enfolds the area in a white-gray cloak, this is still a prime place to explore and daydream. Bundle up and snuggle close—the cool mist tingling against your cheeks is chilly.

Romantic Option: MCKERRICHER STATE PARK, three miles north of Fort Bragg off Highway 1, (707) 937-5804, is a wondrous assortment of nature's most engaging features: waterfalls at the end of forested trails, grass-covered headlands overlooking the Pacific, white sandy beaches, rolling dunes, and haystack rocks where harbor seals spend the day sunning themselves. Actually, the most outstanding feature of this state park is its distance from Mendocino; the extra few miles make it less popular, giving it a definite kissing advantage.

Little River

Hotel/Bed and Breakfast Kissing

GLENDEVEN INN, Little River
8221 North Highway 1
(707) 937-0083, (800) 822-4536
http://www.innaccess.com/gdi/
Moderate to Very Expensive
Minimum stay requirement on weekends and holidays

Glendeven Inn promises country living at its best. Its ten guest rooms are located in three New England-esque structures poised on verdant meadowland brushed by fresh ocean air. Of special interest are the four airy Stevenscroft annex rooms, with water views, wood-burning fireplaces, high vaulted ceilings, large tiled baths, and French doors leading to sunny private decks. If these rooms don't help set a romantic mood, nothing will. Rooms in the charming historic farmhouse are equally engaging, although road noise from Highway 1 is slightly audible. All of the spacious, handsome rooms feature lovely bay or garden views, affectionate details, and country Victorian furnishings.

After your hand-delivered breakfast of warm homemade muffins, freshly squeezed orange juice, fruit, and a piping hot egg dish, consider taking a refreshing hike to the beach. It is an easy 20-minute walk down to the headlands or to Van Damme Beach. If you're fortunate enough to be staying more than a night or two, you can try both trails, and then return to your favorite—maps are provided by the helpful innkeepers.

Romantic Alternative: STEVENSWOOD LODGE, 8211 Highway 1, (707) 937-2810, (800) 421-2810 (Inexpensive to Very Expensive) is set back from the road on nicely landscaped grounds and offers ten surprisingly contemporary rooms in a small, rustic lodge setting. Though the rooms are sparsely decorated and seem to be designed more for traveling executives (remote-control televisions and phones are the major highlight of every room), the wood-burning fireplaces, outside decks, and partial water views in some of the rooms suggest romantic possibilities. The inn's nicest feature is the colorful local art featured in the gallery-like hallways. Generous evening appetizers, wine, and gourmet breakfasts are served downstairs in the cheerful, firelit common room.

HERITAGE HOUSE INN, Little River
5200 North Highway 1
(707) 937-5885, (800) 235-5885

Expensive to Unbelievably Expensive
Closed December through January
Minimum stay requirement on weekends and holidays

Boasting one of the North Coast's most spectacular panoramas, this renovated farmstead holds a series of small cottages terraced above the Pacific, ensconced on 37 acres of spellbinding waterfront. Almost all of the individually decorated cottages have private entrances and a dazzling perspective of a pristine cove where waves crash against parched, rugged cliffs. Decor, views, and amenities vary from room to room. We were partial to the (unfortunately) higher-priced cottages with better views and more luxurious appointments, including ocean-view decks, fireplaces, and oversized Jacuzzi tubs. Views from cottages designated as Sunset, Seacliff, or Vista are pure inspiration. Views from the Carousel Suite are even more sensational. Throw open the windows to welcome the Pacific's music and sink into the double whirlpool set beneath a starry skylight. A two-sided fireplace warms both the living room and bedroom.

If you've got your heart set on one of the property's exclusive, oceanview suites, book your reservations as soon as possible. The Carousel and Vista suites, for example, require reservations *a full year* in advance. And don't be taken aback by the Unbelievably Expensive room rates— they include breakfast and dinner for two in the elegant dining room perched above the Pacific (see Restaurant Kissing).

LITTLE RIVER INN, Little River
7751 North Highway 1
(707) 937-5942, (888) INN-LOVE
Inexpensive to Unbelievably Expensive
Minimum stay requirement on weekends and holidays

Although all 65 of the Little River Inn's rooms face the ocean, the Inexpensive to Expensive rooms don't measure up to our romantic criteria—the interiors of these rooms are too run-down and hotel-like to be considered for a special interlude. However, rooms in the Very Expensive to Unbelievably Expensive categories are an entirely different story. The higher the price, the greater the distance from the noisy parking lot and highway, and the better the amenities and decor. The most luxurious rooms are set across from the main property, on the ocean side of the highway. Four rooms are located in a contemporary rambler called the Van Damme House, and there is a separate cottage next door, called the Coombs Cottage. Each spacious unit has a wood-burning fireplace, homey country furnishings, open-beam ceiling, two-person Jacuzzi tub, and magnificent ocean views. The Unbelievably

Expensive Coombs Cottage has a fireplace, a tub for two, and sublime privacy, but we think the Van Damme South and Margaret Bullard Rooms (still Very Expensive) are just as nice; they have Jacuzzi tubs placed right beside a window so you can enjoy spectacular views as you soak.

Restaurant Kissing

HERITAGE HOUSE RESTAURANT, Little River
5200 North Highway 1
(707) 937-5885, (800) 235-5885
Expensive to Very Expensive
Breakfast, Lunch, and Dinner Daily; Saturday and Sunday Brunch

If you want to reserve a table at this elegant oceanside restaurant, your best bet is to spend the night at the Heritage House Inn. Dinner and breakfast are included in the price of your stay, and dinner reservations are guaranteed to guests only. Once guests have been accommodated, the restaurant opens to envious nonguests.

Nearly every linen-cloaked table in the restaurant's three dining rooms has a glimpse of the sparkling Pacific below. In one room, chandeliers softly illuminate a painted dome ceiling that endows the restaurant with a feeling of spaciousness. Tall candles and white linens in the remaining two dining rooms contribute to an elegant ambience. The menu changes daily and can include savory starters such as saffron-mussel bisque or crab and smoked almond salad; entrées such as grilled salmon with artichokes, leeks, and pistachios; and, of course, luscious desserts.

Romantic Warning: Due to the difficulty of getting reservations, lunch might be your only option here. Unfortunately, the quality of the food and service at the lunch hour does not compare to dinnertime. We were sorely disappointed with the kitchen's sandwiches, soups, and salads the afternoon we dined here.

Albion

Hotel/Bed and Breakfast Kissing

ALBION RIDGE HUCKLEBERRY HOUSE, Albion
29381 Albion Ridge Road
(707) 937-2374, (800) 482-5532
Inexpensive to Expensive
Minimum stay requirement on weekends seasonally

Ocean views are a prerequisite for many romantic-minded North Coast travelers, but because Highway 1 runs along the water's edge, road noise is almost always an issue at oceanside retreats. Keeping this in mind, you may want to sacrifice ocean views for sublime quiet and stay somewhere off the beaten path. Somewhere like Huckleberry House. Nicely tucked into a forested neighborhood, this recently built cedar home sits beside a well-stocked trout pond. Regardless of the room you choose, the peace and quiet here are certain to calm your senses.

The two suites and small guest room located on the second floor of the main house have a brand-new feeling. The suites, done up in contemporary style with bold prints and bright artwork, feature separate sitting areas, wood-burning fireplaces, concealed televisions with VCRs, wet bars, small refrigerators, feather beds, down comforters, gas fireplace inserts beside the bed, and patios facing the surrounding redwoods. The smaller Tower Room is an affordable and airy option, with a four-poster bed, detached bath, and windows overlooking the pond. A detached cottage offers the warmest and most welcoming interior; an open-beam ceiling gives the room a spacious feeling, while a wood-burning fireplace and a brass bed with a patchwork quilt lend country coziness. A full breakfast is served in the main house or can be delivered to your room.

ALBION RIVER INN, Albion
3790 North Highway 1
(707) 937-1919, (800) 479-7944
Expensive to Very Expensive
Recommended Wedding Site
Minimum stay requirement on weekends and holidays

Spontaneity is sometimes the most memorable aspect of a romantic vacation, but at other times it pays to plan ahead. If you're thinking of taking a trip up the North Coast, we suggest you book reservations at the Albion River Inn immediately (or at least two months in advance). Everybody wants to stay here, and if you're lucky enough to get a room, you'll see why. Fortunately, the inn's popularity in no way diminishes its romantic virtues. Set on a precipice towering above Albion Cove and the Pacific, this New England-style inn offers 20 ocean-view units to choose from. All of the rooms have wood-burning fireplaces, elegant country touches, floral linens, down comforters, cozy robes, and complimentary wine and coffee, and all but two rooms have private decks with superlative views. Six of the luxury rooms have Jacuzzi tubs for two with ocean vistas, while several others have two-person soaking tubs. All guests have access to the inn's private headland pathway, which leads to expansive vistas of water and sky. If, after a long day of touring, you want a secluded, first-class place to watch the sky turn fiery red as the ocean thunders against the shore below, this is the place to be.

A generous breakfast of home-baked breads, homemade granola, eggs cooked to order, breakfast potatoes au gratin, fresh fruit, and juices, served in the inn's waterfront restaurant (see Restaurant Kissing), is included with your stay. Dinner here is another romantic must. The food is as delicious as the view is mesmerizing.

Restaurant Kissing

ALBION RIVER INN RESTAURANT, Albion
3790 North Highway 1
(707) 937-1919, (800) 479-7944
Moderate to Expensive
Dinner Daily

Albion River Inn shares its glorious clifftop setting with this highly acclaimed restaurant, also perched above the ocean. Expansive views help make this stylish dining room a worthwhile romantic venture. Although the number of tables limits intimacy, the amorous mood is enhanced by candles at every table and soft piano music on Friday and Saturday nights. (At dusk on weekends you might also catch glimpses of a bagpipe player in a kilt on the bluff.)

The menu's focus on fresh seafood prepared in both Mediterranean and Far Eastern fashion is unique in these parts. Mediterranean flair is deliciously evident in dishes like Pacific snapper sautéed with rock shrimp, capers, and basil, or grilled king salmon topped with herb-pesto cream, while the Asian influence shines in the Thai-style rock shrimp cakes with coconut-curry dipping sauce or lime-and-ginger-grilled jumbo prawns topped with cilantro-garlic butter. Everything is thoroughly satisfying, yet the chef's light touch should leave you with enough room for dessert. Even if you don't think you can eat another bite, you'll be sweetly tempted by caramelized coconut bananas in warm rum-caramel sauce served with French vanilla ice cream, or tangy rhubarb-and-wildberry cobbler topped with homemade lemon-poppyseed ice cream.

THE LEDFORD HOUSE RESTAURANT, Albion
3000 North Highway 1
(707) 937-0282
Moderate to Expensive
Dinner Wednesday-Sunday

You would never guess it from just driving by, but this modest rambler is one of the loveliest places to dine along the entire North Coast. Situated on a bluff with spectacular ocean views, The Ledford House Restaurant is a peaceful place to linger over dinner and romance the night away. Soft jazz filters in from the mellow bar area, single long-stemmed roses adorn every table, and candlelight casts flickering shadows on whitewashed walls, infusing the dining room with warmth. When the area is shrouded in fog (which occurs more often than some would like to admit), Ledford House becomes even more cozy and inviting.

Although the kitchen should be commended for its extremely creative Euro-Californian dishes, they sometimes miss the mark. Soup or salad accompanies your meal, but both were oversalted the night we were there. The main courses regained our esteem. Sautéed sea scallops presented on crispy sweet potato pancakes spread with avocado butter and tomato-ginger salsa were different and delicious, and the roasted duckling with fresh raspberry-tarragon sauce was done to a tee. The interesting menu, amorous atmosphere, and gracious wait staff make The Ledford House Restaurant a wonderful place to spend a memorable evening.

Elk

Hotel/Bed and Breakfast Kissing

ELK COVE INN, Elk   💋💋💋
6300 South Highway 1
(707) 877-3321, (800) 275-2967
Moderate to Expensive
Minimum stay requirement on weekends and holidays

Views from this gingerbread-trimmed bed and breakfast are stunning, and sunset will leave you speechless (which makes kissing that much easier). Set above a driftwood-scattered beach and facing ancient rocks that jut out of the sea, Elk Cove Inn offers six rooms in the main house plus four neighboring cabins. Wood paneling, arched ceilings, down comforters, and floral linens create a homey feeling in the second-story main house rooms, and each has a private standard bath. Dormer windows in two of the rooms face windblown cypresses and the shimmering sea; the other four rooms overlook the inn's grounds and gardens. Luckily, those who don't have an ocean vista from their room can enjoy a bird's-eye view from the rooftop deck.

Higher on the kissing scale are the three small guest cottages, which are perched at the edge of a bluff for even closer views. (The structures aren't actually individual cabins—they are more like duplexes—but they do offer a high degree of privacy and extremely cozy interiors.) Two have bay windows, high beamed ceilings, skylights, and wood stoves, and all of them have fluffy feather beds and down comforters. Glider benches are placed along the bluff for ocean gazing, there is a charming gazebo, and steps lead to the beach below for sunset walks and seaside smooches.

Warm hospitality and freshly baked goodies are another important part of your stay. Breakfast is served at separate tables in the wood-paneled ocean-view dining room. The delicious array of homemade scones, fruit parfaits, and gourmet egg dishes will leave you satisfied until dinner, or at least late afternoon, when appetizers, wine, and beer are served. Hot beverages can be prepared in your own room, and bedtime is accompanied by port and chocolates. Now *this* is living!

GREENWOOD PIER INN, Elk
5928 South Highway 1
(707) 877-9997
Moderate to Very Expensive
Minimum stay requirement on weekends

Lush flower and herb gardens border walking paths that zigzag through the Greenwood Pier Inn's peacefully landscaped grounds, leading you past an eclectic assortment of uniquely crafted redwood cottages set on a bluff above the ocean. Several cottages are inhabited by gift and garden stores, while another houses a cafe that makes good use of the fresh vegetables, herbs, and edible flowers grown here year-round. To our delight, the cottages perched closest to the cliff's edge are reserved exclusively for overnight guests who want to indulge (privately) in the staggering views of the untamed ocean below. Mismatched country fabrics, antiques, and knickknacks blend with funky, artistic touches to create an eccentric mood in each of the property's 12 cottages. Many have fireplaces or wood-burning stoves, and knotty pine paneling; some have private decks, stained glass windows, and canopied beds. Hand-thrown sinks and deep blue tiles add pizzazz to the otherwise very nondescript bathrooms. In the Sea Castle, Oriental rugs cover terra-cotta-tiled floors and inlaid stones accent pink walls. A spiral staircase leads to the second story, where you'll find an ocean-view soaking tub. Private decks jut daringly out over the precipice from North Sea Castle, South Sea Castle, and the Cliffhouse, and soaking tubs on the second stories of all three survey panoramic views of the coast. The smaller, less expensive rooms in the main building have decent views, but they are noticeably more run-down and not nearly as desirable for a romantic encounter. (Sometimes you really do get what you pay for.)

In the morning, a continental breakfast is delivered to your room for you to enjoy at your leisure. Although breakfast in bed is an affectionate option, enjoying your morning meal in a glorious garden perched at the edge of the Pacific may be reason enough to get out of bed. We forced ourselves to put on robes so we could enjoy freshly baked breads and muffins in this serene setting, overlooking enormous ocean-carved rocks and the brilliant blue sea.

Romantic Suggestion: During your stay, be sure to eat at the property's casual **GREENWOOD PIER CAFE** (see Restaurant Kissing) to enjoy the fruits of the beautifully landscaped grounds.

GRIFFIN HOUSE AT GREENWOOD COVE, Elk
5910 South Highway 1
(707) 877-3422
Moderate to Expensive
Minimum stay requirement on weekends

Clustered behind a friendly Irish pub, where you might expect a parking lot, are seven wee 1920s cottages. Don't expect anything too fancy here. Each small unit is modestly decorated with country calico prints and the interiors could use updating, but wood-burning Franklin stoves and incredible ocean views from three of the cottages offer romantic potential. These ocean-view cottages, set at the bluff's edge, are the only ones we recommend. Both Greenwood and Donohue have queen-size brass beds and private decks overlooking the endless Pacific. Matson has a private deck with the same great view, plus a window-side clawfoot tub, but only a double bed. If you need to spread out to be truly comfortable, these units are probably too snug for you, but the views are spectacular, the pub is a convenient and fun place for a nightcap, and the prices are relatively reasonable. A hearty full breakfast is delivered to your door in the morning.

HARBOR HOUSE—AN INN BY THE SEA, Elk
5600 South Highway 1
(707) 877-3203
Expensive to Unbelievably Expensive; No Credit Cards
Minimum stay requirement on weekends

Constructed of redwood in 1916, the Harbor House Inn is balanced at the top of a stunning oceanfront bluff with astonishing views of haystack boulders and sea-worn rock arches that rise above the ocean's ever-changing surface. Unfortunately, the ten guest rooms pale in comparison. Even the nicest rooms are homey and mismatched, decorated with time-worn antiques, fabrics, and drab-colored linens. Still, the fireplaces and breathtaking views found in most of the rooms do provide some romantic allure. Other amenities include the

Lookout Room's private ocean-view deck and the ensured seclusion of the self-contained Seaview and Oceansong Cottages, which also have semi-private decks, fireplaces, and full ocean views.

Other romantic draws here are the full gourmet breakfast and four-course dinner included with your stay. (Nonguests are welcome for dinner, too.) A sweeping bay window in the fireside dining room looks out to the rugged shoreline and the mesmerizing surf. Prix fixe dinners change nightly, but might include Thai lemongrass soup, pepper cheese bread, mixed garden greens with citrus vinaigrette, followed by salmon fillets in phyllo with a Parmesan mornay sauce, polenta, and fresh asparagus spears. A light peach crisp is a perfect finale to your perfectly prepared meal. Breakfast includes delicious hot baked dishes, fresh fruit, pastries, coffee, tea, and juice. After breakfast or dinner, we recommend taking a romantic walk hand-in-hand along the property's spectacular beach.

SANDPIPER HOUSE INN, Elk
5520 South Highway 1
(707) 877-3587
Moderate to Very Expensive
Minimum stay requirement on weekends

Even if the Sandpiper House didn't have such an outstanding assortment of amorous touches, the awesome view would still warrant your attention. But wood-burning fireplaces, bay windows, down comforters, canopied beds, and a complimentary bottle of wine the first night of your stay add to the blissful setting. The five sunny rooms are all decorated with soft floral fabrics, antiques, and fresh flowers. Strange as it seems, the original master bedroom, Woodland Rose, is the only room that doesn't have a water view; instead it looks out onto Highway 1. Greenwood Cove was once so busy that when the original owners built this home in 1916, a peaceful meadow view was preferred. Oh, how times have changed, and thankfully the four other rooms face the now-quiet cove.

A garden path leads to the private entrance of the enchanting Evergreen Suite. This luxurious room boasts French doors that open to a small deck with gorgeous ocean and garden views, crisp white linens on a canopied bed, a wood-burning fireplace, and a two-person soaking tub (also with a view). The Clifton Room has a shower instead of a tub, but the large bay window facing the gardens and ocean beyond is a real treat. Headlands has a lovely private patio, and Weston, perched at the top of the house, features a magnificent view from your pillow. Colorful flower gardens cover the grounds, and a charming outdoor sitting area overlooks the ocean. Beach access is shared with the neighboring **HARBOR HOUSE INN** (reviewed elswhere in this section), and if a few trips up and down these steps has your muscles begging for mercy, consider having a massage—an on-site appointment can easily be arranged. In the morning a two-course gourmet breakfast is served in the dining room, and afternoon tea and evening sherry are also included with your stay.

Restaurant Kissing

GREENWOOD PIER CAFE, Elk
5928 South Highway 1
(707) 877-9997
Moderate to Very Expensive
Breakfast, Lunch, and Dinner Daily

Lunch spots are difficult to come by in this region, particularly in the off-season. Thank goodness for the Greenwood Pier Cafe, where you can fill your growling stomachs with hearty, healthy meals accented with herbs and vegetables from the property's lavish gardens. You're in for a treat with piping hot vegetable soup, tasty pasta, sandwiches and salads made from the freshest ingredients, and scrumptious homemade desserts. Sunlight floods into the casual, airy dining room through surrounding windows that overlook the beautifully landscaped grounds.

Romantic Warning: Come prepared to linger; the wait staff can be exceedingly laid-back and leisurely (bordering on rude).

Manchester

Hotel/Bed and Breakfast Kissing

VICTORIAN GARDENS, Manchester
14409 South Highway 1
(707) 882-3606
Moderate to Very Expensive

Not at all visible from the road, Victorian Gardens Inn is a striking black-and-white Victorian set among 92 acres of meadows and forest. From the moment you arrive, quiet serenity envelops you, as the gracious hosts welcome you like a personal guest in their beautifully appointed residence. Although the home itself is thoroughly Victorian, the interior is not done in typical Victorian fashion. Instead of going the traditional route, which can sometimes be stuffy and overdone, the innkeepers here have created a refreshing blend of old and new. Polished hardwood floors, Persian rugs, hand-stenciled wallpapers, and exquisite artwork fill the main floor, and the same stylish elegance continues in the four guest rooms upstairs.

Sloped ceilings, hardwood floors, and lace curtains prevail throughout, but the spacious Master Bedroom is the premier suite. Distant ocean views can be enjoyed from a comfortable sitting area, shiny brass fixtures sparkle on the clawfoot tub, and a fluffy down comforter warms the queen-size bed. The Northwest Bedroom has a huge private tiled bath, queen-size bed with sumptuous linens and a down comforter, and ocean and pastoral views from the large soaking tub for two. The other two bedrooms, Golden and Poppy, share a bath. If a private bath isn't a top priority for you, Golden is a fine option, with a wrought-iron queen-size bed and wicker chairs set beside a bay window that showcase awesome sunsets. Poppy has two twin-size beds (not exactly conducive to kissing). Full breakfasts are served in the elegant dining room beside a crackling fire, and early evening brings wine and hors d'oeuvres.

Romantic Suggestion: Once you get comfortable here (it won't take long), you need not even step out for dinner. We highly recommend the six-course gourmet Italian meal lovingly prepared by the resident chef/innkeeper. Your innovative Italian host prepares historically authentic classics such as thin slices of ham rolled around diced potatoes, carrots, and green beans with homemade mayonnaise; *vincisgrassi,* which is hand-rolled pasta stuffed with savory wild mushrooms; and succulent roasted pork loin wrapped in porcetta. Desserts are equally mouthwatering. To keep things interesting, a new menu is presented daily, and many of the ingredients are plucked right out of the garden. Each course is served family-style in the fireside dining room, but if you call early enough, you can reserve a table for two. As you would expect from the attention to detail here, fine china, linens, crystal, and silver accompany your meal, and so does fine wine.

The only requirement for dinner is that you must request it at least a day in advance. The price is $50 per person (not including tax and gratuity, but it does include wine and additional beverages, making it an excellent value). Dinner is also open to nonguests on the same basis (24-hour advance reservations given based on availability—no drop-ins).

Point Arena

Hotel/Bed and Breakfast Kissing

WHARF MASTER'S INN, Point Arena
785 Port Road
(707) 882-3171, (800) 932-4031

Moderate to Unbelievably Expensive
Minimum stay requirement on holidays

This quiet, tree-covered hillside is where the wharf master once surveyed the comings and goings of fishing vessels in Arena Cove Harbor below. Now the site of the sprawling Wharf Master's Inn, the hillside hosts a handful of dark wood two-story buildings that overlook the still-bustling harbor. While the buildings' weather-beaten exteriors are noticeably run-down, the property's 23 spacious guest rooms are impressive and immaculate. Done up with pastel color schemes and country accents, every room has a sumptuous four-poster bed and a private deck with views of the ocean or the courtyard. All but two rooms have large, beautifully tiled Jacuzzi tubs and fireplaces. Unrivaled water and sunset views make the original wharf master's refurbished 1870s Victorian home irresistibly romantic and undeniably the best (albeit most expensive) spot to kiss on the property.

Romantic Note: Breakfast is not included with your accommodations. Although this is a bit of an inconvenience, it also allows for cheaper rates.

Romantic Alternative: Formerly a lifesaving station, **COAST GUARD HOUSE HISTORIC INN**, 695 Arena Cove, (707) 882-2442, (800) 524-9320 (Inexpensive to Expensive) proudly overlooks the marina and Arena Cove. The six small guest rooms in this venerable Cape Cod–style home are comfortable, but the heavy Mission-style furniture and Arts-and-Crafts touches make them feel more utilitarian than luxurious. Opt instead for the Boathouse, a separate little cottage with gold sponge-painted walls, high ceilings, a potbellied stove, jetted two-person tub, and all the privacy you could hope for. A full breakfast is delivered to Boathouse guests and can be enjoyed on a private patio facing the ocean.

Restaurant Kissing

PANGAEA, Point Arena
250 Main Street
(707) 882-3001
Moderate; No Credit Cards
Dinner Wednesday-Sunday

If it weren't for the delectable seasonal specialties, such as pumpkin soup scented with clove and lime or free-range chicken roasted in wine and Provence herbs, we might not have even mentioned this earthy, laid-back establishment. However, the excellent food and the fact that it is one of the very few dining options in town make Pangaea a good choice for a fun evening. The interior is an eclectic mix of New Age and funky, with track lighting, black-and-white wicker chairs, and bare tables. Bizarre photographs dot the walls, and a shrine of dripping candles burns behind a bar that takes up half of the room. Don't be put off by our description, however, as odd as all of this may sound. The staff is friendly and knowledgeable, and your meal will be memorable.

Gualala

One surefire way to spot tourists in this region is to hear how they pronounce Gualala. Don't worry; locals won't hassle you if you say it wrong, but the correct pronunciation is "wah-LA-la." Gualala is a Native American word that means "water coming down place." Luckily, the phrase does not mean you should expect rain (it is sunny here an average of 300 days a year); instead it refers to the place where the Gualala River meets the sea. Gualala offers a number of good overnight options and several excellent restaurants, which is surprising considering how small this friendly coastal village feels.

Hotel/Bed and Breakfast Kissing

BREAKERS INN, Gualala
39300 South Highway 1
(707) 884-3200, (800) 273-2537 (in California)
Expensive to Very Expensive
Minimum stay requirement on holiday weekends

As you pull into Breakers Inn's parking lot, you may feel apprehensive about our recommendation. The nondescript exterior gives no indication of the impressive suites that await. In fact, from the outside this could be any seaside motel or apartment complex. Inside, it is a completely different story. Each of the 27 rooms is decorated according to a theme, from San Francisco (a stunning room with elegant cream furnishings, a king-size carved sleigh bed, and beveled glass windows) to Virginia (a Colonial-style room featuring wingback chairs and a mahogany four-poster bed). Themes aren't limited to American styles: Japan has a two-person jetted corner tub made of rare Japanese cypress, and Provence has rattan furnishings and an intricate iron bed. Basically, Breakers Inn offers something for everyone.

Other advantages include the fact that every room has a spectacular view with a large patio facing the Gualala River estuary, the sandy beach, and the pounding surf. Radiant-heated floors warm every room, and several also have wood-burning fireplaces and whirlpool tubs for two. Our only complaint is the unimpressive continental breakfast. Fortunately, the fresh fruit and storebought pastries that are served in the main lobby can be taken back to your room, where the view, the privacy, and a cup of coffee help make up for the limited selection.

INN AT GETCHELL COVE, Gualala
36101 South Highway 1
(707) 884-1936
Expensive to Very Expensive
Minimum stay requirement on holidays

One of the newer properties on the coast, the Inn at Getchell Cove is a stunning Victorian showpiece. Recently renovated, the pale green turn-of-the-century home sits just up from the highway and faces the ocean across the busy road. From the flawless garden to the gleaming hardwood floors and impeccably restored antiques in the elegant common rooms, the owners of this impressive bed and breakfast have given every detail their undivided attention. Beautifully patterned linens and bushels of comfy pillows ornament spectacular hand-carved antique beds in each of the inn's five cozy guest rooms. Colorful wallpaper accents and pretty pastel carpets add crisp finishing touches. Each room has its own lovely tiled bathroom, although one is detached and located just down the hall. The largest room (the Sunrise Suite) boasts a two-headed shower and antique claw-foot tub.

Like everything else at Getchell Cove, the gourmet breakfast is impeccable, served to guests at one large table in the elegant, formal dining room. Hot baked dishes, gooey pastries, and fresh fruit are a perfect prelude to a day of biking, kayaking, canoeing, rafting, hiking, shopping, and whatever else you might have in mind for your day on the coast.

NORTH COAST COUNTRY INN, Gualala
34591 South Highway 1
(707) 884-4537, (800) 959-4537 (in California)
Moderate to Expensive
Minimum stay requirement on weekends and holidays

Set at the edge of busy Highway 1, this terraced weathered redwood home scales a forested hillside and provides many of the essentials for a romantic escape. Private decks trailing with vines lead to French doors that open into each of the four spacious suites, two of which have partial ocean views (across the busy highway). High peaked ceilings and open beams give the eclectic rooms, filled with country knickknacks and antiques, a feeling of spartan spaciousness. Cloth throw rugs warm the wood floors, and patchwork quilts dress up the antique four-poster beds. All four rooms have fireplaces, skylights, and fully equipped kitchenettes. Although it's a tad smaller than the others, we were partial to the Gallery Room, which has the most privacy due to its location farther up the hillside (this also means it is subject to the least amount of traffic noise). A delicious full breakfast is served privately to every room in the morning for the most intimate dining possible.

One of the property's best features is a charming lighted pathway, trimmed with flowers and greenery, that winds up the hillside to a sequestered hot tub guaranteed to soak tired spirits back to life. At the hillside's crest you'll find a gazebo and deck furnished with comfortable lounge chairs, where the only audible sound is the wind whispering through the trees.

ST. ORRES INN, Gualala
36601 South Highway 1
(707) 884-3303
Very Inexpensive to Very Expensive
Minimum stay requirement on weekends

Finding words that succinctly express the architectural intrigue of this inn is a challenge. Across the highway from a cloistered sandy cove, this structure appears suddenly out of nowhere, a fascinating hand-carved, wood-and-glass Russian-style chalet. Stained glass windows in two intricately crafted towers twinkle in the daylight; inside, prismatic light bathes the interior in a velvety amber glow. Varied guest accommodations range from eight simple, sparse rooms in the main house that share baths (and are not recommended) to 12 little cottages scattered about the grounds. Each cottage has its own spirit and tone, with rustic furnishings, a small kitchen, and varying color schemes. Some have unobstructed ocean views, while others have skylights, sundecks, fireplaces, and sunken tubs. Having said all this, we must mention that although rustic simplicity has its charm, the interiors of the cottages could use some sprucing up.

A full breakfast, including homemade granola and freshly baked bread, is delivered in a large basket each morning.

Romantic Note: Make your reservations early. In summer the cottages are booked up to eight weeks in advance.

Romantic Suggestion: Dinner at **ST. ORRES RESTAURANT** (see Restaurant Kissing) is a romantic must.

SEACLIFF, Gualala
39140 South Highway 1
(707) 884-1213, (800) 400-5053
Expensive
Minimum stay requirement on holiday weekends

Seacliff's four modern cedar structures sit on an oceanfront bluff overlooking the mouth of the Gualala River. It looks like an ordinary apartment complex from the parking lot, but once you step inside and get a load of the extraordinary view, you'll see why this is a fabulous place to kiss and kiss and kiss ...

Sixteen units are available. The eight rooms on the first floor are less expensive, but those on the second floor have vaulted ceilings and superior views from corner decks. Since the decor in all of the units can only be described as standard (brown carpet, modest furniture, and drab color schemes), we recommend spending the additional $25 per night to get a room on the second floor—the vaulted ceiling helps create an open and airy feeling. Regardless of the floor you choose, each room has a private patio, wood-burning fireplace, king-size bed, and a two-person whirlpool tub where you can watch sea gulls swoop overhead as you revel in the perfectly unobstructed ocean view.

WHALE WATCH INN, Gualala
35100 Highway 1
(707) 884-3667, (800) 942-5342
http://www.jans-journeys.com/whale/
Very Expensive to Unbelievably Expensive
Minimum stay requirement on weekends and holidays

Many modern hotels and resorts are reminiscent of suburban condominium developments: functional, but not necessarily romantic. The refreshingly artistic Whale Watch Inn is a fresh interpretation of contemporary architecture. Each of the five wooden buildings is stained a weathered seaside gray that harmonizes with the landscape. Sounds of the careening surf echo through the property, which is set above the rugged shoreline and sandy inlet of Anchor Bay. Just 134 steps separate you from the beach below (although it feels more like 200 coming back up).

Eighteen suites are available, each endowed with a unique style. Our favorites are the eight recently renovated suites in Pacific Edge, the main building, and the two rooms in the Quest building. Although the decor varies dramatically, from contemporary to classic, each room offers stunning views and a wood-burning fireplace; some have private decks and whirlpool tubs-for-two. Two rooms in the Whale Watch building are very small, but each has a little woodstove, the view is astounding, and the price is right (though still in the Very Expensive category). Rooms in the Sea Bounty and Cygnet House deserve some romantic consideration, but are not nearly as stylish or well put together as the more recently decorated ones.

A delicious gourmet breakfast is served in the privacy of your room, where you can savor ocean views and, as the name suggests, occasionally sight a pod of whales.

Restaurant Kissing

THE OLD MILANO HOTEL RESTAURANT, Gualala
38300 Highway 1
(707) 884-3256
http://www.intercoast.com/business/milano.html
Moderate to Expensive; No Credit Cards
Call for seasonal hours.

As you veer off the highway and start down the sandy driveway toward the ocean, you will readily appreciate the enveloping seclusion of this modest turn-of-the-century restaurant. Besides its wondrous location (a stone's throw from the edge of an ocean bluff), this restaurant's most irresistible attribute is its enthusiasm for antique country finery. Every corner of the dining area reveals a memento from the past; the cozy tables are draped in rose linens and topped with oil lanterns, and a roaring fire crackles in the river-rock fireplace.

The creative menu changes daily but is consistently delicious. We enjoyed an appetizer of grilled oysters served with barbecue sauce, then moved on to grilled tiger prawns served with citrus butter, and marinated pork tenderloin grilled and topped with nectarine chutney. After dinner, take a stroll through the gardens and along the bluff to admire the celestial scenery.

Romantic Note: Old-fashioned authenticity continues in the nine guest rooms at **THE OLD MILANO HOTEL** (Inexpensive to Expensive). The six rooms above the restaurant share two baths, but if you don't mind sharing the facilities, Rooms 1, 4, and 6 have great views. The master suite offers a private bath and a sitting area with incredible ocean views. A little cottage unit is set beside lovely gardens, and a cozy caboose-turned-guest-room is an option for train lovers (although neither has a view). Bright quilts and mixed floral wallpapers and fabrics in each small room may be a bit too old-fashioned for some tastes, but everyone loves the cliffside hot tub (available for private soaks), the beautifully cared-for gardens, and the outdoor sitting area with two chairs facing the rugged coast. The owners are also planning to add several new ocean-view rooms with fireplaces and private baths in the near future. Time seems to stand still at a place like this.

ST. ORRES RESTAURANT, Gualala
36601 South Highway 1

(707) 884-3303
Expensive; Credit Cards for lodging guests only
Call for seasonal hours.

St. Orres' Russian-inspired architecture is anything but ordinary, and the restaurant exemplifies this property's flair for the unusual. A three-story-high wooden tower, adorned with stained glass windows and stenciled wood-work, houses a dramatic dining room, ideal for romancing the night away. Trailing plants hang from the walls, and the atmosphere is formal yet entirely warm. Distant views of the ocean are visible from some of the candlelit two-person tables clustered at the base of the tower. Dinner here is a prix fixe three-course delight, with unusual entrées like wild boar stuffed with dates and walnuts, served with homemade apple-ginger chutney from St. Orres' orchards; a grilled vegetable tart in a flaky pastry shell with fresh corn beignets and a smoked tomato sauce; or grilled Sonoma County quail marinated in tequila, served with yam and green onion pancakes, quail wontons, and a blood orange–jalapeño pepper glaze. The specialty here is wild game of the North Coast, but a couple of vegetarian options are also available.

TOP OF THE CLIFF, Gualala
39140 South Highway 1
(707) 884-1539
Moderate to Expensive
Lunch and Dinner Daily

You'll wonder why we're sending you to this little redwood shopping center, but take a closer look. On the second floor you'll see Top Of The Cliff, one of the newest and most welcome additions to the Gualala dining scene. The small restaurant and bar holds only 12 tables, but each one has a view of the ocean. Tables right beside the windows have the best vantage point, but every seat is good and there is no indication that Highway 1 and a busy parking lot are right outside. Glass oil lanterns, flowers on each table, and low lighting create a casual but intimate atmosphere.

Seafood, steak, and pasta dishes are served in extremely generous portions, and each meal includes warm bread, hot soup, and fresh salad. The halibut baked with crab and Brie was richly satisfying, but unfortunately left no room for dessert. We were sorry to miss the chocolate-raspberry cheesecake—we hear it's divine.

Outdoor Kissing

KAYAKING, Gualala
Adventure Rents, behind the Gualala Hotel

(707) 884-4386, (888) 881-4386
Gualala Kayak, 39175 South Highway 1 (next to the Chevron station)
(707) 884-4705
Prices start at $25 per kayak

Whether braving ocean waves and currents or just meandering up the Gualala River, lovers of the great outdoors will thoroughly enjoy a kayak excursion. A paddle upriver is perfect for spotting ospreys, great blue herons, and brown pelicans; if you're lucky you may see river otters playing in the water. There is room in each kayak to bring along a picnic lunch (see the following Romantic Suggestion), and if you have a waterproof container for your camera (a plastic bag will do), the photo opportunities are innumerable. Canoes are also available.

Romantic Warning: River kayaking is fine for beginners, but sea kayaking is for the more experienced only.

Romantic Suggestion: Those interested in exploring Gualala's spectacularly private beaches might want to pack a lunch and make a day of it. **THE FOOD COMPANY**, 38411 Robinson Reach, (707) 884-1800 (Inexpensive), located right off Highway 1 in Gualala, is an excellent place to purchase a carry-out gourmet lunch. Whether it's wild mushroom lasagne, deep-dish pizza, or a tempting chocolate soufflé roll with mocha cream, you're sure to find something appetizing. (So appetizing, in fact, that it might be gone before you reach the beach.) Call on the day you plan to picnic and the friendly staff can usually put together something delicious for you. The price for two is typically under $20, not including wine.

ROTH RANCH, Gualala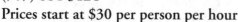
37100 Old Stage Road
(707) 884-3124
Prices start at $30 per person per hour

Roth Ranch provides healthy, energetic horses for gallops along logging trails lined with redwoods, rhododendrons, and wild azaleas. Prices are reasonable for rentals by the hour. If an hour just isn't long enough, request a three-hour excursion that includes a picnic lunch (optional) along the rushing Gualala River. When the river is low (usually toward the end of summer), the ocean beach is accessible.

Sea Ranch

Hotel/Bed and Breakfast Kissing

SEA RANCH ESCAPE, Sea Ranch

60 Sea Walk Drive
(707) 785-2426, (800) SEA-RANCH
Moderate to Unbelievably Expensive

Views of the thundering surf crashing onto Sea Ranch's rugged, rocky shoreline can be best appreciated from the seclusion of your very own luxury rental home. Sea Ranch Escape's vacation properties are some of the prettiest we've seen, scattered along more than ten miles of exquisite coastline. Ranging from cozy cottages tucked among trees to enormous ocean-front homes equipped with every imaginable luxury and amenity, you're sure to find something to match your budget and personality. Most of the homes are newly built, stylishly outfitted, and stocked with all the basic necessities (a full kitchen, towels, linens, blankets, firewood, etc.). Many have spectacular ocean views, decks, fireplaces or wood-burning stoves, and even Jacuzzi tubs. They also come with all the privacy in the world—what more could you need?

SEA RANCH LODGE, Sea Ranch
60 Sea Walk Drive
(707) 785-2371, (800) 732-7262
Moderate to Expensive
Minimum stay requirement

The boundless drama of the Pacific Ocean harbors plenty of romantic possibilities, and the closer your accommodations are to this magnificent shoreline, the better. They don't get much closer than Sea Ranch Lodge, nestled on a bluff directly above the sand dunes and ocean. Though the lodge's common areas are modestly appointed with low-slung couches and dated artwork, gorgeous unhindered views from the solarium and a raging fire in the stone hearth in the piano bar provide all the inspiration you'll need. Guest rooms are rather nondescript, with knotty pine walls, patchwork quilts, and small standard baths, but the extraordinary views, occasional fire-place or Jacuzzi tub, and lack of television and telephones give the otherwise basic hotel rooms some romantic promise. Better yet, renovations are cur-rently underway, which should make some of the lodge's dated distractions a moot point.

Romantic Note: Sea Ranch's **POINTS RESTAURANT** (see Restaurant Kissing) offers excellent cuisine and the same divine ocean views.

Restaurant Kissing

POINTS RESTAURANT, Sea Ranch
60 Sea Walk Drive, at the Sea Ranch Lodge

(707) 785-2371, (800) 732-7262
Moderate to Expensive
Breakfast, Lunch, and Dinner Daily; Sunday Brunch

Views of windswept, undulating sand dunes that reach down to the fringes of the turbulent ocean surf are the highlight of Sea Ranch Lodge's restaurant, with its wall of towering windows. Impressionistic seascapes mimic the views. Although fresh flowers and crisp white linens adorn every table, the restaurant retains an exceedingly casual, lodge-style ambience. Breakfast, lunch, and dinner are served daily, but dinner is by far the most romantic meal, especially if your reservation corresponds with the sunset.

We especially enjoyed the lentil and sun-dried tomato spinach salad; Mediterranean pasta served with baby summer squash, shiitake mushrooms, and artichoke hearts; and, most heavenly of all, the Chocolate Landslide— rich milk chocolate and pecans topped with fresh raspberries and whipped cream. After you've eaten, head to the fireside room, where you can relish the warmth of a fire flickering in the stone fireplace, or take in more delicious ocean views in the adjacent solarium.

Fort Ross

Hotel/Bed and Breakfast Kissing

FORT ROSS LODGE, Fort Ross
20705 Highway 1
(707) 847-3333
Very Inexpensive to Very Expensive
Minimum stay requirement on weekends for some rooms

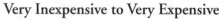

Encircled by rolling meadows dotted with wildflowers and dried golden brush, this very casual destination offers some affordable, affectionate options. Because of its great prices and child-friendly policy, Fort Ross Lodge caters mostly to families (especially during summer vacation). However, if you're on a budget and you don't mind the slight motor-lodge feel, you're in luck. All 16 units in "The Lodge" have simple floral or paisley linens (some could use replacement); amenities such as a small refrigerator, coffeemaker, and television; and sliding glass doors that open to a private, enclosed deck with a barbecue for your use. The best rooms (the King and Queen Rooms numbered 5 through 8 and 14 through 17) overlook the unobstructed beauty of the Pacific Ocean, and some have a fireplace or a little hot tub on a private patio. A glass-enclosed hot tub with the same view is available for all guests. Another favorite feature for all guests is a mowed path leading to the edge of 150-foot coastal cliffs where you can watch the waves crash on the shore or catch a stupendous sunset.

Six more units are set in "The Hill" building, across the street on a forested hillside. These rooms are billed as the more romantic (and more expensive) suites because they are designated "adults only" and four of them have in-room spa tubs. Due to the location, a walk to the shore isn't an immediate option, but a tree-framed view of the sea is still visible from all but one room. These rooms are decorated in a more contemporary style (floral prints on black backgrounds), and feel like studio apartments where you can host your own private party for two.

Romantic Note: When making reservations, you should know that Rooms 9 through 12 and Room 19 have no view at all. Also, be sure to ask about midweek discounts and specials.

Cazadero

Hotel/Bed and Breakfast Kissing

TIMBERHILL RANCH, Cazadero   😚 😚 😚 😚
35755 Hauser Bridge Road
(707) 847-3258
Unbelievably Expensive (price includes breakfast and dinner)
Minimum stay requirement on weekends
Closed January
Recommended Wedding Site

If you're hoping to escape the pressures of the daily grind (and who isn't when it comes to romance?), you couldn't have chosen a better destination. Nothing about this pastoral ranch is remotely reminiscent of the real world (except maybe the price tag). Poised at the top of a ridge above the Sonoma coast, Timberhill Ranch encompasses 80 serene wooded acres of nature's finest greenery.

Secluded among trees, the ranch's 15 handsome cedar log cabins are rustic yet elegant, with knotty pine walls, colorful handmade quilts, tiled wood-burning fireplaces, and (best of all) views of sensational sunsets from private decks. Amenities like oversized tiled bathrooms and mini-bars complete with fridges stocked with tasty refreshments add to your comfort. Hike to your hearts' content through seemingly endless acres of rambling woodland (beyond the ranch itself are 6,000 acres of protected wilderness, where dozens of footpaths wind through redwood forests, past shimmering ponds and fields of wildflowers in adjacent **SALT POINT STATE PARK** and

KRUSE RHODODENDRON RESERVE). You can also make use of the property's premier tennis courts or simply enjoy the scenery from the soothing comfort of a 40-foot heated pool and nearby steaming Jacuzzi tub.

Although the room rates seem quite steep, keep in mind that they include an ample continental breakfast brought to your cottage every morning and a six-course evening meal served in the inn's handsome dining room, which is filled with intimate tables set with silver and crystal. Meals here are remarkable. On any given day the menu may include a noteworthy chilled artichoke appetizer with tarragon and Maine crab; a robust old-fashioned split-pea soup; perfectly seared Chilean sea bass; wonderful grilled swordfish with a black bean and roasted corn relish; homemade mango sorbet as a palate refresher; and, for dessert, strawberry buttercream cake. Consider a walk around the grounds between courses, especially if you can catch the sunset.

Jenner

If it weren't for the spectacular vistas, the sleepy little town of Jenner would be little more than a big curve in the road where the Russian River meets the sea. Calm river waters, a sandy shoreline, and, of course, the sparkling Pacific Ocean give Jenner a special identity all its own. There aren't many kissable overnight options, but you should at least consider stopping for lunch to get your fill of this incredible scenery.

Restaurant Kissing

JENNER BY THE SEA RESTAURANT, Jenner
10400 Highway 1
(707) 865-1192
Moderate
Call for seasonal hours.

In any other setting this restaurant might be a little too rustic, too casual, and too near the highway for a romantic dinner. Here on the Sonoma coast, however, almost any restaurant with a large fireplace and hearth, windows that survey the meandering Russian River emptying into the Pacific (albeit beyond the highway), and a kitchen staff that prepares execptionally fresh seafood dishes is indeed a special spot and worth a kiss or two. Hanging plants trail around the room and black lacquered chairs sit at each of the linen-draped tables. Dishes such as a zesty cioppino and scallops sautéed with black olives, garlic, wine, and pecans are served by an efficient, friendly staff.

Romantic Note: Under the same management, **JENNER INN AND COTTAGES**, 10400 Highway 1, (707) 865-2377, (800) 732-2377 (Inexpensive to Expensive) offers a variety of bed-and-breakfast accommodations, from entire homes to individual units within houses. With their outdated, mismatched furnishings, even the most expensive vacation rentals are far too rustic to be awarded with any lips; however, many of them are set right on the sparkling shore of the Russian River estuary with incredible views of the beach and ocean. Call and ask for a brochure that describes what is available, because saving money and/or being this close to the water might be more important to you than glistening chandeliers and sumptuous linens.

RIVER'S END, Jenner
11048 Highway 1
(707) 865-2484
Moderate
Breakfast, Lunch, and Dinner Daily

Views of swirling white water and turbulent eddies that explode over and around the rock outcroppings of the Pacific Ocean can change at twilight into a placid, almost surreal, composition. As sunset nears, a single path of sunlight glosses the surface, illuminating the water and the horizon, with the hills veiled in darkness. Evening announces its finale with a crescendo of colors that fade slowly to black. From the deck, dining room, or solarium lounge of the River's End restaurant, perched at the edge of the Russian River estuary, this daily, sparkling performance is yours to behold. The menu offers traditional seafood items; our meal was just average, but with the glistening ocean outside, we found it easier to forgive the kitchen's shortcomings.

Outdoor Kissing

GOAT ROCK STATE PARK, Jenner

From Highway 1, watch for signs to Goat Rock State Park.

This dramatic location would have been awarded our premium four-lip rating except that, like many other state parks, it is so packed with people during the summer and on weekends that privacy is hard to find. Still, this place is so alluring that you shouldn't let the crowds deter you. Here the milky green and blue waters of the Pacific crash into the surf and meet the mouth of the Russian River estuary. Water laps on both sides of this small strip of beach, and massive rocks protrude from the sea where colonies of sea lions and seals sometimes bask in the sun.

Romantic Suggestion: There might be fewer people at **SHELL BEACH**, just south of Goat Rock State Park. A beat-up trail leads down to this little section of sand, which is best visited at low tide, when there are diverse tide pools to study. Also, you should be able to find some shells to take home as mementos of a day of fun in the sun. Just make sure that a little crustacean isn't living in the shell you choose.

Pocket Canyon

Hotel/Bed and Breakfast Kissing

APPLEWOOD INN, Pocket Canyon
13555 Highway 116
(707) 869-9093, (800) 555-8509
http://www.applewoodinn.com
Moderate to Very Expensive
Minimum stay requirement on weekends

Built in 1922, this Mediterranean-style pink stucco home once served as a private family estate. Today its European allure and historic elegance enchant guests year-round. Footpaths wind through the lovingly landscaped property, past a stone courtyard with a burbling lion's-head fountain and a large outdoor swimming pool set among spartan stands of trees.

Nine of the inn's 16 guest rooms are located in the spacious, meandering original building. Appropriately, these rooms exude historic authenticity, with English-style antiques, dark wood accents, canopied beds, and brightly-colored fabrics. Several rooms in this building have private balconies, and most have views of the landscaped grounds. We prefer the seven austere rooms in the newer building, which are much more stylish and contemporary. Here, brightly colored walls make an unusual backdrop for eye-catching artwork, and thick down comforters drape sensuous sleigh beds. All of these rooms have gas fireplaces and Jacuzzi tubs or double-headed showers in spacious, modernistic bathrooms inlaid with gorgeous tilework.

In the morning, a vast array of hot breakfast entrées like sautéed apples, Brie omelets, and eggs Florentine are served along with pastries and fresh fruit in the airy dining room of the main building. Dinner is also served here Tuesday through Saturday evenings.

Occidental

Hotel/Bed and Breakfast Kissing

INN AT OCCIDENTAL, Occidental
3657 Church Street
(707) 874-1047, (800) 522-6324
http://www.innatoccidental.com
Minimum stay requirement on weekends

Notorious for his exuberance and enthusiasm, the innkeeper here has used his energy, attention to details, and artistic flair to create a work of art. Set high on a redwood-covered hillside overlooking the small historical town of Occidental, this beautifully restored gabled Victorian home brims with country charm. Oriental carpets cover the hardwood floors, and country knickknacks and antiques fill common areas where guests can lounge in overstuffed sofas and enjoy the warmth of a crackling fire in a brick hearth. Outside, the flower-laden veranda furnished with comfortably cushioned white wicker furniture is a perfect spot to enjoy views of the valley and town below.

There is nothing the conscientious innkeeper has overlooked. Even the smallest of the inn's eight guest rooms is convincingly elegant, with unusual but attractive color schemes that reflect the warm hues of the nature photographs and artwork that adorn the walls. Antique collections vary from room to room, complementing the contemporary mood with a historical flavor. Fluffy down comforters cover sumptuous feather beds, and rich chocolates and a decanter filled with sweet liqueur await guests at their bedside tables. In the Cut Glass Room, sliding French doors open onto a private patio, garden, and six-person hot tub. A corner fireplace glows in the airy Quilt Suite, which also features a ten-foot ceiling and Jacuzzi spa built for two. A canopied four-poster mahogany queen-size bed distinguishes the fireside Tiffany Suite, our favorite room of all.

Awaken in the morning to the enticing aromas of freshly baked pastries, orange pancakes, and other gourmet delights served family-style in the formal dining room. When the weather is warm, you can enjoy this repast outside on the veranda.

Romantic Note: Our only complaint about this lovely bed and breakfast is that noise carries a little too easily from room to room. We were distracted by a nearby television for a good part of the evening we were here.

Bodega Bay

Perched above the rocky coast, Bodega Bay and an array of other small towns dot this shoreline, boasting spectacular views, wonderfully romantic accommodations, and several marvelous beaches accessible from Highway 1. Keep watch for the "COASTAL ACCESS" signs, which will direct you to secluded, windswept beaches—enticing to beachcombers and romantics alike.

Hotel/Bed and Breakfast Kissing

BAY HILL MANSION, Bodega Bay
3919 Bay Hill Road
(707) 875-3577, (800) 526-5927
Inexpensive to Very Expensive
Minimum stay requirement on holidays

Weddings are a specialty at the Bay Hill Mansion; so are sunsets, so even if it's not your big day, the view west at twilight will reward you for staying here. We aren't sure why the word "mansion" is included in this bed and breakfast's name, because the term suggests gilt-edged refinement and a substantial estate, which you won't find here. What you will find are seven comfortable guest rooms in a contemporary Victorian-style home set on a hillside above the village. Soft pastels, dainty florals, and both modern and antique touches decorate every room. We recommend only the four rooms with private or detached private baths; the other three rooms share one bath. The Whale Watch and Jenner's Reach rooms are in the turrets so they have a circular shape and expansive windows. The slightly larger Honeymooner's Hideaway holds some of the prettiest antiques in the house.

In the evening, wine, appetizers, and, of course, glorious sunsets draw guests to the main-floor parlor, with its immense woodstove, homey furnishings, and expansive bay window. In the morning, a full gourmet breakfast is served family-style in the dining room, where more wonderful windows overlook the ocean and Bodega Bay.

BODEGA BAY AND BEYOND
VACATION RENTALS, Bodega Bay
1400 Highway 1, in the Pelican Plaza
(707) 875-3942, (800) 888-3565
http://www.sonomacoast.com
Moderate to Unbelievably Expensive
Minimum stay requirement

It's hard to believe that the owners of these spectacular custom-built homes don't live here year-round, but their loss is your romantic gain. These dream homes can become a reality with just one phone call to Bodega Bay and Beyond. Every one of the rental company's properties is located in Bodega Harbour, a community of stylish, contemporary homes with water views, adjacent to an 18-hole golf course. No matter which you select, you will be surrounded with luxury.

All 29 of the attractive homes are beautifully furnished and equipped with everything you could ever need and more: full kitchens, TV/VCRs, wood-burning fireplaces, firewood, even barbecue grills. Listen to the distant blare of the fog horn from the deck of the Sea Cottage, which looks past the 15th green to the beach and bay. More water views, ample sunlight, stylish decor, and extra touches like double-headed showers and plush linens are some of the enticing features of Cedar Grove. Gull Haven has three bedrooms and baths, a wet bar, two fireplaces, a CD player, pool table, and spacious decks. Harbor Nest, which is slightly more rustic than some of the other rental homes, is popular with couples because of its large hot tub on an outside deck and cozy knotty pine interior.

Romantic Note: A two-night minimum is required, but we recommend staying longer and taking advantage of the generous midweek specials (four nights for the price of three).

BODEGA BAY LODGE, Bodega Bay 💋💋
103 Coast Highway 1
(707) 875-3525, (800) 368-2468
http://www.wlodging.com
Moderate to Very Expensive
Minimum stay requirement on weekends

At first glance, Bodega Bay Lodge looks like little more than a run-of-the-mill highway motor lodge, but a closer look will reveal its wondrous water views and remodeled interior. Even the lobby is surprisingly upscale and comfortable, outfitted with overstuffed sofas snuggled next to a large stone fireplace, floor-to-ceiling bookshelves, and winsome sculptures of frolicking dolphins.

Perched atop an oceanfront bluff, the lodge's 78 guest rooms survey gorgeous views of Bodega Bay and the windswept sand dunes of the adjacent **DORAN BEACH REGIONAL PARK** and bird sanctuary. Only the occasional sound of the harbor horn interrupts the remote peace of this sprawling property. Distinctive touches like shell lamps and seascape sculptures add individuality to the hotel-style rooms, which are done in shades of green and furnished with rattan. Every room has a private deck overlooking the water, and most have the romantic luxury of wood-burning fireplaces. Televisions, coffeemakers, plush white towels and robes, and the added convenience of a refrigerator and wet bar are appreciated amenities. Seashore vegetation defines trails that meander through the property to an exercise room, sauna, outdoor pool, and glass-enclosed whirlpool with an open-top gazebo and ocean views.

Romantic Suggestion: After a day spent enjoying the lodge's spectacular beachfront, we recommend a candlelight dinner at the property's very own

DUCK CLUB RESTAURANT (Moderate to Expensive) which serves breakfast and dinner daily. An immense river-rock fireplace warms this bay-view dining room, which is also decorated with duck sculptures and paintings. Large (a little too large) circular tables are draped in white linens. Trained in Italy, the chef is well known for his seafood ravioli served with lobster saffron cream, and other culinary seafood creations.

Bodega

Hotel/Bed and Breakfast Kissing

SONOMA COAST VILLA, Bodega
16072 Coast Highway 1
(707) 876-9818, (888) 404-2255
http://www.scvilla.com
Expensive to Very Expensive
Minimum stay requirement on weekends
Closed January

You can't miss this prodigious property, conspicuously nestled in 60 acres of rolling hills scattered with oak trees and grazing cattle. Sonoma Coast Villa's red tiled roofs, terra-cotta and stucco exterior, and terraced grounds and courtyard are reminiscent of a Mediterranean mansion. Two affectionate yellow Labs greet guests inside the elegant front lobby. Here, a circular staircase leads up to a tower library, brimming with dog-eared novels, homey knickknacks, and panoramic windows that showcase lovely views of the surrounding countryside. From the lobby, a shaded walkway lined with cactus plants and palm trees proceeds past a scintillating outdoor swimming pool to six ranch-style guest rooms with enormous wood-burning fireplaces.

In contrast with the palatial, elegantly landscaped grounds, the rooms' interiors are somewhat bland and mismatched, with neutral color schemes, slate floors, and stucco walls. Skylights and vaulted ceilings, private entrances and baths, TVs and VCRs, fireplaces, and private patios in several of the rooms help enliven the otherwise lackluster mood. To further spice up the villa's romantic potential, we recommend nibbling on afternoon hors d'oeuvres in the privacy of your own room, sharing a late-night dip in the large indoor communal Jacuzzi tub, and going for a moonlit walk through the lavish property. Continental breakfast is included, served at two-person tables in a charming public dining room adorned with dried flower arrangements.

Romantic Suggestion: Once you've made yourselves comfortable, there is no need to get in your car in search of a romantic dinner site. Known for its reasonably priced and delectable prix fixe meals, the villa's own **SONOMA**

COAST RESTAURANT (Moderate to Expensive) is footsteps away and serves dinner nightly. Flickering candles and white linens accentuate intimate sitting arrangments in the handsome dining room. Savor an appetizer of Bodega goat cheese with smoked eggplant and spinach, sautéed salmon and prawns for an entrée, and puffs filled with French vanilla ice cream and accompanied by chocolate salsa and berries for dessert. After your meal, take an easy stroll through the luscious grounds, which abound with ideal places to kiss.

Marshall

Hotel/Bed and Breakfast Kissing

POET'S LOFT, Marshall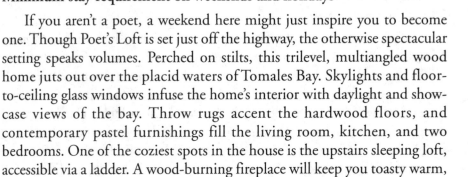
19695 Highway 1
(415) 453-8080
Moderate; No Credit Cards
Minimum stay requirement on weekends and holidays

If you aren't a poet, a weekend here might just inspire you to become one. Though Poet's Loft is set just off the highway, the otherwise spectacular setting speaks volumes. Perched on stilts, this trilevel, multiangled wood home juts out over the placid waters of Tomales Bay. Skylights and floor-to-ceiling glass windows infuse the home's interior with daylight and show-case views of the bay. Throw rugs accent the hardwood floors, and contemporary pastel furnishings fill the living room, kitchen, and two bedrooms. One of the coziest spots in the house is the upstairs sleeping loft, accessible via a ladder. A wood-burning fireplace will keep you toasty warm, as will the spacious outdoor hot tub, which also offers a sweeping panorama of the bay and Point Reyes Peninsula. If this doesn't fuel your poetic inclinations, nothing will.

Romantic Warning: This is a vacation rental, not a bed and breakfast. Guests must provide their own food and linens. However, if you are from out of town, linens and towels can be provided for an extra charge.

Inverness and Point Reyes Station

Bordering the **POINT REYES NATIONAL SEASHORE** (see Outdoor Kissing) and Marin County, Inverness and Point Reyes are the entry points into this gorgeous coastal area. Scattered along the shore of Tomales Bay, these two quaint villages harbor numerous waterside and hillside romantic retreats. Even though this region is sparsely populated and particularly quiet in the winter months, it is too well traveled in the spring and summer. Nevertheless, if you can ignore the crowds or travel off-season, a stay at one of the special bed and breakfasts in the area can be utterly romantic and memorable.

Hotel/Bed and Breakfast Kissing

BLACKTHORNE INN, Inverness Park
266 Vallejo Avenue
(415) 663-8621
http://www.blackthorneinn.com
Moderate to Very Expensive
Minimum stay requirement on weekends

Like a child's tree house, only better, the Blackthorne Inn is a four-story wooden castle with twin turrets, peaked gables, and multipaned windows that feels as if it were nesting high in the treetops. Outside, an octagonal tower is surrounded by an expansive redwood deck, complete with a Jacuzzi tub and a fire fighter's pole that descends to the drive below. Inside, classical music casts a cultivated spell in the spacious living room, with its immense stone hearth and vaulted open-beam ceiling.

Skylights, stained glass windows, and exposed wood walls are some of the highlights found in each of the five guest rooms. Two rooms (with a shared bath) are situated on the main floor; a spiral staircase leads up to the more private ones. The Lupine Room is divinely cozy, with a sloped ceiling and its own entrance, while the Overlook has small outdoor terrace and a small Juliet-style balcony overlooking the living room. The top-of-the-line (and top-of-the-house) unit is the Eagle's Nest, which occupies the octagonal tower; windows on all sides look out to the treetops, and a steep ladder climbs to a private sundeck. (The only drawback to renting the Eagle's Nest is that the bathroom lies across a 40-foot-high outdoor walkway—a potentially chilly jaunt in the middle of the night.) A jetted hot tub is available to all guests until 11 P.M., when it is designated for the private use of guests in the Eagle's Nest.

A full breakfast is served buffet-style every morning and can be enjoyed on the deck, weather permitting, or in the sunny breakfast room at your own table for two.

DANCING COYOTE BEACH
GUEST COTTAGES, Inverness
Sir Francis Drake Boulevard
(415) 669-7200
Moderate; No Credit Cards
Minimum stay requirement on weekends

Nestled on the shore of Tomales Bay, this getaway is the perfect retreat when you're in need of quiet time together. Dancing Coyote's four adjoining beachfront cottages are sheltered from the busy road by a stand of sturdy pine and cypress trees that climb a small hillside. A lovingly landscaped garden enfolds a small outdoor deck furnished with wooden lounge chairs where guests can enjoy close-up views of pelicans swooping down to the water's edge.

Decorated in pastel shades of peach and green, Acacia, Birch, and Beach are three lovely two-story cottages with all the right romantic touches: wood-burning fireplaces, cozy loft bedrooms, two private decks, abundant skylights, and floor-to-ceiling windows (the closer the cottage is to the water, the better the view). A less expensive, slightly more rustic studio cottage, called Skye, is outfitted with rough-hewn wood beams and walls, a small sleeping loft (big enough for just a bed) with a glimpse of the bay, and a funky but surprisingly invigorating outdoor shower. Breakfast provisions are provided for guests to eat at their leisure in the privacy of their own small galley kitchen. Each cottage has access to private beachfront a few feet from its front door. However, keep in mind that your sense of privacy is minimized when all four cottages are occupied and neighboring guests are trekking past to reach the beach. If this is a romantic distraction, take advantage of the fact that all of the windows have Venetian blinds.

GRAY'S RETREAT, Point Reyes Station
11559 Highway 1
(415) 663-1166
Expensive
Minimum stay requirement on weekends

Framed by flower gardens and a dusty horse pasture, this renovated two-story cedar barn was once the original Point Reyes schoolhouse in 1870. Today, the lower floor of this building has been beautifully transformed into an idyllic country retreat, just right for two. Sunshine streams through expansive multipaned windows in the living room and adjacent spacious kitchen, enhancing the golden color scheme and terra-cotta-tiled floors. Funky art, eclectic furnishings, floral fabrics, and a wood-burning stove blend to create a stylish, cheerful ambience. Cozy up in the four-poster bed covered with inviting, rich linens in a separate bedroom or dazzle your beloved with your culinary talents in the fully equipped gourmet kitchen (provisions are your responsibility). Views of Point Reyes' surrounding countryside are plentiful, and French doors in the bedroom and the dining area open onto a private wooden deck that overlooks the pasture, where a gentle-tempered donkey grazes.

Romantic Alternative: If Gray's Retreat is booked, consider the property's other option, **JASMINE COTTAGE**, (415) 663-1166 (Expensive), surrounded by herb, flower, and vegetable gardens, and a flock of clucking chickens that provide fresh morning eggs for guests. The tiny, self-contained wood cottage is charmingly cozy, with lace curtains, a wood-burning stove, a full kitchen stocked with tasty breakfast items, Oriental rugs strewn over a rock floor, and a floral-cushioned window seat with views of the garden. Another romantic perk is the hot tub situated just outside, secluded behind a latticed-wood fence. Though it feels like the country, don't forget that the innkeeper's home is just on the other side of the garden.

HOTEL INVERNESS, Inverness
25 Park Avenue
(415) 669-7393
Moderate to Expensive
Minimum stay requirement on weekends

You'd never guess from the unassuming name or classically restored exterior of this historic building that the Hotel Inverness is one of a kind. When it comes to interior decorating, the owners of Hotel Inverness have boldly gone where few innkeepers have dared to go. If something fun and different is part of your romantic agenda, consider staying here. Three vividly attired rooms are located on the second story. Sunny yellow dominates the first room, bright red covers the walls in another, and a gorgeous blue graces the third. The yellow room is too reminiscent of a kid's playroom to be very romantic, but the red room is truly striking, and the tranquil blue room, with a private deck and a lovely seashore painting that covers most of one wall, is especially inviting. Two more rooms, larger than the others, were nearing completion when we last visited; one has a private deck and both have sitting areas, antique furnishings, and rich color schemes of chocolate and taupe. (These rooms will also have two queen-size beds, which isn't necessarily a romantic setup, but you will appreciate the extra space.) Each room has a distinct character, but bent willow furniture, striking local art, and fun touches are a constant throughout. An expanded continental breakfast is delivered to your room; if it's a sunny morning, you can ask to have it served on the common deck area.

MANKA'S INVERNESS LODGE, Inverness
Argyle Avenue and Callendar Way
(415) 669-1034, (800) 585-6343
Moderate to Expensive

Since Manka's Inverness Lodge runs one of the sexiest restaurants in all of Northern California (see Restaurant Kissing), it's no surprise that its overnight accommodations are equally seductive. Eleven units are available in and around this turn-of-the-century hunting lodge set on a densely forested hillside. The rooms incorporate romance into the hunting lodge theme (authentic right down to real fur rugs, stuffed fish, and hunting trophies) with huge unpeeled log beds, rough-hewn wood walls, cozy fireplaces, and bold hunting prints and plaids. (The four rooms located directly above the restaurant are subject to too much crowd noise during dinnertime, but are entirely intimate after-hours or on Tuesday and Wednesday nights, when the restaurant is closed.) Two cabins on the property make distinctive retreats for embracing, particularly the Fishing Cabin, with its Adirondack-style furnishings and a tub for two that faces a glowing fireplace.

Breakfast is not included with your stay, but the restaurant is open every morning from 8:30 A.M. until 10:00 A.M., and prices range from $5 to $11 per dish. A morning meal of, say, eggs scrambled with shiitake mushrooms and local goat cheese, accompanied by homemade wild boar sausage and cream biscuits, should more than prepare you for the day (don't worry; lighter options are also offered). If you're impressed with what the kitchen produces in the morning, plan ahead by making reservations for dinner, when Manka's chefs really shine.

Romantic Alternative: Manka's also operates the **CHICKEN RANCH** (Very Expensive to Unbelievably Expensive), a rustic 1850s cabin set at the edge of Tomales Bay. This one-bedroom home, named for its original use, is the oldest building in all of West Marin. Although the cabin's interior shows some wear and tear, features like its waterside location, wraparound deck with trailing vines, and resident "guard pony" (Duke, a Shetland pony who has lived there over 30 years) add an incredible amount of charm.

MARSH COTTAGE BED AND
BREAKFAST, Point Reyes Station
(415) 669-7168
http://www.coastaltraveler.com
Moderate; No Credit Cards

As you might deduce from the name, this small, weathered wood cottage sits on the shore of a marsh on Tomales Bay. Although the cabin is situated just off a fairly busy road, a fence deflects most of the traffic noise. Cattails, wild flowers, and long, honey-colored grasses grow around the cabin, framing a nature lover's paradise. Country prints and fabrics, a wood-burning fireplace, and French doors that open onto a sundeck overlooking the marsh enhance the cabin's natural mood. A two-person hammock swinging out-side provides the perfect spot to bird-watch or witness the sun setting over the rolling hills across the bay.

A more than generous breakfast of fresh orange juice, homebaked bread or muffins, seasonal fruits, milk and granola, a basket of eggs, cheeses, tea, and coffee awaits guests in the semimodern, fully equipped kitchen. Your only complaint here will be the fact that you can't stay longer.

THE NEON ROSE, Point Reyes Station
Overlook Road
(415) 663-9143, (800) 358-8346
http://www.neonrose.com
Expensive; No Credit Cards

Thankfully, the only neon to be found at this private country retreat is one red rose, set above the bedroom's arched door frame. Situated in a supremely serene neighborhood, the Neon Rose caters to lovers who really want to escape the city—neon lights included. Pass through a flourishing flower garden into the self-contained one-bedroom cottage, which commands sweeping views of Point Reyes and the bay beyond. The sparse interior features hardwood floors, soft colors, skylights, and chic appointments. All of the conveniences of home, such as a full kitchen, nice stereo system, and tele-phone, are here, plus cozy touches like a living area warmed by a woodstove, a small bedroom with a queen-size bed and plush down comforter, and a jetted tub in the bathroom. A generous continental breakfast is supplied for you to prepare at your own pace. Neon Rose provides peace, quiet, and a healthy dose of relaxation. What more could a city-weary couple ask for?

PATTERSON HOUSE, Inverness
Sir Francis Drake Boulevard
(415) 669-1383
Moderate to Expensive
Minimum stay requirement on weekends

Authentic bed and breakfasts are a rare commodity in Point Reyes and Inverness, where a recent explosion of self-contained rental cottages has over-taken the market. Although Patterson House can't compete with the privacy of a secluded cabin, it compensates with hands-on service, traditional amenities, and the historical perspective that bed and breakfasts are famous for.

Built in 1916, this Craftsman-style, brown-shingled home is perched high on a quiet hillside across the road from Tomales Bay. An eclectic mix-ture of rustic, Victorian, and modern appointments gives the five guest rooms a modest, homey disposition. Thick white eyelet comforters cover queen- and king-size beds, and Oriental carpets accent hardwood floors in some of the rooms. All of the rooms have small private baths with pretty tilework, pedestal sinks, and antique claw-foot tubs. Several rooms have private decks with views of the bay, where you can sit and inhale the scent of trailing wisteria under the moon and stars. You can also stargaze from the communal hot tub set outside on a large deck, although your privacy may be interrupted by other couples with the same idea. Continental breakfast is a family affair, served to guests at one large table in an old-fashioned dining room warmed by a raging fire in the hearth.

SANDY COVE INN, Inverness
12990 Sir Francis Drake Boulevard
(415) 669-2683, (800) 759-2683
Moderate to Very Expensive

Sandy Cove Inn is aptly named, due to its location just off a stretch of sandy shore along Tomales Bay. The weathered gray Cape Cod–style home is enveloped by four acres of country landscape and abundant herb and flower gardens, and tall trees completely conceal it from the road. Two resident sheep lounge amidst the gardens, adding to the pastoral charm of this place, and the innkeepers' careful attention to detail ensures a peaceful, romantic stay. From the wine and cheese in your room upon arrival to evening turndown service to the abundant breakfast the following morning, no detail is slighted.

There are only three guest rooms, each with its own private entrance, queen-size bed, free-standing fireplace, private tiled bath, telephone, stereo, small refrigerator, and coffeemaker. Antique pine and wicker furnishings, hardwood floors, and rich colors lend a rough-hewn elegance to every room. Vaulted ceilings in the second-story North Room and South Room supply an open, airy feel, while the ground-level West Room has a private deck, larger bathroom, and outdoor shower big enough for two.

Breakfast, a savory event, may include warm gingerbread with lemon curd, crème fraîche, and applesauce, or oatmeal pancakes with raspberries and rosemary-chicken-and-apple sausage. Those who like to rise and shine privately will appreciate that this feast can be delivered to your room. Otherwise, it is served at two-person tables in the lovely solarium, with its bountiful greenery and flowers. Either way, breakfast will leave you feeling ready for a day of exploration and discovery in this wondrous area.

SEA STAR COTTAGE Inverness
Sir Francis Drake Boulevard

(415) 663-1554
Very Expensive
Minimum stay requirement on weekends

A 75-foot-long wooden walkway stretches over the tidal waters and leads to the door of this petite, weathered cottage. Comfortable, albeit timeworn, furnishings and a corner woodstove give warmth to the living room, which faces placid Tomales Bay. The adjacent bedroom features a four-poster queen-size bed with a down comforter, and a small bathroom is adorned with blue and white tiles. The overall effect is somewhat sparse and mismatched, but don't despair; the absolute *best* place to kiss here is in the sunroom that spans the front of the building, where a large hot tub is bubbling and ready. From this vantage point, watch a variety of seabirds fly or float by. A breakfast of fresh juice, fruit salad, quiche, and almond croissants is left in the kitchen and can be enjoyed in the simple breakfast room.

Romantic Warning: The Inverness Yacht Club, located right next door, has a long dock that is bound to infringe on your privacy. Also, time and the elements have taken their toll, but with its on-the-water location, Sea Star Cottage still gets bookings despite the lofty price tag. The location certainly *is* special, but at these rates, finer appointments would be in order.

SMITTY'S COTTAGES ON THE BEACH, Inverness
12790 Sir Francis Drake Boulevard
(415) 663-9696, (415) 669-1554
Expensive

At first glance, Smitty's two beachfront cottages seem an unlikely setting for a romantic encounter. Situated just footsteps from a busy road, the cabins' weathered exteriors and neglected grounds are hard to ignore. But much to our surprise, our first impressions were forgotten after one peek at the cabins' lovely, upscale interiors. Richly colored Oriental carpets cover gleaming hardwood floors, and French doors open onto private decks overlooking tranquil Tomales Bay. Contemporary, stylish artwork graces beige-sponged walls, and dried flowers, baskets, and antiques accent the cabins' cozy, cheery living areas. A ladder in one cottage leads to a snug sleeping loft, and cushy down comforters drape the beds in both units. Breakfast fixings are provided ahead of time in fully equipped modern kitchens, where copper teakettles sparkle against fresh white tiles.

VISION COTTAGE, Point Reyes Station
Sir Francis Drake Boulevard
(415) 663-1554
Expensive

Camouflaged by old-growth Bishop pines and cypresses at the top of a hushed, tree-laden hillside, this self-contained cottage specializes in quiet seclusion. Although the shores of Tomales Bay are nowhere in sight, neither is the highway, which adds to your sense of solitude and supreme privacy. A large black stove heats the cottage's rustic interior, which is outfitted with knotty pine walls, floor-to-ceiling windows, and a mismatched assortment of country knickknacks and antiques. Handmade quilts and down comforters cover antique pine beds in two separate, sparsely appointed bedrooms. Though it's a far cry from polished, all of the amenities required for a romantic getaway are here for the taking: a welcome plate of fresh fruit and chewy chocolate chip cookies, a full kitchen stocked with continental breakfast provisions, and two decks that survey views of the surrounding forest. Best of all, you can soak uninterrupted for hours in an oversized outdoor Jacuzzi tub under a canopy of blinking stars in the night sky.

Restaurant Kissing

MANKA'S INVERNESS
LODGE RESTAURANT, Inverness
Argyle Avenue and Callendar Way
(415) 669-1034, (800) 585-6343
Expensive
Breakfast Daily; Dinner Thursday-Monday

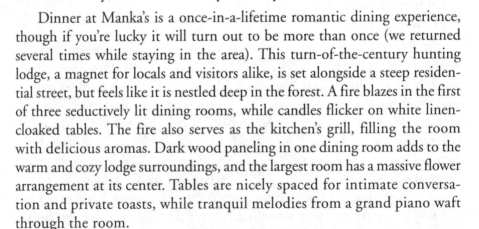

Dinner at Manka's is a once-in-a-lifetime romantic dining experience, though if you're lucky it will turn out to be more than once (we returned several times while staying in the area). This turn-of-the-century hunting lodge, a magnet for locals and visitors alike, is set alongside a steep residential street, but feels like it is nestled deep in the forest. A fire blazes in the first of three seductively lit dining rooms, while candles flicker on white linen-cloaked tables. The fire also serves as the kitchen's grill, filling the room with delicious aromas. Dark wood paneling in one dining room adds to the warm and cozy lodge surroundings, and the largest room has a massive flower arrangement at its center. Tables are nicely spaced for intimate conversation and private toasts, while tranquil melodies from a grand piano waft through the room.

The menu features seasonal specials. Appetizers such as clam and mussel soup with fennel and cilantro puree or grilled polenta with local wild mushrooms are just the beginning. Entrées such as the house-cured grilled pork chops with mashed potatoes, Italian black cabbage, and pear-kumquat chutney, or fireplace-grilled wild sturgeon served with smoky sweet pepper broth are excellent and thoroughly satisfying. But you won't want to forgo dessert. Strawberries with amaretto cream and Belgian chocolate, or creamy cheesecake with warm caramel sauce and toasted pecans will be calling your name.

Romantic Note: Reservations are highly recommended. Monday is designated "Casual Night," with a sampler menu featuring smaller portions and lower prices (in the Moderate range), an absolute steal in our opinion.

Outdoor Kissing

POINT REYES NATIONAL SEASHORE
Bear Valley Visitor Center
(415) 663-1092

Just off Highway 1, about 35 miles north of San Francisco.

Those who had never heard of Point Reyes National Seashore became acutely aware of the area in October 1995, when a raging forest fire threatened to destroy the park and surrounding towns. For eight days, fire crews painstakingly fought the blazes, and in the end, 45 homes and structures were lost and 14 percent of the park was burned. Amazingly, no lives were lost, and the park is quickly regenerating. The damage is hardly apparent from the northern district of the park, but the extent of the devastation can be clearly seen from Drake's Beach and the Estero Trail.

Thankfully, despite the fire, the park is as gorgeous as ever. Point Reyes National Seashore is noted for acre after exquisite acre of wild land, filled with winter grasses, chiseled rock, cascading waterfalls, calm sandy beaches, precarious primitive coastline, and turbulent breakers crashing against haystack rocks. Follow one of the many trails that penetrate this prime hiking kingdom; some end near the edge of the land, where the ocean reveals itself nestled between interwoven hills. (Now is the time to kiss.)

There are too many spectacular treks in this area to list each one in this book. The pucker potential is great everywhere in the Point Reyes National Seashore, but some of our favorites are **ALAMERE FALLS, TOMALES POINT**, the **POINT REYES LIGHTHOUSE** (reviewed in the Whale Watching entry), and **WILDCAT BEACH**. Each spot is dramatically different from the others, but their natural glory is worth discovering for yourselves. Helpful park rangers at the Bear Valley Visitors Center can give you specific hiking information.

Romantic Warning: Realistically, not everyone who wants to find romance owns hiking boots or, for that matter, sturdy thighs and a disposition that can survive the walk. Be sure to find a route that suits your ability.

Romantic Suggestions: Another romantic destination is **HEART'S DESIRE BEACH**, in the Tomales Bay State Park, right on Tomales Bay. Do the views from this tranquil, sparkling bay live up to the beach's name? Go and see for yourselves.

Rent a pair of horses for $20 per hour at **FIVE BROOKS STABLES**, 8001 Highway 1, (415) 663-1570, three and a half miles south of Olema. This is a fabulous horse ranch with hourly rentals at Point Reyes National Seashore.

Some people consider oysters to be a powerful aphrodisiac. We won't argue either way, but if you like these mouthwatering mollusks, stop at **JOHNSON'S OYSTER COMPANY**, 17171 Sir Francis Drake Boulevard, (415) 669-1149, just off the Sir Francis Drake Highway in Point Reyes National Seashore, or the **TOMALES BAY OYSTER COMPANY**, 15479 Highway 1, Marshall, (415) 663-1242. There is nothing fancy about either of these establishments, but you can purchase extremely fresh oysters that have just been plucked from the bay.

WHALE WATCHING

Numerous viewpoints line the Coast Trail in the Point Reyes National Seashore, but Point Reyes Lighthouse, (415) 669-1534, at the end of the Sir Francis Drake Highway, is a particularly outstanding vantage point to watch whales.

If you have always longed to witness firsthand the passage of whales on their yearly migration, then the Northern California coast is a great place to fulfill your cetaceous fantasy. December to April is the best time to witness this odyssey, particularly when the weather conditions are clear and sunny. Be sure to go early in the morning, about the time the sun is warming the cool morning air. As you stand at the edge of a towering cliff, you will have a tremendous view of the coastline. Find a comfortable position, snuggle close together, and be patient.

Take in the open, endless ocean, lined with staggered cliffs dotted with green and gold chaparral for as far as the eye can see. Allow your vision to slowly scan the calm, azure waters. Suddenly, in the distance, breaking the stillness of a silent, sun-drenched morning, a spout of water explodes from the surface. A giant black profile arches boldly against the blue sea, followed by an abrupt tail slap and then all is calm once more. It's hard to explain the romance of that moment, but romantic it is. Perhaps it's the excitement of observing such an immense creature gliding effortlessly through the water with playful agility and ease. Or perhaps it's the chance to celebrate a part of nature's mysterious aquatic underworld together.

Olema

Hotel/Bed and Breakfast Kissing

POINT REYES SEASHORE LODGE, Olema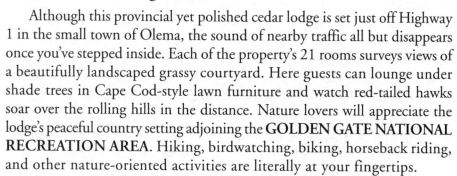
10021 Coastal Highway 1
(415) 663-9000, (800) 404-LODGE (in California)
http://www.placestostay.com
Inexpensive to Very Expensive
Recommended Wedding Site

Although this provincial yet polished cedar lodge is set just off Highway 1 in the small town of Olema, the sound of nearby traffic all but disappears once you've stepped inside. Each of the property's 21 rooms surveys views of a beautifully landscaped grassy courtyard. Here guests can lounge under shade trees in Cape Cod-style lawn furniture and watch red-tailed hawks soar over the rolling hills in the distance. Nature lovers will appreciate the lodge's peaceful country setting adjoining the **GOLDEN GATE NATIONAL RECREATION AREA**. Hiking, birdwatching, biking, horseback riding, and other nature-oriented activities are literally at your fingertips.

If you can afford to indulge, a handful of spacious two-story suites have separate sleeping lofts with sensuous feather beds, wood-burning fireplaces, whirlpool tubs, and the added luxury of breakfast delivered to your doorstep. If a splurge is out of the question, you won't be disappointed with the lodge's less expensive rooms, many of which feature tiled wood-burning fireplaces and whirlpool tubs. All of the rooms are enhanced by natural wood accents, plush down comforters, lovely antiques, and balconies or terraces that open onto the quiet courtyard. Couples traveling together should consider the lodge's free-standing cottage (which can accommodate up to six people), with its ample outdoor Jacuzzi tub, eclectic modern decor, TV and VCR, and a large glass-enclosed shower with twin showerheads.

You probably have your own ideas about how to spend the evening, but just in case, the game room downstairs is equipped with an antique billiards table and plenty of puzzles and games. Unless you've booked a suite (where breakfast is served to your room), you can wake up to a deluxe continental breakfast served in a sunny dining room that opens to the courtyard and is warmed by an immense stone hearth crowned with dried flowers.

ROUNDSTONE FARM, Olema
9940 Sir Francis Drake Boulevard
(415) 663-1020
http://www.coastaltraveler.com

Moderate to Expensive
Minimum stay requirement on weekends
Closed December

We were immediately drawn to Roundstone Farm's rural landscape, where flocks of red-winged blackbirds nest by a tranquil pond, and Connemara and Arabian horses graze in surrounding golden pastures. Named after a district of western Ireland, this ten-acre ranch offers a hushed refuge for those seeking to escape the city. Guests can savor views of the pastoral scenery through a wall of windows in the inn's homey communal living room and adjacent outdoor deck, or from the privacy of their own room.

Built to serve as a bed and breakfast, the inn was designed with seclusion in mind; the five guest rooms are situated on different levels of the guest wing, and all are equipped with private standard baths. Although the outdated linens and eclectic decor are a little worn and could use some sprucing up, Roundstone Farm still deserves its reputation as a romantic destination. You can't argue with views of the sun setting in the distance over Tomales Bay, or with the warmth of a crackling fire in the hearth (found in four of the five guest rooms). A full breakfast, including fresh baked goods, is served family-style in the airy dining room or on the garden patio, depending on the weather.

Restaurant Kissing

OLEMA INN RESTAURANT, Olema
10000 Sir Francis Drake Boulevard
(415) 663-9559
Moderate to Expensive
Lunch and Dinner Daily; Sunday Brunch

A polished dining room may seem out of place in this neck of the woods, but formality in the midst of country life is exactly what you'll find at the Olema Inn. Tapered candles and fresh flower arrangements top the linen-covered tables, and attractive sconces and dried floral wreaths line the walls. French doors open to a pretty garden patio where lunch and dinner are served during warm months, and the tables are nicely spaced for quiet conversation. The unchanging menu is on the small side, but everything is consistently good. Try the fettuccine with scallops and prawns in a creamy pesto sauce, or the pan-roasted trout topped with mandarin orange relish and toasted pine nuts. You won't be disappointed (unless you don't save room for dessert).

Romantic Note: Overnight accommodations are also available at **OLEMA INN** (Moderate). Upstairs are six small guest rooms, each with a simple interior and antique touches. Although the inn's past is colorful, travelers with romance (not history) on their minds should stay at one of the nearby places that has received our *kiss* of approval (see Hotel/Bed and Breakfast Kissing).

Stinson Beach

Although technically part of Marin County, this area is the gateway to the North Coast. Until recently, the only way to stay in Stinson Beach (without moving there) was to spend the night with local friends or rent a vacation home. Several bed and breakfasts have since opened, but this seaside town, located within the **GOLDEN GATE NATIONAL RECREATION AREA**, is happily far from overdeveloped. **STINSON BEACH STATE PARK,** three miles of sandy white beach, is crowd-crazed in the summer, but you can still take off your shoes, close your eyes, and bask in the sun and sand. San Francisco is barely an hour away and the Golden Gate Bridge is in clear sight, but you'll feel light-years away from the city.

Hotel/Bed and Breakfast Kissing

CASA DEL MAR, Stinson Beach
37 Belvedere Avenue
(415) 868-2124, (800) 552-2124
Moderate to Very Expensive
Minimum stay requirement on weekends

Succulent tropical foliage and flowering cactus fill the beautifully landscaped grounds of this towering Mediterranean-style villa, and a terraced stone pathway leads to bright and sunny accommodations. Casa del Mar ("house of the sea") is not a traditional bed and breakfast; the upbeat atmosphere is like a breath of fresh air. Vivacious local art adorns the six colorfully decorated guest rooms, each with a queen-size bed, down comforter, brightly patterned linens, and private patio. Ocean views (beyond rooftops) from terra-cotta-tiled patios make the Shell Room and the Heron Room especially attractive, while the smaller, more affordable Hummingbird Room has a serene view of neighboring Mount Tamalpais.

The spacious, top-floor Penthouse Suite has exquisite views of both the mountain and the ocean from cement patios on each side of the building, but the decor is comparatively spartan. Instead, opt for the Garden Room.

Although it is on the lowest level, it has a decent ocean view from a quaint garden patio, and its other advantages include a private entrance, wood-burning fireplace, and small kitchen. Breakfast can be delivered to either the Penthouse or the Garden Room, but for everyone else, the delightfully creative, full breakfast, which might include apple-ricotta pancakes flavored with cinnamon, or homemade blueberry and poppyseed coffee cake, is served fireside on the airy main floor.

Wine Country

Wine Country is approximately an hour and a half northeast of San Francisco. From the city take Highway 101 north (over the Golden Gate Bridge) to Highway 37 east. Highway 37 connects with the St. Helena Highway (Highway 29), which heads north through the Napa Valley, and with the Sonoma Highway (Highway 12), which accesses the Sonoma Valley.

Hills in this holiday countryside are given over to vineyards and the succulent grapes they produce. Once you visit this region you will understand the vivacious, impetuous temperament that is the hallmark of California's Wine Country: its robust regard for living life to the fullest. The boroughs and hamlets of the area are well-stocked with an enormous selection of bed and breakfasts, restaurants, spas, wine tasting rooms, hot-air balloon companies, and the most remarkable picnic turf around. Deciding where to concentrate your time (and what time of year to visit) is the most difficult part of traveling here. Each season brings on a new, completely different array of colors and sights. In spring, dormant gravepines awaken to fields of golden mustard. By summer, the vines are draped in full green foliage and the warm temperatures keep visitors at a constant flow. Fall brings the celebration of the annual harvest (called the "crush" by folks in these parts), and the grape leaves start to turn golden. Winter, the quietest season, is when the vines become dormant again and the splaying branches are trimmed back to a craggy stalk. Winter can be a good time to come because of the light traffic and the ease of getting reservations, but be forewarned that the weather can be iffy and many establishments close or have limited hours (particularly during the month of January). Still, any time of year, Wine Country offers future memories.

Romantic Consideration: The number of wineries scattered throughout these picturesque hills and valleys is staggering. Even if you were merely to sip your way in and out of tasting rooms for a week, you would make only a nominal, intoxicating dent in the possibilities that exist here. Because this book is about sentiment and not necessarily about choosing a vintage wine, we've selected a handful of wineries, some lesser known and off the beaten path, and others well-known and more highly trafficked but still noteworthy. Either way, winery reviews are listed under Outdoor Kissing for each respective town. These are the places we found to be the most appealing for tasting and embracing, both the wine and each other.

Romantic Suggestion: The wineries are scattered throughout the valley (not exactly within walking distance of one another), so you will probably be driving. A single taste of wine is barely a gulp, but sips add up quickly. Please, know your limits and do not drink and drive. One option that is not only safe but also a lot of fun is to have a limousine drive you around for an afternoon. Many limousine companies operate throughout the valley. In Napa Country, a reputable company that can do two-person tours is **ANTIQUE TOURS**, (707) 226-9227. In Sonoma County, consider using **BAUER'S TRANSPORTAION**, (415) 522-1212, (800) LIMO-OUT, or **STYLE 'N COMFORT LIMOUSINE**, (707) 578-3001, (800) 487-5466. Regardless of the company you choose, prices range from $30 per hour on weekdays to $60 per hour on weekends.

Napa Valley

The heavily trafficked St. Helena Highway winds through most of the towns in the Napa Valley, detracting from the quiet splendor of the area. Nevertheless, the abundance of gorgeous wineries, charming bed and breakfasts and inns, and world-acclaimed restaurants found in the beautiful surrounding countryside of the Napa Valley make this area one of Northern California's most sensational places to pucker up. Great information packets about the Napa Valley can be obtained from the **NAPA VALLEY CON-FERENCE AND VISITORS BUREAU**, 1310 Napa Town Center, Napa, CA 94559, (707) 226-7459.

Napa

It would be nice if the Napa Valley's namesake town was more peaceful and country-like, but the truth is that Napa is where most of the locals come to shop and do business. Consequently, shopping plazas, fast-food stops, and gas stations abound. Thankfully, affectionate establishments also exist here—you just have to know where to look.

Hotel/Bed and Breakfast Kissing

BLUE VIOLET MANSION, Napa
443 Brown Street
(707) 253-2583, (800) 959-2583
http://www.virtualcities.com
Expensive to Very Expensive
Minimum stay requirement on weekends and holidays

A pretty white gazebo rests on the manicured front lawn of this blue and white Queen Anne–style Victorian. Inside, fantasy-inspired touches from around the world will intrigue all romantic spirits who come to stay. The elaborate gold front-door frame, embossed leather wainscoting, Oriental carpets, and modern sculptures and art in the main foyer make it clear that this is not your run-of-the-mill bed and breakfast. Of the nine distinctive rooms located on the second floor, three have gas fireplaces, two have large Jacuzzi tubs, and one has a deep Oriental soaking tub. All of them contain an eclectic mix of antiques. Five more rooms were recently added to the third floor, now affectionately called the Camelot floor. Rooms up here are done in a King Arthur theme, with exquisite antiques, gas fireplaces, stained glass windows, and private baths, all of which boast two-person Jacuzzi tubs.

The full, two-course breakfast might include fresh fruit, sweet cakes for starters, and an egg dish, French toast, or waffles as a tempting main course. Before your morning meal, take a cup of coffee and sit out in the gazebo to watch hot-air balloons grace the morning sky with their flashes of bright color.

Romantic Suggestion: If playing lord and lady of the manor appeals to your *Masterpiece Theater* sensibilities, the innkeepers will happily play along. A totally private, candlelit dinner can be served in your room or in the formal dining room; ask the innkeepers for complete details.

CEDAR GABLES INN, Napa
486 Coombs Street
(707) 224-7969, (800) 309-7969
http://www.historicinns.com/cedar
Moderate to Expensive

If Shakespeare were alive today and touring the Napa Valley, you can bet he would be staying at the Cedar Gables Inn. Renaissance England drips from every inch of this ominous, dark brown shingled mansion trimmed in white and hidden by immense pine trees. Stepping through the large front doors, guests are engulfed by the sheer grandeur of the rich burgundy carpeting, dark redwood walls, tall leaded windows, Gothic-style antiques, and eclectic collectibles. Guest rooms are on the second and third floors, up a massive carpeted stairway. Don't miss the quaint sitting area tucked away on the mezzanine level, or the full suit of armor standing guard for all who pass.

Each room offers exquisite antiques, lush carpeting, and opulent fabrics in rich, warm tones. All rooms have private baths (four have two-person Jacuzzi tubs), and three rooms have wood-burning fireplaces. Our favorite room is the utterly sensuous and dramatic Churchill Chamber, done in delicious shades of black, tan, and cream, with intricately designed antiques and a two-person whirlpool tub. On the other end of the home is a sixth guest room; although this room is located away from the others, it is not as warmly decorated.

Breakfast is served in a bright, black-and-white-tiled sunroom with separate two-person tables clothed in crisp white linens. A variety of homemade baked goods, fresh fruit, and a hot entrée of French pancakes, almond French toast, or the owner's own popular "egg mess," are only some of the delectable treats you may encounter.

CHURCHILL MANOR, Napa
485 Brown Street
(707) 253-7733
Inexpensive to Expensive
Minimum stay requirement on weekends
Recommended Wedding Site

Tall, perfectly manicured hedges effectively conceal this stately mansion in welcome privacy. The pretty fountain, immaculate lawn, and towering white columns offer a lasting first impression. Once you enter the mansion itself and glimpse the two elegant parlors on the main floor, with their high ceilings, intricately carved columns, velvet-draped windows, original fireplaces, stunning antiques, and ornate chandeliers, you know your stay will be a grand one.

Victorian opulence continues in nine of the ten upstairs guest rooms, which feature antique bedroom sets, private baths, and pretty floral linens. A claw-foot tub sits beside a fireplace in both Victoria's and Rose's rooms; Dorothy's Room has dark wood furnishings, including a four poster bed; and Edward's Room, the largest and handsomest, also has a fireplace and claw-foot tub. The Bordello Room, as you might guess, doesn't adhere to Victorian standards, nor does it display the understated elegance of the rest of the house (in fact, there is nothing understated about it at all). The king-size brass bed, dressed in red and black satin, and the black-and-red-tiled Jacuzzi tub for two are a bit much in our opinion, but the innkeepers assured us that a lot of couples are crazy about this room. Take a look and judge for yourselves.

Step into the marble-floored sunroom for a full breakfast that may include a gourmet vegetable omelet or orange-zest French toast with maple syrup and honeyed sour cream. On warmer days, this morning feast can be enjoyed on the huge veranda that wraps around the entire front of the house. Fresh-baked cookies in the afternoon, wine and cheese in the evening, and the availability of bicycles and croquet gear enhance your stay.

THE HENNESSEY HOUSE, Napa
727 Main Street
(707) 226-3774
Moderate to Expensive
Minimum stay requirement on weekends

Standing tall among the ordinary buildings on Main Street, this blue-and-gray Queen Anne Victorian houses a pleasant bed-and-breakfast inn. A manicured lawn and colorful flower beds frame the main residence, where six rooms decorated with a mismatched combination of beautiful antiques and ordinary furnishings are located. Features include high ceilings, warm fireplaces, cozy feather beds, stained glass windows, and claw-foot tubs. Unfortunately, traffic noise is audible in many of the rooms. The adjacent Carriage House holds four more rooms, all offering more privacy and more space, along with whirlpool tubs for two, lovingly restored antiques, and private entrances. Sport and hunting themes give these rooms a more masculine feel: the Bridle Suite has an equestrian theme, while the Fox's Den is decorated with an English hunt in mind.

A full gourmet breakfast is served in the dining room beneath a beautiful hand-painted, stamped tin ceiling. Creatively prepared entrées await each morning, along with homemade granola, fruit yogurt, and fresh baked goodies such as orange scones, pineapple-ricotta muffins, and strawberry nut bread.

LA BELLE ÉPOQUE, Napa
1386 Calistoga Avenue
(707) 257-2161
Moderate to Expensive
Minimum stay requirement on weekends and holidays

This charming Queen Anne–style home is situated in a quiet residential neighborhood. A consistent Victorian theme runs through six of the seven guest rooms, which are located on the first and second floors. Some of these rooms have 20-foot ceilings, hardwood floors covered with Oriental area rugs, floral linens, beautiful Victorian antiques, and sitting areas with authentic stained glass windows. All have standard private baths, and two have wood-burning fireplaces. Located in the basement, near the common area and a small wine-tasting room, is the seventh room, done in a more contemporary style with floral linens, dark green carpeting, a small sitting area, and a spacious bathroom. Even though this suite is close to where wine and hors d'oeuvres are served nightly, it is by far the most spacious and private this inn has to offer.

On sunny mornings, a full gourmet breakfast is served on the front porch in the midst of fragrant flowers, or inside the formal dining room at one large table.

LA RESIDENCE, Napa
4066 St. Helena Highway (Highway 29)
(707) 253-0337
http://www.virtualcities.com
Expensive to Very Expensive
Minimum stay requirement on weekends

Casual refinement and great kissing potential abound at La Residence. Two impressive buildings, a cedar-shingled manor (called the French Barn) and a stately mansion (appropriately named the Mansion), hold 22 beautifully appointed rooms. The 11 rooms in the French Barn feature French and English pine antiques, muted color schemes, and subtle Laura Ashley linens and wallpapers. Rooms in the Mansion live up to the elegant exterior of the building with polished dark wood furnishings, ten-foot ceilings, chandeliers, and white shutters. Fireplaces and patios or verandas are highlights in every room, and each private bath includes all the usual comforts.

Brick paths throughout the property invite you to admire the well-tended grounds, punctuated with rose trellises and grape arbors. A casual wine-and-cheese hour is held nightly on the back patio (or in the second-floor salon, depending on the weather).

You might consider a dip in the pool on hot afternoons, but a much more affectionate option would be a moonlight soak in the Jacuzzi tub behind the mansion, where you can stargaze and luxuriate any time of year. In the morning, a full breakfast is served to individual tables in the French country dining room.

Romantic Note: Considering the proximity to the highway, road noise is hardly noticeable inside your room (especially in rooms facing away from the highway). Obviously, traffic can be heard from any of the outside patios, but a wall of trees fronting the property at least conceals the road from your view.

OAK KNOLL INN, Napa
2200 East Oak Knoll Avenue
(707) 255-2200
Very Expensive to Unbelievably Expensive
Minimum stay requirement on weekends

If you're headed to the Napa Valley specifically for romance, this is the place to kiss and kiss and kiss some more. Oak Knoll Inn is one of those incredibly special places that epitomize all that is good about bed and break-fasts. The tree-lined drive and wrought-iron gates that welcome you only begin to suggest the splendor found here. Besides the handful of other guests, there is nothing else for miles around but the fertile vineyards, lush meadows, and quiet woodlands of the Napa Valley.

Once you enter the courtyard area, where two wings of suites overlook an aqua blue swimming pool, steaming spa, and vineyards in the distance, you will realize that you have stumbled upon a one-of-a-kind retreat. Each of the four spacious suites has a remarkable 17-foot-tall vaulted ceiling, a wood-burning fireplace set into inlaid stone walls, a gorgeous bathroom with marble floors, a plush king-size bed smothered in soft pillows and fine linens, comfortable contemporary furnishings, and French doors that open onto the inner courtyard. The two units at each end also feature a dramatic 12-foot cathedral window facing acres of neighboring vineyards.

The evening wine-and-cheese hour with gourmet goodies and freshly made appetizers could almost serve as dinner. (Not only is your hostess wonder-fully hospitable, she is a great cook.) A local winemaker periodically joins the merriment to personally answer questions and share vintages.

Not surprisingly, breakfast is a gourmet's delight. Different entrées are served each morning; we sat at the fireside in the dining room and savored chocolate "tacos" filled with fresh seasonal berries and homemade papaya sorbet, followed by Anaheim chile quiche served with chorizo, black beans, cilantro salsa, and corn muffettes. On warmer mornings, the outside deck serves as the dining room and hot-air balloons occasionally float overhead. Such serenity isn't found just anywhere.

Romantic Suggestion: Service is another one of Oak Knoll Inn's specialties, and the innkeepers are eager to make your visit to the Napa Valley memo-rable. If you've never been to the area before (or even if you come here regu-larly but want to see some different wineries and restaurants), put your schedule in their capable hands. You won't be disappointed with the itinerary they put together for you.

OLD WORLD INN, Napa
1301 Jefferson Street
(707) 257-0112, (800) 966-6624
Moderate to Expensive
Minimum stay requirement on weekends

If the path to your heart is through your stomach, you'll be smitten by the Old World Inn. Afternoon tea including cookies and a bountiful assort-ment of homemade treats will more than satisfy your sweet tooth, the early evening wine and hors d'oeuvres fest might encourage you to postpone dinner, and (as if you haven't been spoiled enough), a chocaholic's dream of a dessert buffet is set out before bedtime. After sampling these delectable creations, even the latest risers will be eager to get up for breakfast the following morning; breakfast is served buffet-style at intimate tables for two.

In the stairwell that leads to your room, "WELCOME HOME, ROMANCE SPOKEN HERE" is stenciled on the wall, setting a loving, relaxed mood for your stay. Each of the eight cheerful rooms is unique, but charming stenciled walls, comfortable furnishings, and a complimentary bottle of wine are found in every one. Some of the stencil work could use some touching up, but when you see how intricate the painting is, you'll see what an involved task this would be. The cozy Garden Room features large skylights and a private entrance; Stockholm has a private sunroom with a spa tub for two; Birch is extremely pretty, with a white eyelet bedspread and small stand-up balcony; and Anne's Room, appointed in blue and peach tones, has a dramatic floor-to-ceiling canopied bed. If your room doesn't have a private spa, you can enjoy the huge outdoor hot tub.

Romantic Warning: The Old World Inn's location on a busy downtown street is hardly tranquil, especially if you have a room facing Jefferson Street. Traffic thins out after dark, but road noise becomes apparent again in the early-morning hours.

Restaurant Kissing

ATLAS PEAK GRILL, Napa
3342 Vichy Avenue
(707) 253-1455
Moderate to Expensive
Dinner Tuesday-Sunday

Although its name is not particularly suggestive of romance, the Atlas Peak Grill is one of those unique, out-of-the-way places that caters mostly to locals. Be assured: this little restaurant is filled with congenial charm. Flowering gardens hug the vine-covered French country exterior of the elfin stone and brick cottage. Inside, two small dining rooms with low wood-beamed ceilings, massive iron chandeliers, and rough-hewn stucco walls are separated by a small open bar. Small paned windows look out to a quaint backyard area accented by colorful wandering roosters, trailing foliage, and wheelbarrows filled with flowers. The menu offers a variety of European dishes, including fresh seafood and homemade pastas. The herb-crusted sea bass in a rich fennel sauce, pork medallions in Marcella raisin sauce, or saffron-seafood risotto with crab, scallops, and prawns are sure to please the most discriminating gourmets. Service is attentive and gracious.

AUGUSTINO'S, Napa
3253 Browns Valley Road
(707) 224-0695
Moderate
Lunch Monday-Friday; Dinner Daily

A commonplace strip mall is not where you'd expect to find this warm dining spot, but here it is. Augustino's is about as cozy as it gets. Knotty pine walls, painted wood floors, candles at every table, and a two-sided stone fireplace aglow in the center of the room create an enchanting atmosphere. The menu consists of mostly meat options, such as wine–braised chicken, beef stewed with wine and seasonal vegetables, or a traditional cassoulet with sausage, duck and pork. If you're not a meat lover, the fresh fish of the day or the pasta with seasonal vegetables are both satisfying choices. After you've spent a long day touring the Napa Valley, Augustino's offers plenty of warmth and relaxation.

Romantic Suggestion: If you want to check out the incredible picnic spots available in the Napa Valley, consider stopping at **GENOVA DELICATESSEN**, 1550 Trancas, (707) 253-8686 (Inexpensive) for picnic goodies made to order. Allow the friendly and energetic staff to create a delicious sandwich on your choice of fresh bread, with Italian-style meats and cheeses. Appetizing salads are also plentiful, including three bean, marinated mushroom, coleslaw, potato, and macaron, to name a few. If you're hankering for a more substantial meal, one of the fresh pasta dishes, offered with a variety of sauces, will leave you more than satisfied.

BISTRO DON GIOVANNI, Napa
4110 St. Helena Highway (Highway 29)
(707) 224-3300
Moderate to Expensive
Lunch and Dinner Daily

Bistro Don Giovanni is one of the many Napa Valley restaurants that have built a reputation as stylish destinations for fine food and fine wine. Thankfully, the owners of this Italian eatery have also made efforts to create a nice level of warmth in their dining room. Regretfully, the tables are too packed in for our taste, the booths need higher backs to create some privacy, and the noise level can get out of hand on busy nights. Still, even if kissing between courses isn't a viable option, you can at least savor homemade ravioli filled with basil, ricotta, and Parmesan in a light lemon cream, or a rich seafood risotto. Jazzy music, pale yellow walls, terra-cotta tile floors, and a corner gas fireplace may inspire some romantic inclinations for later.

LA BOUCANE, Napa
1778 Second Street
(707) 253-1177
Expensive
Dinner Monday-Saturday
Closed January and holidays

The memory of fresh strawberries drenched with red wine still make our mouths water when we think of our delicious experience at La Boucane. The setting, in an old Victorian home, is nothing out of the ordinary, but the service is attentive and the French cuisine exquisite. The simple but memorable strawberry dessert was the perfect finale to a satisfying meal of crevettes (shrimp) Provençale, avocado salad, and freshly puréed cream of vegetable soup. A meal here will leave you feeling *magnifique.*

Outdoor Kissing

CARNERO'S ALAMBIC DISTILLERY, Napa
1250 Cuttings Wharf Road
(707) 253-9055
$2 tour; no tasting

From Napa, travel south on Highway 29. Take the Highway 12/121 exit and head west. Travel approximately 1.3 miles and turn left onto Cuttings Wharf Road. The distillery is less than a mile down, at the end of the road.

If you're finally tired of "pouring" over the innumerable merlots, chardonnays, and fine cabernet sauvignons in the area, take a trip to the Carneros Alambic Distillery for something different: the making and aging of fine brandy. Be sure to take the short tour that begins in the visitors' center, starting with a demonstration depicting the unique process of creating brandy. You'll then be led outside to a rustic stone building called the Still House, where the distillation tanks are kept. Sunlight dances off these beautiful copper tanks as they concentrate wine into brandy. The tour finishes in the dimly lit barrel house, filled with the aroma of aging brandy. Barely audible Gregorian chants, piped through hidden speakers, help set the perfect mood. Sadly, brandy tastings are not available, but you could purchase a bottle for a delightful nightcap on another romantic occasion.

DOMAINE CARNEROS, Napa
1240 Duhig Road

(707) 257-0101

http://www.domaine.com

$4-$6 tasting fee (includes full glass of wine and light appetizers)

Just off Highway 121/12 (the Carneros Highway), at Duhig Road.

Carneros is the winegrowing region spanning the base of the Napa and Sonoma valleys. Many people use the Carneros Highway to get to and from Napa or Sonoma without realizing there are worthwhile places along the way. Domaine Carneros, an imposing winery that specializes in sparkling wines, is one such place (that is, if you want an elegant and somewhat formal tasting experience). Perfectly trimmed hedges and stately stone fountains frame the stairway leading to the chateau. Marble floors, brass-edged tables, and crystal chandeliers adorn the tasting salon, which functions more like a cafe. Hors d'oeuvres and crackers accompany your sparkling glass of champagne. In the warmer months you can sit outside on a terrace and enjoy your bubbly along with an exquisite vineyard view.

THE HESS COLLECTION WINERY, Napa
4411 Redwood Road

(707) 255-1144

$2.50 tasting fee

Take Highway 29 north, turn left at the stoplight onto Redwood Road, and follow signs to The Hess Collection Winery. The winery is approximately six miles from Highway 29.

A fine wine should be lingered over, and so should this exceptional winery and contemporary art gallery, located on a quiet side road far removed from the rush of Highway 29. The Hess Collection Winery seduces you into slowing your pace with its self-guided tour. A 12-minute audiovisual presentation demonstrates the Hess philosophy of grape growing and winemaking; three floors showcase Donald Hess's contemporary art collection, filled with many provocative and intriguing pieces. As you walk through the gallery, windows interspersed with the works of art allow you to view the winemaking operation. Sadly, picnic tables are not provided here, but a leisurely walk in the garden courtyard may be just the tranquil escape you are looking for.

Don't even think of leaving without tasting one of the award-winning vintages in the sparse tasting room. You will soon find out why all of Napa is buzzing about The Hess Collection wines.

JARVIS, Napa
2970 Monticello Road

(707) 255-5280, (800) 255-5280

$10 tasting fee
Tours and tasting by appointment only

From the St. Helena Highway (Highway 29), turn east onto Trancas. Just beyond the intersection for the Silverado Trail there is a fork in the road; go to the left and you will come to a three-way stop where Trancas becomes Monticello Road. Go straight on Monticello Road and travel approximately four miles. The gates to the winery and a call box are on the left.

Jarvis is a stunning example of what a person with a vision, a passion for wine, and an unlimited expense account can create. Come here to see how the other half lives, or, perhaps more appropriately, the other one percent. The imposing entrance to the wine caves looks like something out of a James Bond movie. Massive arched doors open to the caves, and modernistic bronze sconces line the walls. This is where the tour begins. Toward the center of the tunnels, a stream with waterfalls flows, both for looks and practical reasons—the running water helps maintain the cave's natural humidity. The tour continues into a grand room called the Crystal Chamber, used for social gatherings. Immense dazzling amethysts and crystals at each end of the room are quite a sight to see. Finally, after stopping for a glimpse of the fiber-optic chandelier in the ladies room (yes, men get to peek for just a moment), you'll be taken to a formal tasting room with a long marble table and elegant royal blue chairs trimmed in gold. There, gourmet cheese and crackers accompany tastings of two or three different wines.

Romantic Warning: All in all, Jarvis is a one-of-a-kind experience, but we must admit that the serious and somewhat pretentious tone became tiresome by the end of the almost hour-long tour. If you are aware of this one drawback in advance and still want to see what Jarvis is all about, you will surely appreciate the unique quality of this winery tour.

MONTICELLO VINEYARDS, Napa
4242 Big Ranch Road
(707) 253-2802, (800) 743-6668
$3 tasting fee (includes logo wineglass)
Recommended Wedding Site

On Big Ranch Road, off Oak Knoll Avenue.

In this bustling valley, Big Ranch Road is a road less traveled, and taking it to the peaceful country setting of Monticello Vineyards can make all the difference. A long driveway, framed by acres of vineyards on either side, leads to a stately Colonial brick mansion and neighboring informal tasting room. After touring and sipping, check out the picnic area, which is concealed by white lattice. A garden full of roses blooms beside the picnic tables, and several old walnut trees provide shade on sunny days. If you plan ahead and bring your own lunch, all you'll need is a bottle of wine, available in the tasting room, of course. Isn't life in Wine Country wonderful?

NAPA VALLEY WINE TRAIN, Napa
(707) 253-2111, (800) 427-4124
http://www.napavalley.com/winetrain.html
Sit-down Lunch, Dinner, and Weekend Brunch: Unbelievably Expensive (includes train fare, tax, and gratuity)
Deli cart: Expensive
Closed the first week of January

Call for reservations and directions.

Although it is probably the most touristy excursion in the Napa Valley, the Napa Valley Wine Train can be a lot of fun. Your journey begins at the train depot in downtown Napa. You'll leave the station's tapestry sofas, tasting area, and small art gallery to board a line of 1915 Pullman cars. Each car has been carefully and beautifully restored with glowing mahogany paneling, polished brass, stenciled ceilings, etched glass partitions, and gold and burgundy velvet draperies. Depending on which tour you choose, you will be directed either to the dining car or the lounge car first. Tables line each side of the dining car, so everyone has a window seat. Polished silver, fine bone china, and perfectly pressed white linens enhance the elegant setting, and silver candle lanterns and single red roses are the crowning romantic touches.

Dinner begins with an appetizer; then select one of three entrées. Our dinners, salmon Florentine baked in puff pastry and Angus beef tenderloin marinated in cabernet, fresh herbs, and garlic, were delicious, and the service was very good. Dessert, on the other hand, was a completely different story. For this last course and coffee, we were moved to a different, but still very elegant, car with plush, tufted gold velvet chairs facing picture windows. Thin slices of plain cheesecake and chocolate silk cake hardly compared to the gourmet dinner we had enjoyed earlier, and service was extremely slow. Perhaps our irritation was heightened by the fact that it was completely dark outside, so we couldn't enjoy any scenery, and the slow-moving trip (lasting a minimum of three hours) started to drag by the end.

Romantic Note: Brunch and lunch excursions are also available, meaning you need not be on the train after dark. The view of the vineyards *is* one of the best parts of the Napa Valley Wine Train (although the train's route parallels Highway 29, so if you have driven through the valley you have probably seen these sights). If you prefer to ride the dinner train, which departs at 6:30 P.M. and returns at 10 P.M., we recommend doing so in the warmer months, when the days are longer. Another option, either day or night, is to just come along for the ride and pick up something in the deli car. Another car is devoted to wine tasting. For $5, you can try four wines from their extensive selection.

Romantic Bonus: Due to the popularity of the wine train tours, stops along the route have been added. Passengers can now disembark at various wineries to stretch their legs and whet their palates on the latest vintages.

SILVERADO TRAIL

This stretch of highway follows the east side of the Napa Valley, starting from the south in the town of Napa, and going north to Calistoga.

Only two major roads traverse the Napa Valley: the St. Helena Highway (Highway 29) and the Silverado Trail. At some points these roads are separated by only one or two miles, but in spirit and atmosphere they are eons apart. Highway 29 is just that, a highway, encumbered with cars, billboards, tourists, gas stations, and other "civilized" necessities. In contrast, the Silverado Trail is a meandering drive through nature at its most charming: contiguous, undulating hillsides endowed with a profusion of vineyards, forests, and olive groves. As you map your course through the wine country of Napa Valley, it would be a grievous mistake not to allow enough time to cruise along the Silverado Trail more than once. The wineries tucked away in the network of backroads are less commercial and more personal than those that line the main road. Plus, when you do require provisions or restaurants, the towns of Napa, Yountville, Oakville, Rutherford, St. Helena, and Calistoga are practically across the street.

WILLIAM HILL WINERY, Napa
1761 Atlas Peak Road
(707) 224-4477
Free tasting by appointment

From north- or southbound Highway 29, take the Trancas exit and head east. Follow Trancas until it turns into Monticello, then turn left onto Atlas Peak Road. The winery is on the left, directly across from the Silverado Country Club.

Not every winery in the Napa Valley has great views to accompany its wine-tasting facility. To its romantic credit, William Hill takes advantage of a remarkable setting with an attractive tasting room. Placed on top of a grassy embankment, this small winery overlooks verdant hills peppered with symmetrical rows of grapevines and sprawling shade trees, while mountains stand guard in the distance. Inside, faux antique painted walls and a terra-cotta floor create a lovely atmosphere for tasting. Massive windows look down on hundreds of wooden barrels filled with aging wine. Black wrought-iron picnic tables are set outside near the gravel parking lot, overlooking the inspiring panorama. If you're lucky, you might snatch up the only table set away from the others, on a soft lawn; it's a spectacular place for sunset watching.

Yountville

Yountville is one of the few Napa Valley towns to veer off the St. Helena Highway. This fact alone endows Yountville with a distinctive quiet charm. There are boutiques and galleries to peruse, not to mention several very romantic locales.

Hotel/Bed and Breakfast Kissing

CROSS ROADS INN, Yountville
6380 Silverado Trail
(707) 944-0646
Very Expensive
Minimum stay requirement on weekends and holidays

If your day of kissing in Wine Country has left you walking on air, ascend to the Cross Roads Inn—a sprawling, contemporary wood house set high above the rolling, vineyard-laden valley. The view from its spacious, firelit living room and redwood deck is enchantingly mellow. Enjoy magnificent sunsets from the guest rooms' double whirlpools and private decks. (Views don't get much better than this!) The only other property in Wine Country that even begins to compete with this vantage point is the very exclusive Auberge du Soleil in the neighboring town of Rutherford. However, the view is the only thing these two properties have in common—their styles and atmosphere are very different.

While Auberge du Soleil caters to a very upscale crowd, Cross Roads Inn offers four homey guest rooms with a comfortable, albeit lived-in, feeling. The upper-floor Puddleduck Room, with a pink bedspread and mirrored closet doors, has a two-person Jacuzzi tub with windows on either side looking over the valley to the west and a wild ravine to the north. Features like whirlpool tubs for two, private decks, full breakfasts delivered to your room, afternoon tea, and evening brandy and chocolates help to make up for some of the out-of-date decor, but with prices in the Very Expensive range you may expect more. Still, the view really is amazing, and if that is of premier importance (and you aren't traveling on a limited budget), then Cross Roads

Inn is worth your romantic consideration. Hiking trails above the inn climb up to Atlas Peak, where views get even better, stretching as far as San Francisco on clear days.

MAISON FLEURIE, Yountville
6529 Yount Street
(707) 944-2056, (800) 788-0369
Moderate to Very Expensive

Trailing ivy covers the brick and stone exterior of Maison Fleurie, one of the latest additions to Yountville's bed-and-breakfast scene. Four Sisters Inns (which also operates San Francisco's White Swan Inn and Petite Auberge) purchased this property several years ago, and as usual they have turned a once-tired bed and breakfast into a luxurious getaway. The 100-year-old Main Building sits next to two other small brick buildings, named the Old Bakery and the Carriage House. Charming French country details like delightful murals, elegantly rustic antiques, warm color schemes, and floral linens appoint each of the 13 rooms, which are spread among the three buildings. Four of the most spacious rooms are in the Old Bakery. Each has a king-size bed, gas fireplace, and small patio or deck surveying the outdoor pool and spa area. The two Carriage House rooms have private entrances and queen-size beds; one also has a gas log fireplace. Seven more rooms, some fairly small, are located on the upper floor of the Main Building and have easy access to the expansive sundeck overlooking acres of nearby vineyards. Whichever room you select, afternoon wine and hors d'oeuvres and evening turndown service are part of the impeccable package.

Breakfast is another notable element of a visit to Maison Fleurie. It can be delivered to your room for breakfast in bed, or you can venture to the flower-filled lobby of the Main Building, where the full breakfast is served buffet-style. A crackling fire warms the terra-cotta tile floors in this adorably provincial room, and tables for two allow a semiprivate morning affair. A stay at Maison Fleurie is like visiting the French countryside, without the language barrier.

OLEANDER HOUSE, Yountville
7433 St. Helena Highway (Highway 29)
(707) 944-8315, (800) 788-0357
http://www.oleander.com
Moderate to Expensive
Minimum stay requirement on weekends

What you see is what you get at this French country bed and breakfast, but what you hear is less pleasant. The sound of cars whizzing by on the adjacent highway is more than irksome; it's distracting. What a disappointment for an otherwise peaceful romantic find. A happy blend of old-fashioned decor with modern architecture and amenities distinguishes all four guest rooms. You can kiss by the fireplace in each accommodation, while high peaked ceilings and private balconies lend a sense of spaciousness to every unit.

After a cup of morning coffee, guests can tiptoe to the backyard for a wake-up soak in the hot tub. Every so often, a loud *whoosh* pierces the tranquility of the morning, and a brightly colored hot-air balloon floats overhead. Later, guests can meet in the dining room for hearty breakfast specialties like fresh strawberries, cinnamon-apple flan, and locally made chicken sausage.

VINTAGE INN, Yountville
6541 Washington Street
(707) 944-1112, (800) 351-1133 (in California),
(800) 982-5539 (elsewhere in the U.S.)
http://www.vintageinn.com
Very Expensive to Unbelievably Expensive
Minimum stay requirement on weekends and holidays

Soft classical music breezes through the Vintage Inn's serene lobby, with its plum-colored chairs, brick hearth, and high peaked open-beamed ceiling. Fountains, reflecting pools, and flowers embellish the apartment-like complex of brick and clapboard buildings. All 80 guest rooms have a some-what new feeling, even though the property was built 11 years ago, but wood-burning fireplaces, warm neutral tones, jetted baths, and small patios make them suitably romantic. A complimentary bottle of wine is included with your stay, and hotel-like amenities such as televisions, refrigerators, and coffeemakers are found in every room. Room service and a concierge are also available. Two-room suites are located in the villas, but we prefer the spacious mini-suites and the upstairs rooms with vaulted ceilings, particularly the ones in the inner courtyard, which are less likely to be bothered by road noise from Highway 29. (These Inner Court rooms are more expensive, but a good night's sleep is worth the $20 to $25 extra—especially if you're willing to spring for the Very Expensive to Unbelievably Expensive room rates in the first place.)

A continental champagne breakfast is served fireside in the lobby every morning. If an effervescent mimosa with breakfast doesn't wake you up, then a dip in the inn's outdoor heated pool should rejuvenate you for a day of wining and dining.

Restaurant Kissing

DOMAINE CHANDON, Yountville
1 California Drive
(707) 944-2892, (800) 736-2892
Very Expensive
Dress code: no T-shirts, jeans, or shorts
Call for seasonal hours.

Domaine Chandon might be the most beautiful place to dine in Northern California. Secluded on the grounds of a country winery, this immense three-terraced dining room spares no expense in its quest for luxury. Inlaid stone walls, arched wood-beamed ceilings and doorways, murals, pink linens, and views of the nearby vineyards combine to create a sensuous, elegant dining climate. If it weren't for the dining room's overwhelming popularity, large size, and poor acoustics (it can get noisy in here), we would have given this restaurant four lips without a second thought. It is still a stunning place to dine, though; the French cuisine, with an emphasis on seafood, ranges from very good to superb, and the sparkling wines are superior. Start with an appetizer of smoked salmon tartare with a fennel salad; move on to caramelized sea scallops with carrots, white corn, and crispy onion rings or seared beef tenderloin with blue cheese potato gratin; then finish with a decadent dessert of hot "gooey" chocolate cake with double vanilla ice cream or banana-coconut cream pie brûlée. Sounds wonderful, doesn't it? If you can get a reservation before prime dining hours, you're likely to find the experience rapturous.

Romantic Suggestion: Even if you do not plan to dine here, visit **DOMAINE CHANDON WINERY**, (707) 944-2280. Although it is located just off Highway 29, a hillside totally conceals the road from view, and the entry to the grounds passes vineyards and a flower-trimmed pond. Tours do not include tasting, but you can purchase champagne by the glass or by the bottle in the Salon, a comfortable outdoor area that looks out to vineyards and oak-covered hills.

Romantic Note: Cabaret performances and evening concerts are periodically offered at the winery. For information on special events such as these, call the winery.

FRENCH LAUNDRY, Yountville
6640 Washington Street
(707) 944-2380
Expensive to Very Expensive
Lunch Friday-Sunday; Dinner Daily

Look closely when searching for this restaurant—French Laundry could easily be mistaken for a private country home. Housed in a lovingly renovated two-story brick building, this restaurant is one of the finest in the Napa Valley. It is also one of the most charming. Colorful modern art, fresh flowers on each table, and multicolored tablecloths add pizzazz to the otherwise provincial setting. A superlative prix fixe meal changes nightly, and you are given several choices for each course. The menu may include chilled English pea soup, sautéed whitefish with potato and apple sauce, butter-poached Maine lobster, or pan-roasted quail with red onion marmalade. For dessert, you may be offered fennel and pear sorbet with a summer fruit salad or the more decadent s'more: milk chocolate mousse with a dollop of homemade marshmallow and old-fashioned graham crackers. Service is faultless, and dinner is a gourmet's dream come true.

Romantic Warning: Due to French Laundry's popularity, reservations are difficult to get, sometimes requiring weeks in advance for a Friday or Saturday night. Most innkeepers are well aware of this fact and are willing to make advance reservations at the restaurant for you when you book a stay at their inn. Planning ahead is important in this case, because you won't want to miss the opportunity to dine here.

MUSTARDS GRILL, Yountville
7399 St. Helena Highway (Highway 29)
(707) 944-2424, (800) 901-8098
Moderate to Expensive
Lunch and Dinner Daily

Mustards' popularity precludes it from being considered either intimate or romantic, so why would we send you here? Despite crowds and a boisterous atmosphere, the extensive wine list and inventive menu (offering dishes like steamy Thai mussels in coconut, basil, and mushroom sauce) will appeal to those looking for a fun, relaxed lunch spot. If you don't mind an audience, you might even be able to sneak in a kiss across the table.

Outdoor Kissing

ABOVE THE WEST HOT-AIR BALLOONING
6744 Washington Street
(707) 944-8638, (800) 627-2759
http://www.nvaloft.com
Rates start at $185 per person
Reservations Required

Nobody will argue that a hot-air balloon ride is the best way to get enthralling views of Wine Country. The early-morning launch time may seem like a deterrent at first, but once you witness the glow of sunrise over the colorful valley, you'll be thrilled to be awake, alive, and floating along above acres of Wine Country.

A hot-air balloon adventure could feel a little too close for comfort if the two of you were squashed into a balloon basket with a large handful of other people. Above the West takes a special approach to ballooning, recognizing that crowds can be a deterrent to those who only have eyes for each other. By limiting the number of passengers allowed on every flight (their maximum is six), they cater to those who are looking for a more intimate experience. True romantics can even reserve an entire balloon for two (this costs extra, of course), plus the pilot. What better way to celebrate your love?

Romantic Note: Read Above the West's brochure carefully when you make a reservation so you are aware that balloons can be launched only when the weather allows. Also note that hats are recommended for particularly tall people (the burner above your heads puts out a lot of heat) and jackets are advisable.

S. ANDERSON WINERY, Yountville
1473 Yountville Crossroad
(707) 944-8642, (800) 428-2259
$3 tasting fee

From northbound Highway 29, turn right onto Madison Street, which dead-ends at Yount Street. Turn left onto Yount and then make a quick right onto Yountville Crossroad. The winery is one and a fourth miles down on the right, just before you come to the Silverado Trail.

As you tour Wine Country, you might hear terms like "mossy," "chewy," or, our personal favorite, "barnyard" used to describe the taste and smell of a fine wine. At S. Anderson Winery, these terms are accompanied by a healthy dose of humor. This is not to say that the people at S. Anderson don't take themselves seriously. On the contrary, this endearing family-owned and -operated winery would not be where it is today if they did not take their business extremely seriously. The hour-long tour, complete with generous tastes of their famous champagnes and wines, is as insightful as it is entertaining. The tour begins in the main house, where the winemaking facility is, then proceeds through the vineyards and into the dramatic champagne caves. These ancient caves, boasting 18-foot ceilings, exposed volcanic rock walls, uneven cobbled floors, and more than 400,000 bottles of some of the finest champagnes in the valley, are by far the biggest highlight of any tour in the valley. Incredible! The darkness is punctuated with bare lightbulbs strung on a single black wire and softened by the glow of candles flickering against the barren walls.

You might enter these magical caves under the impression that champagne is only for special occasions, but beware: after sipping S. Anderson's latest vintage, you may be convinced that a fine champagne makes any occasion special. After the tour, purchase your own bottle of bubbly, sit at one of the picnic tables surrounded by the scent of fragrant roses, and toast your special time here.

Oakville

Restaurant Kissing

STARS, Oakville
7848 St. Helena Highway (Highway 29)
(707) 944-8905
Expensive
Lunch and Dinner Thursday-Monday

Anyone who keeps up with the California dining scene knows about San Francisco's Stars Cafe and its star chef/proprietor, Jeremiah Tower. After great success in the Bay Area, Stars has become a chain, with more than 40 other Stars restaurants, including this stylish eatery in the Napa Valley. With so many establishments to oversee, one chef can keep an eye on only so many kitchens. We are sorry to report that with the increase in properties, the quality has been slipping. While the sage-roasted chicken with mushroom stuffing was delectable, a bland seared sea bass was delivered to our table only slightly warm. Dessert was also a disappointment: the poached pear we ordered was so firm that it nearly flew off the plate when we tried to slice through it. So much for tender moments.

Outdoor Kissing

MUMM NAPA VALLEY, Oakville
8445 Silverado Trail
(707) 942-3434, (800) 686-6272
Wines sold by the glass

On the Silverado Trail between the Oakville and Rutherford crossroads.

If you have grown weary of chatting with fellow wine enthusiasts and listening to different blending and crushing techniques, you may find a place like Mumm Napa Valley refreshing. In other words, come here if you are looking for a hands-off experience. Mumm's tasting room is run like a restaurant where you can sit at your own table and enjoy a variety of sparkling wines (for a price). Service is efficient, and the location of the patio area, beside lush rows of grapes, makes for a lovely summer setting.

VICHON WINERY, Oakville
1595 Oakville Grade
(707) 944-2811, (800) 228-1395
Free tasting; tours by appointment

From northbound Highway 29, in the town of Oakville, turn left on Oakville Grade. The winery is one mile up on the left.

Neatly arrayed vineyards blanket the sloping hills that surge down into the valley below Vichon Winery; in the distance, forested peaks rise as far as the eye can see. Vichon's tree-shaded picnic area overlooks this bewitching landscape. As long as you're in this setting, you might as well indulge in a very California kind of afternoon; pack a picnic basket that includes fresh cheeses, crusty bread, and sweet, ripe fruit, pick up a bottle of vintage wine, and relish the pleasure of life's goodness.

Romantic Note: Picnic tables here are for the exclusive use of those who purchase Vichon wine, and you must reserve a table in advance (on busy days, put your name on the list while you're tasting wines so you won't have to wait long).

Romantic Suggestion: Speaking of gourmet California-style picnic lunches, **OAKVILLE GROCERY**, on Highway 29 in Oakville, (707) 944-8802 (Expensive) has everything you'll need. The collection of pâtés, cheeses, olives, cured meats, salads, and breads are all luscious to look at, delectable to eat, and, unfortunately, expensive to buy. This is gourmet heaven, but the devil may be behind the inflated price tags.

VILLA ENCINAL, Oakville
620 Oakville Crossroad
(707) 944-1465
Wines sold by the glass

On Oakville Crossroad, between Highway 29 and the Silverado Trail.

Villa Encinal, located on a quiet road between the Napa Valley's two major thoroughfares, provides a casual, quiet setting where you can spend all afternoon sipping and relaxing. Herb gardens, olive trees, and an unusual water fountain made of antique oak barrels give the inner courtyard's tasting and picnic area charm. Redwood picnic tables with canvas umbrellas are sprinkled around the property: some in the courtyard, several alongside rows of grapes, and a couple on a grassy knoll overlooking neighboring vineyards. This is a fabulous place to enjoy Wine Country without a hint of pretense.

Romantic Suggestion: Gourmet picnic lunches can be ordered in advance, so you needn't lift a finger—all you have to do is show up and your basket will be ready. The generous picnics are $16 per person, but if your appetites aren't huge, the sandwich, salad, Napa Valley fruit, and freshly baked dessert are plenty for two. Best of all, if you mention our book, Villa Encinal offers free tastings!

Rutherford

Hotel/Bed and Breakfast Kissing

AUBERGE DU SOLEIL, Rutherford
180 Rutherford Hill Road
(707) 963-1211, (800) 348-5406
Very Expensive to Unbelievably Expensive
Minimum stay requirement on weekends
Recommended Wedding Site

If the words "splurge" and "pamper" come to mind when planning your romantic getaway, Auberge du Soleil may be the place for you. In this case, we hope that the term "unlimited expense account" is also part of your vocabulary. This upscale resort hotel has some of the most well-known, heart-stirring, and certainly first-class accommodations in the area. In fact, the 50 rooms here are all outrageously spacious and beautiful.

Perched on a forested hillside, Auberge du Soleil overlooks the thriving Napa Valley. Forty-eight rooms are spread throughout 11 Mediterranean-style buildings. Twelve suites have Jacuzzi tubs, and all have wood-burning fireplaces and private terraces with stupendous views. These are stunning retreats, with blond wood furnishings and bright interiors, including fuchsia bedspreads, down comforters, and sunny yellow pillows on the California king beds, and bold modern art on the walls. Even though the architecture is southern French, the combination of brilliant colors and rustic touches like terra-cotta-tiled floors and warm taupe walls create a festive Mexican ambience. Two additional rooms located in the main building are slightly smaller and have no fireplace.

Every convenience you can imagine is merely a phone call away. In-room massage treatments are available, there is 24-hour room service, and your room is equipped with a stereo, television with VCR, and gourmet wet bar.

Also on the grounds are a full-service spa, swimming pool and sundeck, and a quiet path leading through an olive grove and sculpture garden. If the rest of Wine Country weren't so inviting, you might want to spend your entire romantic escape here.

Romantic Warning: When we say Unbelievably Expensive here, we really mean *unbelievably* expensive. Breakfast is not included with your stay, and the only time that rates fall into the Very Expensive category (meaning around $250 per night) is in the winter, midweek from December through March. Auberge du Soleil does offer a unique experience in the Napa Valley, but the prices are also the highest in the valley.

Romantic Suggestion: Even if you do not stay overnight, you should spend some time enjoying the view from Auberge du Soleil's decks in the restaurant and lounge (see Restaurant Kissing). Have lunch or an early dinner while daylight still covers the valley.

Restaurant Kissing

**AUBERGE DU SOLEIL RESTAURANT
AND LOUNGE , Rutherford**
180 Rutherford Hill Road
(707) 967-3111, (800) 348-5406
Very Expensive to Unbelievably Expensive
Breakfast, Lunch, and Dinner Daily
Recommended Wedding Site

High above the Napa Valley, perched atop a ridge, Auberge du Soleil has a commanding perspective on the entire countryside. Ensconced in hills blanketed with flourishing olive groves, the restaurant and its neighboring buildings are so well integrated with the landscape that they seem to be organically linked. Walls of cream-colored stucco, light pine-paneled ceilings, wooden tables, and a Spanish-style hearth all add to this elegantly natural effect. The dining room and lounge are designed to supply premium viewing pleasure from every nook and corner. Tables in the lounge are positioned near a fireplace large enough to generate ample warmth. However, weather permitting, the absolute best place to kiss at Auberge du Soleil is on the expansive outdoor deck. A properly timed evening visit will allow you to bask in the watercolor hues of day yielding to night.

The view is a hard act to follow, but meals here are just as satisfying. Although the restaurant's name is French, the menu offers an international variety of dishes with a focus on fresh regional ingredients. Sautéed Petaluma mushrooms make a nice starter, or you may want to try the passion fruit barbecued shrimp. For a main course, the grilled Chilean sea bass and wasabi-crusted ono are excellent choices, and so is the thyme-roasted pheasant with sautéed black trumpet mushrooms and Napa ham. Whether you indulge in a dining adventure here or simply toast each other in the bar, the potential for romance is more than likely—it's guaranteed.

Romantic Suggestion: Rising above Auberge du Soleil is **RUTHER-FORD HILL WINERY**, 200 Rutherford Hill Road, (707) 963-1871 weekdays, (707) 963-7194 weekends. It's located just off the Silverado Trail and up Rutherford Hill Road. This small winery is a heart-tugging spot to bring a picnic with your own tempting specialties for a leisurely lunch and private wine tasting. Spread your blanket in the shade of a leafy tree to capture a splendid view of the valley. Or save your appetite and, as the cool of evening approaches, saunter down to Auberge du Soleil and toast to the beginning of an amorous night.

St. Helena

This picturesque though sizable town embodies everything there is to love about Wine Country. The town's center is lined with boutiques, cafes, restaurants, and a couple of art galleries, while the town's country outskirts are laden with wineries and cozy bed and breakfasts. Of all the towns in Wine Country, St. Helena probably has the most abundant selection of places to explore, eat, stay, and (last, but never least) kiss.

Hotel/Bed and Breakfast Kissing

CHESTELSON HOUSE, St. Helena
1417 Kearney Street
(707) 963-2238
Inexpensive to Moderate
Minimum stay requirement on weekends

Just two blocks from St. Helena's town center, this blue-and-white Victorian bed and breakfast has old-fashioned flair. Firelight warms the parlor and adjacent dining area, where the considerate innkeeper leaves tea and cocoa out for late arrivals. Three of the four guest rooms located on the main floor have floral linens or patchwork quilts, brass or antique beds, and beautifully restored wooden furniture. To experience the inn's most romantic retreat, step downstairs into the lovely secluded Shadow Suite, bright and airy with crisp white and green linens, emerald green carpeting, and ceiling-high bay windows that frame the bed's headboard. A two-person Jacuzzi tub in the bathroom is the best part of the suite.

In the morning, awake to a gourmet breakfast of fresh fruit, sweet breads, and baked eggs or Dutch babies. You can enjoy your morning meal in the privacy of your own room or at a large table in the main parlor.

HARVEST INN, St. Helena

1 Main Street
(707) 963-9463, (800) 950-8466
http://www.harvestinn.com
Expensive to Unbelievably Expensive
Minimum stay requirement on weekends and holidays

Flowering gardens and manicured lawns edge the brick walkways that meander through the Harvest Inn's lovely grounds to clusters of English Tudor-style buildings. Brick chimneys, spiral turrets, and iron lanterns enhance the European atmosphere, and tall trees completely conceal the inn from the view of Highway 29. Unfortunately, the 55 guest rooms do not begin to match the charm of the landscaping. Mismatched calico wallpapers, leather furniture, contemporary sofas, and oak tables and chairs are found in even the most expensive suites. Most rooms do have wood-burning fireplaces that help enhance the mood, but poor lighting makes the brick wall hearths and oak floors feel heavy and dark rather than warm and glowing. Still, rooms with patios adjacent to the 14 acres of vineyards behind the inn are noteworthy romantic possibilities. Up-close views of symmetrical rows of grapevines and the sun setting behind the Macaymas Mountains in the distance make up for some of the decorating shortcomings. The same views can be enjoyed from the dining room's deck. A standard continental breakfast buffet is presented in the inn's wood-appointed dining room, framed by stained glass windows and warmed by a large brick fireplace. Two outdoor swimming pools and Jacuzzi tubs are also available for guests.

INK HOUSE, St. Helena

1575 St. Helena Highway (Highway 29)
(707) 963-3890
Moderate to Expensive
Minimum stay requirement for select rooms

Authenticity is the hallmark of this grand, three-story, yellow Victorian built in 1884. (Some feel its real claim to fame is the fact that Elvis Presley filmed *Wild in the Country* here in 1959, but if you are not partial to the King, do not panic—there is no Elvis paraphernalia in sight.) Wrought-iron gates and landscaped gardens surround the home, lending privacy to the wraparound veranda, though the neighboring highway is still visible and audible. Inside, the noise seems to disappear. The main floor offers two cozy parlors brimming with antiques and a warm fireplace. The seven guest rooms on the main and upstairs floors are all individually decorated with soft colors; lace half-canopies and curtains; queen-size antique wood, brass, or wrought-iron beds; eclectic antiques; and Oriental carpets. For the best views (and the best kissing), climb upstairs to the observatory at the top of the house. Furnished with comfortable white wicker chairs and area rugs over hardwood floors, the room is encircled by windows that allow panoramic views of the vineyards below.

In the morning, a delicious array of freshly baked breads and muffins, a hot entrée, and plenty of coffee and tea are served in the dining room at one large table, or by the fireplace in one of the parlors.

THE INN AT SOUTHBRIDGE, St. Helena
1020 Main Street (Highway 29)
(707) 963-3646, (800) 520-6800
http://www.placestostay.com
Very Expensive
Minimum stay requirement seasonally

Judging from its sister property, the celebrated Meadowood resort, the newly built Inn at Southbridge is sure to be a hit. Located near the heart of St. Helena on Highway 29, this two-story Mediterranean-influenced inn is very different from pastoral Meadowood. Still, the staff here strives for the same level of quality and service (which is saying a lot). All 21 spacious guest rooms have vaulted ceilings, Shaker-style furnishings, pale yellow or sage green interiors, wrought-iron lamps, down comforters, and wood-burning fireplaces. The newness of the inn and the minimalist decor create a somewhat cool atmosphere, but the simplicity of the rooms is refreshing.

If your hearts are set on a quiet country setting, the Highway 29 location is a drawback. (If your budget allows, you should consider Meadowood instead.) However, guests' privacy and comfort are a top priority, and you will not be disappointed. Guest rooms are well soundproofed, and landscaping efforts in the courtyard continue. Also, the inn is within easy walking distance of downtown St. Helena, numerous wineries, and many restaurants.

Romantic Note: Guests can access the swimming pool and fitness center at Meadowood, just minutes away ($15 per person; $25 per couple). Meadowood's spa treatments, croquet, tennis, and golf privileges are also available for an additional charge.

   Romantic Suggestion: For a casual bite to eat, try **TOMATINA**, (707) 967-9999 (Moderate to Expensive), located on the inn's ground level. Mediterranean cuisine is the specialty, and even though the atmosphere is more festive than intimate, the chef is reputed to be one of the best in the valley.

LA FLEUR, St. Helena   💋💋
1475 Inglewood Avenue
(707) 963-0233
Expensive
Minimum stay requirement on weekends

   Bountiful roses line the circular drive fronting La Fleur, a pale blue 1882 Victorian tucked nicely away from Highway 29. Choose from seven guest rooms, each done in a different theme. A majestic, billowing crown valance over the bed and a stunning floor-to-ceiling black marble hearth enhance the Prince Edward Room; rococo gilt mirrors and wall sconces highlight stenciled walls, and a claw-foot tub awaits in the bath. The Library Room is decidedly Victorian, with the original tile fireplace, cool green walls, shelves lined with books, and swag drapes crowning a bay window that looks out to the rose garden. The brightest, sunniest room in the house is the Vineyard Room, where grapes are stenciled on the walls and expansive windows overlook the vineyards. Every room appeals to a different taste, and all offer a good deal of charm, but they could also use some attention, such as paint touch-ups, a good deep carpet cleaning, and the updating of some linens.

   In the morning, a glorious full breakfast buffet is presented in the main-floor sunroom. Marble-topped tables for two fill this cheerful room, and antique plates line the walls. After breakfast (or whenever you choose), a romantic bonus to your stay is a private tour and tasting at the petite Villa Helena winery next door.

   Romantic Warning: La Fleur's answering service is less than helpful, and more often than not, the bed and breakfast's calls are forwarded there. If you need immediate customer service or you need to be somewhere that allows you to be easily reached, this could be a problem. Granted, being left alone can be conducive to romance, but it is reassuring to know that personal service is available when needed (and in a bed and breakfast, hands-on service is expected).

MEADOWOOD, St. Helena
900 Meadowood Lane
(707) 963-3646, (800) 458-8080
http://www.placestostay.com

Unbelievably Expensive
Recommended Wedding Site

Although the address states St. Helena, Meadowood is discreetly tucked into the forested foothills of the Napa Valley, nowhere near a highway or any potential noise (except perhaps the occasional thwack of a tennis racquet). This grand dame of Wine Country is reminiscent of an elegant Cape Cod resort, with its tiers of gables, gray clapboard siding, and sparkling white trim and balustrades. Meadowood believes in the three Rs: refinement, relaxation, and rejuvenation. Manicured croquet lawns, a nine-hole golf course, seven tennis courts, two swimming pools, a state-of-the-art fitness center, and a full-service health spa are all available to guests. Eighty-four rooms are scattered amongst the resort's 250 wooded acres. Thirteen rooms overlook the croquet lawns, 17 cottages (each holding four private suites) are set around the property, and several Hillside Terrace rooms provide the ultimate in privacy. Private entrances, stone hearths and wood-burning fireplaces in most rooms, private balconies, cathedral ceilings with skylights, and subtle, softly hued interiors create a sense of serenity. Down comforters, gourmet honor bars, and air-conditioning ensure comfort. Even the tile floors in the bathrooms are heated, so as not to startle your toes.

Meadowood is one of the most expensive places to stay in the Napa Valley, but a place as grand as this validates the old cliché "You get what you pay for." For a special occasion or if you want to splurge, Meadowood justifies the expense.

Romantic Suggestion: A visit to Meadowood would not be complete without a dinner in **THE RESTAURANT** (see Restaurant Kissing).

VINEYARD COUNTRY INN, St. Helena
201 Main Street (Highway 29)
(707) 963-1000
Expensive to Very Expensive
Minimum stay requirement on weekends

Move this beautiful, relatively new Mediterranean-style inn a little farther away from the highway and you couldn't ask for more. Other than its poor location, no detail has been overlooked. All 21 guest rooms are gracious two-room suites, situated in a complex of two-story stone buildings. The bedrooms have full baths, four-poster beds, and sumptuous down comforters; the sitting areas are equally attractive and comfortable, with wet bars, large brick fireplaces, and rich green or warm peach color schemes. Some rooms even have private patios that overlook neighboring vineyards. A generous continental breakfast is served to two-person tables in the lovely communal dining room that overlooks the inn's small roadside vineyard on one side and a brick courtyard with an outdoor pool and Jacuzzi tub on the other.

WINE COUNTRY INN, St. Helena
1152 Lodi Lane
(707) 963-7077
http://www.winecountryinn.com
Expensive to Very Expensive
Minimum stay requirement on weekends for select rooms

Situated on a beautifully landscaped knoll overlooking tranquil acres of tree-hemmed vineyards, this dark wood-paneled inn has all the makings for a romantic country experience. The 24 guest rooms, spread among three different buildings, are individually decorated with old-fashioned country accents of calico and floral wallpapers, white wainscoting in the recently renovated bathrooms, and handmade patchwork quilts. Most of the rooms have wood-burning fireplaces and small balconies or decks that view the pastoral natural surroundings. Three rooms have outdoor Jacuzzi tubs set out on private decks, and one has a whirlpool tub in its crisp white bathroom.

The outdoor swimming pool, bordered by colorful flowers and greenery, affords the best views of the vineyards and stunning evening sunsets. We can't think of a better spot for you to enjoy a newly purchased vintage as you dabble your toes in the cool sparkling water.

Mornings feature an extensive buffet breakfast of hot scones and croissants, a hot egg dish, and fresh fruit served in the parlor of the main house by the warmth of a woodstove.

ZINFANDEL INN, St. Helena
800 Zinfandel Lane
(707) 963-3512
Expensive to Very Expensive
Minimum stay requirement on weekends and holidays

Set on a relatively quiet street between Highway 29 and the Silverado Trail, this stone and wood English Tudor–style home is enhanced by a spouting fountain on the manicured front lawn. Guests enjoy the forested surroundings that enclose two acres of gardens, an aviary, two gazebos, a small swimming pool, a hot tub, and a fish pond and waterfall.

Three guest rooms here exude homespun European ambience. The Chardonnay Room has a large stone fireplace, wood-beamed ceiling, large soaking tub, and bay windows overlooking the garden. A tiled Jacuzzi tub, private deck, oak furnishings, and stained glass enhance the Zinfandel Suite.

The third room, Petite Sirah, is indeed petite and not necessarily the best option, due to its detached bath. Snuggly down comforters, a complimentary fruit and champagne basket upon arrival, and a lavish full breakfast (served family-style every morning) add to the personal touches here. While not as upscale as many Wine Country properties, the Zinfandel Inn gives travelers a taste of what an old-fashioned bed and breakfast can offer.

Restaurant Kissing

BRAVA TERRACE, St. Helena
3010 St. Helena Highway (Highway 29)
(707) 963-9300
Moderate
Lunch and Dinner Daily

We say "bravo" to Brava Terrace, for its casual but elegant style of dining and lively menu with something for everyone. Fresh ingredients are blended deliciously to create original appetizers such as Jamaican chicken skewers, or a grilled mushroom, spinach, and corn salad with walnut-garlic vinaigrette. Main courses are just as pleasing, with fresh fish, pasta, and risotto, each prepared differently every day. We found the mushroom ravioli with a lemon vinaigrette outstanding, and the grilled peppered ribeye steak with mashed vegetable potatoes and a red wine sauce is perfect for a healthy appetite. Unfortunately, we have heard reports that the kitchen is inconsistent, and the night we dined the snapper was overdone. Still, the well-spaced tables, prompt service, and warm stone fireplace framed with dried branches and twinkling white lights will help to secure a romantic and enjoyable evening.

Romantic Option: TRILOGY RESTAURANT, 1234 Main Street, (707) 963-5507 (Expensive) is a food lover's paradise. Inside this simple storefront location, ten tightly packed tables draped in white and peach are available for diners who wish to sample authentic French cuisine. Sautéed duck with port and figs or grilled yellowfin tuna with lemon, caper, and dill butter are examples of the traditional lunch and dinner entrées you will find here.

GREYSTONE RESTAURANT, St. Helena
2555 Main Street (Highway 29)
(707) 967-1010
Moderate to Expensive
Lunch and Dinner Wednesday-Monday

Discussions about the CIA occur frequently in the Napa Valley, and it is not because of an abundance of covert activities. Most likely when someone mentions the CIA, it's a reference to the Culinary Institute of America and its fantastic restaurant: Greystone. This newcomer has taken the valley by storm and is becoming a destination in itself.

Formerly the Christian Brothers Greystone Winery, this monumental Gothic stone structure first opened its doors in 1889. Now, after three years and $14 million of renovations, Greystone has opened as a continuing education center for chefs from around the world and, luckily for us, as a first-rate restaurant for visitors from around the world. The atmosphere is entirely festive and usually noisy, with voices resonating off the stone walls and high ceiling, but we found the whole experience so memorable that three lips were still in order. Copper hanging lamps light up bright yellow and royal blue chairs, and an open kitchen allows you to watch the chefs in action. Two acres of organic gardens on the premises provide the freshest produce available, and local products are used in abundance (including an extensive wine list).

The Mediterranean menu is designed so guests can enjoy a variety of dishes, and the prices allow samplings of many flavors. Hot and cold tasting selections like grilled chicken and fennel skewers, and grilled oyster mushroom bruschetta are fabulous, but try to save room for a small pasta dish. The gnocchi served with wild mushrooms, winter squash, spinach, and brown butter are outstanding. Exciting main courses such as Greystone paella with saffron rice, shrimp, mussels, chicken, and chorizo, and grilled rosemary swordfish with warm potato, roasted pepper, and tuna salad are equally savory. Dessert provides the perfect finale; lavender flan with brandied orange slices and a meringue cookie, and pear and date tart with walnut ice cream are two tantalizing selections. It is not always easy to get a reservation at Greystone, but your effort will reap great rewards.

PAIRS PARKSIDE CAFE, St. Helena
1420 Main Street (Highway 29)
(707) 963-7566
Moderate
Lunch and Dinner Wednesday-Monday

Although the atmosphere is more like a casual cafe or espresso bar than a fancy dining establishment, Pairs Parkside Cafe is a lovely place for a light bite or evening dessert and drinks. Votive candles at each bare table help to illuminate the earthy ambience provided by the burnished yellow walls, wrought-iron and wicker chairs, and hardwood floors. New age music whispers soothingly in the background.

The menu offers an international mix of dishes, and service is low-key and friendly. Try the lemon basil roasted salmon on sweet corn polenta with tomato caper compote or the grilled peppered sirloin steak with a blue cheese and caramelized onion tart. The inventive dessert choices include a warm triple chocolate truffle brownie sundae with espresso ice cream and roasted pecans, and warm cinnamon apple crisp with vanilla bean ice cream. Unlike so many other St. Helena restaurants, Pairs Parkside Cafe is not about seeing or being seen, and the peacefulness is a welcome change of pace.

PINOT BLANC, St. Helena   Unrated
641 Main Street (Highway 29)
(707) 963-6191, (888) 907-4668
Moderate to Expensive
Call for seasonal hours.

Time did not allow us to give Pinot Blanc a proper review before this edition went to press, but from the description of the interior and reports of the kitchen's expertise, this new restaurant sounds like a lovely addition to St. Helena's dining scene. As the name suggests, the theme here is wine. A well-known Los Angeles chef came to the Napa Valley to open this restaurant especially for the movers and shakers of the wine industry. That is not necessarily our readership, but it sounds like romantics will also benefit from this newcomer.

An outdoor patio, surrounded by trees, is a pleasant spot. The inside dining room also has a quaint atmosphere with dramatic accents and fresh flower arrangements, but unfortunately the windows face the less scenic main street.

THE RESTAURANT AT MEADOWOOD, St. Helena
900 Meadowood Lane
(707) 963-3646, (800) 458-8080
http://www.placestostay.com
Very Expensive to Unbelievably Expensive
Dinner Daily; Sunday Brunch
Recommended Wedding Site

The Restaurant at Meadowood exudes a rejuvenating serenity and quiet elegance that is rarely found. Simultaneously spacious and intimate, the dining room has high peaked ceilings, plush upholstered chairs, and exquisite table settings. Classical music and a formal but unpretentious staff add to the refinement. The extensive wine selection, including 250 vintages from the Napa Valley alone, will please any palate, as will the four-course extravaganza. A variety of French- and Asian-influenced dishes featuring local ingredients are offered for each course.

Just to give you an idea of what your taste buds can look forward to, our meal started with roasted Hawaiian prawns with wild mushrooms and sweet chile vinaigrette. Seared halibut tournedos with white beans, roasted garlic, and cilantro butter were the second course, and the main course consisted of roasted rabbit tenderloin with fresh bay leaf gnocchi and crispy rabbit confit. For dessert we ordered layered lemon cream brûlée and strawberry sorbet, and double chocolate cake served warm with orange sauce and brown sugar spears. Our relaxed dinner lasted more than two hours, but the waiting was worth every minute, the impeccable food worth every calorie, and the wonderful experience worth every penny.

SHOWLEY'S AT MIRAMONTE, St. Helena
1327 Railroad Avenue
(707) 963-1200
Moderate to Expensive
Lunch and Dinner Tuesday-Sunday

The Yountville–Rutherford–St. Helena sector of Wine Country has its share of award-winning restaurants. The local, regional, and international crowds that flock to this part of the world keep a handful of stressed chefs very busy. It is a feat to continually execute smashing meals that keep pace with the finicky palates of these visiting connoisseurs. Showley's, though not as in-vogue as some of the other restaurants in the area, does a superior job of keeping up with the demand while providing a low-key, pleasant atmosphere. Inside this large, unembellished white stucco building is a simple, subdued interior featuring local artwork, French country touches, and a creative locally inspired menu. Grilled Japanese eggplant with caramelized onions, capers, pesto, and sun-dried tomato confit makes an interesting start to a meal of roasted garlic chicken or apple wood and rosemary–smoked pork in chipotle sauce with rosemary aioli. Portions are generous, and service is congenial and professional.

TERRA RESTAURANT, St. Helena
134 Railroad Avenue
(707) 963-8931
Expensive to Very Expensive
Dinner Wednesday-Monday

Antiques and icons of the past do not automatically promote thoughts or actions that are conducive to kissing (or even hugging, for that matter). But blend the artifacts of days gone by with appropriate contemporary flourishes, and you have all the romantic atmosphere you could ever need.

Terra effortlessly achieves that heartwarming balance. The century-old stone building has a noble yet unpretentious aura. As you enter, it feels as if you're setting foot in a miniature French castle. The wood beams that loom overhead, the burnt red tile floor, and the stone walls are complemented by contemporary paintings and fixtures. Here is a setting fit for award-winning cuisine. The menu lists an exotic assortment of fresh fish and game, accompanied by intriguing sauces and side dishes. The grilled salmon fillet with Thai red curry sauce and the sake-marinated sea bass with shrimp dumplings are both exquisite. You will not be disappointed by the desserts either—the chocolate bourbon ice cream sandwich with chocolate fudge sauce is to die for.

TRA VIGNE, St. Helena
1050 Charter Oak Avenue
(707) 963-4444
Moderate to Expensive
Lunch and Dinner Daily

In an epicurean region like Wine Country, fine wine goes hand in hand with fine food. Many restaurants in the Napa Valley have achieved success with that concept, combined with a stylish atmosphere in their dining rooms. Unfortunately, stylish interiors and romance don't always go together. Some of the most popular places in the valley have incredible food, great wine lists, and chic interiors, but they lack warmth and intimacy. Tra Vigne is a perfect example of this. Reservations are nearly impossible on weekend nights, and even if you can get a table, the noise in the dining room discourages closeness. Still, if you must dine in a restaurant that everyone has been talking about for years, an evening at Tra Vigne may be in order.

Trailing ivy covers the handsome brick exterior of Tra Vigne, and wrought-iron gates open to a brick courtyard. Inside, 25-foot ceilings, a stunning oak bar, and towering wrought-iron–embellished French windows create a very impressive, almost overwhelming setting. The tables are individually spotlighted from above, and every detail is attended to with sophistication and panache, including the food. Lobster tortellini and clams in a tomato-saffron broth; cracker-thin pizza with caramelized onions, thyme, and Gorgonzola cheese; and braised short ribs with soft garlic polenta are all tantalizing and beautifully presented.

Romantic Alternative: It is not nearly as grand as the interior dining room, but a quieter and more casual dining option is Tra Vigne's small outside eatery known as **CANTINETTA DELICATESSEN**, (707) 963-8888 (Inexpensive to Moderate). Wrought-iron tables and chairs are set beneath trees in the small brick courtyard, and a great selection of Italian breads, cheeses, and meats is available. Takeout is also an option if you just want to get back to your room or are planning a picnic.

Outdoor Kissing

BALE GRIST MILL STATE HISTORIC PARK, St. Helena
(707) 942-4575
$5 day-use fee

On the west side of Highway 29, a few miles north of downtown St. Helena.

You won't see any grape arbors at this cool, forested park a short drive and a world away from the area's sun-soaked vineyards. Stroll along restful paths that meander past a gurgling stream hemmed with wildflowers in early spring. One easy trail leads to a restored wooden grist mill with a 36-foot waterwheel; tour the mill together on weekends to experience life in simpler times. Or follow the path through meadow and forest to a kissing spot that nature has saved just for you.

BURGESS CELLARS, St. Helena
1108 Deer Park Road
(707) 963-4766
Free tasting; open by appointment only

From the Silverado Trail going north, turn right onto Deer Park Road. As you wind up the mountain toward the town of Angwin, look on the left side of the road for the entrance to Burgess Cellars.

There are many reasons why you should visit one winery rather than another. If you are a consummate oenophile, you may be lured by the exceptional quality of the grapes at a particular vineyard or by the sterling reputation of an established estate. But it is also a treat when you become acquainted with the offerings of a small up-and-coming winery and can take pride in your discovery. Burgess Cellars in the hills of Napa Valley, is one of these wineries. In addition to its winemaking craft, Burgess is famous for striking views of the Napa countryside. Your emotions and your taste buds will soar to new heights here.

FLORA SPRINGS WINERY, St. Helena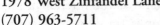
1978 West Zinfandel Lane
(707) 963-5711
Free tasting by appointment
Recommended Wedding Site

From southbound Highway 29, turn right onto West Zinfandel Lane.

You'll find this attractive winery far from the hustle of Highway 29, surrounded by spectacular views of rolling vineyards. Several picnic tables are set in a charming brick courtyard, surrounded by copious flowers and dotted by sturdy shade trees. Beyond a stone fountain lies the cozy tasting room, with dark wood accents and friendly, unpretentious service. Sip to your hearts' (and palates') content, with tastes of Flora Spring's complex merlot, a beautifully blended Sangiovese, or Soliloquy and Trilogy, both blends of several different varieties of fruit.

JOSEPH PHELPS VINEYARD, St. Helena
200 Taplin Road
(707) 963-2745, (800) 707-5789
http://www.jpvwines.com
Free tasting by appointment

From St. Helena, follow Highway 29 south approximately one mile. Turn east onto Zinfandel, then turn north onto the Silverado Trail, and then turn east onto Taplin Road. Look for signs to the winery on the left.

Wind up and away from the busy Silverado Trail to this large and unpretentious winery with natural wood accents, Oriental-style landscaping, and beautiful views, set on a verdant, secluded hillside. Joseph Phelps is one of the only wineries along the Silverado Trail that escapes traffic noise completely. Wine tastings are served exclusively as part of a tour, but to join in you only need to make a reservation. An adjacent outdoor terrace presides over a stunning view of a sparkling lake enclosed by vineyards and rolling hills; it's an inspiring spot for a picnic.

MERRYVALE VINEYARDS, St. Helena
1000 Main Street (Highway 29)
(707) 963-2225
http://www.merryvale.com
$3-$5 tasting fee, $10 wine seminar by appointment only

Just north of the St. Helena town center, on the east side of Main Street (Highway 29).

There is nothing particularly outstanding about Merryvale Vineyards in terms of its location or picnic facilities. But the entertaining and extremely educational two-hour winemaking seminar with extensive tasting is well worth the time. Guests learn how to understand and appreciate the taste of a wine's many different components, such as its tannin and sugar content, how it was aged, and what it was stored in. If you are not in the mood for a two-hour-long seminar, visit the attractive tasting bar, which features a nice array of Merryvale wines. On your way out, you may want to check out the charming gift shop filled with delightful souvenirs of the valley.

ST. CLEMENT WINERY, St. Helena
2867 St. Helena Highway (Highway 29)
(707) 967-3033, (800) 331-8266
$2 tasting fee

From St. Helena, follow the St. Helena Highway north. The winery is on the left.

Neatly cropped vineyards climb toward this picturesque Victorian perched at the crest of the hillside. The house's original living quarters are filled with antiques and serve as a quaint tasting room. Once you've filled your glasses, wander outside to the porch swing or to the picnic tables arranged around the patio and terraced grounds, and drink in lovely views of the surrounding countryside along with your wine.

Romantic Suggestion: In the busy summer months it is a good idea to call ahead to reserve a picnic table. At less busy times, you only need to let your hosts know you are on the premises, then go out and enjoy the expansive hillside grounds.

Calistoga

There is no other place in the United States quite like Calistoga, California. The entire town is dedicated to the rejuvenation of the body and spirit through an ingenious variety of treatments. We have added a special "Miscellaneous Kissing" section to highlight spas that offer services just for couples. In addition to spending a day at a spa, which you really should do, devote some time to exploring Calistoga, which has a laid-back atmosphere (even at the height of tourist season) and a fun mix of places to stay, eat, and shop.

Romantic Suggestion: For additional information about Calistoga, call the **CALISTOGA CHAMBER OF COMMERCE**, (707) 942-6333, or visit the town's Web site: http://www.napavalley.com.

Hotel/Bed and Breakfast Kissing

CHRISTOPHER'S INN, Calistoga
1010 Foothill Boulevard (Highway 29)
(707) 942-5755
Moderate to Expensive
Minimum stay requirement on weekends

Although Christopher's Inn is located near a jam-packed intersection of Highway 29, the architect-innkeeper reduced the traffic's impact with numerous soundproofing efforts when he turned these three historic buildings into an English country inn. When you settle in your delightful accommodations for a quiet evening, you will be comforted to find that the street sounds are hardly noticeable.

Gracing most of the ten beautiful guest rooms are intriguing antiques, high ceilings, private entrances accessible through small patios, and gas or wood-burning fireplaces. All rooms have bold Laura Ashley prints that drape the beds and cover the large windows. Unfortunately, there aren't any views to speak of, although the colorful flowers peeking through the windows will surely brighten your stay. In some units the decor is sparse, but supposedly this is because the innkeepers are taking their time to select just the right antiques and details. Mornings are leisurely at Christopher's, with an expanded continental breakfast delivered to your door in a country basket.

There are many new plans in the works for Christopher's Inn, such as the installation of private outdoor Jacuzzi tubs for four of the units, as well as two outdoor Jacuzzi tubs and a pool for all guests to use. Three more units have also been added directly behind Christopher's, in a building called The Arbors. As of now, they are a hodgepodge of a few stunning antiques mixed with the outdated original structure and decor. But have patience; if the innkeepers put as much care and attention into these new units as they did for the first ten, we will be able to give them all rave kissing reviews.

THE ELMS, Calistoga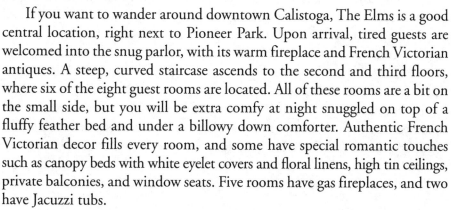
1300 Cedar Street
(707) 942-9476, (800) 235-4316
http://www.theelms.com
Moderate to Expensive
Minimum stay requirement on weekends

If you want to wander around downtown Calistoga, The Elms is a good central location, right next to Pioneer Park. Upon arrival, tired guests are welcomed into the snug parlor, with its warm fireplace and French Victorian antiques. A steep, curved staircase ascends to the second and third floors, where six of the eight guest rooms are located. All of these rooms are a bit on the small side, but you will be extra comfy at night snuggled on top of a fluffy feather bed and under a billowy down comforter. Authentic French Victorian decor fills every room, and some have special romantic touches such as canopy beds with white eyelet covers and floral linens, high tin ceilings, private balconies, and window seats. Five rooms have gas fireplaces, and two have Jacuzzi tubs.

Two other rooms available at The Elms are more private. The Carriage House (also called the Honeymoon Suite) is located next to the main house and has a private entrance, kitchenette, and spacious shower built for two. Private Domaine, on the lower level of the main house, also has a private entrance, plus a Jacuzzi tub and a deck.

A full breakfast is served downstairs in the main house, and later in the day a generous assortment of wines and cheeses is offered beside the fire or outside on the patio.

FOOTHILL HOUSE, Calistoga
3037 Foothill Boulevard (Highway 128)
(707) 942-6933, (800) 942-6933
Expensive to Very Expensive

Certain bed and breakfasts have a way of immediately making you feel right at home—and Foothill House is one such place. Perhaps it's the innkeeper's warm welcome, maybe it's the smell of freshly baked cookies in the air, or it could be the way the world seems to slow down the moment you reach the property. Whatever the reason, special places like this are worth revisiting time and time again.

The modest exterior of Foothill House gives no indication of the coziness and comfort found in each room. There are three rooms in the main house, and each one overflows with everything your sentimental hearts could desire. All three rooms have four-poster beds, a fireplace or woodstove stacked with logs, and Laura Ashley interiors. The recently added Redwood Room also has a two-person whirlpool tub and a private little brick patio. If you go up the tiny hill in the backyard and pass the gazebo, you'll find a separate cottage called the Quail's Roost, with a double-sided fireplace and a whirlpool tub for two beside a tall window that overlooks a waterfall cascading down the hillside. And wait, there's more! After a full day of sweeping your way through the wineries and health spas of this county, you'll return to find gourmet appetizers and wine waiting for you each afternoon. Later, the bed will be neatly turned down, and more wine and the Foothill House's signature ceramic canister of hot, chewy chocolate chip cookies left in your room. (Cookies and wine may sound odd, but taste these phenomenal little gems before forming an opinion.)

In the morning, a beautifully prepared breakfast basket with freshly squeezed orange juice, hot coffee, some kind of inventive egg dish, and warm baked goods can be delivered to your door or served in the congenial sunroom. As you linger over the last morsel of French toast soufflé, homemade biscuits, sun-dried tomato sausage, and fruit soup, you will be revitalized for an encore performance of the day before. The super-hospitable innkeepers will gladly help you plan your day if you so desire.

LA CHAUMIÈRE, Calistoga
1301 Cedar Street
(707) 942-5139, (800) 474-6800
Expensive to Very Expensive
Minimum stay requirement on weekends and holidays

La Chaumière is a charming stucco home turned stylish bed and breakfast, located just four blocks from the town center. Draped in bountiful foliage, it feels more like a country hideaway than you would expect in this neighborhood location. There are two nicely decorated guest rooms in this petite residence, each with a private bath and an eclectic mix of antiques. The common living room is wonderfully cozy, but the space is really too small to share with another couple that you don't know. Our suggestion is to stay here when you are traveling through Wine Country with friends and have the entire house to yourselves. The owners don't live on the property, so you will be quite alone.

Better yet, choose the Log Cabin unit, a private little cottage located behind the house. The highlight of this charming cabin, built in 1932, is the massive redwood tree surrounded by a large deck. A ladder leads up the trunk to another deck set in the tree's boughs where, in warmer months, soothing massage treatments can be scheduled. Inside the cabin, knotty pine walls, Adirondack-style furnishings, and a wood-burning fireplace with a petrified-wood hearth create a cozy, rustic atmosphere. There is a little kitchen for guests to use, and a private bath with a blue-tiled shower stall.

A full two-course breakfast that may include Italian sausage frittata and country potatoes is served in the main house's dining room each morning or may be taken back to your room. Afternoon wine and cheese are also part of your stay.

THE PINK MANSION, Calistoga
1415 Foothill Boulevard (Highway 128)
(707) 942-0558, (800) 238-7465
http://www.pinkmansion.com
Inexpensive to Moderate
Minimum stay requirement on weekends and holidays

If you haven't already guessed from the name, everything about this turn-of-the-century Victorian is a veritable extravaganza of pink. Don't worry if you're not too fond of the color; the ever-present *pinkness* is soft and subtle throughout the entire home.

Painted a soft shade of pink, the main parlor is decorated with an interesting collection of antique angels and cherubs, and Oriental art pieces. Each of the six guest rooms, located on the main and second floors, is outfitted differently. The Angel Room is home to more of the aforementioned collection; the Rose Room Suite features lots of pink and rose paraphernalia (the combination is a bit dated and overdone); and the Oriental Room is decorated in simple, minimalist style with antiques from China and Japan. All of the rooms have private baths and views of the surrounding valley and forest. Three rooms also have fireplaces; two are gas and one is wood-burning.

In the morning, an array of fresh scones, baked apples or pears, and vegetable quiche or French toast, served downstairs in the dining room, will help entice you out of your warm bed. After breakfast, you'll likely want to sneak away to the inviting indoor lap pool, attractively set in an airy sunroom, with a faux antique fresco covering a far stone wall. An outdoor hot tub is also available, located outside in the midst of flowers and greenery.

SCOTT COURTYARD, Calistoga
1443 Second Street
(707) 942-0948, (800) 942-1515
Expensive
Minimum stay requirement on weekends

A thoroughly wonderful experience awaits you at Scott Courtyard, located in a residential neighborhood just two blocks from downtown Calistoga. The seven private suites are located in four pastel yellow cottages clustered around a pool and a garden courtyard. Each room is decorated differently, but they all feature art-deco style, tropical flair, and eclectic antiques that make them reminiscent of 1940s Hollywood bungalows. The Rose Suite has hardwood floors, Oriental rugs, cane furniture, peach-colored walls, and a little gas log fireplace. The Tropical Bungalow also has a gas fireplace, but a different atmosphere is created with bright tropical prints, orange glazed walls, and leather couches.

Artists and would-be artists are invited to let their creative urges flow in the artist's studio, and those looking for relaxation can lounge by the pool or take an evening soak in the hot tub. Wine and cheese are served every afternoon, and full breakfasts are served at individual bistro tables in the main house's dining room. There seems to be something for everyone here, although conservative tastes may be taken aback by the wild style and bold colors. On the other hand, if you are looking for a fun and different bed and breakfast, this is it. In a business where traditional Victorian, country, or contemporary decor rules, Scott Courtyard's rebellious style is like a breath of fresh air.

SILVER ROSE INN AND SPA, Calistoga
351 Rosedale Road
(707) 942-9581, (800) 995-9381
http://www.silverrose.com
Moderate to Expensive
Minimum stay requirement on weekends

Perched on top of an oak-studded knoll, a discreet distance from the busy Calistoga spa scene, the Silver Rose sits on 20 acres of exquisite landscaping that blends in beautifully with the nearby foothills and trees. The impressive rock garden features a flowing waterfall that spills into a huge stone-etched swimming pool adjoining a bubbling Jacuzzi tub. And, of course, framing the entire backyard are hundreds of the striking rosebushes for which the inn is named.

Nine guest rooms are available, and each one is done to perfection in a different fantasy theme. The Safari Room has wall-to-wall jungle prints, a bamboo forest, and net canopy over the bed; the Western Room offers a terra-cotta floor, corner Jacuzzi tub, vaulted ceiling, and a roundup of cowboy paraphernalia; and the Carousel Room has been appointed with its namesake: a beautiful carousel horse. The decor can be a bit much, but each room is exceedingly comfortable and lovingly decorated. Three rooms have two-person Jacuzzi tubs; all feature warm gas fireplaces and pleasant views of the nearby vineyards. A healthy California-style breakfast of fresh fruits, breads, and muffins is served in the inn's spacious common area near a colossal stone fireplace.

The Silver Rose has recently added a small but charming in-house spa that offers a wide range of services. The half-hour massage, fango mud water treatment, and the herbal body wrap are capable of relaxing even the tensest travelers. A second building called Inn The Vineyard has been recently added, located just below the Silver Rose Inn and Spa. This special estate, which opened in the summer of 1996, has 11 theme rooms, private baths, cathedral ceilings, a huge stone fireplace in the great room, an outdoor pool shaped like a bottle of wine, two tennis courts, and a chip and put green. Although we visited before it opened, we feel assured the owners will put just as much loving care into these rooms as they put into the property's original building.

Restaurant Kissing

ALL SEASONS CAFE, Calistoga
1400 Lincoln Avenue
(707) 942-9111

Moderate
Lunch and Dinner Thursday-Tuesday

With its delightful menu and classic interior, this small storefront cafe is an enchanting place to enjoy a romantic dinner for two. Brown shutters, white linens, a black-and-white checkerboard floor, and an open kitchen where busy chefs prepare the night's specialties lend depth to the cozy atmosphere. The entrées are exceptionally light and fresh. We chose the sage-drizzled pan-roasted chicken with autumn vegetables and a garlic au jus, and the penne pasta with smoked chicken, kalamata olives, sun-dried tomatoes, mushrooms, and jack cheese, which were brought to our table by a friendly and knowledgeable server. If the tightly packed tables were farther apart, an evening here could be truly perfect.

CALISTOGA INN, Calistoga
1250 Lincoln Avenue
(707) 942-4101
Moderate
Lunch and Dinner Daily

The Calistoga Inn is like two different restaurants depending on the time of year. In summer, lunch and dinner are served only on the garden patio; in cooler months, the antique-filled main floor of the inn serves as the dining room. Micro-brews from the small Napa Valley Brewing Company (located on the premises) are always available, and the same menu applies both seasons. The pan-roasted, herb-infused chicken with caramelized onions and mashed potatoes is delicious and hearty, while the seafood fettuccine with scallops, shrimp, mussels, and clams in a classic marinara sauce is a flavorful but lighter option. Service is friendly but not always prompt.

Romantic Warning: The low rates for the 18 rooms at the Calistoga Inn are unheard of in Wine Country, but unfortunately we cannot recommend staying here. Noise from the main-floor kitchen, dining room, and bar is a problem. Also, every room has just a double bed and shares a bath.

Outdoor Kissing

CHATEAU MONTELENA, Calistoga
1429 Tubbs Lane
(707) 942-5105
$5 tasting fee

From northbound Highway 29, turn left onto Tubbs Lane. The inn is on the immediate right-hand side of the road.

Picture yourself and your loved one sipping wine and savoring various delectables on your own private island in the middle of a tranquil lake. Sound like a dream? Well, this dream comes true at Chateau Montelena Winery, where two remote islands, replete with big shady trees, Japanese-style gazebos, and picnic tables, are available for your own romantic interlude. Connected to the mainland by a narrow, red lacquered footbridge, the islands beckon to visitors emerging from the castle of a winery that looms above the lake. What more could you ask for?

Romantic Note: Reserving one of these islands costs only foresight, but they are extremely popular, so don't delay. As for picnic provisions, you're on your own, except for the wine you purchase at the winery.

CLOS PEGASE, Calistoga
1060 Dunaweal Lane
(707) 942-4981, (800) 366-8583
http://www.napavalley.com/clospegase.html
$2.50 tasting fee

Located between the Silverado Trail and Highway 29, on Dunaweal Lane.

Clos Pegase is a dramatic, terra-cotta-colored winery named after Pegasus, the winged horse of Greek mythology. As the story goes, Pegasus gave birth to wine and art when his hooves unleashed the sacred Spring of the Muses. The water irrigated the vines and inspired the poets who drank of them. We can't guarantee that you will be moved to verse, but you can enjoy the fine wine here and appreciate the classical Greek and modern sculptures that beautify the petite grounds.

NAPA VALLEY BALLOONS, INC.
(707) 944-0228, (800) 253-2224 (in California)
Prices start at $165 per person

Call for reservations and directions.

Your excursion commences at sunrise, when the air is still and cool (yes, that means somewhere between 5 A.M. and 9 A.M.). As you step into the balloon's gondola, your eyes will gape at the towering, billowing bag of fabric overhead, and your heart will race with wild expectation. Once aloft, the wind guides your craft above countryside blanketed with acres of grapes. Up here, the world seems more serene than you ever imagined possible. You will be startled by the sunrise from this vantage point; daylight awakens the hills with new vigor and warmth. After your flight, a gourmet champagne brunch awaits at a nearby hotel. This isn't everyone's way to start an early morning. But for those who can handle the noise and heat from the overhead flame thrower that fills the balloon with hot air, it is a stimulating way to spend an early morning together.

SCHRAMSBERG VINEYARDS, Calistoga
1400 Schramsberg Road
(707) 942-4558
$6.50 tasting fee (includes three half-glasses of champagne)
Reservations required for tasting and tour

Approximately two and a half miles south of Calistoga, on highway 29, turn west onto Peterson Road and then take an immediate right onto Schramsberg Road.

It is no exaggeration to say that there are dozens of wonderful wineries in the Napa Valley. One of the more distinctive and beautiful is Schramsberg. This 100-year-old estate, located in the Napa Valley highlands, is full of historical and enological interest. The stone buildings of the winery are located far enough away from the traffic of the main road to provide quiet refuge. Because only private tours are allowed, your introduction to the world of champagne will be sparklingly intimate. After you roam through the labyrinth of underground cellars that were tunneled into the rocky ground years ago, be certain to stop at the wine shop. By this point, you will have learned almost all the secrets of *methode champenoise*, so purchase your own bit of effervescent history to share.

Miscellaneous Kissing

LINCOLN AVENUE SPA, Calistoga
1339 Lincoln Avenue
(707) 942-5296
Prices vary, depending on the service

Besides offering spa services that range from a tranquilizing massage to an invigorating rubdown (both will knead away any anxieties you may have brought with you from the city), the staff members are skilled at foot reflexology and acupressure massage. In this ultra-soothing atmosphere, you can custom design services that fit your personal preferences, such as side-by-side herbal blanket wraps, enzyme baths, mineral baths, facials, and more.

LAVENDER HILL SPA, Calistoga
1015 Foothill Boulevard (Highway 29)
(707) 942-4495, (800) 528-4772
Prices vary, depending on the service

Because Lavender Hill Spa specializes in treatments for couples, intimacy and privacy are at the top of its list, and the calming atmosphere adds to a highly intimate and romantic experience. With a variety of treatments to choose from, you'll be able to find the right combination for rejuvenation and renewed peace of mind. We highly recommend the half-hour mud bath, which is actually a wonderful mixture of soft ash and subtly scented herbs, followed by a warm blanket wrap and light foot massage. These treatments take place in the bath house, which is fully insulated for noise protection and warmth. Side-by-side mineral bath tubs and two tables for the after-bath blanket wrap and foot massage await. We also urge you to try the hour-long massage, which was everything we had hoped and then some. The professional staff works serious wonders on tense muscles, and the overall result is simply amazing. A day at Lavender Hill Spa is something you and your bodies will remember forever.

Sonoma Valley

Unlike the towns of the Napa Valley, which are dissected by the St. Helena Highway, Sonoma Valley towns are set off the highway and consequently feel more rural, though less accessible. If you're in a hurry this might be an inconvenience. If you slow down, however, you'll realize that the lack of nearby traffic creates a climate that is much more conducive to romance. More information about the Sonoma Valley is available from the **SONOMA VALLEY VISITORS BUREAU**, 453 First Street East, Sonoma, CA 95476, (707) 996-1090.

Sonoma

Despite its tourist appeal and bustling popularity, the town of Sonoma is still a prime place for a romantic rendezvous. The village itself is wrapped around a park-like square shaded by sprawling oak trees and sculpted shrubbery. Weaving around this central area are flowering walkways, a fountain, a duck pond, and park benches. Beyond the square's perimeter, branching out in every direction, is an array of shops, restaurants, and wineries that have retained much of their original charm.

Romantic Warning: As is the case in most Wine Country towns, summer crowds in Sonoma can be overpowering all week long and unbearable on the weekends. Off-season is the best time to find a degree of solitude as well as cooler, more comfortable weather conditions.

Hotel/Bed and Breakfast Kissing

EL DORADO HOTEL, Sonoma
405 First Street West
(707) 996-3030, (800) 289-3031
Moderate to Expensive
Minimum stay on weekends and holidays seasonally

What the El Dorado Hotel lacks in warmth and personality, it makes up for with privacy, comfort, and convenience. For some travelers (especially ones who aren't wild about the close quarters in many bed and breakfasts), these factors are enough to inspire romantic inclinations. Located at the edge of Sonoma's town square, this hotel has 27 modestly proportioned rooms with four-poster iron beds, pale peach bedspreads, terra-cotta-tiled or hardwood floors, televisions placed on the dressers, and bare walls (except for mirrors framed in bundled branches). Individually, the furnishings are quite stylish, but the way they are combined, without any personal touches, creates a stark effect. French doors in most rooms open to small patios that either overlook the hotel's inner courtyard and its heated pool or the nearby town square. Continental breakfast for two and a split of wine are also included with your stay, and for your added comfort, most of the typical hotel amenities are available.

Romantic Note: RISTORANTE PIATTI, (707) 996-2351 (Moderate), located in the El Dorado Hotel, is a chain restaurant known for its bustling atmosphere and fresh, well-prepared Italian cuisine. This location is no different from the others except that it is incredibly convenient if you are a guest of the hotel.

SONOMA MISSION INN & SPA, Sonoma
18140 Sonoma Highway (Highway 12)
(707) 938-9000, (800) 862-4945
http://www.sonomamissioninn.com
Expensive to Unbelievably Expensive
Minimum stay requirement on weekends

Rigorously scheduled activities, spartan diet food, and militant aerobics instructors do not constitute a romantic getaway. This is not what we have in mind when recommending Sonoma Mission Inn & Spa, and it is not what the staff at Sonoma Mission Inn & Spa promotes. Although a variety of workout classes are offered, a state-of-the-art fitness facility is available, and spa-style items are listed on the menu, guests choose for themselves the type of spa experience they are here for—the only limitation is the price tag.

Unfortunately, guest rooms are less than inspiring, so the only reason to come here *is* for use of the full-service spa or for dinner at **THE GRILLE** (see Restaurant Kissing). Many of the 170 rooms are merely hotel-like, with pastel pink and beige interiors—not exactly what you expect from the grand rose-colored, Spanish Colonial exterior of the building and the elegantly appointed lobby. Historic Inn rooms are on the small side, but they do have more character, with floral bedspreads, half-canopies, and wood shutters; some rooms also have wood-burning marble fireplaces, and larger suites are available. If you can really splurge on spa treatments and a full-service property suits your needs, Sonoma Mission Inn & Spa may be just right for you.

Romantic Note: To give you an idea of what to expect, massage prices start at $79 per person, and "The Revitalizer," a one-hour-and-45-minute package including an herbal body scrub, lymphatic massage, and hot linen body wrap, costs $169. (You will probably end up spending more on à la carte spa treatments than on your standard guest room, which is already expensive.) The spa staff is expertly trained, and if you are here to truly pamper yourselves, we say go for it. The best values are the spa packages that are available Sunday through Thursday nights only. (Be sure to ask for midweek rates, because they won't be volunteered unless you inquire.)

THISTLE DEW INN, Sonoma
171 West Spain Street
(707) 938-2909, (800) 382-7895
http://www.sonoma.com
Moderate to Expensive

A restful retreat just a block away from Sonoma's busy town center, the Thistle Dew Inn is comprised of two turn-of-the-century homes. The common area and the dining room in the main house are appointed with Arts and Crafts–style antique furniture mixed with contemporary effects, and warmed by a cozy wood-burning fireplace. The six guest rooms, divided between the two homes, are filled with more Arts and Crafts antiques, hand-made Amish patchwork quilts, queen-size beds, bright sponge-painted walls, and private bathrooms. Two have gas fireplace and whirlpool tubs; one has just a gas fireplace, and one more features just a whirlpool tub.

Mornings here are a treat, and could feature banana-buckwheat pancakes, fruit-filled oven-baked Dutch babies, mushroom and Brie omelets, or cinnamon-raisin French toast. After breakfast, cactus lovers may want to inspect the inn's greenhouse, where the innkeeper has collected over 400 different species of this prickly plant. Evenings at Thistle Dew Inn are set aside for hors d'oeuvres and pleasant conversation near the warmth of the stone fireplace.

TROJAN HORSE INN, Sonoma
19455 Sonoma Highway (Highway 12)
(707) 996-2430, (800) 899-1925
http://www.innaccess.com/thi/
Moderate to Expensive

Weary wine tasters will immediately feel welcomed upon entering this turn-of-the-century country inn. The spacious sun-filled parlor holds a pleasant mixture of contemporary and antique furnishings, and the glowing hearth creates a warm atmosphere in the evening when you visit with the hospitable innkeepers over refreshments.

Six nice but average guest rooms, all with private baths and contemporary and antique furnishings, vary both in decor and mood. Two that stand out are the airy and feminine Bridal Veil Room, with a white Battenburg lace canopy over the bed, and a woodstove in the corner; and the sensual and inviting Victorian Room, dressed in rich burgundy. In the morning, a full gourmet country breakfast ensures a hearty start to a full day of wine tasting.

VICTORIAN GARDEN INN, Sonoma
316 East Napa Street
(707) 996-5339,(800) 543-5339
http:\\www.victoriangardeninn.com
Inexpensive to Expensive
Minimum stay requirement on weekends

Petite but extraordinary grounds envelop the Victorian Garden Inn, set in a peaceful Sonoma neighborhood only blocks from the town square. Fountains and white iron benches dot the glorious garden, and a trellised brick walkway leads to the front door. If the garden doesn't provide enough cooling shade on summer afternoons, a swim in the large pool behind the house should do the trick or you can retreat to your air-conditioned room.

Four comfortable options are available; we recommend the three units that are detached from the main house (each has a private bath). Top of the Tower is the least expensive of these three rooms, and although it is very small and the bathroom has only a shower, it is quite private, and the high ceilings and pastel blue decor help to create the illusion of more space. The pretty Garden Room features a gas fireplace, cut-lace duvet, wicker furnishings, and a claw-foot tub; and the handsome Woodcutter's Cottage has a high, open-beam ceiling, dark green interior, claw-foot tub, and a wood-burning fireplace. A continental array of locally grown fruit, granola, fresh juice, and pastries is set out in the main dining room every morning. Guests are welcome to take breakfast back to their room or enjoy it on the garden-trimmed patio.

Restaurant Kissing

EASTSIDE OYSTER BAR AND GRILL, Sonoma
133 East Napa Street
(707) 939-1266
Moderate to Expensive
Lunch and Dinner Thursday-Tuesday

Just off the town square, amid boutiques and gift stores, sits the Eastside Oyster Bar and Grill. This extremely popular restaurant is great for a casual, lively encounter that may not be particularly intimate but could be a lot of fun. Oysters are the specialty, of course, but all kinds of seafood are available, ranging from poached mussels in ginger, garlic, and lemongrass broth to grilled tuna served with fresh tomatoes, black olives, and baby artichokes. Other bistro-type dishes are also available, and everything is delectable. Tables in the dining room are a little too close for comfort, but the heated brick patio behind the restaurant is quite charming, especially when plants around the tables are in bloom.

THE GENERAL'S DAUGHTER, Sonoma
400 West Spain Street
(707) 938-4004
Moderate to Expensive
Lunch and Dinner Daily; Sunday Brunch

Set in the heart of Sonoma Valley, a massive yellow and white home houses this premium restaurant. Inside, three dining rooms are separated by tall white columns, and each is painted a cheery shade of yellow, cream, or peach. Twinkling chandeliers and stencils of grapevines trim the ceilings. In the warmer months, you can enjoy your meal on the outdoor patio, which unfortunately faces the parking lot, or at a more private table on the restaurant's wraparound porch.

Starters and entrées include exceptional dishes such as a fillet of beef fajita tamale with an ancho chile sauce; risotto with grilled salmon, wild mushrooms, spinach, cherry tomatoes, and butternut squash; and grilled Pacific salmon with a lobster and basil vinaigrette sauce, served with roasted garlic mashed potatoes. For dessert, the sourdough chocolate cake should not be missed.

THE GRILLE, Sonoma
18140 Sonoma Highway (Highway 12), at Sonoma Mission Inn & Spa
(707) 938-9000

Expensive to Very Expensive
Lunch and Dinner Daily; Sunday Brunch

Sonoma Mission Inn & Spa, where The Grille is located, is one the most impressive structures in the valley. Built in the early 1800s, the warm pink exterior of this Mission-style beauty is enhanced by perfectly maintained grounds. A fleet of expensive cars typically lines the circular drive fronting the inn, an indication of who this property caters to.

As you enter through the casually elegant lobby, take note of the Lobby Bar, where you may want to sit fireside and enjoy after-dinner drinks. The Grille is slightly more formal than the lobby, but the sophistication is without pretense. Recessed lighting, pale peach walls, candles and fresh flowers at every table, and crisp white table linens create an environment that is both refined and serene.

A distinct French influence is evident in the menu, but locally grown products are the main attraction, and, in true spa tradition, several light options are available. Unlike typical spas, however, even the lightest dishes are flavorful and extremely good. The grilled Petaluma chicken breasts with wild mushroom and sweet pepper relish are excellent, as is the roasted duck breast with curried dried cherries and sesame noodles. If you aren't too put off by the scale provided in the bathroom (reminding you that this is a spa), consider one of The Grille's brilliantly presented desserts.

PASTA NOSTRA, Sonoma
139 East Napa Street
(707) 938-4166
Moderate
Dinner Daily

Take a cliché, add a dash of California freshness, and *voila!* you have this delightfully creative and comfortably casual Italian bistro. High peaked ceilings and a series of open rooms hint at the original framework of this former Victorian home, highlighted with little white lights and oil lamps flickering on the tables. Our favorite items on the classic menu are the home-made caramelized carrot pasta, the cream-cheese ravioli, and a baked Maui onion stuffed with sausage and topped with cheese.

Outdoor Kissing

BUENA VISTA HISTORICAL WINERY, Sonoma
18000 Old Winery Road
(707) 938-1266, (800) 926-1266

Free tasting
Recommended Wedding Site

From Sonoma Plaza, head east on East Napa Street. Turn left after the railroad tracks onto Old Winery Road. The winery is about one mile from the plaza; watch for California Historical Landmark signs.

Gather your picnic goodies in Sonoma Plaza: award-winning sourdough; local deli meats and mustards; and scrumptious pesto jack from the **SONOMA CHEESE FACTORY**, 2 Spain Street, (707) 996-1931 (Inexpensive). Once you have provisions, a smooth chardonnay and a peaceful picnic spot, are all you'll need, and both can be found at Buena Vista. Rugged stone walls covered with tangles of ivy lend an ancient feel to this winery. Established in 1857, it is California's oldest. A bevy of picnic tables are set by a woodsy creek and on a hillside terrace, all shaded by sweet-scented eucalyptus trees. The cool tasting room offers a small selection of fine gifts to commemorate your time together; and a mezzanine gallery showcases local art.

GLORIA FERRER CHAMPAGNE CAVES, Sonoma
23555 Carneros Highway (Highway 121)
(707) 996-7256
Wines sold by the glass

Take Highway 101 north and turn west onto Highway 37. At the intersection of Highway 37 and Highway 121, turn north onto Highway 121 and proceed six miles. The champagne caves are on the left side of the highway.

As the name suggests, the focus here is on champagne, an effervescent drink that almost always goes hand in hand with special occasions. Regardless of the occasion, though, any afternoon here is sure to be special. Gloria Ferrer's stunning Spanish-style villa is set a half mile from the highway, at the base of gently rolling hills. After taking a tour of the caves and learning how fine champagne is created, stay and taste some. You are given a full glass of sparkling wine in the spacious tasting room, where plenty of two-person marble-topped tables sit beside a crackling fireplace. Or you can sit, sip, and smooch outside on the vast veranda that faces acre upon acre of grapes.

VIANSA, Sonoma
(707) 935-4700, (800) 995-4740
Free tasting

Take Highway 101 north and turn west onto Highway 37. From Highway 37, take the Napa/Sonoma turnoff to Highway 121 (a left turn); the winery is on the right.

Viansa, a relatively new winery run by the very established Sebastiani winery family, offers not only fine wine but an extensive Italian marketplace where you can purchase gourmet picnic necessities and plenty of edible mementos of your time spent in Wine Country. Fresh herbs and vegetables complement pâtés, salads, and other tasty Italian treats, all made right on the premises. Try one of the freshly baked focaccia sandwiches and a luscious dessert, followed by a smooth cappuccino (if you've already tasted enough wine). You can enjoy this small feast in the casual, brightly lit Italian marketplace inside, but the attractive grounds will beckon you outside. Numerous picnic tables are set beneath a grape trellis, overlooking young grapevines and a 90-acre waterfowl preserve.

Romantic Note: The picnic area is reserved only for people who purchase their picnic items from Viansa.

Glen Ellen

Glen Ellen, a quiet rural community located just off Highway 12, is so small that there isn't much to say about it except that the relaxed country atmosphere is a welcome change of pace compared to city life or even to life in one of the larger Wine Country towns. Still, it does hold a few antique shops and a handful of wineries. Even if you can only spend an afternoon in Glen Ellen, driving through acres of grapes amidst gently rolling hills to get there makes the trip worthwhile.

Hotel/Bed and Breakfast Kissing

BELTANE RANCH, Glen Ellen
11775 Sonoma Highway
(707) 996-6501
Moderate; No Credit Cards

A working farm, vineyard, and down-home bed and breakfast intermingle effectively at this Wine Country destination, making it a truly countrified place to stay. A dusty driveway off the main road winds up to the yellow woodframe farmhouse set in the midst of gentle hills and green pastures. Of the four rooms in this century-old, modestly renovated building, the two upstairs are the most desirable because you can sit on the wraparound deck, eat a hearty breakfast, and survey the lush garden in the front yard. Although the rooms are neither sophisticated nor endearing, they offer unmistakable coziness and comfort. It is primarily the setting of this 1,600-acre ranch, crisscrossed with hiking trails, that makes it ideal for long lazy afternoons and quiet loving evenings.

GAIGE HOUSE INN, Glen Ellen

13540 Arnold Drive
(707) 935-0237, (800) 935-0237
Expensive to Very Expensive
Minimum stay requirement on weekends

The Gaige House, an impressive Italianate Victorian, seems to have taken root in this rural setting. You might want to do the same after staying the night here. An eclectic collection of antiques punctuated with an occasional modern sculpture fills the fireplace-warmed double parlors, providing plenty of conversation pieces when the time comes for afternoon wine and cheese. The nine guest rooms (with plans for two more), are spacious and uncluttered, with comfortable, tasteful furnishings and private modern baths. Some bathrooms have claw-foot tubs, and two rooms have fireplaces and views of the garden. The Gaige Suite is the most grand, with its own vast wraparound deck, a king-size carved mahogany bed with a crocheted canopy, and an immense blue-tiled bathroom with a whirlpool tub large enough for four, but much more romantic with just two. After a day spent wine tasting, refresh yourselves with a dip in the inn's pool or sink into the garden furniture and cool off on a shady section of the lawn. Breakfast is a two-course affair served on the commodious deck or in the sunroom.

GLENELLY INN, Glen Ellen

5131 Warm Springs Road
(707) 996-6720
Inexpensive to Moderate
Minimum stay requirement on weekends

This 1916 railroad inn is a legacy of Glen Ellen's heyday, when San Franciscans considered this woodsy town an invigorating getaway. The inn's setting is still very enchanting, nestled at the base of a steep hill, shaded by the gnarled branches of century-old oak and olive trees. A soothing Jacuzzi tub and a brick courtyard lie in the lower rose garden, and a double hammock swings lazily in the breeze on the more naturally landscaped upper terrace.

Although the architectural design is from an era when standard rooms were smaller, the fresh country decor, Norwegian down quilts, and claw-foot tubs in most of the eight rooms add to the intimacy, and wood-burning stoves in two of the rooms enhance the coziness. Private entrances make it easy to come and go after a late-night dip in the hot tub or a moonlit swing in the hammock.

A full breakfast, served beside the fireplace in the spacious upstairs common room, always includes freshly squeezed juice, baked goods still warm from the oven, and granola. A tasty, more filling main dish such as lemon French toast or a sausage and spinach frittata varies from day to day.

Restaurant Kissing

GLEN ELLEN INN, Glen Ellen
13670 Arnold Drive
(707) 996-6409
Moderate
Call for seasonal hours.

Set inside a Cape Cod—style cottage, this tiny restaurant delivers one delight after another. You'll need to make a reservation early to enjoy an evening in this charming little gem, owned and operated by an equally charming couple (he is the chef and she is the server). Stenciled grape leaves trim the ceilings and white linens while single votive candles grace the tables in the two indoor dining rooms. An indoor sunporch, filled with abundant greenery, is also available. The open kitchen is surprisingly quiet, and the meals produced are truly mouthwatering. The grilled prawns on a bed of fresh pasta with vegetables and a light lemon cream sauce, and the smoked chicken breast wrapped in pancetta and stuffed with white cheddar cheese and lemon sage sauce are both amazingly good. As satisfied as you'll be, the desserts are all too tempting to pass up. The Bailey's Irish Cream mousse scented with chocolate, and the French vanilla ice cream rolled in toasted coconut and drizzled with caramel sauce are unforgettable.

Outdoor Kissing

JACK LONDON STATE HISTORIC PARK, Glen Ellen
2400 London Ranch Road
(707) 938-5216
$5 per car day-use fee

From Glen Ellen's center, head west uphill on London Ranch Road.

Besides being a fascinating historical site, the Jack London State Historic Park offers some of the most pastoral picnic sites around, with lovely wooded paths suitable for an old-fashioned stroll after lunch. Sit at one of the picnic tables set among the trees or bring a blanket and spread it out on the rolling lawn that overlooks the small cottage where London penned many of his famous adventure stories. A forested trail leads to the granite ruins of Wolf House, the castle that London was building for himself and his beloved wife, Charmian. Tragically, Wolf House mysteriously burned down before they could move in, and London died shortly thereafter. Nearby is another grand stone structure, the House of Happy Walls, which Charmian built as a memorial to the love of her life. It holds memorabilia from their life and exotic travels together.

Romantic Warning: In the summer, when tourism is at its peak and the kids are out of school, Jack London's "Beauty Ranch," as he called it, can feel more like a zoo than a park.

Romantic Suggestion: On your way to Jack London State Historic Park, stop at the **BENZIGER FAMILY WINERY**, 1883 London Ranch Road, (707) 935-4046, (800) 989-8890, for free wine tasting and a self-guided tour. Here you can get a brief lesson about winemaking and wander through lush, well-maintained grounds. Watch out for heavy equipment, though; this working ranch gets hectic around harvest time.

Kenwood

Kenwood is another modest village, located north of Glen Ellen on Highway 12. But don't let the small-town look fool you into just driving through. There are several places worth stopping.

Hotel/Bed and Breakfast Kissing

THE KENWOOD INN, Kenwood
10400 Sonoma Highway (Highway 12)
(707) 833-1293, (800) 353-6966
Very Expensive to Unbelievably Expensive
Minimum stay requirement on weekends

If an Italian count and countess were to greet you at the door of the Kenwood Inn, you probably wouldn't be surprised. This Tuscan-style villa is only a few years old, but it looks ancient, as if transplanted from a Mediterranean hillside. Ivy embraces the walls, a rose garden abounds with blooms, and tall hedges and a cement wall conceal the courtyard and its swimming pool, hot tub, and central fountain.

Twelve opulent guest rooms are dispersed throughout several buildings. The decor varies slightly, but dark, rich brocade fabrics, faux marble walls, feather beds, and wood-burning fireplaces are found in every room. Some rooms have small ivy-framed stone balconies that face the lovely garden, pool, and, unfortunately, Highway 12 in the nearby distance. The Italian theme continues in the breakfast room, with its *trompe l'oeil* murals and tapestry-covered high-backed chairs. Here, an Italian-accented two- or three-course gourmet breakfast is served at intimate two-person tables.

Romantic Suggestion: Kenwood Inn also operates a full-service spa adjacent to the reception lobby, if you care to be pampered. A "Togetherness Massage" can be scheduled in your room or you can venture to the spa for a variety of body treatments.

Restaurant Kissing

KENWOOD RESTAURANT, Kenwood
9900 Sonoma Highway (Highway 12)
(707) 833-6326
Moderate to Expensive
Lunch and Dinner Tuesday-Sunday

Whitewashed walls hung with contemporary, impressionistic paintings, a high peaked ceiling with exposed beams, cane chairs, and white linens accent the Kenwood's lovely, elegant dining room. Floor-to-ceiling windows reveal intoxicating views of the pastoral fields and vineyards. Unfortunately, after the dining room fills up with devoted patrons, it loses some intimacy due to noise levels. Because of this, you might want to visit during an off time, for an early luncheon or late dinner.

The international and creative menu features tantalizing choices such as grape leaves stuffed with wild rice and lamb, Bodega Bay bouillabaisse with mixed seafood, and sweetbreads with basil ravioli. All are designed to go well with a glass of the local wines.

Outdoor Kissing

CHATEAU ST. JEAN, Kenwood
8555 Sonoma Highway (Highway 12)
(707) 833-4134, (800) 332-9463
Free tasting

On the east side of Highway 12 (Sonoma Highway).

Getting stuck in a huge tour group is never romantic, which is why we love Chateau St. Jean, an elegant winery estate where you take a self-guided tour at your own leisure. During harvest time you can witness the winemaking process, but regardless of when you visit, you must climb up to the observation tower. From this perspective you have a wonderful view of the expansive vineyards, rolling green hills, and beautifully manicured property. Purchase a bottle of Chateau St. Jean's highly acclaimed wine, choose a prime picnic spot on the lush green lawn, then kiss everyone in your intimate, two-person tour group.

Santa Rosa

Kiss the grape arbors, sleepy hills, and sweet fresh air goodbye, because this is the city. If you're still in a provincial mindset, Santa Rosa can be a disappointment. Not only is it a detour from the country, it is also California's largest city north of San Francisco. Despite this fact, Santa Rosa provides a handful of very distinctive romantic locales, several of which are located on the city's outskirts, which feel like the country again.

Hotel/Bed and Breakfast Kissing

THE GABLES, Santa Rosa
(707) 585-7777
Moderate to Expensive
Minimum stay requirement on weekends and holidays

Three and a half acres of picturesque farmland surround this gabled Victorian Gothic Revival home, so we are tempted to call it a country get-away, but the busy highway zooms along nearby, so we can't. However, once you step inside this lovely inn you will be won over by the beauty of the main parlor and the aroma of afternoon tea. The Gables offers eight remark-able rooms to choose from, plus a cozy cottage next door. The Parlor Suite, located on the main floor, is the largest and most elegant possibility; decorated in hunter green and burgundy, it is equipped with a king-size bed, down comforter, and Italian marble fireplace. The other refined yet unpretentious guest rooms are reached via a curving mahogany staircase. The house features 15 gables that crown keyhole-shaped windows, which are incorporated in the room's decor. Floral wallpapers, richly colored linens, attractive antiques, and private bathrooms accompany every room, and three also have wood-burning fireplaces to warm your toes on cold nights.

Perhaps the most enticing (and most private) accommodation is the self-sufficient cottage adjacent to the main house. Knotty pine walls, a Franklin stove, attractive handcrafted wood furniture, a loft bedroom with a feather bed and down comforter, a double whirlpool tub, and a full kitchen are endearing touches.

To lure you out of your snug bed in the morning, a gourmet country breakfast of fresh fruit, home-baked breads with homemade jam, and an ever-changing hot entrée is served in the formal dining room.

VINTNERS INN, Santa Rosa
4350 Barnes Road
(707) 575-7350, (800) 421-2584

Expensive to Very Expensive
Minimum stay requirement seasonally

Driving to Vintners Inn past well-groomed rows of grapevines feels like passing through a magic portal into southern France. A fountain splashes in the central plaza and brick pathways lead to the Mediterranean-style sand-colored buildings with red tile roofs. (It seems more like a vintner's private estate than a hotel.) The 44 spacious, uncluttered guest rooms are appointed with antique pine and contemporary furnishings; French doors open to brick patios or iron grillwork balconies that overlook 50 acres of surrounding vineyards. Upper-story rooms have high peaked ceilings and oversized oval tubs that invite long soaks. Savor a mellow cabernet by the wood-burning fireplace if you are in a suite, or head to the common-area library, where overstuffed couches provide comfy fireside snuggling. A huge Jacuzzi spa is also available for guests' use, but it is placed so close to the road that traffic noise can be a problem.

A deluxe continental breakfast is served in the reception building every morning. You can enjoy home-baked breads, cereal, yogurt, and fruit in the bright sunroom overlooking the lawns, or savor a Belgian waffle together by the wood-burning hearth beneath a skylit cathedral ceiling.

Restaurant Kissing

JOHN ASH & CO., Santa Rosa
4330 Barnes Road, at Vintners Inn
(707) 527-7687
Expensive
Lunch Tuesday-Sunday, Dinner Daily; Sunday Brunch

The view of the vineyards surrounding this elegant restaurant is almost as enticing as the fruit of their vines. Clusters of candlelit, linen-covered tables overlook the panoramic country scene through floor-to-ceiling windows, as do the tables on the outdoor brick terrace. In the evening, an inviting fire casts a warm glow inside this showcase for Sonoma Valley foods and wines. The menu changes seasonally, but it is as contemporary and fresh as the decor, with choices such as roasted butternut squash and apple soup with cinnamon crème fraîche, Sonoma rabbit braised in red wine, and the grilled salmon with wild mushroom and sun-dried tomato compote. The restaurant is always busy, but service is prompt and professional. Wine for every taste is offered, from private reserves to chardonnay made of grapes from the surrounding vineyards to cognacs blended by John Ash himself.

JOSEF'S RESTAURANT AND BAR, Santa Rosa
308 Wilson Street, at Hotel La Rose
(707) 579-3200
Moderate to Expensive
Lunch Tuesday-Friday; Dinner Monday-Saturday

The locally quarried granite exterior of this 1907 depot hotel wears a somber face, but the parlor and dining room inside are warmly inviting. An ebony grand piano (played by a computer) greets diners with clear, bell-like melodies. The mauve, green, and sand color scheme is restful; the tables are elegantly laid with white linen, fine china, and silver. Relax with an aperitif on the love seat in front of the wood-burning fire to review the European menu, then sit down to savor prawns in Chef Josef's garlic-herb sauce; sautéed chicken topped with lemon, capers, and artichokes; or a classic rack of lamb roasted in a mustard–red wine sauce.

LISA HEMENWAY'S, Santa Rosa
714 Village Court Mall
(707) 526-5111
Moderate to Expensive
Lunch and Dinner Daily

Who would have thought a romantic and elegant new restaurant, specializing in creative world cuisine, could be found in a small shopping mall? Well, we did, and there is nothing "mallish" about Lisa Hemenway's. White plantation-style shutters keep the inside tranquil and unbothered by passing shoppers, while white linen tablecloths, terra-cotta-tiled floors, floral fabric chairs, and soft lighting complete the picture. The lengthy menu is intriguing. Asian rice rolls with rice noodles, crisp vegetables, and sweet chili dip make a perfect starter. The signature main dish of chicken, lemon-grass, and peanut hash rolled in Napa cabbage and served with jasmine black rice and chili-mint sauce is sensational, as is the porcini pansotti pasta with mixed mushroom ragout and a dollop of crème fraîche. The service is as excellent as everything else.

Romantic Warning: Rooms at **HOTEL LA ROSE**, 308 Wilson Street, (707) 579-3200, (800) 527-6738 (Inexpensive to Expensive) don't begin to compare with the restaurant for kissing ambience.

WILLOWSIDE CAFE, Santa Rosa
3535 Guerneville Road
(707) 523-4814

Moderate to Expensive
Dinner Wednesday-Sunday

It would be easy to pass this barn-red roadhouse if you were not aware of the delicacies that await inside. Only a modest sign marks Willowside Cafe, but plenty of people have still managed to discover this much-talked-about little restaurant—and finding it is half of the fun. Polished copper tabletops, hardwood floors, and interesting artwork and lighting create a cosmopolitan, stylish atmosphere that is unexpected in this rural setting. The small menu changes weekly, but beautifully presented California cuisine is the specialty. Ahi tuna tartare with fennel and Dijon mustard is an interesting starter; the Gulf prawns with black beans and citrus salsa are succulent, but the spiciness of the black beans can be overwhelming. The three-cheese buckwheat ravioli with walnut sauce gets points for creativity, but here it's the cheese filling that overwhelms any other flavors in the dish. Dessert—warm apple crisp and pumpkin-chocolate cheesecake—regained our affections. Except for the glowing candles at each table, nice low lighting, and pleasant service, Willowside Cafe is not especially intimate, but it is still worthy of romantic consideration.

Outdoor Kissing

MATANZAS CREEK WINERY, Santa Rosa
6097 Bennett Valley Road
(707) 528-6464, (800) 590-6464
Free tasting

What's different about Matanzas Creek Winery? How about the two million lavender stems that blanket the front hills of the sprawling property? Often compared with the lavender hills found in Provence, the sight (and scent) is simply breathtaking. If you happen to visit in June (which is lavender harvest time), the aroma that wafts through the air is almost as intoxicating as the aging wines. The main building and winemaking facility is set back behind the lavender fields and hidden by tall trees and shrubs. Daily tastings of their latest triumphs are offered, but better yet, purchase a bottle and stroll through the lavender fields arm in arm, or set up a picnic lunch at one of the two tables located at the back of the property in a serene wooded area.

If you want to take more than memories back home with you, visit the main building, where you'll find a whole range of Matanzas Creek products for sale, including bath oils, bath salts, potpourri, sachets, and soaps, all infused with this fragrant purple herb.

Healdsburg

You might assume that if you've seen one small town in Wine Country, you've seen them all. Guess again. Amazingly enough, each town in this area has a character and disposition of its own, which makes traveling here an ongoing surprise. Healdsburg is one of our favorite towns in the Sonoma Valley for several reasons: its charming town plaza and park green are lined with interesting boutiques and restaurants, and the gorgeous surrounding countryside harbors numerous bed and breakfasts and wineries secluded on quiet, winding roads—perfect for kissing. For additional information, contact the **HEALDSBURG AREA CHAMBER OF COMMERCE**, 217 Healdsburg Avenue, Healdsburg CA, 95448, (707) 433-6935, (800) 648-9922 (in California).

Hotel/Bed and Breakfast Kissing

BELLE DE JOUR INN, Healdsburg
16276 Healdsburg Avenue
(707) 431-9777
Moderate to Expensive
Minimum stay requirement on weekends and holidays

The four gabled cottages and the newly built Carriage House Suite at Belle de Jour Inn are equally irresistible and private, but just different enough to make it hard to choose one. Snugly situated next to one another, these crisp white beauties stand out against gentle green hills and bright flowers. All offer modern furnishings mixed with plenty of country charm, along with hardwood floors, sumptuous linens, and private entrances. Our favorite is the recently renovated Carriage House Suite with luscious earth toned linens, a four-poster king-size bed, fireplace, two-person whirlpool tub, and double-headed shower. Coming in a close second is the Terrace Room, which features a high vaulted ceiling, wood-burning stove, and whirlpool tub with a stunning view of the surrounding vineyards and lush greenery.

Breakfast at Belle De Jour is a cornucopia of ever-changing daily delights such as fresh fruit, crab quiche, apple turnovers, and fresh muffins. The morning feast is enjoyed in the innkeeper's country kitchen, inside the adjacent farmhouse.

CALDERWOOD INN, Healdsburg
(707) 431-1110, (800) 600-5444
Moderate to Expensive
Minimum stay requirement seasonally

The inscription on the Scottish crest hanging at Calderwood's back entrance says it all: "RIVIRESCO" ("I flourish again"). Thanks to the present owners, nothing could be closer to the truth. This Queen Anne Victorian inn is nestled in a quiet residential neighborhood, secluded behind cypress and spruce trees. Sip a cool glass of lemonade with your hors d'oeuvres as you relax in a porch swing on the front porch or examine the spacious parlor cluttered with period furnishings and knickknacks.

Custom-designed Bradbury and Bradbury silk-screened wall and ceiling papers enhance the Victorian mood in each of the six guest rooms upstairs. Cozy alcoves, attractive linens, private baths with claw-foot tubs, and period antiques highlight the rooms; one even has a Jacuzzi tub.

Your hosts take cooking seriously and present guests with an opulent full breakfast in the dining room. The tasty special of the day, accompanied by home-baked breads and seasonal fruits, puts the finishing touch on a romantic interlude.

CAMELLIA INN, Healdsburg
211 North Street
(707) 433-8182, (800) 727-8182
http://www.camelliainn.com
Inexpensive to Expensive
Minimum stay requirement on weekends

The Camellia Inn combines Victorian elegance with modern amenities to help fatigued travelers attain a peaceful state of mind. Trimmed with intricate, leaf-motif plasterwork and decorated with Oriental carpets, floral sofas, tapestried chairs, and two marble fireplaces, the double parlors of this 1869 Italianate Victorian home are lovely places in which to enjoy afternoon wine and hors d'oeuvres.

The bouquet of nine individually decorated guest rooms will appeal to almost any bed-and-breakfast connoisseur. All of the rooms have private baths (one is down the hall but still private), and four have Jacuzzi tubs. Beautiful antiques and family heirlooms mixed with some modern furnishings, pretty linens, comfy sitting areas, and gas log fireplaces are found in most. Our favorite rooms are Royalty, with a Scottish half-tester canopy bed, and Tiffany, with Bradbury and Bradbury wall coverings, a four-poster queen-size bed, and a large Jacuzzi tub for two.

A full buffet breakfast, served at one large table in the dining room, always includes a hearty main dish such as quiche or French toast, cinnamon rolls or coffee cake, and plenty of fresh fruit.

Before you sneak off to your room, take a dip in the swimming pool in the backyard. Afternoon refreshments are served outside near the pool in the summer months.

GRAPE LEAF INN, Healdsburg
539 Johnson Street
(707) 433-8140
Inexpensive to Expensive
Minimum stay requirement on weekends

It's hard to miss this refurbished Queen Anne–style bed and breakfast set in an otherwise ordinary neighborhood. Why? Because it is painted lavender with bright purple trim. The inn, a winsome and welcome combination of eccentricity and solace, has seven suites done in seven personalized styles. From the outside it's hard to imagine that there is room for more than one, much less seven, but the accommodations are more than ample. Amenities include sloped ceilings with skylights in the four upstairs rooms, multicolored leaded-glass windows, separate sitting areas, hardwood floors covered with Oriental rugs, and whirlpool baths for two in five of the rooms. Breakfast is a substantial array of egg dishes, oven-roasted red potatoes, fresh breads, fresh fruit, and juice. Early-evening wine tastings of seven to twelve varieties are an added feature, and every Saturday night vintners join in the merriment. An overnight stay here is a surprising combination of fun and old-fashioned romance.

HAYDON STREET INN, Healdsburg
321 Haydon Street
(707) 433-5228, (800) 528-3703
http://www.haydon.com
Inexpensive to Expensive
Minimum stay requirement on weekends

Harbored on a quiet residential street, this gabled Queen Anne Victorian home and its neighboring two-story cottage are a convenient setting for exploring Healdsburg by day and relaxing in elegant comfort by night. The cottage, located behind the home, houses the two most desirable accommodations: the Victorian Room, which has cathedral ceilings, Ralph Lauren paisley linens, a wicker bed, restored antiques, and a two-person Jacuzzi tub; and the Pine Room, which has whitewashed walls, a Battenburg lace canopy over the queen-size bed, and a skylight above the whirlpool tub.

The six guest rooms located in the main house are smaller and less private, but still very romantic. Antique beds and furnishings, cozy down comforters, crisp linens, floral accents, and skylights abound. Our favorite is the Turret Suite, with its bed tucked under the slope of the ceiling, and a claw-foot tub placed next to a warm fireplace.

Breakfast, served in the main dining room and main parlor, is a full, country affair with home-baked breads and muffins, two hot entrées, fresh fruit and juice, and hot coffee and tea.

HEALDSBURG INN ON THE PLAZA, Healdsburg
(707) 433-6991, (800) 431-8663
Expensive to Very Expensive

You may wonder if you are in the right place when you first arrive here. The entrance to the Healdsburg Inn on the Plaza is located in an art gallery and gift shop on the ground floor. (On your way through, be sure to stop and peruse the work of the talented local artists featured here; you may find a token memento to take home.) A staircase leads to the bed-and-breakfast area on the second floor, where ten guest rooms adjoin a mezzanine. Every suite has a private bath, some have gas fireplaces and bay windows, and three rooms share a lovely outdoor balcony. The very romantic Garden Suite, also known as the Honeymoon Suite, is the most recent addition, with a whirl-pool tub for two, corner gas fireplace, and king-size white iron and brass bed. All are affectionately decorated with American antiques, down comforters, firm canopied beds, and cozy sitting areas trimmed in pastel colors and textured country fabrics.

One of the most outstanding features of this inn is the rooftop garden and solarium set above the plaza—a charming setting for a savory buffet breakfast and afternoon wine served with appetizers and snacks. This lovely room is also open to the public for afternoon tea served with richly decadent cake and cookies. If you care to join in, the price is only $5.50 per person.

THE HONOR MANSION, Healdsburg
(707) 433-4277, (800) 554-4667
Expensive to Very Expensive
Minimum stay reqiurement on weekends and holidays

Once in a while we stumble across a place that is so close to flawless, it quickly reminds us why we do what we do. The Honor Mansion is one of those places. Beauty and grace emanate from the very foundation of this white, Italianate Victorian home set in a quiet residential neighborhood under a 100-year-old magnolia tree.

Your first glimpse of elegance comes in the guest parlor, with its deep burgundy wallpaper, crackling fireplace, and period antiques. Five rooms and a private cottage are available at this bed and breakfast, and each accommodation offers tender touches and varied decor. Amenities in all rooms include feather beds with richly colored down comforters, private bathrooms, and exquisite antiques. Our favorite room is the Rose Room, which has dusty rose walls, plush linens and pillows, a claw-foot tub and pedestal sink in the bathroom, and a small outdoor porch. No, wait, maybe our favorite is the precious Angel Room, with a cherub mural in the corner above the bed, and a handmade patchwork quilt; or the Magnolia Room, with a carved four-poster bed, sumptuous cream damask bed covering, and a bird's-eye view of the venerable magnolia. Certainly the most private option is the newly built separate cottage, called Cottage in the Redwoods, with a TV and VCR, king-size bed, fireplace, large soaking tub, wet bar with refrigerator, private patio, and jewel-toned linens.

Early-evening refreshments are served on the outdoor deck, which is furnished with green wrought-iron tables and chairs, and hemmed by colorful gardens and a koi pond. In the back of the home, an outdoor swimming pool promises recreation and relaxation for tired wine enthusiasts.

Morning arrives with an array of fresh breads, fresh fruits and juice, and a delicious hot entrée, and *voila!*—your magical stay at the Honor Mansion is complete.

MADRONA MANOR, Healdsburg
1001 Westside Road
(707) 433-4231, (800) 258-4003
http://www.placestostay.com
Moderate to Very Expensive
Minimum stay requirement in select rooms seasonally

A royal crest adorns the gates that welcome you to this landmark bed and breakfast and restaurant (see Restaurant Kissing)—considered one of the finest in the area. Beautifully landscaped gardens and surrounding woods completely hide the stately 1881 mansion from any sign of the nearby city and highway. The setting is truly majestic and peaceful.

Nearly all of Madrona Manor's 21 rooms, distributed among the three-story Victorian mansion, the adjacent Carriage House, the Garden Cottage, and the Meadow Wood Cottages, have something to offer. Unfortunately, some rooms offer a little less to than others, which makes Madrona Manor a confusing mix of absolutely fabulous rooms and more mediocre accommodations.

Most rooms in the main mansion are stunning, with exquisite period antiques, queen- or king-size beds, tall ceilings and windows, spacious bathrooms, luxurious linens, and large fireplaces. Other rooms in the main mansion fall short, with appointments that look a bit timeworn and drab, and none of the luxuries of the other outstanding rooms. The renovated Carriage House features rooms with fireplaces and intriguing Oriental art, but some have a motel feel and lack romance. We still love Suite 400 in the Carriage House, with its French contemporary furniture, king-size bed, private deck, and Jacuzzi tub with shutters that open to views of the fireplace. The Garden Cottage and Meadow Wood East and West are all very private and spacious, and overlook the painstakingly landscaped herb and rose gardens.

An elegant buffet breakfast with baked scones, fresh fruit, cereals, and coffee and tea is served exclusively to guests in the main house's beautiful dining room.

Restaurant Kissing

MADRONA MANOR RESTAURANT, Healdsburg
1001 Westside Road
(707) 433-4231, (800) 258-4003
http://www.placestostay.com
Moderate to Very Expensive
Dinner Daily

Be sure to arrive 10 or 15 minutes before your dinner reservation so you can wander through the handsomely landscaped grounds of this estate. If it's raining, even better: sit by the fire on an overstuffed sofa in the cozy parlor. The manor's dining room is characterized by high ceilings, rose wallpaper, lace curtains, and intimate tables covered in white linens and scattered throughout the house's original living and dining rooms. Given the stellar ambience, it's no surprise that the food here is divine. Prix fixe menus include specialties like Dungeness crab mousse with scallops and sole, served with a sauce of tomatoes, leeks, saffron, basil, and orange zest; honey-glazed pheasant with wild rice, fresh corn, and polenta on a bed of spinach served with pomegranate sauce; and, for dessert, wild huckleberry puffs with lemon verbena and honey-roasted sunflower seeds baked in phyllo and served with tangerine ice cream. We'd award four lips for the creative selections alone, not to mention the impeccable flavor and presentation.

MANGIA BENE, Healdsburg
241 Healdsburg Avenue

(707) 433-1772
Expensive
Lunch Thursday-Sunday, Dinner Daily

This small Italian eatery overlooks Healdsburg's busy main street, but its warm golden interior is soothing and the food is definitely worthwhile. An appetizer of roasted garlic and black truffle custard with sweet red pepper sauce will arouse your appetite for dishes like braised Pacific salmon with a fresh herb crust. Unfortunately, focusing *only* on each other will pose a bit of a challenge: the small tables are arranged too closely together for intimate conversation.

Outdoor Kissing

RUSSIAN RIVER AREA WINERIES

For maps and information on this area, call the Russian River Region Visitors Bureau, (707) 869-9212, (800) 253-8800, or the Russian River Wine Road Information line, (800) 723-6336.

More than 50 wineries grace the Russian River area, which stretches from the Pacific Coast inland to Healdsburg, then north through Geyserville. Many are family-run operations far off the beaten path, and a pleasure to discover together. The following wineries offer quiet, romantic picnic spots for where you can savor a bottle of wine with the repast you've packed in your basket. *Salud!*

Romantic Note: The following wineries are listed in alphabetical order, not in order of preference or by location. All have something different to offer romance-seeking travelers.

A. RAFANELLI WINERY, 4685 West Dry Creek Road, Healdsburg, (707) 433-1385; open 10 A.M. to 4 P.M. daily. A departure from many of this area's chic and somewhat pretentious wineries, this one is set deep in the country. Although there is no picnic area, you'll enjoy sipping wine in the wood-barn tasting room or wandering through the grounds, which are hemmed with grape arbors.

BELLEROSE VINEYARD, 435 West Dry Creek Road, Healdsburg, (707) 433-1637; open 11 A.M. to 4:30 P.M. daily. Located down a winding farm road and a long gravel drive, two picnic tables sit next to an old red barn overlook rolling vineyards with mountains on the horizon. Roaming chickens and weatherworn antique farm equipment accent the rural setting.

DRY CREEK VINEYARD, 3770 Lambert Bridge Road, Healdsburg, (707) 433-1000, (800) 864-9463; open 10:30 A.M. to 4:30 P.M. daily. Situated on a flatland surrounded by vineyards and sloping hills, you'll find this winery deep in the countryside. Stained glass windows flank ivy-covered stone barns that serve as tasting rooms. When you've selected your wine, head outdoors to the picnic tables, set beneath shade trees on a manicured lawn framed by flower gardens.

FERRARI-CARANO WINERY, 8761 Dry Creek Road, Healdsburg, (707) 433-6700; open 10 A.M. to 5 P.M. daily. Formal flower gardens with perfectly trimmed shrubs line the path to this Italianate mansion where a lovely gift shop and tasting room await. Unfortunately, because this is one of the most upscale wineries in Sonoma Valley, there is no picnic area. But, you can stop and smell the roses while strolling along the brick walkways that pass through the gardens.

HOP KILN WINERY, 6050 Westside Road, Healdsburg, (707) 433-6491; open 10 A.M. to 5 P.M. daily. One of the most romantic picnic spots in the area, these sun-soaked picnic tables border a pond that is surrounded by vineyards and home to a family of mallards. More tables are in the cozy, shaded garden. Wine tasting takes place in the impressive stone historic landmark that was once a hop kiln and now doubles as a small gallery for local art.

KORBEL CHAMPAGNE CELLARS, 13250 River Road, Guerneville, (707) 887-2294, (800) 656-7235; open 9 A.M. to 5:30 P.M. daily. This winery is farther west than most of these wineries, but a superb stop for romance if you're heading to the coast. The tasting room is one of the grandest in the land—a spacious, elegant chamber, complete with crystal chandelier, in a castle-like stone building. Before tasting, take a bubbly tour of the winery or the stunning gardens. Colorful flowers and towering shade trees enhance the picnic area, but noises from the busy street aren't conducive to vintage kissing.

LAMBERT BRIDGE WINERY, 4085 West Dry Creek Road, Healdsburg, (707) 431-9600, (800) 975-0555; open 10:30 A.M. to 4:30 P.M. daily. A roaring fire in a massive stone fireplace helps to warm this large building, which resembles a barn. Rows of barrels line one wall, and the tasting bar is hosted by a casual, unpretentious staff. A gazebo and several picnic tables are set next to the parking lot, but if you look away from the cars you'll see only vineyards. Open daily; free tasting; tours by appointment.

ROCHIOLI VINEYARDS AND WINERY, 6192 Westside Road, Healdsburg, (707) 433-2305; open 10 A.M. to 5 P.M. daily. This is another winery with an intoxicating picnic setting. Spend a lazy afternoon lingering at a table on a shaded patio with an ambrosial view of rolling vineyards backdropped by mountains.

RUSSIAN RIVER WINE ROAD
Highway 128 to Chalk Hill Road

From Healdsburg, follow Healdsburg Avenue north until it becomes Alexander Valley Road. Follow this road to Highway 128 and turn south. Highway 128 branches off to the east; to the west is Chalk Hill Road.

The handful of wineries along this backwoods road are set apart from the rest of the Napa Valley by their isolation and beauty. Coiling through the hillsides and ravines, your path crisscrosses the tributaries and creeks of the Russian River. Along the way, the vineyards, redwoods, and forests take turns revealing their distinctive virtues and profiles. Whenever you see a winery sign along here, consider stopping and resting for a bit under the shade of a tree or in the coolness of a cellar tasting room.

Geyserville

Hotel/Bed And Breakfast Kissing

CAMPBELL RANCH INN, Geyserville
1475 Canyon Road
(707) 857-3476, (800) 959-3878
http://www.campbellranchinn.com
Moderate to Very Expensive
Minimum stay requirement on weekends and holidays

Perched on a hillside overlooking acres of vineyards and lovely countryside, this contemporary home offers some of the best views around. All four guest rooms and the separate cottage have private baths, comfortable but some mismatched furnishings, and king-size beds. Campbell Ranch Inn feels more like a home-stay than we generally like to recommend, but the fantastic view, bucolic setting, and gorgeous gardens that encircle the home are reasons enough to spend a night or two. A large pool and deck area are perfect for hot summer days, and there is also a tennis court for guests to use. Another draw is the innkeeper's culinary skills. A number of delicious homemade desserts are set out every night, and her full breakfasts are extraordinary.

Romantic Note: While the decor is uninspired, you really can't beat the prices. Except for the cottage, rates are all Moderate and Expensive—and as you may have noticed in the rest of this region, anything less than Very Expensive is hard to come by.

HOPE-BOSWORTH HOUSE, Geyserville
21238 Geyserville Avenue
(707) 857-3356, (800) 825-4233
http://www.winecountryinns.com

Moderate
Minimum stay requirement on weekends and holidays

Kissing cousin to the Hope-Merrill House (reviewed below) is the Hope-Bosworth House, located directly across the street. This attractive Queen Anne Victorian has four guest rooms, all with queen-size beds, private baths (one is private but located across the hall), and views of the neighborhood. The Oak Room, with a whirlpool bathtub and a charming country atmosphere, deserves special mention, as well does the Sun Porch Room, with wicker chairs and hardwood floors.

A full country breakfast with fresh breads, a hot egg entrée, and fruit is served in the antique-filled dining room on the main floor.

HOPE-MERRILL HOUSE, Geyserville
21253 Geyserville Avenue
(707) 857-3356, (800) 825-4233
http://www.winecountryinns.com
Moderate to Expensive
Minimum stay requirement on weekends and holidays

Staying in one of the eight rooms at this faithfully and elaborately restored turn-of-the-century Victorian is like stepping back in time. The Eastlake Stick–style home showcases Victorian intricacies alongside modern amenities. Stunning silk-screened Bradbury and Bradbury wall coverings and ceiling papers add the proper flourish to the Sterling Room, while the romance of a whirlpool tub for two enhances the beautiful Peacock Room. The Vineyard View Room has a cozy fireplace and a beautifully restored antique armoire.

Before you indulge in the full, gourmet breakfast of fresh pastries and a hot egg dish, take a dip in the refreshing outdoor swimming pool, set behind the home, near a latticed gazebo and a vineyard.

Romantic Suggestion: For $30, the inn will prepare a gourmet picnic lunch for two. This includes an appetizer, entrée, salad, dessert, fruit, and a bottle of the innkeeper's wine, all packed in a keepsake wicker basket. Reserve ahead to enjoy this delicious experience.

Restaurant Kissing

CHATEAU SOUVERAIN, Geyserville
Independence Lane (Highway 101)
(707) 433-3141
Moderate to Expensive
Lunch and Dinner Friday-Sunday

No matter which Wine Country town you spend the night in, make sure you head north to Geyserville to dine at Chateau Souverain at least once. A stately stone and wrought-iron archway sets the mood as you approach the elegant chateau, set atop a vineyard-laden knoll. Sweep up the regal stone steps to the main dining room, where picture windows on three sides frame a view that is as intoxicating as the nearly 100 fine wines offered here. A massive fireplace, magnificent bent brass chandeliers hanging from a cathedral ceiling, and soft, neutral tones enhance the ambiance. In the warmer months, tables are set on the grand terrace overlooking the vineyards of the Alexander Valley.

The cuisine is equally wonderful, with appetizers like Redwood Hill goat cheese and leek tart with pine nuts, chives, and baby greens, and entrées such as roasted Sonoma chicken with potato-leek gratin, or fresh lemon and black peppercorn tagliarini. We saved room for the frozen chocolate praline mousse cake with chocolate sauce, and highly recommend that you do the same.

" *Every kiss provokes another.* "

Marcel Proust

San Francisco

Shrouded by fog and harbored between the Pacific Ocean and San Francisco Bay, the city of San Francisco pulsates with electricity. Colorful Victorian-style townhouses crowd together in lively hillside neighborhoods, and the arches of the landmark Golden Gate Bridge gracefully ascend above clouds hovering over the bay.

There is truly something for everybody in this distinctive city that thrives on diversity. The options are endless when it comes to luxury hotels and opulent bed and breakfasts, and world-renowned chefs dazzle diners in restaurants all over the city. Wildlife and greenery abound in **GOLDEN GATE PARK** (see Outdoor Kissing), where you can seek refuge from city life in nature's splendor. Depending on your mood, a night on the town in San Francisco can include spending an evening at the theater, symphony, or opera; taking a moonlit walk through the architecturally renowned **PALACE OF FINE ARTS** (see Outdoor Kissing); riding on one of the city's infamous cable cars; perusing the vendors' stands at Fisherman's Wharf; or shopping and exploring the bustling international districts. No matter how you choose to spend your time, San Francisco's sights and sounds are sure to inspire fun, romance, and plenty of kissing.

Romantic Warning: Parking in San Francisco, especially in crowded areas like Union Square or Chinatown, can be a real challenge. Don't let the frustration of searching for a space spoil the day or evening before it begins. If you are downtown or nearby, do yourselves a favor and catch a cab or a cable car, or walk (but go on foot only if you're wearing good walking shoes and are prepared to climb some hills).

Hotel/Bed and Breakfast Kissing

THE ARCHBISHOP'S MANSION, San Francisco   ❤❤❤❤
1000 Fulton Street, at Steiner
(415) 563-7872, (800) 543-5820
http://www.sftrips.com
Expensive to Unbelievably Expensive
Minimum stay requirement on weekends
Recommended Wedding Site

The outside world melts into oblivion as you enter this magnificent mansion turned bed and breakfast. Crossing the threshold, you can see what makes this place so spectacular. A massive foyer, the stained glass dome crowning the formidable three-story staircase, and Noel Coward's grand piano in the hallway are a few of the more notable appointments.

Built in 1904 for the archbishop of San Francisco, the mansion was used to entertain dignitaries from all over the world. Much of its old-world elegance remains today. The formal parlor is ornately furnished with high-backed chairs, a polished wood mantel, an Oriental rug, and gold detailing. An impressive triple-vaulted, hand-painted ceiling is the parlor's main attraction.

Each of the 15 lavish guest rooms is superbly designed for intimacy. In the Carmen Suite, a claw-foot bathtub sits next to one of the mansion's 11 carved-mantel fireplaces. In the Don Giovanni Suite, you'll find a seven-headed shower and a four-poster bed from a French castle. All of the rooms feature choice antiques, graceful sitting areas, embroidered linens, and partial or full canopies gracing the beds. A few even have city views, and two boast Jacuzzi tubs. Each room has been christened with the title of a well-known opera.

A gracious staff serves wine in the parlor, and in the morning a generous continental breakfast is brought to your door. **ALAMO SQUARE** (see Outdoor Kissing) is right across the street if you care for a morning walk. The surroundings and service at the Archbishop's Mansion allow guests to revel in the noble, gilt-edged style of the rich and famous. By the way, the Archbishop's Mansion survived the 1906 earthquake. Its tremor-worthiness alone merits a high kissing score.

THE BED AND BREAKFAST INN, San Francisco
4 Charlton Court, at Union Street
(415) 921-9784
Inexpensive to Expensive; No Credit Cards

Leave behind the urban pace of Union Street and immerse yourselves in this snug, hobbit-like hideaway. Formerly a neighborhood carriage house, the picturesque Bed and Breakfast Inn is tucked into a side street, and its 11 eclectic rooms provide an interesting city escape. Only five have private baths, but all are surprisingly comfortable and quaint, appointed with eclectic antiques and thick down comforters. A few even open onto their own hidden rooftop garden. A spiral staircase in the spacious Mayfair Penthouse winds upstairs to a bedroom with a sloped ceiling and a large, two-person Jacuzzi tub. Another favorite is the wonderfully luxurious and private, self-contained Garden Suite, with a solarium, whirlpool tub that looks onto a garden patio, loft bedroom, and fully equipped, beautifully tiled modern kitchen.

Breakfast is served in the main house's small country-style dining room at cozy two-person tables and is included with every room except the Garden

Suite. (People who opt for this suite don't mind; they can take advantage of their kitchen and make a romantic breakfast at their secluded leisure.) Guests also have the option of having breakfast served directly to their room, an option too tempting for the romantically inclined to resist.

Romantic Suggestion: The multitude of cosmopolitan shopping and dining establishments on Union Street are steps away from the Bed and Breakfast Inn's front door. Browsing hand-in-hand around this area can be a one-of-a-kind shopping extravaganza. From the western edge of the Presidio to Telegraph Hill on the east side, you'll find an endless parade of stores with everything a curious consumer could ever want.

CAMPTON PLACE HOTEL, San Francisco
340 Stockton Street, between Sutter and Post
(415) 781-5555, (800) 235-4300
http://www.placestostay.com
Very Expensive to Unbelievably Expensive

Imagine valet service that unpacks your baggage, brings fresh bouquets to your room, and provides shoe shines. There is only one word for the Campton Place Hotel: aristocratic; and there is only one word for you during your stay: spoiled.

From the marble lobby with Asian accents to the rooftop garden and extravagant dining room (see Restaurant Kissing), the Campton Place Hotel has spared no expense. Except, that is, for the guest rooms. Though attractively decorated in warm tones of gold and browns, the bathrooms and furnishings are fairly standard and not nearly as posh as you might expect for these prices. Suites are larger, but similar in decor. What this hotel does excel at, however, is providing its guests with gracious service and upscale amenities. In addition, the 117 rooms are spread out over 17 floors in an attempt to ensure privacy; from the ninth floor up, there are only four rooms per floor. Just steps from Union Square, the Campton Place Hotel would be a real treat if only it were less oriented toward the business set and more focused on leisurely getaways.

Romantic Note: The lobby area hosts jazz musicians most Wednesday nights.

THE CLIFT HOTEL, San Francisco
495 Geary Street, at Taylor
(415) 775-4700, (800) 65-CLIFT
Very Expensive to Unbelievably Expensive
Recommended Wedding Site

The Clift Hotel has recently changed hands; it is no longer a Four Seasons property, but a Grand Heritage Hotel. Understandably, the new management may find its predecessor a hard act to follow. (Is there anything about most Four Seasons that isn't romantic?) Renovations were underway when we visited, but only time will tell if the Clift will live up to its long-standing reputation for excellent service.

Situated in the theater district not far from Union Square, this regal hotel is simply beautiful. The elegant lobby area is filled with clusters of chairs and leather couches, and huge plants grow in ornately decorated pots. Hanging ivy accentuates the cedar paneling, and the tall ceiling is crowned by a series of crystal chandeliers. Welcoming tones of beige, gold, and brown invite you to discover all this hotel has to offer. Savor a glass of chardonnay in the exquisite **REDWOOD ROOM**, surrounded by walls with a velvet patina and grand redwood burl columns, or dine in the equally posh **FRENCH ROOM** (see Restaurant Kissing).

All 326 rooms are spacious and quiet, with dark wood furnishings, comfortable linens, lavish swagged valances, and large windows that let in plenty of California sunshine. Most rooms feature blue or rose color schemes, with a few mismatched touches here and there. French doors separate the bedroom from the sitting area in both the Petite and Executive suites. If your pocketbook can handle it, we recommend the Deluxe Suite, which features a great view, large marble bathrooms, and a spaciousness that may well be unmatched in the city. Surprisingly, none of the rooms have Jacuzzi tubs or fireplaces, and breakfast is included only in the weekend packages; for prices this steep, you'd think such romantic amenities would be standard.

EDWARD II BED & BREAKFAST, San Francisco
3155 Scott Street, at Lombard
(415) 922-3000, (800) 473-2846
Inexpensive to Moderate
Minimum stay requirement on weekends

The endless procession of cars whizzing by on Lombard Street is enough to make you want to pass this one up. Don't. If you're willing to contend with intense traffic noise, this is one of San Francisco's best kissing bargains. While its prices are comparable to the plethora of nearby economy motels, the Edward II is in a class of its own in every other sense. Stained glass windows add color to the bright and cheerful lobby filled with country knickknacks and cozy clusters of tables and chairs. An adjacent London-inspired pub, ornamented with beautiful green tilework, enhances the property's authentic English disposition.

Although ten of the inn's 31 rooms share baths and are more reminiscent of a European hostel, the remaining accommodations have many of the essentials for a romantic encounter. New carpeting, pretty English antiques, and down comforters give even the smallest rooms elements of charm. We especially appreciated the five largest suites (some are full-size apartments), with their four-poster canopy beds, whirlpool tubs, and additional country touches. Continental breakfast is served each morning in the main lobby area.

FAIRMONT HOTEL, San Francisco
950 Mason Street, at California
(415) 772-5000, (800) 527-4727
Expensive to Unbelievably Expensive
Recommended Wedding Site

You might recognize the legendary Fairmont Hotel even if you've never been there—it's one of the most photographed hotels in the country. Built in 1907, it is also one of San Francisco's oldest and most popular hotels. Cloaked in red, from the deep red carpet to the red velvet couches and settees, the hotel's spectacular lobby sets the stage for romance, illuminated by grandiose crystal chandeliers and flanked by marble columns. Of the 596 rooms here, the newer Tower Rooms are the most inviting, with large picture windows that showcase stunning views of the distant bay, plus attractive antique furnishings, choice linens, and Oriental touches.

In the historic tower, views are limited and the decor is slightly more dated and mediocre. An interesting note: The Fairmont's renowned Penthouse Suite was featured in the *Guinness Book of World Records* for being the most expensive in the world (just uttering the price of $8,000 nearly takes your breath away). The prices for the other rooms are relatively much more reasonable, though still not inexpensive. The Fairmont Hotel's **NEW ORLEANS ROOM** and **MASON'S RESTAURANT** (see Restaurant Kissing) are both wonderful places to dine and listen to jazz.

HOTEL MONACO, San Francisco
501 Geary Street, at Taylor
(415) 292-0100, (800) 214-4220
http://www.travelweb.com
Expensive to Unbelievably Expensive
Recommended Wedding Site

The Cote d'Azur is closer than you think. In fact, if you happen to be in San Francisco's theater district, it's just around the corner. As you enter the gateway of this French-inspired luxury hotel, you'll feel as if you have traveled much farther than California. In the front lobby a life-size portrait of a woman draped in stars and moonlight is visible at the top of a sweeping marble staircase. Just beyond, an ornate chandelier hangs from a cathedral ceiling and floor-to-ceiling mirrors reflect the dreamy hues of a mural depicting hot-air balloons floating amidst clouds. Arm chairs cozied by a raging fire in the hearth invite guests to stay a while. In a second, somewhat cozier common room, flamboyant fabrics and flourishes provide an air of chic opulence. Modern artwork graces the terra-cotta walls, and a second fireplace casts a warm glow over the richly decorated parlor. Wine and cheese are served every afternoon in this handsome room.

You know you're in for something different when you check in at the front desk, which is patterned with Louis Vuitton material. As strange as it sounds, the designers here have done more than pull off the unusual—they've created a showpiece. The 201 extravagant and luxurious guest rooms are works of art, boasting brilliantly colored and intriguingly patterned fabrics and linens. Red-striped canopies hover above fluffy yellow down comforters. Eastern wildlife paintings contrast with green and yellow pin-striped wall-paper. Antique trunks hint of exotic travels, while jetted Jacuzzi tubs in 20 of the suites and showerheads with massage options in the rest of the rooms ensure modern comfort. A full-service fitness center, spa, and beauty services are available to guests, complimentary shoe shines and newspapers are provided, and Nintendos are featured in every room (although we can think of better games to play in these surroundings). You're guaranteed plenty of pampering and lots of imaginative fun at this luxury hotel, where kissing just seems predestined.

Romantic Note: Hotel Monaco's adjacent restaurants, **THE PETITE AND GRAND CAFES**, (415) 292-0101 (Moderate to Expensive), are open daily for breakfast, lunch, and dinner. Toulouse-Lautrec artwork, brass sculptures, and spherical chandeliers create an intruiging environment, but echoing cathedral ceilings and an open kitchen are distracting to say the least—especially when the restaurants are full. We recommend filling up on tasty California cuisine here and relying on the hotel itself to inspire your romantic inclinations.

HOTEL TRITON, San Francisco
342 Grant Avenue, at Bush
(415) 394-0500, (800) 433-6611
Expensive to Very Expensive

If, after Alice went through the looking glass, she had needed a hotel room, she might have stayed at the Hotel Triton. The interior is a combination of surrealistic and unconventional details that offer intriguing sensory stimulation. Chairs with S-shaped backs adorn the lobby, divider screens are painted bright yellow with floating pastel figures, and dance-club music spills from the elevators. Guest-room walls are either white-and-taupe-checked or sponge-painted pink and iridescent gold. Beds are strewn with oversized throw pillows and backed with cloud-shaped headboards. All 140 rooms have up-to-date amenities to make your stay exceedingly comfortable, albeit amusingly eccentric.

For a breath of fresh air, both figuratively and literally, request a room on the seventh floor, otherwise known as the EcoFloor, where the ecologically minded meets the super chic. These rooms come equipped with water- and air-filtration systems, all-natural linens, as well as biodegradable soaps and shampoos.

Hotel Triton also offers three designer suites, all of which are stellar attractions. The Jerry Garcia Suite displays a collection of his fabulous silks, the Wyland Suite is decorated with colorful seascapes and boasts an impressive fish tank, and Suzan Briganti's Love Letter Suite is the perfect spot to rendezvous with your favorite pen pal.

Romantic Note: Next to the hotel is **CAFÉ DE LA PRESSE**, 352 Grant Avenue, (415) 398-2680 (Inexpensive), a delightful blend of European cafe and international newsstand. What better place in which to "espresso" your love?

HOTEL VINTAGE COURT, San Francisco
650 Bush Street, between Powell and Stockton
(415) 392-4666, (800) 654-1100
Moderate to Very Expensive
Minimum stay requirement on weekends

Hotel Vintage Court has one of the cozier hotel lobbies in San Francisco. Circular couches surround a marble hearth where a crackling fire inspires guests to kick off their shoes and relax. Exotic bouquets and classical music complement the tranquil atmosphere, and in the early evening complimentary wine and cheese are served to guests in this quiet setting. Once you've selected your vintage of choice, head upstairs to the newly renovated guest rooms, named after some of California's best-known wineries. Though the names differ, the rooms share the same fresh, countrified decor, with floral draperies accenting large bay windows and matching linens draping queen-size beds. If you're willing to pay just a little bit extra, you can book a suite with an oversized Jacuzzi tub. In spite of the pervasive hotel-style ambience, upscale rooms of this caliber rarely (if ever) go hand-in-hand with such reasonable rates.

Romantic Suggestion: We can't say enough about **MASA'S**, the Vintage Court's restaurant (see Restaurant Kissing). It's a romantic must whether you're an overnight guest here or not.

THE HUNTINGTON HOTEL, San Francisco   ❧❧❧❧
1075 California Street, between Taylor and Mason
(415) 474-5400, (800) 652-1539 (in California),
(800) 227-4683 (in the U.S.)
http://www.travelweb.com
Expensive to Unbelievably Expensive

Our highest recommendation when it comes to kissing in San Francisco goes to the elegant Huntington Hotel, perched on the upper tier of Nob Hill. Originally built as a luxury apartment building, the Huntington has commodious, wonderfully quiet rooms brimming with individuality and romantic flair. The ornate furnishings and deep gold, burgundy, and forest green fabrics create a thoroughly regal atmosphere in every room. Crystal lampshades diffuse soft light over luxurious couches festooned with pillows and designed with snuggling in mind. Oversized mirrors, gilt-framed artwork, and televisions hidden in beautiful dark wood armoires are other handsome features. Many rooms enjoy views of pleasantly manicured Huntington Park across the street, where the sight of locals doing tai chi at dawn inspires guests to slow their pace and enjoy their surroundings.

Although the Huntington's one- or two-bedroom suites fall in the Unbelievably Expensive category, you get what you pay for. You'll want for nothing at this hotel, and the gracious staff ensures that your stay here will be private and thoroughly comfortable.

The Huntington prides itself on playing host to visiting nobility, dignitaries, and celebrities. At the risk of sounding like we're name-dropping, we must mention that we ran into Fabio, the famed romance-novel model, in the elevator. If the so-called King of Romance stays here, need we say more?

Romantic Suggestion: The Victorian mahogany walls and dark green leather chairs of **THE BIG 4** restaurant, (415) 771-1140 (Expensive to Very Expensive) on the Huntington Hotel's main floor look like they belong in a men's club, which isn't particularly romantic. However, the same decor takes on new life when warmed by a crackling fire in the cozy lounge. In this alluring location, listen to a soft piano music and enjoy a nightcap before retiring to your choice accommodations.

THE INN AT THE OPERA, San Francisco
333 Fulton Street, between Gough and Franklin
(415) 863-8400, (800) 325-2708
Moderate to Very Expensive

If you're not already an opera buff, a single evening here might incite your cultural passions and encourage you to become one. It's hard not to get caught up in the excitement of the brilliantly dressed crowds attending a night at the opera just down the street from the inn. Artists, patrons, and opera lovers alike seek refuge after the final curtain at this luxurious spot. The inn's softly stated elegance spoils guests at every turn with inviting overstuffed pillows and comforters, bedside chocolates, and terry-cloth robes. All 48 guest rooms, designed with intimacy in mind, feature queen-size beds with half canopies, muted pastel color schemes, wet bars, and beautifully restored antiques. (Regretfully, we found many of the rooms to be so cozy they bordered on claustrophobic; if this is a concern, you may do better in one of the salon suites, which are slightly larger and offer the convenience of two bathrooms.)

Decorated in regal shades of green and beige, the lobby is home to a beautiful hand-pained French screen, Oriental celadon vases, and an Aubusson rug. Prints from the Paris Opera Ballet are displayed on the walls near the front desk. Even the hallways have curtained windows and raised wallpaper, reminiscent of the narrow corridors leading to box seats at the theater. Classical music is piped into each guest room, and bureau drawers are lined with sheet music. Last, but not least, the gracious service will convince you that this place truly deserves a standing ovation.

A fireside dinner at the inn's sumptuous **ACT IV LOUNGE** (see Restaurant Kissing) is a romantic must. Guests can also admire the handsome surroundings while enjoying the complimentary continental buffet breakfast.

THE INN AT UNION SQUARE, San Francisco
440 Post Street, between Mason and Powell
(415) 397-3510, (800) 288-4346
http://www.unionsquare.com
Expensive to Unbelievably Expensive

Located a half block west of Union Square, this small European-style inn offers cozy comfort and dedicated service. All 30 rooms are appointed with sitting areas, standard baths, Georgian furnishings, and brass lion-head door knockers. Most of the rooms are a bit on the small side and in need of a decorator, except for the choice Penthouse Suite on the top floor, which has its own sauna, deep Oriental soaking tub, fireplace, and wet bar. Several rooms have half canopies; however, the linens and carpets are a bit too motel-like for these tariffs. And don't count on a view, either, unless you enjoy looking out at the brick walls of adjacent buildings.

Painted with murals of bookshelves and lovely garden scenes, the main lobby is too small and too close to noisy Post Street to be relaxing. However, each of the six floors has its own tranquil lounge with a crackling fireplace where morning breakfast, afternoon tea, or hors d'oeuvres can be enjoyed (or taken back to the privacy of your room).

JACKSON COURT, San Francisco
2198 Jackson Street, at Buchanan
(415) 929-7670
Moderate to Expensive
Minimum stay requirement on weekends

A small brick courtyard hemmed with greenery fronts the entrance of this historic brownstone, harbored in one of San Francisco's quieter, more distinguished neighborhoods. Instead of traffic noise, you can actually hear birds chirping in nearby trees. Unique decorative touches impart turn-of-the-century sophistication to this unusual ten-room bed and breakfast. Classical sculptures are displayed in the stone hearth in the cozy front parlor, where guests can lounge on plush red velvet couches and enjoy a lavish complimentary afternoon tea. Continental breakfast is also served here in the morning.

Upon arrival, guests are ushered to their room and welcomed with a bottle of California wine. The eclectic guest rooms have their own charms and differ dramatically from one another. Set just off the parlor, the sunlit Garden Room has dark wood walls accented by a showy marble fireplace (which doesn't actually work). Other romantic features of this room include a sexy glass-enclosed shower and a private outdoor garden patio. In the home's Library Room, a large sitting area is warmed by a wood-burning fireplace. One of the sunniest rooms in the house, the Corner Suite, is appointed with white and beige fabrics and has two comfortable window seats. Luscious linens and comfy antique beds compensate for the discordant style of some of the rooms, like the Buchanan Room with its overbearing beige and white polka-dot accents.

Romantic Note: Because this property is operated as a time-share, reservations are accepted no sooner than two months in advance to allow owners the opportunity to choose the rooms they want well ahead of time. Except for this rule, Jackson Court has the look and feel of a typically run professional bed and breakfast—you'd never know the difference.

THE MAJESTIC HOTEL, San Francisco
1500 Sutter Street, at Gough
(415) 441-1100, (800) 869-8966
Moderate to Expensive

Several million dollars were spent transforming this mansion into a designer masterpiece, and it shows. A mirrored marble entrance leads into a plush lobby area brimming with antique tapestries, etched glass, and French Empire furnishings. You may want to stop here and sip a cocktail at the genuine 19th-century mahogany bar, but don't linger too long—the real romance is waiting for you upstairs.

A hand-painted, four-poster canopied bed dressed in plump feather pillows, fine linens, and plush down comforters is the focal point of each of the 57 elegantly historic rooms. Lace curtains, subtle color schemes, marble bathrooms, and beautiful antiques create an upscale turn-of-the-century ambience. Small crystal chandeliers are suspended from the ceiling of every room, and gas fireplaces lend a warm glow to the 30 spacious suites. Bay windows allow in ample sunlight, especially in the corner rooms, which feature a semicircular wall of tall windows. Our only complaint about this otherwise fastidiously maintained hotel is the fact that it is on busy Gough Street and the windows aren't soundproofed. (Of course, that tends to be the case no matter where you stay in San Francisco.) To avoid undue traffic noise, we recommend the rooms that face somewhat less-trafficked Sutter Street.

Romantic Note: For a very convenient romantic repast, dine at CAFE MAJESTIC (see Restaurant Kissing), located downstairs adjacent to the lobby.

Romantic Suggestion: Take a walk through LAFAYETTE PARK, located at the corner of Octavia and California, three blocks up from the hotel. It is a beautiful oasis with remarkable views and well-tended gardens. Romance novelist Danielle Steel just bought one of the mansions across the street from this inspiring park. Enough said?

THE MANSIONS HOTEL, San Francisco
2220 Sacramento Street, between Laguna and Buchanan
(415) 929-9444, (800) 826-9398
http://www.themansions.com
Inexpensive to Unbelievably Expensive
Minimum stay requirement on weekends

From a distance, the two illustrious mansions enfolded by gardens look similar to other homes in this prestigious San Francisco neighborhood. Upon closer inspection, however, you'll notice peculiar mosaic sculptures in the front yard—your first hint that this property is one of a kind. A live caged parrot greets you in the lobby just past the hotel's Gothic-style doorway, where an eccentric combination of flamboyant flourishes and collector's items is reminiscent of a curiosity shop. A collection of antique pigs occupies the billiard room, and a practiced magician entertains guests nightly on stage in the front parlor. Finally, tucked around the corner, you'll find a thoroughly idyllic, crystal-chandeliered dining area where continental breakfast and dinner are served to guests.

Disappointingly, the common rooms are in much better shape than the rest of the Mansions Hotel. Most of the 21 guest rooms need renovation. The displayed televisions, drab linens, worn carpeting, and standard baths are generally unimpressive. Still, there are redeeming qualities. Beautiful antiques lend old-world charm to many of the rooms; marble fireplaces, private decks or terraces, and a crystal decanter of sherry placed on a bedside table are other romantic highlights. A breezeway connects the first mansion to a neighboring four-story redwood mansion with fewer eccentricites. Here you can relax in the sophisticated communal library, furnished with yellow brocade Queen Anne furnishings or lounge in the sunshine on the outdoor deck and garden patio.

If nothing else, the Mansions Hotel offers an interesting change of pace. Guests get a kick out of the magic show and are intrigued by the ghost rumored to roam the mansions' halls. (Just for the record, we didn't notice anything out of the ordinary, besides the unusual surroundings.)

Romantic Suggestion: After the magic show, enjoy dinner in the lovely **MANSIONS RESTAURANT** (see Restaurant Kissing).

NOB HILL INN, San Francisco
1000 Pine Street, at Taylor
(415) 673-6080
Inexpensive to Very Expensive

Classical music in the cozy lobby of this tiny Victorian-style bed and breakfast takes your mind off the busy thoroughfare just outside, although traffic noise poses more of a distraction in the upstairs guest rooms. To make matters worse, cheap linens and amenities in some of the inn's motel-style guest rooms don't even merit a lip rating. So why do we consider this a find? Approximately half of the inn's guest rooms have attractive linens and enticing fireplaces; some even have sexy marble bathrooms with glass-enclosed showers. And then there's the seductive rooftop Jacuzzi tub, which can be reserved exclusively for an hour to ensure that your sensuous soak will not be interrupted. A generous continental breakfast, served downstairs at individual tables in a cozy wine cellar adjacent to the lobby, is also included with your stay. A bargain like this is bound to inspire a kiss or two as long as you're careful to reserve one of the nicer rooms.

PETITE AUBERGE, San Francisco
863 Bush Street, between Mason and Taylor
(415) 928-6000, (800) 365-3004
Moderate to Very Expensive

A collection of stuffed teddy bears and the smell of freshly baked cookies greet you in the lobby of this winsome, yet practical, downtown hotel. It doesn't matter which of the 26 guest rooms you choose; even the eight smallest rooms, without gas fireplaces, are endowed with the gracious charm of a French country inn. Creamy lace window treatments, thick comforters, and muted color schemes ensure comfort and calm during your stay, and the staff's attention to detail guarantees satisfaction.

As the smell of baked goods suggests, the kitchen takes great care in preparing a full breakfast, served buffet-style in the lower-level French country dining room (late-afternoon wine and hors d'oeuvres are also presented here). Terra-cotta tile floors, an expansive mural depicting a country marketplace, and a glowing gas fireplace in the neighboring parlor add to the charming setting. At Petite Auberge you will never be left hungry, but even if you are, the downtown location is so convenient that the dining options are countless.

Romantic Note: The largest rooms face Bush Street, but they are also more prone to street noise. Thankfully, fairly effective soundproofing efforts have been made throughout the inn, but the smaller rooms at the back of the hotel are still the quietest.

THE PRESCOTT HOTEL, San Francisco
545 Post Street, between Taylor and Mason
(415) 563-0303, (800) 283-7322
Very Expensive to Unbelievably Expensive
Recommended Wedding Site

While the Prescott is much too large to be considered charming or intimate, that doesn't keep the management from trying to make things feel that way. A fire roars in an immense hearth in the hotel's elegant "living room," where Oriental rugs are scattered over beautifully finished hardwood floors. Here, guests can relax in overstuffed love seats and admire the hotel's collection of early California arts and crafts. Twice a month, on Sunday evenings, a local storyteller enchants guests with intriguing tales by the fireside. Complimentary beverages are served here during the day, and wine and cheese are offered in the evening.

Although the Prescott has 165 guest rooms, the hotel feels much smaller due to the fact that there are only a handful of rooms on each floor. Hunter green bedspreads with hints of burgundy, cherry-wood tables and chairs, bowfront armoires, and brass accents are attractive features in the otherwise hotel-style guest rooms. Suites are slightly more expensive, but have more space and the added luxury of Jacuzzi tubs. Your comfort is ensured in all of the rooms, which have every imaginable modern convenience, including color television, VCR, stocked bar and refrigerator, terry-cloth robes, a hair dryer, and nightly turndown service. Guest who stay in the rooms and suites on the more expensive Club Level also receive a complimentary breakfast, hors d'oeuvres and cocktail reception every evening, and use of the exercise facilities. Stationary bicycles and rowing machines can even be delivered to your room upon request—we kid you not!

Roosted at the top of the Prescott is what may be the most extraordinary suite in the city: the Mendocino Penthouse. You'll be instantly enchanted by the rich Edwardian furnishings and hardwood floors in the parlor and bedroom, the grand piano in the formal dining room, two wood-burning fireplaces, and a rooftop deck with a Jacuzzi tub and garden. Staying here is the height of romantic pampering, which makes its Unbelievably Expensive price tag a little easier to swallow.

Romantic Note: POSTRIO (see Restaurant Kissing), located just off the hotel's lobby, is an upbeat, chic eatery with sensational cuisine.

THE RITZ-CARLTON, San Francisco
600 Stockton, at California
(415) 296-7465, (800) 241-3333
http://www.travelweb.com
Unbelievably Expensive
Recommended Wedding Site

If you're in the mood to be waited on, catered to, and simply spoiled, book a night here. This stately neoclassic heritage building has been fastidiously restored and renovated. From the expansive rose garden to the Persian carpets and Bohemian crystal chandeliers, everything is first-class. Dramatically lit Ionic columns grace the hotel's block-long facade. Once you've made an entrance via a semicircular driveway leading to a grand porte cochere, you can't help but marvel at the exquisite 18th- and 19th-century furnishings, fabrics, and antiques decorating the lobby. Just off the foyer is **THE LOBBY LOUNGE,** with pale coral walls and floor-to-ceiling windows; here guests enjoy afternoon tea to the soothing melodies of a classical harp.

All 336 rooms feature pale silk wall coverings, antique-style furnishings, richly upholstered furniture, Italian marble bathrooms with double sinks, and plush terry-cloth bathrobes. Even the "standard" rooms are tastefully decorated in subtle color schemes with large windows and elegant drapery. The 42 spacious suites are the most grand, with separate dining, living, and sleeping rooms, and private balconies that overlook the city. In the 52 Ritz-Carlton Club rooms that fill the eighth and ninth floors, guests are provided with a dedicated concierge and special amenities like complimentary continental breakfast, midmorning snacks, afternoon tea, cocktails and hors d'oeuvres, and late-evening cordials and chocolates.

If you overindulge (or plan to), visit the workout facility, complete with a fully equipped training room, heated indoor pool, whirlpool, and spa. Massage therapy is also offered in case you climb one too many of San Francisco's infamous hills. Basically, everything you need is at your fingertips when you stay at the Ritz.

Single long-stemmed roses grace each table in the Ritz's French-inspired **DINING ROOM**, (415) 296-7465 (Very Expensive). Fabric-covered chairs are clustered around linen-bedecked tables, and the tall windows are adorned with thick drapes. We recommend the duck breast with potato croutons, lavender, rhubarb, and cracked almonds, or the Moroccan-style lamb served with a spicy coriander and parsley sauce. On warm days, **THE TERRACE** (Expensive) offers courtyard seating at white wrought-iron chairs and tables with peach-colored umbrellas. Enjoy contemporary Mediterranean cuisine accompanied by a jazz vocalist and pianist Friday and Saturday evenings. Both dining options are too large and formal to be considered romantic, but the food is wonderful and they couldn't be more conveniently located, unless, of course, you opt for room service.

SHERMAN HOUSE, San Francisco
2160 Green Street, at Webster
(415) 563-3600, (800) 424-5777
Very Expensive to Unbelievably Expensive
Minimum stay requirement on weekends and holidays
Recommended Wedding Site

Kissing here may turn your heart inside out, but so will the bill unless you have an unlimited expense account. An Absurdly Expensive category is more appropriate for many of the rooms in this exquisitely restored 1876 French-Italianate mansion. Still, this is San Francisco's most aristocratically intimate hotel and restaurant. Renovations inspired by the French Second Empire radiate royal ambience, from the grand music room with cathedral ceilings and hardwood floors to the sweeping wood staircase that winds through the center of the home.

Room 301 in the main house is like a king's chamber, with a full canopy bed draped with heavy velvet-lined tapestry draperies; a plush window seat with abundant pillows and billows of drapes above; and an immense bath with a deep, black soaking tub. Other rooms are equally stately, with canopied queen-size beds, wood-burning fireplaces, and luscious fabrics. Stone walking paths lead from the main house, past manicured courtyards with splashing fountains and a gazebo, to the quiet confines of the Carriage House. We fell instantly in love with the Thomas Church Garden Suite on the lower level, which is enveloped by multilevel gardens. Two walls of windows allow lots of daylight into this striking suite, appointed with latticed walls, wicker furnishings, slate floors, teak-trimmed jetted tub, and a free-standing fireplace.

If you're hesitating because of the steep price tag, keep in mind that the sumptuous surroundings are unparalleled anywhere else in San Francisco. You might want to save up for a special celebration you'll never forget.

SPENCER HOUSE, San Francisco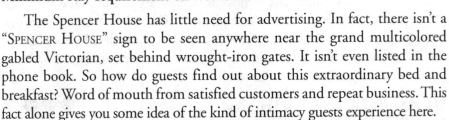
1080 Haight Street, at Baker
(415) 626-9205
http://www.sirius.com/~bjc
Moderate to Expensive
Minimum stay requirement on weekends

The Spencer House has little need for advertising. In fact, there isn't a "SPENCER HOUSE" sign to be seen anywhere near the grand multicolored gabled Victorian, set behind wrought-iron gates. It isn't even listed in the phone book. So how do guests find out about this extraordinary bed and breakfast? Word of mouth from satisfied customers and repeat business. This fact alone gives you some idea of the kind of intimacy guests experience here.

Although the Spencer House has all the trappings of a noble Victorian— spacious firelit parlors, wood floors, Oriental carpets, and period antiques— its real focus is on comfort. All six guest rooms have feather beds, rich fabrics, and private baths; some have large bay windows that offer glimpses of the Golden Gate Bridge peeking over the city rooftops. Bradbury silk-screened wall and ceiling coverings, crisp linens trimmed with antique lace, gas and electric chandeliers, and a collection of gorgeous antiques contribute to the authentic but fantastically comfortable Victorian climate. And the hospitality doesn't stop there. A delicious breakfast of eggs ranchero with salsa or Belgian waffles topped with warm strawberries is served at one long table in the wood-paneled dining room. It's no wonder they don't need to advertise!

THE WARWICK REGIS HOTEL, San Francisco
490 Geary Street, at Taylor

(415) 928-7900, (800) 827-3447
Moderate to Very Expensive

Set in the heart of San Francisco's theater district, the Warwick Regis Hotel couldn't be more conveniently located. Its reputation for romance, however, has more to do with its enticing, luxurious atmosphere. The Warwick combines old-world charm with modern amenities to create an exceedingly comfortable yet elegant climate. All 80 regal guest rooms are decorated with comfortable antiques, lace curtains, textured wallpaper, and black marble bathrooms. Some of the exceptionally romantic suites have balconies, canopied beds, and fireplaces. Complimentary continental breakfast is served downstairs at the chic **LA SCENE CAFE** (see Restaurant Kissing). Once you've satiated your romantic inclinations, you'll appreciate that the Warwick is just a short walk from much of what San Francisco is famous for: Union Square, the cable cars, art galleries, exclusive shops, fabulous restaurants, and, of course, the theaters.

Romantic Note: When making your reservations at the Warwick, ask about the different romantic packages (including theater packages). These include such extras as valet parking, dinner at La Scene Cafe, red roses on your pillows with turndown service, and charming mementos.

WHITE SWAN INN, San Francisco
845 Bush Street, between Mason and Taylor
(415) 775-1755, (800) 999-9570
Expensive to Very Expensive

Magically, the White Swan Inn brings the English countryside to life in the heart of downtown San Francisco. The 26 guest rooms are masterfully decorated with stately antiques, floral and striped wallpapers, dried flower wreaths, and lace curtains. Personal touches like turndown service (complete with chocolates left on your pillow), homemade cookies available day and night, and soothing bath salts in every bathroom make this one of the most endearing bed and breakfasts in the city. Every room has a gas log fireplace as well. The two spacious Romance Suites, each with a separate dressing area, canopied queen-size bed with a down comforter, and even more flowers and lace, are particularly inviting. A bottle of champagne is part of the Romance Suite package, although every room comes with complimentary drinks in a small refrigerator.

As wonderful as the guest rooms are, you should venture downstairs to the handsome fireside library in the afternoon. High tea and an abundance of appetizers are served daily. A full breakfast buffet is also presented downstairs in the cozy dining room, where individual tables provide ample privacy. Overall, the White Swan Inn effectively sustains the illusion of being a small European boutique hotel. Unless you look out a window (or open one for that matter—Bush Street is an extremely busy thoroughfare), you may forget you're within walking distance of Union Square. Such convenience, comfort, and charm can't be found everywhere.

Restaurant Kissing

ACQUERELLO, San Francisco
1722 Sacramento Street, between Van Ness and Polk
(415) 567-5432
Expensive
Dinner Tuesday-Saturday

Appropriately named *Acquerello,* the Italian word for "watercolor," this cozy Italian restaurant is as pretty as a painting. A small handful of tables topped with candles, white linens, and pale pink china are surrounded by cream-colored walls softly illuminated by wall sconces and graced with simple artwork. An exquisite pastel floral arrangement at the front entrance adds a dash of color to the otherwise unassuming surroundings.

While the setting alone may whet your romantic appetite, Acquerello offers an innovative selection of Italian dishes flavored with the freshest ingredients of each season. If it's available on the night you dine, don't miss the pumpkin gnochetti with black truffles and sage, or the homemade green onion fettuccine with salmon in a spumante sauce. The wine list is extensive, and the courteous staff is always willing to help you select the perfect wine to accompany your meal.

ACT IV LOUNGE, San Francisco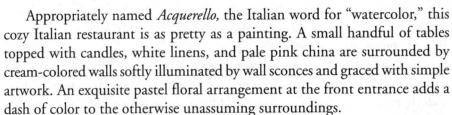
333 Fulton Street, between Gough and Franklin, at the Inn at the Opera
(415) 553-8100
Expensive to Very Expensive
Breakfast, Lunch, and Dinner Daily; Cocktails Daily; Sunday Brunch

After an exhilarating night at the opera, pamper yourselves a bit more at this bastion of refinement and gourmet cuisine. The handsome interior is accented by a marble fireplace, mahogany pillars, and muted lighting that gently illuminates the room. Belgian wall tapestries, low ceilings, and live piano accompaniment add to its old-world charm.

Comfortable chairs and leather sofas are positioned around a handful of tables. Wherever you end up sitting, you and your companion will enjoy the delights of the ensuing meal—from appetizers to after-dinner drinks. The menu changes frequently, but we were thrilled with the duck and pheasant in caramelized onions served in a puff pastry shell, and the angel-hair pasta with prawns, scallops, and caviar. Delicious encores include the tarte tatin covered with spun sugar and the warm chocolate truffle torte. You'll be kissing before you know it.

Romantic Suggestion: For equally sumptuous and romantic accommodations, we suggest the guest rooms upstairs at the **INN AT THE OPERA** (see Hotel/Bed and Breakfast Kissing).

ALAIN RONDELLI, San Francisco
126 Clement Street, between Second and Third Avenues
(415) 387-0408
Expensive
Dinner Tuesday-Sunday

This chic, upscale restaurant serves excellent French cuisine in a fast-paced atmosphere typical of San Francisco. On any given evening, you're sure to find noisy crowds packed into the tiny dining room or couples conversing at the bar. Green shutters, tables covered with white linens, and cream booths decorate the softly lit restaurant. Chef Alain Rondelli's masterpieces are pleasing to both eye and palate. Each meal is personally introduced to you by the chef, and served on mirrored plates. Service can be intrusive, offering more attention than a couple looking for privacy really needs.

BACCO, San Francisco
737 Diamond Street, between 24th and Elizabeth
(415) 282-4969
Moderate to Expensive
Dinner Daily

View the sunset from San Francisco's breathtaking **TWIN PEAKS** (see Outdoor Kissing), then dine at nearby Bacco's, one of the few romantic restaurants in this part of town, to top off the evening. The cozy storefront dining room exudes archetypal Italian charm. Eclectic Italian art, masks, and triangular wall sconces embellish terra-cotta walls, and single flowers brighten simply dressed tables covered with white linens. Picture windows lined with flowerboxes look out to the residential street beyond. Like the ambience, the kitchen's menu is simple but appealing, featuring delicious antipasti and pasta specialties.

BIX, San Francisco
56 Gold Street, an alley between Pacific and Jackson, off Montgomery
(415) 433-6300

Moderate
Lunch Monday-Friday; Dinner Daily

You will feel as though you've been transported back to the '40s once you step over the threshold of Bix's back alley entrance, and that's the point. This two-story restaurant and jazz club is highlighted by Corinthian columns, cathedral ceilings, and an expansive mural of a '40s dance floor. Jazz is the theme here, and if you're looking for great entertainment to accompany an excellent meal, you've come to the right place. While you're partaking of well-prepared dishes accented with a few unusual ingredients (the bananas Foster with vanilla ice cream and rum is heavenly), you can also listen to a torch singer, saxophone player, or jazz pianist. Sometimes the volume makes soft, romantic conversation impossible, but it won't prevent you from snuggling up close in the cozy, cushioned booths set along the upstairs wall.

BONTA, San Francisco
2223 Union Street, between Fillmore and Steiner
(415) 929-0407
Moderate to Expensive
Dinner Tuesday-Sunday

Cozy is the operative word at this exceedingly tiny storefront trattoria with ten tables. Bonta's small size, however, is no indication of its big reputation. Tiled floors and marble-topped tables create a casual yet polished climate, accented with striking contemporary artwork, candles, and angel figurines. Unfortunately, when the restaurant is operating at full capacity (which is most of the time), the din of other diners can be distracting. So where's the romance? If the way to your heart is through your palate, you'll fall in love with Bonta at first sight (or should we say taste?). All of Bonta's menu items are handmade on the premises, including the fresh pastas and enticing desserts. We recommend the homemade tortellini or ravioli. For dessert, the fresh pear crisp warmed in the oven and served with a scoop of hazelnut gelato literally melts in your mouth.

CAFE MAJESTIC, San Francisco
1500 Sutter Street, at Gough
(415) 776-6400
Moderate to Expensive
Breakfast and Dinner Daily

Local polls have named Cafe Majestic one of San Francisco's "most romantic" cafes more than once, and we're not surprised. More a restaurant than a cafe, the Majestic's tasteful interior is characterized by a lofty orna-mented ceiling, Corinthian columns that separate its three dining rooms, and muted pink and green tones. Long-stemmed red roses at every table add to the romantic spirit. In the evenings, a talented pianist makes music on the baby grand in the corner and encourages special requests. Don't be shy—he's willing (and able) to play just about anything!

Although the kitchen strives hard to please, we recommend steering clear of breakfast. (We were disappointed when we were served stale, day-old pastries the mornings we dined here.) Fortunately, dinner is a completely different story. Sautéed crab cakes with roasted bell pepper aioli, and the salmon fillet stuffed with prawn mousse and baked in puff pastry are two of the tempting items you can choose from. Service is excellent, and desserts are divine.

CAFE MOZART, San Francisco
708 Bush Street, between Powell and Mason
(415) 391-8480
Moderate to Expensive
Dinner Tuesday-Sunday

Thick red velvet and timeworn embroidered white curtains hang in the windows, secluding diners from the busy street. One of San Francisco's more intimate restaurants, Cafe Mozart has a mere ten tables, each draped with white linens and set with fine china, silver, crystal, and a single red rose. Antiques, paintings, and delicate chandeliers enrich the interior, and music by the restaurant's namesake is a delightful accompaniment to every meal.

The French cuisine is flavorful and beautifully presented. Try the wonderful chicken mushroom marsala, or the duck de Provence with its sweet orange sauce. Another scrumptious dish offers tender morsels of lamb on a bed of hot linguine, garnished with carrots, pineapple, and basil leaves. The dessert tray is a masterpiece in itself; select from among chocolate-hazelnut torte, berries topped with amoretto-flavored whipped cream, and other sweets presented on a silver platter. (Hint: The warm chocolate cake with roasted banana sauce is a lip-warming production.) This is a remarkably romantic place for a special occasion, even if the occasion is simply that the two of you are together.

CAMPTON PLACE RESTAURANT, San Francisco
340 Stockton Street, between Sutter and Post
(415) 955-5555
Expensive to Very Expensive
Breakfast, Lunch, and Dinner Daily

Campton Place Restaurant is an exceptional culinary landmark where the elite come for very serious dining and very intense romancing. Its elegance and refinement are dazzling. Extravagant floral arrangements and gilded mirrors surround tables set with crystal and freshly cut roses. Large potted plants, exquisite vases, and etched glass partitions are precisely positioned around the room. The extremely formal service and regal setting call for Miss Manners–approved etiquette—don't even *think* about committing a faux pas at this place!

The American cuisine is sublime. Crab cakes, caviar, and venison are merely preludes to the entrées. Tempting dishes include the grilled veal and the diver scallops with roasted eggplant and East Indian spices. If you'd like, you can also visit Campton Place Restaurant for breakfast. Its atmosphere is less stuffy in the morning: you could drop your napkin twice and no one would blink an eye.

Romantic Note: For the same formal style in accommodations, consider splurging on overnight reservations at the deluxe **CAMPTON PLACE HOTEL** (see Hotel/Bed and Breakfast Kissing).

THE CARNELIAN ROOM, San Francisco
555 California Street, at Montgomery, at the Bank of America Building
(415) 433-7500
Very Expensive
Dinner and Cocktails Daily; Sunday Brunch

Fifty-two floors above it all, the Carnelian Room's distinctive glass-enclosed lounge offers mesmerizing views of San Francisco. For a stellar experience, arrive just before sunset as the last light of day casts striking shadows across the city. The dramatic vista provides a heartfelt backdrop to the lounge's opulent interior, resplendent with rich walnut paneling and 18th- and 19th-century artwork. Views are accessible from both the restaurant and bar, the latter being a more economical kissing windfall. You can count on the Carnelian Room's gilt-edged service to be gracious and accommodating, no matter what you decide. The kitchen strives to please with a small, eclectic menu that includes items like butternut squash ravioli, pan-roasted Chilean sea bass, and decadent desserts (the chocolate and banana flying saucer is as delicious and unusual as it sounds).

If you've got a special proposal in mind, consider renting the private Tamalpais Room for $50. Here you'll find a cozy table set for two, a cushy love seat, and a green-and-red light outside the room that you control, summoning your own personal waiter only when you require service.

CHEZ MICHEL, San Francisco
804 North Point, at Hyde
(415) 775-7036
Moderate to Expensive
Dinner Tuesday-Sunday

With its striking color scheme, artsy flair, and delectable French cuisine, Chez Michel is an attractive place to wine and dine the night away. Come prepared to snuggle, for the cramped seating may not allow otherwise. Several black-and-white-checked booths fill the tiny dining area; however, a single U-shaped booth at the central rear of the restaurant may be your best bet for finding some semblance of privacy. Contemporary black-and-white drawings hang in stark contrast against the dark walls, which have been painted deep blue and black. The blond wood accents serve to lighten up the room and enhance the restaurant's chic simplicity.

Appetizers range from duck leg confit to poached pearl oysters to crab flan. Entrées include pheasant breast stuffed with duck mousse, and you should not pass up the warm decadent chocolate cake for dessert.

THE CLIFF HOUSE, San Francisco
1090 Point Lobos Avenue
(415) 386-3330
Moderate
Breakfast, Lunch, and Dinner Daily
Recommended Wedding Site

Busloads of camera-laden tourists flock to the Cliff House to witness stunning ocean views at the height of the afternoon. To avoid being overrun (or run over) by crowds, we recommend visiting in the early evening, when there isn't a wait for a table with a view. Floor-to-ceiling windows in the Cliff House's several dining rooms showcase incomparable panoramas of the forceful, roaring ocean colliding against the jagged black rocks below. You'll be tempted to linger as you watch seals and other aquatic life frolicking happily in the waves or basking in the sun on Seal Rock (a spectacle that is vastly superior to any aquarium).

Rich red draperies and glowing candlelight create a romantic setting in the main dining room, which is appointed with dark wood detailing and tall, leafy plants. Slightly more casual and crowded, a second upstairs dining room shares the same magnificent views. Ocean vistas are the Cliff House's main specialty, but the standard seafood fare should improve after a recent overhaul designed to upgrade the kitchen's quality and menu presentation.

CLUB 36, San Francisco
345 Stockton Street, between Post and Sutter, at the Grand Hyatt
(415) 398-1234
Inexpensive to Moderate
Cocktails and Appetizers Daily

Hovering 36 airy floors above the city, this cocktail lounge overlooks the bay facing Fisherman's Wharf and Coit Tower. Club 36 doesn't open until 4 P.M., but after a day of working, shopping, or sightseeing, it is a good place to sit back and gaze at the city from afar. Sink into one of the burgundy leather chairs to soak up the casual atmosphere, stunning view, and soothing piano music played nightly from 9 P.M. to 1 A.M. This is a wonderful place to begin or end your evening out together in San Francisco.

THE COMPASS ROSE, San Francisco
335 Powell Street, between Geary and Post,
at the Westin St. Francis Hotel
(415) 774-0167
Inexpensive to Moderate
Lunch, Afternoon Tea, and Evening Appetizers Daily

Act out your favorite scenes from *The Phantom of the Opera* in a deep-cushioned settee with just enough room for both of you. This lavishly decorated lounge turned restaurant is located in the heart of San Francisco's theater district, set just off the lobby of the regal St. Francis Hotel. Dark wood and black marble pillars enhance the effect of the Compass Rose's ornate cathedral ceiling. Hand-painted decorative shoji screens, oversized vases, and other exquisitely restored Eastern artifacts lend privacy to handfuls of plush wingback chairs, love seats, and settees grouped around antique tables. The dimly lit atmosphere is warm and sensuous any time of day, especially when a string trio mesmerizes listeners with soothing melodies. High tea, an impressive affair served from 3 P.M. to 5 P.M. daily, includes finger sandwiches, scones, berries with Grand Marnier cream, and petit fours. Dinner features a small variety of gourmet appetizers and entrées such as ginger-roasted prawns served with pineapple salsa or baked monkfish flavored with mussels and clam sauce.

CYPRESS CLUB, San Francisco
500 Jackson Street, between Columbus and Montgomery
(415) 296-8555
Expensive to Very Expensive
Dinner Daily

As our waitress so aptly put it, the Cypress is a "1940s supper club gone wild." Wild is actually an understatement. As you reach for the contorted handle on the bronze door and peel back the black velvet curtains shielding the entrance, prepare your senses for overload. Colorful stained glass windows and busy contemporary murals contrast with dark wood paneling and wide columns. Cloud-shaped pillows and brightly colored upside-down ice cream cones hang from the ceiling. Masked copper wall sconces shed light on copper-accented cushioned booths that surround the sunken interior and provide the most privacy in the tightly packed dining room. A talented jazz trio performs nightly, and their swinging rhythms blend with the buzz of conversations around you. Due to the unbelievable crowds, kissing isn't exactly a comfortable option here, but the engaging surroundings and astounding cuisine are well worth the trip. Start with the Yukon gold potato soup served with truffles and truffle oil and proceed to a heavenly cornucopia of vegetables served with butternut squash risotto, lentils, and potato pancakes. Asian vegetables, lyonnaise potatoes, apricot naan, and huckleberries add unique flavors and accents to every dish. Don't forget to save some room: desserts here are sweetly satisfying.

EMPRESS OF CHINA, San Francisco
838 Grant Avenue, between Clay and Washington
(415) 434-1345
Moderate
Lunch and Dinner Daily

Bustling fruit stands and gift shops brimming with international knick-knacks line the narrow streets of San Francisco's Chinatown. The area is well worth a visit for the interesting sights and sounds alone, although noise and crowds (not to mention parking challenges) pose too much of a distraction for a romantic rendezvous. But don't completely overlook the possibilities of an amorous evening in Chinatown—there is romance to be found here, after all.

An elevator at the Empress of China takes you six stories above the hustle and bustle, delivering you into a distinctly mysterious setting. You'll pass through a pagoda in the upstairs entrance, where a small pine tree reaches toward the light filtering through a glass dome overhead. Soothing Oriental music wafts through the ornately decorated interior, fashioned after ancient Oriental architecture. A priceless assortment of antiques and temple artifacts fills the spacious dining rooms, Chinese lanterns illuminate the hallways, and peacock feathers brighten gold-accented walls. Floor-to-ceiling windows line the exterior wall, showcasing views of the bay and of homes climbing the hillside beneath Coit Tower—an especially beautiful sight when the sun has set and the twinkling lights emerge in the dark.

In spite of the intriguing ambience, it is apparent that years of serving hundreds of loyal patrons have taken their toll, from the worn linens to the weary and sometimes impatient wait staff. Even so, the Empress of China is a frequent award-winner for its cuisine. The chefs highlight fragrance, color, and flavor in their preparation of such Chinese favorites as almond chicken and lobster in garlic sauce.

FLEUR DE LYS, San Francisco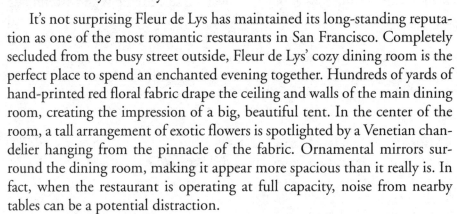
777 Sutter Street, between Jones and Taylor
(415) 673-7779
Expensive to Very Expensive
Dinner Monday-Saturday

It's not surprising Fleur de Lys has maintained its long-standing reputation as one of the most romantic restaurants in San Francisco. Completely secluded from the busy street outside, Fleur de Lys' cozy dining room is the perfect place to spend an enchanted evening together. Hundreds of yards of hand-printed red floral fabric drape the ceiling and walls of the main dining room, creating the impression of a big, beautiful tent. In the center of the room, a tall arrangement of exotic flowers is spotlighted by a Venetian chandelier hanging from the pinnacle of the fabric. Ornamental mirrors surround the dining room, making it appear more spacious than it really is. In fact, when the restaurant is operating at full capacity, noise from nearby tables can be a potential distraction.

In spite of its decidedly French disposition, the kitchen also flirts with Mediterranean accents. From truffled vichyssoise to sea bass with a ratatouille crust, every dish is cooked to perfection, artistically presented, and served by a gracious staff that truly wants you to delight in your dining experience.

FOURNOU'S OVENS, San Francisco
905 California Street, at Powell, at the Stanford Court Hotel
(415) 989-1910
Expensive to Very Expensive
Breakfast, Lunch, and Dinner Daily; Saturday and Sunday Brunch

Breakfast, brunch, lunch, or dinner, you can always expect a gourmet repast at Fournou's Ovens. The Mediterranean-style restaurant is handsomely decorated with tiled floors, tapestries, paintings, colored dishes, and 18th-century French Provençalantiques. High-backed chairs, candle lanterns, and fresh flowers complement each table. Set within a small alcove in the main dining room, accented by garlic braids and hanging copper skillets, are several European-style roasting ovens decorated with blue-and-white Portuguese tiles. As you dine, you can watch as the chef bakes bread for each evening's meal.

Fournou's Ovens is really a series of small dining rooms, and depending on your mood, you can select a setting that matches the experience you have in mind. Sit in one of the formal dining rooms for a quiet candlelight tête-à-tête. For a casual breakfast or lunch, sit in the airy solarium; through its conservatory-style windows you can watch the cable cars ascending and descending Nob Hill.

The chefs here prepare contemporary American cuisine that is best described as hearty and flavorful. Rack of lamb is a house specialty, along with poultry and seafood dishes. For a meal on the lighter side, we recommend the ricotta gnocchi with organic vegetables in olive juice, or the clams with linguine, tomatoes, and basil. One of the city's best maple creme brûlées is here as well, so save room for dessert.

Romantic Note: Fournou's Ovens has one of the most extensive wine lists in the world, with over 20,000 bottles housed in its wine cellar.

THE FRENCH ROOM, San Francisco
495 Geary Street, at Taylor, at The Clift Hotel
(415) 775-4700, extension 256
Expensive to Very Expensive
Breakfast Daily; Dinner Tuesday-Sunday

This majestic dining room, once the epitome of grandeur and elegance, has obviously fallen from grace since it came under new ownership. In regard to tug-at-your-heartstrings ambience, the French Room remains one of the loveliest dining rooms in San Francisco, and if we were judging on this basis alone it would merit at least four lips. The room is accentuated with rich wood paneling, beautiful fabrics, elegant table settings, and classical pillars rising to lofty ceilings set off by stunning crystal chandeliers. Elegant folds of drapery adorn the windows, and potted plants abound. Soft lighting and classical music conspire to create a heartwarming backdrop for any amorous occasion.

But despite its gorgeous setting, the service and food simply leave too much to be desired. First of all, the service is painfully slow; plan on a good two hours for a full-course meal, whether you want a leisurely pace or not. (This place definitely is not an option for those rushing off to the theater.) Second, the bumbling wait staff is not up to the standards of such an elegantly formal restaurant. Our tuxedo-clad waiter couldn't seem to remember the daily specials, and his inappropriate comments throughout the evening were bothersome. Third, the food, although artistically presented, borders on mediocre to inferior. And for these prices (or any price), you deserve better. Every entrée we attempted to order came with a warning as to why we might not enjoy it. Once we did decide on a meal, we were disappointed anyway. Even dessert was unappetizing.

Hopefully, in time, the French Room will manage to regain its previous reputation for excellent service and consistently wonderful food. In the meantime, consider yourselves warned.

Romantic Alternative: Adjacent to the dining room is the dimly lit **REDWOOD ROOM** (Inexpensive to Moderate). This art deco cocktail lounge is similarly handsome, with high ceilings, plush lounge chairs, and carved redwood paneling adorned with immense reproductions of Gustav Klimt paintings. In the evenings, the lounge features live piano music.

GARDEN COURT, San Francisco
2 New Montgomery Street, between Second and Third,
at the Sheraton Palace Hotel
(415) 546-5010
Expensive to Unbelievably Expensive
Breakfast and Lunch Daily; Afternoon Tea Wednesday-Saturday;
Dinner Tuesday-Saturday
Recommended Wedding Site

Crystal chandeliers hang from a leaded glass dome ceiling, illuminating the mirrored doors, gold leaf sconces, marvelous flower arrangements, and marble columns that enhance the Garden Court. Overstuffed sofas and chairs provide relaxed, intimate seating in the back of the room. Tables in the front appear more proper, draped elegantly in white and graced with fine china and fresh flowers. Though the ornate splendor of this palatial room might well surpass that of any other dining room in San Francisco, unfortunately so do the prices. To best appreciate the gorgeous surroundings without spending a fortune, you might consider opting for high tea instead of dinner. Astonishingly, the white glove service here is among the slowest we've encountered in all of San Francisco. (For the prices you pay, this feels almost intolerable.)

GAYLORD INDIA RESTAURANT, San Francisco
900 North Point Street, at Ghirardelli Square
(415) 771-8822
Expensive
Lunch and Dinner Daily

Serene Indian music and authentic Eastern ambience make you feel that you've been transported across the globe to India, when in fact you've just walked up to the second floor of the Chocolate Building in San Francisco's Ghirardelli Square. One of the few lip-worthy spots in this tourist mecca, Gaylord's offers all the right ingredients for an intimate dining experience. Hand-carved figurines, antiques, and artifacts from India fill the poshly decorated dining room, which overlooks San Francisco's harbor and Fisherman's Wharf below. Candle lanterns glow atop cozy tables draped with pink linens, many placed next to bay windows that showcase engaging water views. Although we found the service to be more aloof than friendly, we weren't dissuaded from enjoying the kitchen's traditional East Indian menu, from aromatic curries and freshly baked breads to dal and vegetable samosas.

JULIUS' CASTLE, San Francisco
1541 Montgomery Street, north of Union Street
(415) 392-2222
Moderate to Expensive
Dinner Daily

Yes, we know this is a tourist trap (and we all know tourist traps are antithetical to kissing), but the spectacular views from this castle nestled on Telegraph Hill below the famous Coit Tower are worth mentioning. Bay windows in the series of upstairs dining rooms survey unobstructed views of San Francisco Bay and the Golden Gate Bridge. Crystal chandeliers shed soft light above linen-cloaked tables in the somewhat timeworn Victorian-style dining room, distinguished by mauve walls and dark wood paneling. Although nearly every table has a view, most of them are crowded much too close together for romantic preferences. If you're having trouble overlooking the crowds, turn your attention to the delectable French menu. You're sure to appreciate the delicately sautéed abalone with a lime infusion and chives or the broiled swordfish with garlic, tomatoes, herbs, and peppers.

KISS, San Francisco
674 Eighth Street, between Brannan and Townsend
(415) 552-8757
Moderate
Lunch Monday-Saturday; Dinner Monday-Friday

How could we pass up a restaurant with a name like this? The theme is displayed in a sensuous, citified version of Gustav Klimt's famous painting called *The Kiss*. Beneath a white canopied ceiling, an expansive mural depicts a man and woman embracing atop a skyscraper. Dried flowers, greenery, and

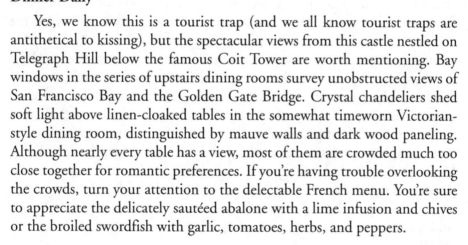

angel ornaments also warm up the simple dining room of this otherwise stark, cafe-like restaurant, appointed with modern track lighting and white linens. Unfortunately, the tables are arranged a little too close together for comfortable displays of affection (you'd think they'd know better with a name like Kiss).

The menu changes weekly, but is typically quite good. We didn't find fault with the breast of pheasant with black currant sauce; the tomato-herb pasta with crabmeat in a puff pastry shell covered with spinach purée, sun-dried tomatoes, and melted Swiss cheese; or, last but not least, the sweetly delicious Grand Marnier soufflé.

LA FOLIE, San Francisco
2316 Polk Street, between Green and Union
(415) 776-5577
Very Expensive
Dinner Monday-Saturday

You can't help but like this enticing French restaurant from the moment you see it. A soft glow illuminates the mullioned windows, and boxes of flowering plants hang from the second story. Inside, puffy clouds adorn the sky blue ceiling, and coral-colored faux marble walls provide a backdrop for beautiful contemporary artwork. Lots of snug tables for two are packed a little too close for comfort in vintage California fashion; half-curtained windows help conceal the bustling sidewalk and crowds outside. This eclectic yet charming mix truly exhibits the "folly" expressed in the restaurant's name. The food is fabulously French with striking flavors. If you're in the mood to splurge and sample a little of everything, consider the "Discovery Menu," which includes five courses, or the "Chef Menu," which can be prepared especially for you upon request. Even if you dine à la carte, you won't be disappointed with items like roasted sea scallops served with Yukon gold potatoes, or a crab, avocado, mango, and tomato "gâteau."

LA NOUVELLE PATISSERIE, San Francisco
2184 Union Street, at Fillmore Street
(415) 931-7655
Inexpensive; No Credit Cards
Breakfast and Lunch Daily; Dinner Friday-Saturday

Now and then, rather than having a romantic destination, it is better to have a starting point and an open mind. If you find yourselves feeling adventurous one morning and decide to venture out in search of new places to kiss, we suggest you begin at La Nouvelle Patisserie. You can't miss this charming French bakery, mostly because so many other people are headed there too. Inside, plenty of small marble tables fill the room. Breathe in the robust aroma of freshly brewed coffee and choose from the dozens of pastries, breads, fresh fruit tarts, truffles, cakes, and chocolates waiting for you.

Later in the day, lunch specials, salads, sandwiches, pâtés, and crêpes are also offered. This place is usually packed, but you can take your treats along on the next leg of your journey.

LA SCENE CAFE, San Francisco
490 Geary Street, at Taylor, at the Warwick Regis Hotel
(415) 928-7900
Expensive
Breakfast and Dinner Daily

This chic cafe, located on the main floor of the **WARWICK REGIS HOTEL** (see Hotel/Bed and Breakfast Kissing), is a lively spot for an après-theater cocktail or dessert. Dark wood accents, white linens, and soft lighting surround you, as you gaze at (and try to identify) drawings of cinema and theater stars of yesteryear. La Scene offers an enjoyable menu, with a prix fixe theater dinner for those in a rush to arrive before the curtain rises. Unfortunately, the tables are too close together and the atmosphere is too noisy to encourage much intimacy. La Scene is best visited after dinner, especially Wednesday through Saturday evenings, when live piano music fills the bar area.

THE MAGIC FLUTE, San Francisco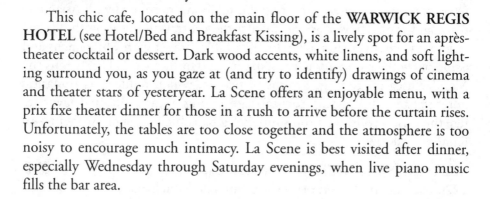
3673 Sacramento Street, between Spruce and Locust
(415) 922-1225
Inexpensive to Moderate
Lunch Monday-Friday; Dinner Monday-Saturday

Angelic and charming, this restaurant offers a refreshing contrast to the numerous formidable, highbrow dining establishments in San Francisco. Daylight streams into the front dining room, where cozy two-person tables are tucked into alcoves and arranged with privacy in mind. Windows in the back dining room look out to a garden courtyard hemmed with shrubs and greenery, accented by the sound of water trickling from a stone fountain. Dried vines and large watercolors depicting San Francisco scenes ornament the warm peach-colored walls, and filigree chandeliers softly illuminate both of the airy, countrified dining rooms. Your sentiments will easily expand to blend with this engaging atmosphere as the evening slowly unfolds. Pasta and risotto are the kitchen's specialties, but we would be remiss if we failed to mention the chef's dedication to serving extraordinarily delicious desserts.

THE MANDARIN, San Francisco
900 North Point, at Ghirardelli Square
(415) 673-8812
Moderate to Expensive
Lunch and Dinner Daily

Unknown treasures await behind the brick exterior of the Mandarin. Enter through the main courtyard of Ghirardelli Square and ascend to the second floor past displays of Chinese artifacts. The mostly brick interior is accented by several monochromatic walls of white, purple, red, and yellow that provide welcome splashes of color. Loosely thatched bamboo partitions separate a series of interconnecting dining rooms decorated with Asian art-work and exotic flower arrangements; the central dining room holds the restaurant's circular Mongolian fire pit. Tables are set with white linens and equipped with lazy Susans to assist in dining "family style." (This means the Mandarin caters to large groups of people, which reduces its romantic potential by a lip or so.) You can't go wrong with traditional favorites like the spring rolls, won ton soup, kung pao chicken, or chow mein—to name only a few.

MANSIONS RESTAURANT, San Francisco
2220 Sacramento Street, between Laguna and Buchanan,
at the Mansions Hotel
(415) 929-9444
Breakfast and Dinner Daily
Inexpensive to Unbelievably Expensive

If you're looking for a little magic, you've come to the right place. Your dining experience at the Mansions Restaurant begins with a bona fide magic show, featuring a professional magician who entertains dinner guests with disappearing acts, ghosts, and snow blizzards (even in July) in the parlor of a playful, museum-like mansion. After the show, guests are ushered to an adjacent dining room where a handful of tables are arranged in a stained glass alcove overlooking a flower garden dotted with mosaic-tiled sculptures.

The menu, or "Main Act," might include a fresh fillet of salmon roasted and wrapped in parchment paper, or fresh jumbo prawns served in an ocean of garlic salsa. In accordance with the restaurant's unique surroundings, the "gold rush" desserts are equally unusual, and actually topped with 24-karat gold!

Romantic Note: Accommodations at **THE MANSIONS HOTEL** (see Hotel/Bed and Breakfast Kissing) are also delightfully different and worth looking into.

MASA'S, San Francisco
648 Bush Street, between Powell and Stockton,
at the Hotel Vintage Court
(415) 989-7154
Unbelievably Expensive
Dinner Tuesday-Saturday

Masa's lip-worthy reputation as one of the best spots in San Francisco to romance the night away is well earned. It doesn't get more formal or more intimate (or more expensive, for that matter) than this dimly lit dining room. Deep red walls and rich red draperies embrace a small handful of tables elegantly appointed with crystal, china, and silver. Because there are so few tables here and such a large wait staff, patrons are indulged and catered to, almost to the point of excess. The fresh, succulent lobster, shrimp, and scallops appetizers will literally melt in your mouth. From the roasted monkfish to the grilled Maine lobster or swordfish, every dish is a masterpiece. Desserts are equally astonishing, especially the decadent dark chocolate cake served with Tahitian vanilla sherbet. If you're willing to pay these kind of prices (the prix fixe dinners start at $70 per person), we can't think of a better place to wine and dine your beloved. For this reason, you'll need to book your reservation several months in advance.

MASON'S, San Francisco
950 Mason Street, at California, at the Fairmont Hotel
(415) 772-5233
Expensive
Dinner Daily

The lobby of the Fairmont Hotel is refined and luxurious, but its signature restaurant is suprisingly subdued. Attractive brass and blond oak furnishings and the allure of low lights and fresh flowers create an appealing but understated ambience. Tables harbored by the windows have quintessential San Francisco views of the cable cars on California Street. Our favorite kissing attractions here are the cozy two-person tables and overstuffed sofas surrounding a grand piano in Mason's lounge, where jazz musicians entertain nightly. A congenial staff serves delicious entrées from a small, select menu that includes elegant, delicious dishes such as champagne-braised salmon or fresh truffle torte filled with black summer truffles.

Romantic Suggestion: If you're not in the mood for jazz, consider dining at the Fairmont Hotel's second restaurant, **BELLA VOCE RISTORANTE AND BAR**, 950 Mason Street, (415) 772-5000 (Expensive to Very Expensive), which serves breakfast and lunch daily. Silk tapestries and candlelight highlight an authentic Tuscan climate in which to enjoy delicious northern Italian cuisine and fresh seafood.

MCCORMICK AND KULETO'S, San Francisco
900 North Point Street, at Ghirardelli Square
(415) 929-1730
Moderate to Expensive
Lunch and Dinner Daily

McCormick and Kuleto's location in touristy Ghirardelli Square has always been a romantic drawback. But the intriguing views of the water and the Bay Bridge, together with the elegant interior, are worth a closer look. The restaurant is large and airy, with dark wood, brass accents, and abundant green plants. Crowded and noisy best describes the atmosphere, but tables are situated far enough apart to allow for some semblance of privacy. Huge floor-to-ceiling picture windows accented with stained glass grant amazing views from the main dining room; on a clear evening you can watch the water sparkle as the sun slips away into the distance. You can easily overlook the tourists with a view like this!

An incredible selection of fresh seafood and an impressive wine list can make it difficult to decide what to order, so here are some helpful hints. For a delectable starter, try the crawfish cakes with Cajun remoulade. Both the ahi tuna with pickled ginger and the sea bass with capers, olives, and tomatoes are delightful entrées, but the seafood stew with crab, mussels, clams, crawfish, and prawns is also a winner.

METROPOLITAN RESTAURANT, San Francisco
248 Sutter Street, between Grant and Kearney
(415) 982-6440
Moderate to Expensive
Lunch and Dinner Monday–Friday

Don't be surprised if the Metropolitan changes its name in the near future—it appears to be having a serious identity crisis. Originally named Lascaux and designed to suggest the famous cave in France that contains some of the world's oldest paintings, the restaurant was subsequently transformed to look like the interior of the Statue of Liberty. Now it exudes an erratic combination of the two designs. A staircase descends from the city street into this cave-like setting, where arched ceilings and soft candlelight create an unusual but surprisingly enticing ambience. Tiled floors run throughout the series of connecting dining rooms filled with nicely spaced tables covered with pink and white linens and flickering candles. Contemporary art and exotic flower arrangements are unexpected highlights. A fire blazing in the huge stone hearth completes this present-day cavern.

The Metropolitan's eclectic nature continues with the menu. You'll find everything from baked Brie to pears poached in port with Gorgonzola cheese. Most entrées prove to be tantalizing, but those in the know always order the homemade gnocchi or the salmon baked in phyllo pastry. The desserts are decadent and certainly delicious enough to justify the temptation. You can share—there's something especially sweet about one plate and two forks.

After dinner, a nightcap at the lively bar is a gratifying way to end the evening. A pianist or jazz ensemble provides the music; the rest of the evening's entertainment is left to your discretion.

NEW ORLEANS ROOM, San Francisco
950 Mason Street, at California, at the Fairmont Hotel
(415) 772-5259
Moderate
Cocktails and Appetizers Daily

For a wonderful, reasonably priced evening of tripping the lights fantastic, follow your ears to the New Orleans Room. This is where you'll hear swing at its best: smooth, intoxicating renditions that will make you sway to the beat like never before. Colorful art surrounds a large stage in this dimly lit cabaret, filled with cozy, cushioned settees made for two. Reservations for this popular nightspot are highly recommended.

NIEMAN MARCUS ROTUNDA
RESTAURANT, San Francisco
150 Stockton Street, at Geary, at Nieman Marcus Department Store
(415) 362-4777
Moderate to Expensive;
American Express or Neiman Marcus Credit Cards Only
Lunch and High Tea Daily

Who would ever guess that you could find a great place to pucker up in a department store? Believe it or not, there is a wonderful kissing place in Nieman Marcus. On the fourth floor, under a spectacular stained glass dome, the Rotunda Restaurant provides a respite from the shopping crowds and offers an invitation to romance. Slip into a cozy booth or select a table draped in white linen and accented with a pale pink rose, near the floor-to-ceiling windows overlooking Union Square. The dining room serves delightful lunches and light meals, but in our opinion, afternoon tea at the Rotunda is the ideal interlude. In a world where late-afternoon romance is too often overlooked because of busy schedules, you'll discover teatime can be a leisurely treat.

Romantic Warning: The Rotunda is mostly frequented by shoppers, which can give the restaurant something of a "women's club" atmosphere.

PANE E VINO TRATTORIA, San Francisco
3011 Steiner Street, at Union
(415) 346-2111
Moderate
Lunch Monday-Saturday; Dinner Daily

There's much more to Pane E Vino than bread and wine. Its quaint, authentically Italian atmosphere invites devoted hearts to partake in the pleasures of an evening together. Two small dining rooms comprise the restaurant, although the one in back is more romantic with its brick fireplace, clay tiled floor, low lighting, and beamed ceiling. A sideboard adorned with fresh flowers and aged cheeses adds rustic charm. Accommodating waiters, most with thick Italian accents, are always happy to make recommendations if you have difficulty deciding. You'll soon discover that the food is delicious (especially the pastas), the wines are wonderful, and the atmosphere is certainly for lovers. The restaurant really should be named Pane E Vino E Amore!

PLUMPJACK CAFE, San Francisco
3127 Fillmore Street, at Greenwich
(415) 563-4755
Expensive
Lunch Monday-Friday; Dinner Monday-Saturday

Despite its name, PlumpJack Cafe is not a cafe and there is no "plump Jack" to be found anywhere. It is more accurately described as an elegantly sophisticated restaurant known for its chic interior. Decorated almost exclusively in taupe and gray, the dining room features cylindrical columns, elegant floral arrangements, and spherical ceiling lamps. A handsome chenille-covered booth hugs the large windows overlooking Fillmore Street, and the closely spaced tables are draped with white linens and accented with fresh roses. A curvy iron window treatment, almost medieval in nature, is connected to a transparent screen and displayed in the front window.

PlumpJack offers French and Italian cuisine, from a mussel-filled risotto to duck confit and roasted duck breast. Other noteworthy dishes include the salad of roasted wild mushrooms and the Yukon Territory arctic char served with savoy cabbage, pancetta, potatoes, and pearl onions. Delicious food and innovative decor make this a popular (and somewhat noisy) place for romance.

THE PLUSH ROOM, San Francisco
940 Sutter Street, between Hyde and Leavenworth, at the York Hotel
(415) 885-2800
Moderate
Cocktails Wednesday-Saturday

Remember those late-night black-and-white movies from the 1940s, where hearts were lost, found, broken, and mended, all at a quiet table in the corner of a jazz club? Dramatic music in the background would reach a crescendo just in time for the lovers to join in a torrid embrace. The Plush Room keeps alive this tradition of steamy jazz and soothing contemporary ballads in an appropriately classy, intimate setting. Tables and booths are set beneath a stained glass ceiling, and the large stage seems to spill out into the audience. Whether or not you are a jazz connoisseur, you'll be tempted to share one of the dark mauve booths with your partner. Just don't be surprised to discover that words will be of no practical use all evening long.

POSTRIO, San Fancisco
545 Post Street, at Mason
(415) 776-7825
Very Expensive to Unbelievably Expensive
Breakfast and Lunch Monday-Friday; Dinner Daily; Saturday and Sunday Brunch

Postrio is an upbeat dinner option for couples who are looking for a good time rather than quiet togetherness. Everything about Postrio resembles a theatrical production. Diners make their entrance down a sculpted iron staircase to the main dining room. The "set" is an artistic array of colors, textures, and lighting designed to stimulate the senses. Plush, fabric-finished booths alternate throughout the room with striking tables draped in white linen and accented with black chairs. Modern art decorates the walls, while green plants and exotic flowers add even more color. Wolfgang Puck, world-renowned chef and owner of Postrio, is without doubt the "director" of this production. His "producers" in the large, open kitchen deserve standing ovations for their dramatic, award-winning interpretations of California cuisine. Meals are served by a lively "supporting cast" that wishes to assist your performance. It's up to you to decide how to play out the evening, but don't forget to end with a curtain call for the scrumptious desserts. (We highly recommend the caramelized banana and peanut napoleon.)

Romantic Alternative: The upstairs bar at Postrio serves gourmet pizzas and lighter fare until 1:30 A.M. It's the perfect place for a bite to eat and a quick kiss or two after a genuine night at the theater.

RISTORANTE BUCA GIOVANNI, San Francisco
800 Greenwich Street, at Mason and Columbus
(415) 776-7766
Moderate to Expensive
Dinner Tuesday-Sunday

Simple rustic charm is the romantic allure of this Italian hideaway. A rather nondescript upstairs area features a handful of tables and a bar, but we recommend taking the stairs down to the basement dining room. Here, low curved ceilings, brick-lined walls, and dim lighting create an intimate cave-like setting favorable for romantic interludes. Photographs adorn the brick walls, wine racks line the entryway, and a rich burgundy color scheme prevails throughout. Guitar music adds the final touch. Our only hesitation is that the tables are very close to each other, so plan on sharing your romantic mood with others nearby.

Pasta entrées at Buca Giovanni are authentically delicious, especially the round ravioli stuffed with Gorgonzola and eggplant, served in a light basil sauce. You can also choose from an elaborate selection of seafood and meat dishes, such as the baby lobster tails or the rabbit sautéed with porcini mushrooms.

SILKS, San Francisco   ❤❤❤❤
222 Sansome Street, between Pine and California,
at the Mandarin Oriental Hotel
(415) 986-2020
Moderate to Expensive
Breakfast and Dinner Daily; Lunch Monday-Friday

To reach Silks, pass through the Mandarin Oriental Hotel's lovely lobby and ascend an elegant sweeping staircase. A tuxedo-clad waiter greets you at the top and ushers you to a table for two in this small, exceedingly formal and contemporary dining room. A splendidly ornate wood table crowned with a lavish floral bouquet provides a classic centerpiece, surrounded by clusters of tables set far enough apart to allow for a considerable amount of intimacy. Modern artwork and colorful hand-blown glass candleholders add an unusual effect. We spent a good part of the evening in an animated discussion (in between kisses, of course), attempting to determine the subject matter of an enormous brass sculpture set against one wall of the dining room. You'll find the food here to be almost as imaginative as the artwork. Silks' kitchen combines French techniques with Oriental ingredients and California zest, but presentation is the specialty. Your taste buds will delight in the results, from the poached pear and apricot compote for breakfast to the Thai coconut-lemongrass soup and sweet potato ravioli.

Romantic Option: The **MANDARIN ORIENTAL HOTEL**, (415) 885-0999, (800) 622-0404 (Unbelievably Expensive) is an outstanding, albeit business-oriented, place to stay while you are in San Francisco. Guest rooms are located on the top 11 floors of the 48-floor twin towers of the California Center. Every room has an unbelievable view, and some have marble bathtubs with the same celestial perspective of the city.

TOMMY TOY'S, San Francisco
655 Montgomery Street, between Washington and Clay
(415) 397-4888
Expensive to Very Expensive
Lunch Monday-Friday; Dinner Daily

"Elaborate" is the only word that adequately describes the decor at Tommy Toy's. The restaurant is patterned after the 19th-century Dowager Empress' reading room, and she obviously knew how to live. Each dining room is separated by etched glass partitions and filled with exquisite Asian art pieces, shojis, fabrics, and tapestries. Such ornate surroundings create an almost museum-like atmosphere. Hand-painted candle lamps and fresh flowers accent each pink-linened table.

You'll certainly be treated like royalty at Tommy Toy's. Hostesses dressed in long kimonos greet you at the door, and tuxedo-clad waiters give you their utmost attention throughout the evening. The service is truly amazing. Don't be surprised if a small troupe of waiters wheels a tray alongside your table and dramatically unveils your meal. Just about everything on the menu earns high marks for both taste and artistic presentation. Try the pan-fried foie gras with sliced fresh pear and watercress in a sweet pickled ginger sauce, or sample the breast of duckling smoked with camphorwood and tea leaves and served with a plum wine sauce. Vegetables are consistently prepared to perfection. Tommy Toy's successfully combines Chinese cuisine with French flair. What other Chinese restaurant serves such succulent Peking duck with crêpes for the main course, and then a perfectly fluffy, smooth chocolate mousse for dessert?

YOYO BISTRO, San Francisco
1611 Post Street, at Laguna, at the Radisson Miyako Hotel
(415) 922-7788
Expensive
Breakfast, Lunch, and Dinner Daily

The Japanese word *yoyo* refers to a wide expanse of ocean. From the entrance on the second story, the restaurant opens before you like a vast sea as you descend the staircase into the depths of the main dining room. High ceilings and wood columns rise up around you, and flying fish hang near the windows. The eclectic mix of French bistro, Asian influences, and contemporary fixtures tends to clash rather than enhance the restaurant. European artwork is displayed alongside Japanese murals, while modern lamps hang above chairs of natural wood. Both chopsticks and bread are brought to the table before your meal. White linens and candles adorn each table, and jazz plays in the background.

Sample tantalizing *tsumami*, small dishes of food that are typically eaten with cocktails; a separate menu is devoted solely to *tsumami* at Yoyo Bistro. Try the sesame-spinach salad, ahi tuna tartare, or oysters on the half shell with wasabi-tobiko mignonette, or order from the bistro menu. We recommend the "flower" broth with prawns, spinach, and lemon for starters, followed by the red curry melted duck. Also excellent is the roasted halibut served with green papaya salad, coconut broth, and cilantro pesto.

VIVANDE RISTORANTE, San Francisco
670 Golden Gate Avenue, between Van Ness and Franklin
(415) 673-9245
Moderate
Lunch and Dinner Daily

Located several blocks from San Francisco's opera house, Vivande is often brimful of opera-goers dressed to the hilt. Given the kind of crowds it draws, Vivande is surprisingly jocular. Patrons enter through a wood door carved to look like a yawning mouth. Murals depicting court jesters adorn the soft yellow walls, accented with unusual striped orange and yellow lamps. An open kitchen and bar add to the commotion of the usually packed dining room, but immense red velvet booths in the back of the restaurant ensure enough privacy for at least one passionate kiss. The kitchen strives to please with its typically Italian fare, ranging from penne pasta and fettuccine to risotto served with oven-roasted butternut squash and zucchini.

Outdoor Kissing

ALAMO SQUARE, San Francisco

At the corner of Fulton and Steiner Streets.

San Francisco is famous for its numerous parks scattered throughout the city, in places where you would least expect a group of trees or lush green grass. Take time to enjoy one of these welcome patches of nature in quiet, tree-dotted Alamo Square. This park, perched high above the city, offers a most remarkable view of San Francisco. On a sunny day, it's a lovely spot for a picnic.

ANGEL ISLAND, San Francisco
Ferries from San Francisco, Vallejo, or Tiburon
(415) 546-2810 (San Francisco and Vallejo),
(415) 435-2131 (Tiburon)
$5-$10.50 for the ferry

Become castaways for a day on this angelic island in the middle of San Francisco Bay. The ferry ride alone is worthy of a windswept kiss. Once on the island, you can leave the lively little marina and ascend primitive trails to private panoramas of the San Francisco skyline or Marin's forested hills. Bring along a picnic lunch to enjoy in a sun-soaked meadow. With its six-mile perimeter trail and rugged climb to a 360-degree view of the Bay Area, Angel Island is sure to yield a secluded kissing spot.

GOLDEN GATE BRIDGE, San Francisco

Lincoln Boulevard, Park Presidio Boulevard, and Lombard Street all merge onto the Golden Gate Bridge. There is a parking area just east of the toll booths, where you gain entrance to the walkway across the bridge.

Walking over the venerable, symbolically soaring Golden Gate Bridge is an exhilarating, unforgettable journey. This monumental structure offers views that can only be described as astonishing. From this vantage point you can survey the city's physique while you balance high above it, unencumbered by buildings or earth. The Pacific Ocean, 260 feet below, is an endless blue apparition framed by the rugged curve of land north to Marin and south to San Francisco. As unbelievable as it sounds, the gusts of wind up here can cause the reinforced, Herculean steel cables to sway to and fro. This is one place where, without even kissing or touching, you can really feel the earth move—and it won't be from an earthquake, either. On a clear, sunny day, just once in your lives, put on your walking shoes and discover this one for yourselves.

GOLDEN GATE PARK, San Francisco
Recommended Wedding Site

Between Lincoln Way, Fulton Street, Stanyan Street, and the Pacific Ocean.

For those who know this vast acreage of city woodlands and gardens, it is possible to imagine that Golden Gate Park and Romance are themselves an adoring couple. There is so much to see in this diverse three-mile-long park that even in a day you can only scratch the surface. Nevertheless, any of the park's varied attractions can provide a prelude to an enchanting day together. One place to start is the **STRYBING ARBORETUM**, a horticultural wonderland of plants and trees from all over the world. Another remarkable city escape is the **JAPANESE TEA GARDEN**, where an exotic display of Japanese landscaping gives you a tranquil reprieve from urban life. While school is in session, the **CHILDREN'S PLAYGROUND**, with its extraordinary carousel, offers adults a grand backdrop for playtime. The **CONSERVATORY OF FLOWERS** is a stunning structure that houses many of the earth's most brilliant colors and plant life. Wherever you find yourselves, this magical San Francisco park is the foremost outdoor spot of the city.

GOLDEN GATE PROMENADE, San Francisco

Golden Gate Park Promenade winds for three and a half miles around one of the most astounding scenic routes the Bay Area has to offer. This walkway extends from **AQUATIC PARK** at Fisherman's Wharf to **FORT POINT** under the Golden Gate Bridge. If there is a lover's lane to be found anywhere in San Francisco, it would be the projection of land at Fort Point. As you gaze out to the golden rocky hills, the vast lengths of the Golden Gate and Bay bridges, the glistening blue water, and the formidable cityscape, there is little else to do but move closer and kiss.

PALACE OF FINE ARTS, San Francisco
Recommended Wedding Site

Bordered by Lyon, Bay, Baker, and Jefferson Streets.

Nothing in San Francisco compares to the European splendor of the Palace of Fine Arts. Erected in 1915 for the Panama Pacific International Exposition, it was not built to last. When the structure began to crumble in the late 1960s, San Franciscans, who had come to cherish the Palace, raised enough money to restore it, making it a permanent city landmark. Reminiscent of European architecture, the mock-Roman rotunda is supported by mammoth Corinthian columns and flanked by majestic colonnades. Walking paths lead beneath the dome and around the adjacent lagoon, where ducks and swans are often seen gliding. This setting, ethereal any time of day, is especially romantic at night when the spellbinding architecture is lit up by spotlights.

Romantic Option: A few blocks away, on Marina Boulevard, between the Yacht Harbor and Fort Mason (Cervantes and Buchanan Streets), a grassy stretch of land called **MARINA GREEN** hugs the bay. On warm weekends, if you don't mind crowds, it's a good place to watch sailboats, fly a kite, or simply sit and enjoy the sunshine.

PIER 39, San Francisco

At the foot of Beach Street, at Embarcadero.

OK, call us kids; we won't be insulted. After all, sometimes it is easier to see the joy of life through the eyes of a child. In the case of Pier 39, if you don't use a younger viewpoint, all you're likely to see is a sizable tourist attraction. Try our approach instead, and spend your time eating cotton candy, riding on the carousel, or driving the bumper cars. Investigate the teddy bear store, home to more than 2,000 of these huggable creatures, or watch mimes, magicians, and musicians perform while you wrinkle your nose at the smell of the sea and squint at the sparkling reflection of the sun on the ocean. On a nice day, you're sure to see sailboats whipping across the water with the wind.

On the tourist side of things, more than 100 specialty shops line the two-story boardwalk. There are at least a dozen eating spots for every taste and budget, and as an extra incentive many of the restaurants have views of the bay. Pier 39, if you're willing to adjust your biases and be young at heart, can be a pretty neat place.

Romantic Suggestion: Take a cruise on exquisite San Francisco Bay. **THE BLUE AND GOLD FLEET**, (415) 705-5444, is docked at Pier 39's west marina; scenic, very touristy excursions depart frequently. You won't be alone, but if you concentrate on the scenery the crowds will be much less apparent. For more privacy, rent your very own boat for the evening through **DOCKSIDE BOAT AND BED**, (415) 392-5526, (800) 4-DOCKSIDE (see Oakland Hotel/Bed and Breakfast Kissing).

THE PRESIDIO, San Francisco

Bordered by the Pacific Ocean, San Francisco Bay, Lyon Street, West Pacific Avenue, and Lake Street.

It started in the 1700s with the Spanish settlers. Then, the Presidio was their northern military post. Now, the Presidio is home base to the U.S. Army's Sixth Division. Fortunately for those who are inclined to kiss in the great outdoors, the Presidio is not just a military installation. This beautiful corner of San Francisco contains hundreds of acres of lush lands and is open to the public. There's much more to the Presidio than you can see on foot, so start by driving around the grounds on roads lined with redwood and eucalyptus trees. Next, do yourselves a favor: park the car, clasp hands, and go for a walk. You might choose to stroll by some of the historical sites and displays. Maybe you'll opt for an open area with views of the Golden Gate Bridge and the Pacific Ocean. Or perhaps you'll select the residential area, where old yet immaculate base houses (still occupied) evoke the nostalgic feeling of days long past.

TELEGRAPH HILL, San Francisco

From Union Street, head east up Telegraph Hill.

If you live in or visit San Francisco regularly, there is probably one place that symbolizes for you what this city is all about. For some it's Fisherman's Wharf, for others it's Union Square, for some eccentrics it may be Alcatraz. For kissing, we nominate Telegraph Hill.

The top of Telegraph Hill is where the famous Coit Tower presides over the city. This fluted, reinforced concrete column, built in 1933, is noted for its interior murals depicting historic San Francisco scenes. An elevator takes visitors to the top of the tower, and from this vantage point you get a sense of the city's passionate personality and dynamic energy, as well as its orderly, well-contained physique. You will also be exposed to a lot of other sightseers, who may obscure the view and reduce your hope for a romantic moment. But then again, when you actually witness the sights and sounds from this pinnacle, you may find that the crowds around you don't seem to matter. It's worth a try!

Romantic Suggestion: When you've finished admiring this hallowed view, make sure you have made nearby dinner reservations at **JULIUS' CASTLE** (see Restaurant Kissing). If you haven't, the North Beach area is overflowing with Italian restaurants and Italian bakeries that tantalize the senses.

TWIN PEAKS, San Francisco

Follow signs for Scenic Route 49, which will direct you to this hilltop setting.

They don't call this the scenic route for nothing. As you follow signs for Scenic Route 49, you'll drive (it would take hours on foot) up a steep, winding grade that climbs far above the city, eventually culminating at a peak that feels like the top of the world. San Francisco looks almost minuscule from this lofty perspective, which overlooks truly breathtaking panoramic views of the Golden Gate Bridge and Marin County, reaching even as far as the Northern Coast. On clear days, the views are awe-inspiring. Though this aerie is by no means a secret, it is still much less frequented than some of San Francisco's other scenic lookouts. We saw several couples smooching without concern, which inspired us to do the same.

" *With a kiss, let us set out for an unknown world.* "

Alfred de Musset

Marin County

An escape from the city is closer at hand than you might think. A quick drive across the famous Golden Gate Bridge takes you from the crowded urban streets of San Francisco to the picturesque waterfront towns of Sausalito and Tiburon and the forested hills of Mill Valley, Larkspur, and Greenbrae. Whether you've got shopping to do or just want to spend some quality time communing with Mother Nature, Marin County offers something for just about everyone.

Romantic Suggestion: One way to get to Marin without getting stuck in traffic is to take the **GOLDEN GATE FERRY**, (415) 332-6600. The ferry leaves from the San Francisco Ferry Building, located at the foot of Market Street, and makes its way across the bay every day of the week. For kissing purposes, we recommend traveling during off-peak hours on weekdays. However, even when the boat is thick with commuters, the ferry feels like a genuinely San Francisco way to sightsee in the Bay Area.

San Rafael

Hotel/Bed and Breakfast Kissing

GERSTLE PARK INN, San Rafael
34 Grove Street
(415) 721-7611, (800) 726-7611
Moderate to Expensive

Once the site of a traditional English-style estate built in 1895, the Gerstle Park Inn is ensconced on one and a half acres in a quiet residential neighborhood, overlooking the sleepy town of San Rafael. Redwood trees (the oldest redwoods in town) lend ample shade to the expansive gardens and orchards. Deer are frequently seen peacefully grazing on the property.

Due to its small size, romantic amenities, and emphasis on privacy, the Gerstle Park Inn strikes the right balance of intimacy and professionalism. Leaded glass doors open into lovely common rooms, where gleaming hardwood floors are accented by handsome Oriental carpets. A fire rages in the large marble hearth, and richly colored mauve walls set off Asian vases and artifacts.

All eight moderate-size guest rooms have private baths and have been lovingly decorated with bright colors, country furnishings, eclectic Oriental accents, and fresh bouquets. Four rooms have Jacuzzi tubs and most have serene views of the gardens or San Rafael's hills. Harbored on the lower floor, the Lodge Suite has its own private entrance and a deck appointed with wrought-iron furniture. Bright yellow floral linens and wallpaper have a cheery effect. In the bathroom, steps climb up to an enticing soaking tub with gold fixtures and a separate glass-enclosed shower.

In the Gerstle Suite, French doors open onto a private patio and flower gardens. An immense shower–steam bath is an unexpected luxury in the cozy bathroom, where Oriental rugs warm the tiled floor. A private staircase winds upstairs to our favorite room of all: the elegant Redwood Suite, with green-striped wallpaper, beautiful antiques, a luxurious king-size bed, Jacuzzi tub, and a private deck overlooking the gardens.

Breakfast includes gourmet specialties like stuffed crêpes, served at cozy two-person tables in the snug breakfast room. After you've eaten more than your fill (it's impossible not to), stretch your legs in neighboring **GERSTLE PARK**, where four acres of trails traverse the tree-covered hills.

Greenbrae

Restaurant Kissing

JOE LOCOCO'S, Greenbrae
300 Drakes Landing Road
(415) 925-0808
Moderate to Expensive
Lunch Monday-Friday; Dinner Daily

Known more for its delicious Italian cuisine than its quiet atmosphere, Joe LoCoco's caters to those whose stomachs are the key to their hearts. As you pass the open kitchen in the front entrance, you may be overcome by the irresistible aromas wafting through the dining room. And the food is as good as it smells! The focus here is hearty, not heavy, and the kitchen turns out marvelous homemade pastas and fresh seafood dishes. We especially enjoyed the grilled Tuscan bread, served with wild mushrooms and fresh herbs, and the spinach fettuccine layered with four cheeses.

Noise from the adjacent open bar and kitchen combined with the loud shouts of hurried waiters pose serious romantic distractions for those look-ing for quiet conversation. Otherwise, the dining room, bathed in the soft glow of candlelight, is arguably romantic. Artwork depicting food adorns the peach-colored walls, and exquisite floral arrangements add another gentle touch of color. Large windows at one end of the dining room showcase views of the marina across the street and Mount Tamalpais in the distance. If you're willing to overlook the noise factor, you won't be disappointed.

Larkspur

Restaurant Kissing

BOLERO, Larkspur
125 East Sir Francis Drake Boulevard
(415) 925-9391
Moderate
Lunch and Dinner Daily

The structure that houses Bolero was built more than a hundred years ago. Back then it was the Green Brae Brick Kiln, and it supplied bricks for such San Francisco landmarks as Ghirardelli Square, the Cannery, and the St. Francis Hotel. Now, a century later, and after more than a million dollars in renovations, Bolero retains its historic charm while offering all the contemporary advantages of an alluring Spanish restaurant.

Guests are greeted at the door by the hospitable wait staff and offered a seat at the bar or in the more intimate dining room. Shaped like a large tunnel, the dining room has solid brick walls and a curved brick ceiling. As you'd expect in such a place, it's dark, but low light is reflected off the walls from colorful sconces. White linens and blown glass artwork add their own share of brightness to the room. Although the restaurant is rather large, the tables are situated to provide a secluded feeling. Another brick tunnel in back serves as the restaurant's wine cellar.

Bolero's chefs prepare several different types of paella, from the traditional paella Valenciana to more elaborate seafood or hunter-style creations. One type of paella features an entire Maine lobster, split and cooked in a spicy tomato-garlic-sherry sauce. Other delicious entrées include jumbo prawns and pork chops. Everything about Bolero invites you to linger for a while in a place where the past provides the setting for modern-day romance.

If you're in the mood for live entertainment, you may wish to sit at the bar, where you can witness authentic flamenco dancing every Friday and Saturday night. Why not do as the Spanish do and order a few *tapas* while you watch?

LARK CREEK INN, Larkspur
234 Magnolia Avenue
(415) 924-7766
Moderate

Lunch Sunday-Friday; Dinner Daily; Sunday Brunch
Recommended Wedding Site

As you wind through Larkspur's remote wooded neighborhoods, you may be surprised to come across this yellow frame home on what would otherwise be another curve in an out-of-the-way country road. In spite of its remote location, the Lark Creek Inn is one of the North Bay's more renowned dining spots. Its reputation is well deserved, and the home's countrified ambience is perfectly conducive to a romantic interlude. The main dining room features pale hardwood floors, crisp white linens, and a glass-domed ceiling shaded by lofty redwoods. Colorful abstract artwork adds a contemporary touch. Windows surround the adjacent sunroom, which is somewhat cozier. When the weather warms up, the restaurant's garden, situated near a babbling creek, serves as an extension to the dining room.

Then, of course, there is the unforgettable food. The moment you enter the restaurant, enticing aromas hint at the delights listed on the ever-changing menu. Brunch specials include dishes like baked brioche French toast stuffed with pears and pear butter. Lunch and dinner are equally creative, with selections such as buttermilk fried rock cod sandwiches served with spicy remoulade, housemade ravioli, Hood Canal oysters laced with malt vinegar dressing, and oven-roasted crab with chile-lime drawn butter and beans baked in the coals.

Mill Valley

Home to a handful of restaurants, art galleries, and boutique stores, the small town of Mill Valley is a charming place to spend an afternoon. Nature enthusiasts will appreciate Mill Valley's rural setting. Red-tailed hawks soar above the rolling hills, and vistas of the mountain peaks and valleys in this region are simply spectacular. **MOUNT TAMALPAIS** and nearby **MUIR WOODS** are ideal for a variety of day hikes (see Outdoor Kissing). We have only one warning: Be prepared to contend with crowds on weekends, particularly on clear blue summer days.

Hotel/Bed and Breakfast Kissing

MILL VALLEY INN, Mill Valley
165 Throckmorton Avenue
(415) 389-6608, (800) 595-2100
Expensive
Minimum stay requirement on weekends

Mill Valley's one and only downtown inn is set near the foot of Mount Tamalpais and surrounded by redwood, eucalyptus, and oak trees. The inn is advertised as a European-style pensione, and its stucco exterior fits this description to a tee (except that it's in Northern California and not Europe). Flowerpot-adorned balconies and natural wood accents grace the building's facade, hinting at the wonders inside.

Sixteen guest rooms are situated around an interior atrium rising from the covered parking garage at street level to the third floor. Half of these rooms face the street and have narrow wrought-iron balconies, while the rest have wider balconies and overlook a forested area. Two private cottages are surrounded by redwood trees and front a gentle creek. All the rooms have queen-size beds, tiled bathrooms (some with skylights), and French doors. Fireplaces and Franklin woodstoves are found in several of the rooms as well.

"Environmentally friendly" and "eco-chic" are perhaps the best phrases to describe the inn's decor. All of the natural wood furnishings have been handcrafted by local artisans, including the "distressed" armoires and the sleigh beds. The look is truly stunning, especially when you discover that many of the rustic touches have been created from leftover materials and natural fabrics. For example, mirrors are framed with old window frames, lamps are constructed from manzanita branches, and coat racks are made out of old-fashioned doorknobs. Bed frames are made of either wrought iron or natural wood, and crowned with woodsy wreaths.

Continental breakfast is catered by nearby **PIAZZA D'ANGELO RISTORANTE** (see Restaurant Kissing) and served on the inn's Sun Terrace. This partially covered sundeck looks out on tall redwoods and Papermill Creek. With its Indian slate floors, stylish umbrellas, and maize-colored teak tables, the Sun Terrace is a perfect place to enjoy a morning repast or al fresco dining any time of the day.

Romantic Warning: Due to the inn's location in downtown Mill Valley, traffic noise can be a problem in rooms facing the street. Some evenings you may also hear (whether you want to or not) live music from a popular night spot down the street.

MOUNTAIN HOME INN, Mill Valley

810 Panoramic Highway
(415) 381-9000
Moderate to Expensive
Recommended Wedding Site

Views don't get much better than this. Set high above the trees on a ridge of Mount Tamalpais, the Mountain Home Inn surveys a lush sloping valley, the Golden Gate Bridge, San Francisco, and the Marin Hills in the distance. Hawks soar overhead, and the only sound you'll hear is the wind rustling through the branches of the surrounding trees. Nature artwork, wood-paneled walls, and wood accents are part of a mountain lodge motif in the ten guest rooms; all boast views of the breathtaking setting. Even the smallest guest rooms are worth mentioning: some have their own fireplace, whirlpool or large soaking tub, and private deck. Our favorite room of all (and the most secluded) is the Canopy Room, appointed with a king-size four-poster bed made of actual tree trunks and draped with a canopy and a plush down comforter. A skylight built into the cathedral ceiling allows in ample natural light, while shutters conceal a whirlpool tub open to the bedroom with views of the tree-laden hillside beyond. Dried flower wreaths and bouquets enhance the rustic but elegant mood.

A bountiful breakfast here might include entrées like French toast or home-made bagels with smoked salmon, served in the property's elegant (and very popular) dining room. Whether or not you decide to spend the night here, lunch or dinner at the Mountain Home Inn is a delicious way to savor the views (see Restaurant Kissing).

Restaurant Kissing

EL PASEO, Mill Valley
17 Throckmorton Avenue
(415) 388-0741
Expensive
Dinner Daily

Don't be fooled by the Spanish name; El Paseo is nothing like the cantina you'd expect. Instead, it's one of the loveliest, most intimate *French* restaurants in Northern California. Potted plants front the entrance to this ivy-laced refuge tucked behind a brick courtyard in the charming town of Mill Valley. Inside, low ceilings with exposed dark wood beams accentuate the dining room's deep, rich decor and brick walls. Bottles of wine are tucked into nooks and crannies around the restaurant, and candles flicker in over-sized wineglasses at every table. Authentic French offerings such as escargots with blue cheese butter or sautéed prawns flamed with brandy are served on hand-painted china and are guaranteed to satisfy. It's not surprising El Paseo has won a number of well-deserved culinary awards. It is equally deserving of its four-lip rating for romance in our book. We can't think of a better environment to express your love and enjoy fine food.

MOUNTAIN HOME INN RESTAURANT, Mill Valley
810 Panoramic Highway
(415) 381-9000
Moderate to Expensive
Call for seasonal hours.
Recommended Wedding Site

Situated on the north side of Mount Tamalpais, this contemporary wood-and-glass restaurant and lodge stands guard over the sloping East Bay hills. Excellent food and sublime views create a rare dining experience in this handsome, refurbished building with vaulted redwood ceilings and huge windows. Dried flowers and crisp linens embellish every table in the elegant dining room on the lower floor, which is warmed by a large tiled fireplace. A second dining room is located just off the bar (which can sometimes get noisy), next to another fireplace. When the weather is warm, you can relish the sunshine and spectacular views on the casual outdoor deck. Soups, salads, and seafood are the specialties at lunchtime, and dinner continues in similar California fashion with items like grilled eggplant and broiled salmon. Walnut-chocolate mousse is an absolute must for dessert!

Romantic Note: The Mountain Home Inn also has ten cozy guest rooms worthy of your romantic consideration (see Hotel/Bed and Breakfast Kissing).

PIAZZA D'ANGELO, Mill Valley
22 Miller Avenue
(415) 388-2000
Moderate
Lunch and Dinner Daily

In spite of its exceedingly casual and noisy atmosphere, Piazza D'Angelo offers some of the best Italian fare this side of San Francisco. Modern in appearance, the restaurant's series of crowded dining rooms are accented with red tile floors, modern artwork, and colorful low-hung lamps. Bottles of olive oil, Tuscan pottery, and other Italian knickknacks adorn a partition that runs through the center of the busy restaurant. In the warmer months, you can enjoy a sunny Italian repast in an open-air section of the dining room or outside on a tiled patio. The delicious scent of Piazza D'Angelo's individual pizzas and pasta specialties floats from the open kitchen to tantalize and entice you. Go ahead and give in—you'll be glad you did!

Outdoor Kissing

MOUNT TAMALPAIS STATE PARK
Panoramic Highway

(415) 388-2070
Recommended Wedding Site

Take Highway 101 north to Marin County. Turn off at the Stinson Beach-Highway 1 exit and follow the signs for Muir Woods and Mount Tamalpais.

If you long to be surrounded by nature, you need only cross the Golden Gate Bridge into Marin County and drive along Highway 1 to the crest of Mount Tamalpais. This is without question one of the most absorbing drives in the area. Coiling along the edge of this windswept highland, each turn of the S-shaped road exposes another vantage point from which to scan wondrous views of overlapping hills cascading down to Marin. As you continue your excursion, you can remain in the car or venture out into the hills with a picnic in hand. The **STEEP RAVINE TRAIL**, which begins at the Pantoll Station on the Panoramic Highway, is a magnificent deep-forest journey to views of the ocean and bay. Here, in the midst of earth's simple gifts, a loaf of bread, a jug of wine, and your beloved are all you need.

MUIR WOODS NATIONAL MONUMENT
Panoramic Highway
(415) 388-2595
Recommended Wedding Site

Take Highway 101 north to Marin County. Turn off at the Stinson Beach-Highway 1 exit and follow the signs for Muir Woods.

Donated to the federal government in 1908, this well-preserved parcel of redwoods was declared a national monument by President Theodore Roosevelt. Set in the hushed splendor of Redwood Canyon, Muir Woods boasts 560 acres of undisturbed forest and six miles of walking paths. Hawks float overhead in abundance and sunlight filters through the leafy cathedral canopy. Chipmunks, blue jays and other beautiful birds, and black-tailed deer are frequently seen in this shady forest where redwoods dominate. Redwood Creek runs year-round, trickling down from the peaks of Mount Tamalpais to provide sustenance to the trees and animals that live here. Even in the height of summer, you can find secluded spots to admire nature's handiwork and enjoy each other's company in this magical preserve.

Tiburon

Tiburon has the bright reputation of being the sunny spot of the Bay Area. Not always but often, when other parts of San Francisco and Marin County are veiled in fog, Tiburon is basking in sunshine. Located along the waterfront, the main part of town is brimming with restaurants and shops that can provide plenty of things for you to see and do during your visit here.

Marin County has several outdoor sanctuaries. If you're in Tiburon, stop by the **RICHARDSON BAY AUDUBON CENTER**, 376 Greenwood Beach Road, (415) 388-2524. Housed in a charmingly restored Victorian, the center has a picture-perfect setting by the water. A short loop trail leads you up to the crest of a hill for a scenic panorama of Angel Island, San Francisco, Sausalito, and the coastal mountains.

Restaurant Kissing

CAPRICE RESTAURANT, Tiburon
2000 Paradise Drive
(415) 435-3400
Expensive
Dinner Daily
Recommended Wedding Site

Dining at Caprice feels almost like setting sail on a boat. Taking advantage of its perch above the gently swirling waters of Raccoon Strait, a wall of windows in the dining rooms looks out to unobstructed views of Angel Island, San Francisco, and the Golden Gate Bridge suspended in the distance. Tables spaced with privacy in mind hug the windows, ensuring that everyone has a share of the remarkable setting.

Dinner here is always an enamored event. Glass lanterns glow atop every table in the softly lit restaurant, and background jazz sets the right tempo for romance. The celebrated chef wins patrons over every time with his creative international cuisine. Appetizers like Dungeness crab quesadillas are just the beginning. We enjoyed the simple but delectable portobello mushroom sandwich almost as much as the seared scallops braised with cucumbers and leeks and served in a ginger-butter sauce. Vegetarians will appreciate the chef's special touch with vegetables and legumes.

Caprice is very popular on weekends, so reservations are a must. If you happen to arrive early (which we recommend), you can enjoy a glass of wine beside the hearth in the entryway or downstairs next to a raging fire in a massive rock fireplace.

Romantic Suggestion: After brunch or an early dinner, continue up Paradise Drive until you reach **PARADISE BEACH PARK**. This quiet, wooded little corner of the world overlooks the distant hills beyond the bay and the San Rafael Bridge. Depending on the time of day and the season, this place could be yours alone, and there is enough strolling and picnicking turf here to make it a significant lover's point of interest.

GUAYAMAS, Tiburon
5 Main Street
(415) 435-6300
Inexpensive to Moderate
Lunch and Dinner Daily; Sunday Brunch

In every way, Guyamas reflects a south-of-the-border feel and flavor. This casual waterfront restaurant, named for a Mexican fishing town, emphasizes authenticity instead of Americanized versions of Mexican food. Menu selections include tamales, pork wrapped in banana leaves, fresh fish served with chile-tomato butter, and green chiles stuffed with chicken and raisins. Some dishes may sound more exotic than the usual tacos and burritos, but be adventurous—they are all delicious.

Choose a table in the casual contemporary adobe dining room, which is accented with bright colors and a corner fireplace, or sit outside on the second-story waterfront deck. The patios are warmed with gas heaters, making them pleasant even on cool nights. Blooming bougainvillea climbs over whitewashed log beams, pots of cactus are placed around the deck, and pastel colors set a calming mood. A stunning view of the bay and San Francisco makes outdoor dining even more irresistible. Guyamas may not be fine dining, but you'll find that sitting back, enjoying the view, and relaxing is very easy to do. All this, and you get a great meal!

TUTTO MARE, Tiburon
9 Main Street
(415) 435-4747
Moderate
Lunch and Dinner Daily

Chain restaurants typically are not places we recommend for romantic interludes. However, when it comes to restaurants like Tutto Mare, on Tiburon's village waterfront, it is an altogether different story. Water views, a simple interior, and fresh menu items make this Italian eatery one of the most pleasant, albeit casual, restaurants in Marin County. The gray interior provides a subtle background, but the open kitchen and large number of tables can make conditions clamorous on busy days. We recommend dining on the second-story deck overlooking the ferry dock, Angel Island, and San Francisco's skyline in the distance.

Tutto mare is Italian for "all things of the sea." Accordingly, the menu offers a variety of seafood items, from steamed mussels in white wine and garlic broth to crab and shrimp ravioli in fennel cream sauce. Individual pizzas and other Italian dishes are also available.

Sausalito

Sausalito is often described as a "vast beautiful view of San Francisco." It's true that this little waterfront town is one of the best vantage points from which to ogle the city skyline. Sausalito is also an enjoyable place to escape from the hustle and bustle of San Francisco and browse through stylish boutiques, gift stores, and art galleries.

Hotel/Bed and Breakfast Kissing

CASA MADRONA HOTEL, Sausalito
801 Bridgeway
(415) 332-0502, (800) 567-9524
http://www.casam.com
Moderate to Very Expensive
Recommended Wedding Site

Casa Madrona's Victorian-style property meanders up a residential hillside set above sparkling Sausalito Bay in the heart of Sausalito. As you climb to your accommodations on a tiered walkway enfolded by greenery and a trickling fountain, this multilayered hotel reveals its many personalities. Guest rooms display the creative work of no fewer than 16 local designers, and each room is more interesting than the last. (Describing all 35 rooms here would require a book in itself.) The 1,000 Cranes Room's spartan Japanese-style decor artistically incorporates ash and lacquer design elements. In the Katmandu Room, purple carpeting and oversized lounge cushions accentuate a bed cozied beneath a skylight. Brimming with Eastern artifacts, secret alcoves, and mirrors, this room also offers the luxury of a fireplace and a soaking tub for two. In the Casa Cabana, a bright orange color scheme creates a Southwestern ambience where cactus plants look right at home. There is even a houseboat rental available!

At the top of the hill, the property's original Victorian home and surrounding cottages offer relatively subdued accommodations, ranging from Gramma's Room (which looks as old-fashioned as it sounds) to the English Gate Cottage, filled with old-world antiques and overlooking incredible harbor views. No matter what theme strikes your fancy, most of the rooms sport romantic amenities like private decks with brilliant sunlit harbor views, fireplaces, and seductive spa tubs. Complimentary continental breakfast is served in Casa Madrona's elegant restaurant, **MIKAYLA** (see Restaurant Kissing), which commands panoramic views of the bay.

THE INN ABOVE TIDE, Sausalito
30 El Portal
(415) 332-9535, (800) 893-8433
Very Expensive to Unbelievably Expensive

Aptly named, the contemporary wood-shingled Inn Above Tide sits directly above San Francisco Bay in the picturesque town of Sausalito. Built with views in mind, the inn has 30 modern guest rooms, all with floor-to-ceiling picture windows that survey panoramic water views with San Francisco's skyline twinkling in the distance. Potted rosebushes and beautiful hand-carved lounge chairs adorn private waterfront decks adjacent to most of the rooms. Binoculars allow you to catch closer glimpses of the seabirds and sailboats passing by. Ultra-contemporary fabrics and furnishings accentuate the cheery, oversized guest rooms. Boutique pillows decorate king-size beds in all of the rooms and swaths of sheer fabric drape a king-size canopied bed in the luxury suite. Twenty-four rooms have fireplaces, stylishly tucked into rounded brick turrets. The private bathrooms are beautifully decorated, and many feature deep circular soaking tubs.

Sample Napa and Sonoma vintages during "wine hour" in the afternoon on the communal sundeck. A generous complimentary breakfast is delivered to your doorstep in the morning and can be enjoyed at your leisure, along with the morning newspaper.

Romantic Suggestion: The Inn Above Tide offers "Moonlight Serenade" romantic packages, which include extras like chilled champagne, sunset wine service, fireside massages, and delayed check-out times.

Restaurant Kissing

MIKAYLA, Sausalito
801 Bridgeway, at the Casa Madrona Hotel
(415) 331-5888
http://www.casam.com
Moderate to Very Expensive
Dinner Daily; Sunday Brunch
Recommended Wedding Site

Even if you can't stay overnight at the lovely Casa Madrona Hotel, a meal at the property's Mediterranean restaurant is a heart-stirring alternative. Colorful Laurel Birch artwork adorns peach stucco walls in the simply adorned dining rooms, complemented by floor-to-ceiling windows that showcase panoramic views of Sausalito Bay and the San Francisco skyline. While nearly every table has a glimpse of the water, tables closest to the windows offer the most exceptional views. Every table is draped with elegant white linens and topped with a lone orchid set afloat in a clear glass bowl. Small and eclectic, the gourmet menu features seafood with a Mediterranean influence, from grilled salmon to cornmeal-crusted bluenose sea bass. After you've sampled the food and the views to your hearts' content, take a stroll through the town of Sausalito. Or, if you are staying at the hotel, head back to your private, individualized haven at Casa Madrona (see Hotel/Bed and Breakfast Kissing).

SCOMA'S, Sausalito
588 Bridgeway
(415) 332-9551
Moderate to Expensive
Lunch Thursday-Monday; Dinner Daily

A dynamite location on the shore of Sausalito makes Scoma's a sure thing for an enticing encounter. Classic seafood dishes like saucy cioppino or steamed clams in white wine and garlic are served in two nautically inspired dining rooms. The tables are packed in far too tightly for any degree of intimacy, but if you wait for one in the sunny glass-enclosed dining room, your eyes can savor the magnificent view as you enjoy your meal. Service is efficient but hurried (when you see the volume of people going in and out of here, you'll understand why). After dinner, walk along the shore (the pace may depend on how much you ate) to gaze at San Francisco's city lights and the moon's reflection on the water.

Romantic Alternative: HORIZON'S, 558 Bridgeway, (415) 331-3232 (Moderate) has a more casual, bar-like atmosphere that offers the same outstanding view as Scoma's. The dark wood interior is set off by a wall of windows that open onto an outdoor deck poised directly over the bay. From here you can survey the entire area, from the Bay Bridge to the home-covered hills of Tiburon. The atmosphere is relaxed, but a cup of coffee or cocktails from this vantage point could turn out to be an inspiring affair.

THE SPINNAKER, Sausalito
100 Spinnaker Drive
(415) 332-1500
Moderate
Lunch and Dinner Daily
Recommended Wedding Site

Situated on a rocky point next to the Sausalito Yacht Harbor, the Spinnaker enjoys tremendous views of Sausalito and distant San Francisco.

Floor-to-ceiling windows span the entire length of one wall; this allows diners to watch sailboats and ships slipping by against the picturesque backdrop of the city skyline, which dazzles after nightfall on clear evenings. The views nearly make up for the dining room's bland, somewhat dated interior. While the seafood, pasta dishes, sandwiches, and burgers are always satisfying, they remain secondary to the splendid waterfront location, where couples can and should fill up on romance.

Romantic Alternative: If **THE CHART HOUSE**, 201 Bridgeway, (415) 332-0804 (Moderate to Expensive) sounds familiar, it's because almost every major city has one. Even so, we've never seen a Chart House with a better view than the one in Sausalito. Huge picture windows frame the bay and the San Francisco skyline, the steak and seafood fare is always good, and in our opinion the salad bar here is one of the best in the Bay Area.

Outdoor Kissing

MARIN HEADLANDS
Northwest of the Golden Gate Bridge
(415) 331-1540

From the north: Heading south on Highway 101, take the last Sausalito exit and follow signs to the park. From the south: Heading north on Highway 101, take the Alexander Avenue exit and follow San Francisco signs under the freeway; then follow signs to the park.

What is it about the Golden Gate Bridge that evokes passion in all who see it? Find out for yourselves by visiting the Marin Headlands. A precipitous road hugs the cliff above this graceful sculpture of a bridge. Several viewpoints are perfect for windblown kisses in front of the Golden Gate, with the San Francisco skyline as a backdrop. It's a magical scene when the fog rolls in, cradling the arching span and city skyscrapers in cottony billows of mist. Intrepid romantics can continue on the winding road to the edge of the Pacific, hike inland to secluded, grassy picnic spots, or comb rocky beaches while exchanging sea-swept caresses.

RODEO BEACH AT THE MARIN HEADLANDS
(415) 331-1540

Head north from San Francisco on Highway 101. Take the Alexander Avenue exit and follow San Francisco signs under the freeway; then follow signs to Marin Headlands.

This expanse of white sandy beach is not a secret among locals, but you can be effectively alone during most weekdays before summer vacation releases eager kids from the classroom. It's hard to believe this scenic area is so close to the city. Jasper and agate are scattered along the shore, and Bird Island, just a short distance from shore, is often blanketed with fluttering white seabirds. In the distance, rolling hills and jagged cliffs make distinguished tableaux against the bright blue sky. Dozens of hiking trails wind over intriguing terrain to breathtaking panoramas. You won't be at a loss for ways to spend time here; prepare yourselves for the elements (namely sun and wind) and enjoy long, loving hours together.

Romantic Note: GOLDEN GATE NATIONAL RECREATION AREA, (415) 331-1540, contains more than 70,000 acres of protected coastline, pristine woodland, regal mountains, rugged hillsides, and meticulously maintained city parks. It is hard to believe that such a massive nature refuge exists so close to San Francisco. Hiking, picnicking, swimming, and any other outdoor activity you can think of is possible in this awesome stretch of land that offers something for the most ardent wilderness lovers or tamest urban dwellers. Thanks to Mother Nature and the Golden Gate National Park Association, this awesome area is yours to enjoy to the fullest.

Romantic Possibility: Nearby **MUIR BEACH STATE PARK** is a much-frequented expanse of white sandy shoreline. While long smooches are probably out of the question, you can still claim your own spot, lie back, listen to the ocean's serene rhythms, and concentrate on each other.

*"I have found men who didn't
know how to kiss. I've always found
time to teach them."*

Mae West

East Bay

Just across the Bay Bridge, the East Bay stretches from Point Richmond south to the Livermore Valley. In between are Berkeley, home of the well-known University of California Berkeley campus, and the mini-metropolis of Oakland. The East Bay may not be a total escape from the city, but if you only have a weekend to spare, it is extremely convenient. You will find also that the East Bay is home to several establishments worth your romantic consideration.

Point Richmond

Hotel/Bed and Breakfast Kissing

EAST BROTHER LIGHT STATION, Point Richmond
117 Park Place
(510) 233-2385
Unbelievably Expensive; day use is $10 per person
Open Thursday-Sunday

Red sky at morning, sailors take warning; red sky at night, a sailor's delight. If you want to have a ringside view of the ocean's fickle nature or watch the comings and goings of the local fishermen, you can do so in authentic style at East Brother Light Station bed and breakfast. Located on the rocky shores of East Brother Island in the strait separating San Francisco Bay from San Pablo Bay, the 1873 lighthouse is on the National Register of Historic Places. Income from the bed and breakfast is used to preserve the island's buildings and boats. Guests can spend the night in the cream-and-white Victorian house connected to the lighthouse.

Although sparsely decorated, the four guest rooms have queen-size beds with brass frames and ordinary linens. Breathtaking views of the water are definitely the highlight of each room. Unless you don't mind sharing a bathroom with a neighboring couple, request one of the two upstairs rooms featuring private baths. From the common area, ascend a spiral staircase to the light tower, where you can enjoy magnificent views of Mount Tamalpais and the San Francisco skyline. The island offers plenty of restful activities to occupy your time; visitors enjoy fishing, observing the surrounding wildlife, and browsing in the parlor library. Tours of the island are provided by the innkeepers as well.

Overnight accommodations include a ten-minute boat ride from the Point San Pablo Yacht Harbor to the island, hors d'oeuvres upon arrival, a four-course dinner, and breakfast. (Lunch is served only to guests staying two or more nights.) Day visits to the lighthouse are available Friday through Sunday.

Romantic Warning: Due to the island's limited water supply, showers are reserved for guests staying more than one night. In addition, the U.S. Coast Guard's electronic foghorn operates 24 hours a day between October 1 and April 1. Earplugs are provided for guests, but light sleepers may be awakened throughout the night.

Oakland

Oakland romance might seem like an oxymoron. True, Oakland doesn't have the allure or charisma of downtown San Francisco or Wine Country, and we have to agree that by and large downtown Oakland doesn't hold much fascination for those seeking affectionate encounters. Still several semi-romantic locales can accommodate certain amorous agendas.

Hotel/Bed and Breakfast Kissing

THE CLAREMONT RESORT AND SPA, Oakland
Ashby and Domingo Avenues
(510) 843-3000, (800) 551-7266
http://www.claremnt.com
Very Expensive to Unbelievably Expensive

Nestled in the Berkeley Hills and enfolded by acres of deftly cultivated gardens and palm trees, this colossal plantation-style mansion is reminiscent of a European castle. Epic in scale and style, the hotel's exterior can appear overbearing and impersonal if you have something smaller and more intimate in mind. One problem for couples is that large resorts like the Claremont lend themselves to conventions and tour groups. Feeling like part of a software association's annual meeting doesn't exactly make kissing a top priority. This famous hotel and tennis club is an exception to that rule ... well, at least in part.

The Claremont definitely attracts its share of convention-goers and businesspeople (87 percent of its clientele, in fact), but don't let this stagger-ing statistic deter you from seeking romantic possibilities here. All guests at the Claremont have the opportunity to engage in any and all of the available indoor and outdoor activities. There are many. Tennis courts, an Olympic-size swimming pool, a nearby golf course, saunas, hot tubs, a full-service spa, a state-of-the-art exercise room, a fully equipped weight-training room, and a fitness center offer invigorating ways to spend the day getting healthy and being active together. This isn't the place to come, however, if you want to lock yourselves away in a luxurious room for a weekend. The 239 rooms have 1980s-style decor, lightweight bedspreads, splashy pastel prints, and a standard, somewhat dreary hotel feeling. Some suites have views of Berkeley's hills, the lovely garden grounds, or the distant San Francisco skyline, but the view alone does not justify the cost of these otherwise nondescript rooms. Still, you may want to come to the Claremont Resort and Spa with healthful intentions of being good to yourselves and to each other. Spa Romance packages make it easy (but not exactly affordable) to plan an East Bay getaway.

    Romantic Suggestion: In the spirit of health, the **PAVILION RESTAU-RANT**, Ashby and Domingo Avenues, (510) 843-3000 (Moderate to Expensive) serves light California cuisine, including a selection of "spa portions" that have the calories already calculated. Located next to the hotel lobby, this convenient dinner option allows you to enjoy stirring views of palm trees and San Francisco's distant skyline (especially nice at sunset).

DOCKSIDE BOAT AND BED, Oakland
77 Jack London Square
(510) 444-5858, (800) 4-DOCKSIDE
http://www.boatandbed.com
Expensive to Unbelievably Expensive
Minimum stay requirement on weekends and holidays

    Whether you fancy sailboats or luxury motor yachts, you can kiss like a millionaire (at least for an evening) on your boat of choice in this industrial, though surprisingly quiet, Oakland port of call. Our 35-foot sailboat would have been a dream come true if the intimate accommodations had been less rustic and confining. More spacious boats cruise into the Unbelievably Expensive category, but they can be a better way to go if you're willing to share the romance of the evening with another like-minded couple. Complete with several private staterooms, modern furnishings (including stereos), and private baths, a large yacht can provide ample space and privacy for two couples. Continental breakfast, packed in a picnic basket, is delivered to your boat in the morning.

    When making reservations, ask about the "snooze and cruise" packages. These often include romantic extras like private charters on the bay, limousine service, special floral bouquets, and on-board massages. Catered candlelight dinners aboard are also available, although they can be quite expensive; another option is to stroll through the picturesque marina to one of the many (less expensive) restaurants and cafes clustered along the waterfront.

Dockside Boat and Bed also offers similar accommodations at Pier 39 in San Francisco, (415) 392-5526, (800) 4-DOCKSIDE. Including both sites, there are ten boats from which to choose, ranging in size from 35 to 68 feet. Most boats have queen-size beds, and some feature lovely teak interior paneling. Whether you decide to dock near Jack London Square in Oakland or near Pier 39 in "the City," you're sure to experience fantastic views of the San Francisco skyline.

WATERFRONT PLAZA HOTEL, Oakland
Ten Washington Street, at Jack London Square
(510) 836-3800, (800) 729-3638
http://www.waterfrontplaza.com
Expensive to Very Expensive

A romance package designed just for kissing is the year-round specialty at this recently opened hotel, harbored along Oakland's industrial waterfront in Jack London Square. Champagne and chocolate-dipped strawberries are the prelude to an amorous stay in a spacious waterfront-view room. (Be sure to request a room with a view—not all of them have one.) Appointed with bleached pine furnishings and cheery linens, many of the 144 contemporary guest rooms also have gas fireplaces. Corner suites with wraparound balconies and gorgeous water views are particularly enticing. Televisions with VCRs, mini-bars, coffee makers, and access to a public fitness center, sauna, and pool are all provided to ensure that the only thing you need to complete the scene is each other. In the morning, a continental breakfast is delivered to your room. You're also given two complimentary nightshirts, which, in this setting, are most likely to go home with you unworn.

In spite of the romance packages offered here, this hotel draws an almost exclusively business-oriented clientele, particularly on weekdays. You are likely to be the only two people here with something other than business on your minds.

Restaurant Kissing

IL PESCATORE, Oakland
57 Jack London Square
(510) 465-2188
Moderate
Lunch and Dinner Daily; Saturday and Sunday Brunch

Marina yachts rock with the waves and twinkling harbor lights are reflected on the water just outside the window of this Italian eatery, which serves up a touch of magic in the evenings. White linen tablecloths and crystal wine goblets add a dash of elegance, while the nautical theme and wood-paneled interior remain refreshingly unpretentious. Portholes and a ship's steering wheel add to the illusion that you're on a boat. The friendly, down-to-earth wait staff serve up delicious seafood and Italian fare. Antipasti specialties such as grilled eggplant marinated in fresh herbs provide the perfect start to dinner, which might continue with pasta topped with scrumptious smoked salmon or baby clams in white wine. Seafood entrées featuring calamari, salmon, and scallops will whet your appetite for more waterfront romance.

SCOTT'S SEAFOOD GRILL AND BAR, Oakland
No. 2 Broadway, at Jack London Square
(510) 444-3456
Expensive
Lunch and Dinner Daily; Sunday Brunch

A veritable parade of sailboats, tugs, motor yachts, and even a seal passed by in the estuary outside our window at Scott's. This classy, upscale seafood restaurant can get a bit crowded at times, but don't let that distract you from the fabulous view. Request a seat at one of the cozy booths lining the windows; that way you'll be away from the noisy kitchen, but close enough to the lounge area to appreciate the performing jazz trio (Sunday brunch only) or live piano music (every evening). Lanterns and white tablecloths top each table, while gold dome-shaped chandeliers hang from the maroon ceiling.

A basket of freshly baked breads promptly arrives at your table (the poppyseed muffins are especially scrumptious). For your entrée, choose from a diverse selection of fresh seafood. Scott's extensive menu includes everything from cod, salmon, and trout to Hawaiian favorites like ahi tuna, swordfish, and mahimahi. As for the steamed Manila clams, we fell for them hook, line, and sinker.

Outdoor Kissing

JACK LONDON SQUARE, Oakland
Event information line: (510) 814-6000

From Interstate 880 south: Take the Jackson Street exit, turn right at the first light onto Jackson, and then turn right onto Second Street. From Interstate 880 north: Take the Broadway exit, turn left onto Broadway, and continue four blocks to Jack London Square.

Although romantics often prefer the solitude of less-populated destinations, once in a while they may wish to join the crowds and visit a popular local attraction. In a city where amorous options are few and far between,

Jack London Square may be such a place. This up-and-coming area along Oakland's estuary provides a waterfront home for an abundance of restaurants, shops, and museums. At its center stands an immense Barnes & Noble bookstore; at the southeast end is Jack London Village, a series of specialty shops in a turn-or-the-century setting. Festivities and events are scheduled all year round, and every Sunday you'll find a delightful farmers market.

Walk along the sunny boardwalk or tour Franklin D. Roosevelt's restored presidential yacht, otherwise known as the "Floating White House." If you would rather not be landlocked, rent a canoe or kayak or take a guided tour of the Inner Harbor and Estuary. In addition, you can catch the Alameda/Oakland ferry, which provides daily service to Alameda, Pier 39, and San Francisco.

LAKE MERRITT, Oakland

From San Francisco, take the Bay Bridge to Interstate 580 east. Take 580 toward Hayward and exit at Grand Avenue. Grand Avenue eventually winds its way into the park.

Ask anyone in the East Bay area if downtown Oakland has any amorous potential and you'll probably hear the same answer: no. If you ask about Lake Merritt, however, people tend to whistle a different tune. Surrounded by 155 acres of park, Lake Merritt is located in, yes, downtown Oakland. Its surprising setting is ideal for picnicking, strolling, canoeing, or myriad other outdoor activities. Autumn is perhaps the best time to discover this city oasis, when the leaves slowly change and frame the lake in vibrant shades of gold and orange.

Start an afternoon here with a picnic near the water, then try a sailing lesson or take a tour on a miniature stern-wheeler. At **CHILDREN'S FAIRYLAND**, which attracts as many adults as kids, puppet shows, amusement rides, and scenes from your favorite fairy tales provide lively diversions. Don't be too disappointed when you find the afternoon has slipped away while many sections of this domain remain unexplored. You'll have to return a few times to see it all, but that leaves you with something to look forward to next time you happen to be near downtown Oakland.

Berkeley

People flock from across the country to visit U.C. Berkeley's beautiful campus, set beneath the verdant, rolling Berkeley Hills. This can be a lovely place for a picnic, particularly in the summer, when the student population dwindles significantly. A small array of additional romantic locales are also worth a visit.

Hotel/Bed and Breakfast Kissing

GRAMMA'S ROSE GARDEN INN, Berkeley
(510) 549-2145
http://www.fractals.com
Moderate to Expensive

A name like "Gramma's Inn" might not conjure up romantic images, but don't be too quick to judge. This Tudor-style bed and breakfast actually comprises five restored mansions, cottages, and carriage houses centered around a garden courtyard and set just off busy Telegraph Avenue. English country gardens and literally hundreds of blooming rosebushes fill the sprawling property and lend an appreciated pastoral touch to the urban surroundings.

There is something for everybody at Gramma's, which offers 40 rooms with a variety of amenities and styles. Dark wood detailing accents the historic Faye Building, built in 1906. Rooms in this building exude turn-of-the-century elegance, with old-fashioned wallpapers, hand-sewn quilts, and country-style furnishings. Claw-foot tubs, colorful stained glass windows, and working fireplaces are additional enticing period touches. A circular window seat in the spacious upstairs bedroom provides beautiful views of the surrounding hills and distant bay.

Ivy winds around the exterior of the renovated Carriage House, our favorite building on the property. Terra-cotta-tiled floors and hand-painted tiled fireplaces lend a French country feeling to the units here, where French doors open to private garden patios. Rose-colored walls give each room a warm blush, highlighted with cathedral ceilings and lovely, plush linens. Rooms in the Garden Building and Cottage Building are more contemporary, with high ceilings, gas fireplaces, hand-painted tilework in several rooms, and modern linens and carpeting.

Due to the vast number of rooms and wide range of amenities found here, be specific when you're making a reservation. Not all of the rooms have private baths, enticing views, or fireplaces. Don't be shy about asking if these are prerequisites for your romantic interlude.

You won't find fault with the elaborate wine and cheese plate set out each afternoon or the complete breakfast of baked dishes, delicious breads, and homemade preserves served in the property's **GREENHOUSE RESTAURANT**, 2740 Telegraph Avenue, (510) 549-2145 (Inexpensive to Moderate). Enjoy this morning repast with your beloved at a private two-person table, set overlooking the lovely colorful gardens. The Greenhouse Restaurant also serves up delicious California cuisine for Sunday brunch and dinner Tuesday through Saturday.

Restaurant Kissing

CHEZ PANISSE, Berkeley
1517 Shattuck Avenue
(510) 548-5525
Expensive
Cafe: Lunch and Dinner Monday-Saturday
Restaurant: Dinner Monday-Saturday

Many restaurant reviewers say that if you eat out only once in San Francisco, Chez Panisse should be the place (even though it happens to be in Berkeley). Well, far be it from us to argue with the edible truth. If delicious French cuisine is your idea of a romantic meal and you happen to be on the east side of the bridge, the food and atmosphere are definitely worth your while.

Chez Panisse offers two dining alternatives with two entirely different menus. The first option is an upstairs cafe that offers a casual à la carte menu of soups, salads, and a limited selection of entrées. Our favorite dining spot in this area is a cozy alcove set aglow with lanterns and filled with a handful of tables. The other choice is the downstairs dining room, which has similar decor but a much more elaborate prix-fixe menu. Begin your meal with an aperitif and a salad of prawns and wild mushrooms with saffron or grilled guinea hen breast with a riesling sauce. Top it all off with a citrus compote with Lavender Gem sherbet.

Romatic Note: Due to Chez Panisse's outstanding reputation, you may have to book your reservations a month in advance, particularly if you want to dine on a weekend.

FONTINA CAFFÉ ITALIANO, Berkeley
(510) 649-8090
Moderate
Lunch and Dinner Daily

Fontina Caffé Italiano is an agreeable spot for some informal romancing. The restaurant consists of two dining rooms that share a single fireplace, with an open bar along one wall near the entrance. The brick walls are adorned with everything from modern posters and acrylic landscape paintings to strings of garlic and peppers. White linens and bottles of olive oil top each of the nicely spaced tables. A small outdoor seating area is also available; unfortunately, its location on a busy street and the table umbrellas sporting beer logos detract from its romantic appeal. Choose from a selection of pasta, chicken, fish, and veal dishes, and don't forget to ask about the daily dessert specials.

SKATES ON THE BAY, Berkeley
100 Seawall Drive
(510) 549-1900
Moderate
Lunch and Dinner Daily; Sunday Brunch

San Francisco has one of the world's most stunning skylines. One way to really appreciate it is to go east across the Bay Bridge. From Skates on the Bay's dining room, you can observe the Golden City's dazzling profile, defined by the expansive blue bay and steep urban hills lined with steel-and-glass skyscrapers. Windows envelop nearly three-quarters of the dining room, so nearly every table has a glimpse (at the very least) of the prime views. Chandeliers and track lighting illuminate the crowded dining room, which is filled with circular booths and closely spaced tables. (It's obvious that the view from here is no secret—you're likely to find yourselves competing for reservations and dining in a crowd.) This can make for an exceedingly noisy and cluttered environment, but thank goodness the food is good (we loved the Cajun fettuccine and fresh focaccia). You'll be tempted to stay for dessert so you can linger over the city's lights a little longer.

Romantic Suggestion: After dinner, leave the crowds behind and walk along the water's edge to a nearby pier jutting out into the bay. Follow your instincts to the end of the dock, where the city skyline beckons to you from across the bay. This is one of the best places to kiss we've found yet.

Outdoor Kissing

BERKELEY MUNICIPAL ROSE GARDEN, Berkeley
Recommended Wedding Site

From San Francisco, take the Bay Bridge east and stay on Interstate 80 going north. Take the University exit east. Go straight to Shattuck Avenue and turn left. At Hearst Street, turn right. From here your last turn is a left onto Euclid, which you follow to the top of the hill.

The Berkeley Municipal Rose Garden is an enchanting realm filled with color and fragrance. From its upper level, you can gaze over an amphitheater of nature's splendor. As you make your way down the stairs, passing one rosebush after another, the scented air surrounds you. This is prime kissing territory, especially in the summer. The sedate setting is so expansive that even when others are around, you can almost always find an empty park bench. You can spend a few moments (or a few hours) enjoying views of acre after beautiful acre of this earthly paradise.

TILDEN REGIONAL PARK, Berkeley
(510) 525-2233

From Oakland, take Highway 24 through the Caldecut Tunnel. Exit onto Fish Ranch Road and follow this to Grizzly Peak Boulevard. Look for entrance signs to Tilden Regional Park on the right; several entrances are located along Grizzly Peak.

Nature's majesty is always close at hand in the Bay Area, and Tilden Regional Park is no exception. One of the most expansive earthy getaways in the area, the park encompasses more than 2,000 acres of forested trails, gardens, and picnic grounds. A hand-in-hand stroll through the park's Botanical Garden is simple romance at its best. Peaceful pathways wind through terraced plantings of native California blooms and trees, and ardent hikers can find their own private paradise along the more rugged trails. Picnic spots abound throughout the park; just drive until you find one that suits your fancy. With so many romantic possibilities, Tilden Regional Park offers a welcome respite from nearby civilization.

Lafayette

Hotel/Bed and Breakfast Kissing

LAFAYETTE PARK HOTEL, Lafayette
3287 Mount Diablo Boulevard
(510) 283-3700, (800) 368-2468
http://woodsidehotels.com
Expensive to Unbelievably Expensive

From the freeway the Lafayette Park Hotel looked like an impressive Swiss chalet, but because it was visible from the highway we were worried. After all, a love nest that borders a highway or a busy road is potentially a pigeonhole when it comes to romance. In this case, however, our skepticism was unfounded. The moment our weekend began, the freeway may as well have never existed.

High above the lobby, skylights illuminate a hand-carved staircase that winds its way down three stories, and a profusion of fresh flowers bring soft color and life to the elegant decor. Our brightly appointed room had a vaulted ceiling and a wood-burning fireplace, though we must say we were disappointed with the thin bedspreads and standard hotel furnishings. Exploring further, we found three charming courtyards: one built around an Italian marble fountain, another surrounding a stone wishing well, and the third with a large swimming pool and whirlpool spa. Adjacent to the lobby is the

DUCK CLUB RESTAURANT, 3287 Mount Diablo Boulevard, (510) 283-3700, (800) 368-2468 (Moderate to Expensive), which offers American cuisine in an admirable atmosphere. After dinner, a latte or cappuccino in the lounge, near the cobblestone fireplace, is a wonderful way to round out the evening.

Restaurant Kissing

TOURELLE, Lafayette ❦❦❦
3565 Mount Diablo Boulevard
(510) 284-3565
Moderate
Lunch Monday-Friday; Dinner Daily; Sunday Brunch

Perfectly trimmed hedges and ivy-covered brick mark the entrance to Tourelle, an engaging bistro with a charming courtyard. The courtyard itself would be delightful for a leisurely lunch or an intimate evening interlude if it weren't for the nuisance of nearby traffic. Thankfully, all distractions dissolve away inside, where two dining rooms offer different experiences. One room has an informal, lively feel, with a glass roof and a big open kitchen; the other is a beautiful, casually elegant dining room with towering vaulted ceilings, and brick walls. Selections from the smoker, grill, and oak-fired pizza oven are the specialties here, but everything on the menu is worth trying. The Spanish-style fish and mussel stew in a spicy tomato pepper broth is excellent, and the homemade Italian sausage raviolis with porcini mushroom broth and white truffle oil are to die for.

Walnut Creek

Hotel/Bed and Breakfast Kissing

SECRET GARDEN MANSION, Walnut Creek ❦❦❦❦
1056 Hacienda Drive
(510) 945-3600, (800) 477-7898
Expensive to Unbelievably Expensive
Recommended Wedding Site

Grand, immaculately white wrought-iron gates open to allow passage into this mansion's three-acre grounds. Deer fashioned from grapevines are set on the lawn beside the front entrance, and they are not the only creatures guests will happen upon during their stay. The abundant handcrafted animals (rabbits in particular) are an integral part of the inn's theme.

Inside, an impressionistic portrait of the inn hangs above the mantel in the grand Victorian parlor, where a plush settee and comfortable chairs are placed before a wood-burning fireplace. Guest rooms are entirely unique (our room had an original metal safe that now serves as a closet) and highlighted with romantic details, from billowing canopies to private balconies to a cupid fresco. Each of the seven suites has a special attraction. The Victorian-inspired Terrace Suite is warmed by a white brick hearth. French doors in the Summer House open to a flowery porch-like bathroom where you can indulge in a bubble bath in the claw-foot tub, and Juliet's Balcony has its own private little balcony and a sunny bathroom with a raised claw-foot tub. The irresistible Estate Suite is warmed by a wood stove and has a sizable black marble bathroom with a jetted tub for two, double pedestal sinks, and fluted brass fixtures; after some good clean fun, climb a small platform to reach the four-poster brass bed, smothered in a goose-down comforter.

No detail has been overlooked. Over a delicious full breakfast, served to individual tables in the cheery tea room or outside on the terrace on warmer days, you'll notice that even the glasses are delicately etched with gold. (If you prefer having breakfast delivered, that can be arranged in all but two of the guest rooms.)

Romantic Suggestion: The Secret Garden Mansion now offers formal tea service every Friday, Saturday, and Sunday from noon until 1:30 P.M. ($18 per person), so even if you aren't a guest you can come and sample the sweetness of this place (at least for an afternoon). The **SECRET GARDEN TEA ROOM** is utterly charming, with hardwood floors, floral table linens, a pretty wall fountain, and, best of all, an elaborate wall mural that depicts a blooming summer garden. Finger sandwiches, warm scones with Devonshire cream, and other authentic English treats accompany your hot tea, and everything is beautifully presented on fine china and polished silver. Again, the gracious staff leaves no detail undone. Tea guests are invited to view guest rooms (if any are available), but be forewarned: after one peek you will surely want to spend the night.

Restaurant Kissing

MASSIMO RISTORANTE, Walnut Creek
1604 Locust Street
(510) 932-1474
Moderate to Expensive
Lunch Monday-Friday; Dinner Daily

Massimo Ristorante, a downtown eatery, is really two restaurants in one: Massimo on the first floor (at street level) and Maximillian on the second. Massimo is a stylish dining room with white linens, geometric-print upholstered booths, mirrors along one wall, and an open bar. Italian specialties are served in this casual yet sophisticated atmosphere.

For those of us with amorous intentions, the Maximillian Room upstairs is the more romantic option. Soft lighting, exposed brick walls, French country touches, and pale pink table linens create a significantly warmer ambience than downstairs. There are no windows in this cozy room to remind you that you're in downtown Walnut Creek, so you may as well order something from the classic French menu and imagine yourselves in a Parisian bistro.

Danville

Restaurant Kissing

BRIDGES RESTAURANT, Danville
44 Church Street
(510) 820-7200
Expensive
Lunch Friday; Dinner Daily

Bridges' Asian-inspired California cuisine is so good that it draws overwhelming crowds (which, needless to say, are not the least bit conducive to kissing). The closely arranged tables in the chic ultra-contemporary dining room are another romantic hinderance. The seating situation is better in the warmer months, when you can choose a table outside on the garden terrace, surrounded by trees, a burbling fountain, and strands of tiny white lights.

If it is so packed and noisy, why do we consider Bridges an acceptable place to kiss (or at least spend a semi-romantic evening)? Once you taste your meal, you will immediately understand. The seafood is always fresh and beautifully prepared. We recommend the sautéed salmon with a cognac–passion fruit sauce served on a bed of jasmine rice. Or try the three-tiered meal of sautéed white prawns and stir-fried chicken with snow peas and oyster mushrooms, seafood samplers, and a trilogy of sorbets served in a Japanese bento box. Each savory bite will help you forget about the clamorous surroundings. And don't leave without dessert: the passion fruit ice cream with warm coconut and macadamia nut coffee cake is heavenly.

San Ramon

Restaurant Kissing

MUDD'S, San Ramon
10 Boardwalk
(510) 837-9387
Moderate
Lunch Monday-Friday; Dinner Tuesday-Sunday; Sunday Brunch

While the name of this earthy San Ramon restaurant may not be particularly romantic, the atmosphere is charming, service is pleasant, and the food some of the lightest and freshest we've had. Tables adorned with candle lanterns are scattered across several connecting dining rooms with curved wood ceilings and terra-cotta tile floors. Request a window seat or a table outside on a warm day so you can appreciate the flourishing herb and edible flower garden that spans the back of the restaurant. A trail winds through the gardens if you care to take a mini–nature walk before or after your meal.

Freshness, creativity, and, of course, flavor are the kitchen's hallmarks. The grilled free-range chicken marinated in sweet onions, garlic, lemon, and wine, and the ratatouille cassoulet, with a wide variety of fresh sautéed vegetables served over white beans and topped with toasted bread crumbs, are enough to convince you to come back again and again.

Pleasanton

Hotel/Bed and Breakfast Kissing

EVERGREEN, Pleasanton
9104 Longview Drive
(510) 426-0901
Expensive to Very Expensive

Have you ever dreamt of living in a woodsy, upscale neighborhood close enough to the city to be convenient but distant enough to be removed from all of the city's pressures? Pleasanton is just that kind of community, and Evergreen is the perfect place to have a taste of the good life. Set in a quiet wooded area, this impressive cedar and oak home is tucked into a hillside with trees and shrubbery all around. Large windows and a vaulted ceiling with skylights on the airy main floor allow the natural splendor outside to complement the interior. Shiny hardwood floors in this common area are warmed by a crackling fireplace, and plush couches provide a relaxing place to sit and discuss dinner plans.

The four guest rooms all exhibit the same comfortable elegance found in the main floor parlor. Of particular romantic interest is the top-floor Grandview Suite, a spacious, extremely comfortable room with a corner fireplace, an antique king-size sleigh bed, a tiled bathroom with a two-person Jacuzzi tub and double headed shower, views of the surrounding treetops, and a private deck where you can sit and enjoy it all. Hideaway, the other romantic's retreat, has a pine four-poster king-size bed, cream and beige accents, and an oval Jacuzzi tub for two. This room also has a deck, but it faces the driveway, so it is not as private as the Grandview Suite's. The two remaining guest rooms are the least expensive, partially because they have simple bathrooms without Jacuzzi tubs, and the beds are queen-size instead of king-size, but also because they are smaller. The cozy country interior of the Retreat Room makes for a comfortable getaway, but the Library's dark fabrics make this choice feel slightly confining. Fortunately, even if you choose a room without a tub for two, a large spa on the large outside deck is available for all to enjoy.

A generous expanded continental breakfast is served buffet-style on the main floor. Stone-topped tables with wrought-iron chairs are set in a sunny breakfast area, or you can take a tray back up to your room. Either way, you should feel invigorated after a good night's sleep and inspired by the natural beauty around you.

Romantic Suggestion: Not only is Evergreen's location great due to the seclusion, but it is also right next to **AUGUSTIN BERNAL PARK**, 8200 Golden Eagle Way, (510) 484-8160. If you think your calves can handle an uphill walk, it is only about 45 minutes to the top of Pleasanton Ridge from Evergreen, and the view from the top is awesome. After catching your breath, you'll find this an excellent place to kiss.

Livermore

Outdoor Kissing

LIVERMORE VALLEY, Livermore

From southbound Interstate 680, exit onto eastbound Interstate 580 and drive to the Livermore Avenue exit.

Escape the citified hustle of the Bay Area in the quiet Livermore Valley's wine region. Unlike the Napa and Sonoma valleys, this area has remained relatively undeveloped, and it serves as a refuge for a number of wineries nestled among rolling hills speckled with oak trees and cattle. A mere hour's drive from nearly anywhere in the Bay Area, the Livermore Valley makes for an ideal kissing excursion.

Romantic Suggestion: If the weather makes picnicking impossible, consider eating at the casually chic **WENTE VINEYARDS RESTAURANT**, 5050 Arroyo Road, (510) 447-3696 (Moderate). Floor-to-ceiling windows offer views of the surrounding hillsides and vineyards, the service is affable, the wine list excellent, and the Italian food notable.

South of San Francisco

Woodside

Restaurant Kissing

BELLA VISTA, Woodside
13451 Skyline Boulevard
(415) 851-1229
Moderate to Expensive
Dinner Monday-Saturday

The winding scenic drive to Bella Vista is half the fun of dining here. Although the weathered wood paneling and carpets are as timeworn in appearance as the restaurant's exterior, the floor-to-ceiling windows in two of the three dining rooms command endless views of a rolling procession of redwood trees and the distant blue outline of the bay. Arrive before sunset so you can have dinner as darkness begins to veil the area in velvety black. If you've timed things just right, you'll have finished your scallops sautéed in white wine and be taking your first exquisite bite of chocolate soufflé just as the lights of the towns below begin to twinkle.

Outdoor Kissing

FILOLI GARDENS AND ESTATE, Woodside
Canada Road
(415) 364-2880
$10 per person
Reservations Required
Call for seasonal hours.

Filoli Gardens is about 25 miles south of San Francisco. From Interstate 280, take the Edgewood Road exit west, then turn right onto Canada Road and drive 1.2 miles to the entrance.

Filoli's 16 acres of gardens evoke passion in all who visit. The gardens are laid out in a sumptuous Italian-French design, with parterres, terraces, lawns, and pools that form a succession of garden rooms. More than 20,000 plants are added annually to ensure year-round splendor. The Chartres Cathedral Garden recreates a stained glass window with roses and boxwood hedges; the Woodland Garden is Eden revisited. The wisteria-draped mansion is similar to a European summer palace. Original furnishings and items from the Getty and de Young museums recall an era of grand luxury. If you feel a sense of *déjà vu*, it may be because you have seen Filoli portraying the classy Carrington estate on television's *Dynasty*, or perhaps you kissed here in your most pleasant dreams.

Portola Valley

Restaurant Kissing

IBERIA, Portola Valley
190 Ladera-Alpine Road
(415) 854-1746
Moderate to Expensive
Lunch and Dinner Daily

Don't reread your directions—you're supposed to be in a shopping mall. We admit it's an unusual location for a romantic restaurant, but you won't have any qualms once the owner of this distinctive Spanish restaurant has greeted you and ushered you to the table of your choice. Everything about this restaurant is authentically Spanish, from the ambience to the menu to the wait staff. European knickknacks fill the cozy dining room, set overlooking a small grove of trees. Leaded glass partitions lend privacy to cozy tables set with lovely hand-painted dishes. Although the menu changes periodically, we recommend the poached salmon in sweet vermouth sauce and the unusual amost dessert-like lobster dishes served in a sauce of saffron, chocolate, and nuts.

Palo Alto

Hotel/Bed and Breakfast Kissing

GARDEN COURT HOTEL, Palo Alto
520 Cowper Street
(415) 322-9000, (800) 824-9028
http://www.gardencourt.com
Expensive to Very Expensive
Minimum stay requirement seasonally
Recommended Wedding Site

Escape the street noise of downtown Palo Alto in a Mediterranean-style villa built around an enclosed courtyard. All 62 guest rooms here have balconies, many of which overlook the flower-filled courtyard below. Though we were especially partial to the rooms with courtyard views, we must warn you that they directly face rooms on the opposite side of the hotel. (For the utmost privacy, you'll have to shut the curtains.) Even the rooms that face the busy street are infused with sunlight and laden with luxurious appointments: canopied beds draped with luscious fabrics and plush down comforters, large arched windows, and contemporary furnishings. Six suites have fireplaces and seven have Jacuzzi tubs; all abound in romantic potential.

Saratoga

Surrounded by forest and parkland, Saratoga is an idyllic escape from the city. Tall trees shade the picturesque small-town streets, lined with Victorian storefronts and well-tended gardens and homes. Saratoga's main thoroughfare, **BIG BASIN WAY**, is surprisingly small, but teeming with award-winning restaurants that score as high on the kissing scale as they do on the culinary scale. Saratoga has more than enough romantic possibilities to fill a superlative afternoon or weekend interlude.

Romantic Warning: Due to the growing popularity of the Paul Masson concert season, there are times when Big Basin Way is a traffic bottleneck, the likes of which are not supposed to happen outside the city. Keep your schedule loose if you happen to be here at the end of a concert. Simply park your car and have a snack or sip cappuccino at any of the dining spots along Big Basin Way.

Hotel/Bed and Breakfast Kissing

THE INN AT SARATOGA, Saratoga
20645 Fourth Street
(408) 867-5020, (800) 543-5020
Expensive to Unbelievably Expensive

Nestled in the heart of picturesque Saratoga, this handsome inn strikes a perfect balance between the intimate warmth of a bed and breakfast and the comfortable practicality of a hotel. All 45 suites have private balconies and windows that overlook a creek flowing through a small forest of sycamore, maple, and eucalyptus trees. Upscale hotel furnishings and amenities provide everything seasoned travelers require and romantics yearn for, including luxurious tiled Jacuzzi tubs in seven of the rooms. Complimentary wine and refreshments are served every afternoon in the plush lobby downstairs. A complimentary buffet-style continental breakfast is served here in the morning, but there aren't always enough tables to go around. Consider taking breakfast back to the privacy of your own room.

Restaurant Kissing

LA FONDUE, Saratoga
14510 Big Basin Way
(408) 867-3332
Moderate
Dinner Daily

La Fondue effortlessly lives up to its reputation as a unique restaurant. More unusual than it is romantic, the colorful dining room filled with moons, suns, and stars draws its theme from Greek mythology. Who would guess that in an atmosphere like this the menu would offer nothing but fondues? The air is laden with delicious aromas, and the fondue selection is limitless, from standard cheese or teriyaki sirloin fondue to white chocolate fondue. If you're wondering if fondue can be romantic, take notice of the restaurant's "fondue rules," which state: "If a lady loses her cube in the fondue, she pays with a kiss to the man on her right." Just make sure you're not seated next to strangers.

LA MÈRE MICHELLE, Saratoga
14467 Big Basin Way
(408) 867-5272
Moderate to Expensive
Lunch and Dinner Tuesday-Sunday; Sunday Brunch

When making reservations at La Mère Michelle, you will have to specify whether you want to eat indoors or outdoors. It's a difficult choice. Subdued and elegant, the dining room is highlighted by sparkling crystal chandeliers, fine art, and mirrored walls. Here, candles flicker at intimate tables cloaked in white linens. Though it is much more casual, the candlelit patio is equally enticing, encircled by a short brick wall embellished with periwinkle blue flowers and overlooking Saratoga's charming storefronts. The traditional French menu and enchanting atmosphere of either dining room are sure to please. No matter where you choose to sit, the savory baked seafood mornay with fresh scallops, shrimp, crab, and prawns will taste divine.

LE MOUTON NOIR, Saratoga
14560 Big Basin Way
(408) 867-7017

Moderate
Lunch Saturday; Dinner Daily

Le Mouton Noir is anything but the black sheep of Saratoga's restaurant row. A combination of pink paisley and Laura Ashley prints lends a country feel to this very intimate Victorian dining room. French-inspired California cuisine and elaborate desserts are served with care, and the food is delectable. Whether you have lunch here, with sunlight streaming through the many windows, or bask in the glow of a candlelight dinner, Le Mouton Noir is a delightful romantic discovery.

THE PLUMED HORSE, Saratoga
14555 Big Basin Way
(408) 867-4711
Expensive
Dinner Monday-Saturday

Each of the intimate dining rooms at the Plumed Horse has unique detailing and character. One brims with Victorian antiques and opulent red velvet furniture; another has weathered wood walls and stained glass windows. Appropriately, horse paraphernalia and horseshoes are displayed everywhere. Best of all, the Continental cuisine with a heavy French influence rarely disappoints. We recommend the toasted Cypress Grove goat cheese with a sun-dried tomato ratatouille, the lobster bisque, and the crisp baked salmon with poached oysters on a bed of spinach. (Wow!)

Romantic Note: The wild at heart can go dancing after dinner on Friday and Saturday nights in the **CRAZY HORSE SALOON**, located next door.

RESTAURANT SENT SOVÍ, Saratoga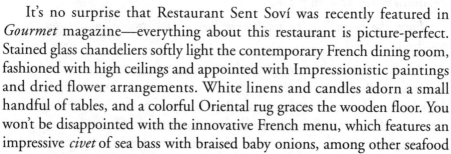
14583 Big Basin Way
(408) 867-3110
http://www.sentsovi.com
Moderate to Expensive
Dinner Tuesday-Sunday

It's no surprise that Restaurant Sent Soví was recently featured in *Gourmet* magazine—everything about this restaurant is picture-perfect. Stained glass chandeliers softly light the contemporary French dining room, fashioned with high ceilings and appointed with Impressionistic paintings and dried flower arrangements. White linens and candles adorn a small handful of tables, and a colorful Oriental rug graces the wooden floor. You won't be disappointed with the innovative French menu, which features an impressive *civet* of sea bass with braised baby onions, among other seafood and meat-based entrées. Dessert shouldn't be passed up here—the passion fruit soufflé with champagne is especially tantalizing.

Outdoor Kissing

HAKONE GARDENS, Saratoga
21000 Big Basin Way
(408) 741-4994
$3 parking on weekdays, 10 A.M.-5 P.M.;
$5 parking on weekends, 11 A.M.-5 P.M.
Recommended Wedding Site

Take Big Basin Way through town; about a mile up the road you will see a turnoff sign on the left side of the street.

We missed it the first time we visited Saratoga, but after several friends who had been there admonished us for not checking out the Hakone Garden, we returned for what they said would be an unbelievable outing. We searched valiantly for the turnoff sign. Finally we saw it and followed it to one of the most serene settings we've ever seen, a horticultural utopia, pure and simple and sublime.

Redwood trees stretch to the sky, sheltering a sculptured landscape of exquisite flora and fauna. In the center of the garden is a blue pond where sleepy carp, a Japanese symbol of love and longevity, languish in the still water. White-water lilies float over the surface, and a cascading waterfall fills the air with mild, tranquilizing music. The garden is edged with wood-fenced walkways adorned by sweet-smelling flowers. The contemplative mood of the area makes it prime territory for a walk with the one you love. Six picnic tables are also provided, where you can enjoy a light snack from the winery's gift shop.

MOUNTAIN WINERY, Saratoga
14831 Pierce Road, at Highway 9
(408) 741-5181
Recommended Wedding Site

From Big Basin Way, turn left onto Pierce Road and follow the signs to the main gate.

Perched above the idyllic town of Saratoga, up a steep and winding country road, Mountain Winery covers some of the most august, sun-drenched earth in the entire South Bay. Everything here seems almost too picture-perfect. Graceful trees rustle in the soft breezes. Grapevines arc across the mountainside, disappearing from sight as the land curves to meet hill after hill. Perhaps the only flaw in this majestic setting is that the winery is not open to the public except during special events. Then again, for most of the spring, summer, and part of fall, that's not a problem. Every year, the winery presents a spectacular summer concert series featuring entertainers who appeal to almost every audience. Past concerts have showcased the soulful sounds of Ray Charles, classy jazz vocals from the legendary Ella Fitzgerald, the country stylings of Ricky Skaggs, and the soothing instrumentals of talented Kenny G. Regardless of what you choose to hear, there is something miraculous about listening to music in the mountains with a clear sky and the sweeping countryside as your only backdrop.

Romantic Warning: On a summer day, sitting in an unshaded spot can lead to meltdown. Try to find protected seats or bring a sun visor, sunglasses, and towels. At night, however, the mountain breezes can be cooler than you might expect. An extra sweater will keep shivers at a minimum.

Romantic Note: If wedding bells are in your future, facilities and services for large groups are available here, through a separate company located adjacent to the winery. Call **CHATEAU LA CRESTA RESTAURANT**, (408) 741-5526, for details. This restaurant does only banquets or catering and is not open to the public.

Campbell

Restaurant Kissing

CAMPBELL HOUSE, Campbell
106 East Campbell Avenue
(408) 374-5757
Moderate to Expensive
Lunch Tuesday-Friday; Dinner Tuesday-Saturday

Housed in a 60-year-old Spanish-style villa with arched windows and a lovely fireplace, this cozy restaurant provides a homey atmosphere, attentive service, and delicious food, all in just the right proportions. Campbell House's cuisine is rumored to be some of the best in the South Bay area, and the rumor is well founded. Twelve intimate tables set off by dark wood paneling and dried flower wreaths provide a perfect setting for enjoying fresh seafood or grilled homemade Italian chicken sausage with blue cheese polenta.

San Jose

You might be wondering why anybody would go to the silicon capital of the world for anything other than computer software. We actually wondered the same thing—until we stumbled across several very romantic finds ... and thankfully, there wasn't a computer in sight.

Restaurant Kissing

BELLA MIA RESTAURANT, San Jose
58 South First Street
(408) 280-1993
Moderate to Expensive
Lunch and Dinner Daily; Saturday and Sunday Brunch

Thirteen thousand square feet of romantic possibilities await you at this newly renovated turn-of-the-century restaurant, a diamond in the rough (as they say), set among the rundown storefronts of downtown San Jose. Wood and brick lend a handsome air to the downstairs dining room, though sounds drifting past the open kitchen can intrude on quiet conversation. If you're serious about wining and dining, head upstairs, where tables are arranged under skylights in the mezzanine or in a beautiful back dining room warmed by a fireplace and accented with candles and rich green wallpaper. The Italian menu has something for even the pickiest palates—the freshly baked focaccia and award-winning salmon ravioli with ricotta and herbs are both musts.

EMILE'S, San Jose
545 South Second Street
(408) 289-1960
Moderate
Lunch Friday; Dinner Tuesday-Saturday

Ultra-modern track lights illuminate a massive floral arrangement in the center of Emile's chic dining room, appointed with an ornate sculpted ceiling, tapestry-covered chairs, and wall mirrors. Proudly dubbed "San Jose's best," this newly opened restaurant offers a creative mix of contemporary European cuisines. Due to its extreme popularity and consequent crowds, the setting doesn't exactly feel intimate, but the food more than compensates. The menu changes weekly, but two of the delectable dishes offered are grilled salmon served with fresh black linguine and porcini mushrooms in a saffron cream sauce, and grilled portobello mushrooms served with whipped Gorgonzola potatoes, artichoke hearts, and slow-baked roma tomatoes in a wild mushroom sauce.

Romantic Note: Just around the corner from Emile's is an exceptionally charming Italian eatery called **PASQUALE'S**, 476 South First Street, (408) 286-1770 (Moderate). Stained glass windows line the entrance to the small brick dining room, which is cluttered with modernistic frescos and knick-knacks. You'll appreciate the cozy ambience, as well as the savory Italian fare.

LA FORÉT, San Jose
21747 Bertram Road
(408) 997-3458
Moderate to Expensive
Dinner Tuesday-Sunday; Sunday Brunch

Just a short drive away from the high-tech world San Jose is famous for, La Forét is one of the prettiest restaurants in the area. Located outside the city limits, the restaurant sits next to a creek in what was the first two-story adobe hotel in California. White tablecloths drape cozy tables topped with red roses in the restaurant's three different dining rooms, which survey views of a wooded landscape. A sublime French menu offers a wide range of pheasant, chicken, duck, and pasta entrées, and the service is outstanding. Soft candlelight will cast a gentle spell as you lovingly share your evening here.

" *Soul meets soul on lovers' lips.* "

Percy Bysshe Shelley

Lake Tahoe and Environs

Glistening in the foothills of the High Sierra peaks, Lake Tahoe is the largest alpine lake in North America: 22 stunning miles long and 12 miles wide. The climate too is alpine in nature, which means summers are warm and dry and winters cold and snowy. Spring and fall can be a little of both. The area's breathtaking scenery, fishing, swimming, skiing, hiking, and, yes, gambling lure tourists of all kinds—especially those looking for romance.

Romantic Warning: During the off-season, when the weather is too cold for swimming in the lake but too warm for snow, many establishments are closed, especially on the north and west shores, where gambling does not keep visitors coming year-round. Always call in advance.

NORTH SHORE

Incline Village, Nevada

The affluent residential neighborhood of Incline Village sits on the Nevada side of Lake Tahoe. On this side of the state line, most hotels put their energy into providing captivating casinos rather than romantic rooms, so lodging options are limited. One advantage of staying here is that the area is self-contained: skiing, shopping, swimming, and boating are all nearby.

Hotel/Bed and Breakfast Kissing

HYATT REGENCY LAKE TAHOE
RESORT HOTEL, Incline Village
Country Club Drive and Lakeshore Boulevard
(702) 832-1234, (800) 233-1234
Very Expensive

Unlike the more developed shores of South Lake Tahoe, the North Shore has retained its natural forested setting. You'll actually enjoy a moonlit stroll along the curved paths that lead from this modern high-rise through the woods, past earth-toned cottages, to the lakeshore. The Hyatt typically caters to an executive clientele, but a unit in one of the 24 lakeside cottages could inspire a lot more than a business meeting. Wood furnishings, richly colored decor, stone fireplaces, and private decks with up-close views of the sparkling lake create an alpine lodge look and an amorous mood.

The 458 guest rooms in the 12-story main building are a cross between a charming inn and a standard hotel, with blond pine furnishings, rich floral spreads, plenty of playful throw pillows, and lake or mountain views. On the Regency floors, complimentary afternoon wine, liqueurs, hors d'oeuvres, and an expanded continental breakfast are served in the private common room.

Restaurant Kissing

LONE EAGLE GRILL, Incline Village
111 Country Club Drive, at the Hyatt Regency Lake Tahoe
Resort Hotel
(702) 831-1111
Moderate to Expensive
Lunch and Dinner Daily; Sunday Brunch

Although the Lone Eagle is owned by the Hyatt, it is set apart from the high-rise hotel and nestled in the woods on the lakeshore. Fires raging in two river-rock fireplaces spread warmth throughout the airy dining room, despite the soaring 25-foot open beam ceilings. Windows wrap around two sides of the restaurant, and diners risk becoming mesmerized by the shimmering facets of Lake Tahoe, as dazzling as sapphires on a necklace. Every candle-topped, linen-draped table offers this glorious view.

Duck is a specialty here, served with your choice of Oriental, orange, lingonberry, or green pepper sauce. The extensive menu has something for everyone, including seafood and meat dishes.

Outdoor Kissing

DIAMOND PEAK CROSS COUNTRY
AND SNOWSHOE CENTER, Incline Village
Mount Rose Highway (Route 431)
(702) 832-1177
$14 for an adult day-pass

From Incline Village, drive five miles out of Incline Village along the Mount Rose Highway (Route 431) toward Reno. Near the crest of the mountain, park in the highway turnout. Follow signs to the center, which is located just up the path in the woods.

If a kiss gives you that top-of-the-world feeling, just wait until you kiss at Diamond Peak. High on a mountaintop, groomed cross-country ski trails lead through pristine forest to spectacular, eagle's-eye views of crystalline Lake Tahoe and its ring of snowcapped peaks. Even beginners will find rentals, lessons, and one easy trail here; try the rolling intermediate trails if you can laugh together at your snow-softened falls. Along the intermediate Vista View loop, climb up aptly named "Knock Your Socks Off Rock" and you'll know what kissing on top of the world is all about. Tables are provided at the base of the rock for chilly but heartwarming picnics.

Romantic Alternative: Several marked cross-country ski trails varying in difficulty are located on the western shore of the lake in the **TAYLOR CREEK FOREST SERVICE AREA**, (916) 573-2600. Our favorite is the one that leads past the eagle wintering area to the lakeshore. Follow the lakeshore, then circle back through the rustic but grand historic estates built in the 1920s. Along this forested shoreline, you'll never guess that casinos are just a short drive away. Be sure to buy a $3 Sno-Park permit in South Lake Tahoe for parking at Taylor Creek.

Crystal Bay

Restaurant Kissing

SOULE DOMAIN RESTAURANT, Crystal Bay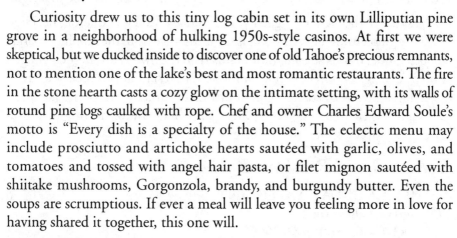
(916) 546-7529
Expensive
Dinner Daily

Curiosity drew us to this tiny log cabin set in its own Lilliputian pine grove in a neighborhood of hulking 1950s-style casinos. At first we were skeptical, but we ducked inside to discover one of old Tahoe's precious remnants, not to mention one of the lake's best and most romantic restaurants. The fire in the stone hearth casts a cozy glow on the intimate setting, with its walls of rotund pine logs caulked with rope. Chef and owner Charles Edward Soule's motto is "Every dish is a specialty of the house." The eclectic menu may include prosciutto and artichoke hearts sautéed with garlic, olives, and tomatoes and tossed with angel hair pasta, or filet mignon sautéed with shiitake mushrooms, Gorgonzola, brandy, and burgundy butter. Even the soups are scrumptious. If ever a meal will leave you feeling more in love for having shared it together, this one will.

Tahoe Vista

Tahoe Vista doesn't offer much more than a busy street of wall-to-wall businesses. Most likely you'll quickly travel through here and won't feel inspired to linger, unless you want to do some shopping.

Restaurant Kissing

LE PETIT PIER, Tahoe Vista
7252 North Lake Boulevard
(916) 546-4464
Expensive to Unbelievably Expensive
Dinner Wednesday-Monday

Development along the lake is so dense in Tahoe Vista that you could easily miss this gem of a French restaurant, perched literally at the water's edge. Inside, the incredible views and the savory aromas are a welcome invasion of the senses. A lantern glows at each table, and the contemporary decor is enhanced by white linens and modern artwork. Generous prix fixe meals are offered; a typical feast might consist of Oregon smoked salmon, soup, spinach and dried apricot salad with balsamic vinegar dressing, pheasant Souvaroff for two, and a delectable dessert. Individual entrées and single dishes prepared for two are also available.

Squaw Valley

From Highway 80, take Highway 89 south to Squaw Valley Road. Turn left and drive two miles to a fork in the road; veer left and then take the first right.

Nestled at the base of jagged peaks, Squaw Valley is one of the High Sierras' most picturesque settings. It is some distance from the sapphire sparkle of Lake Tahoe, but its soaring mountains rival the Swiss Alps in their rugged beauty. A village of hotels, condominiums, and restaurants is tucked away in the valley, along with stables, golf courses, and other recreational facilities. Although this first-class ski resort first gained renown for hosting the 1960 Winter Olympics, sports buffs convene here year-round.

Hotel/Bed and Breakfast Kissing

PLUMPJACK SQUAW VALLEY INN, Squaw Valley
1920 Squaw Valley Road
(916) 583-1576, (800) 323-7666
Moderate to Very Expensive
Minimum stay requirement on weekends and holidays

Originally built for Olympic contestants in 1960, this two-story, wood-shingled lodge is strategically situated at the base of the mountain, next to the gondola and the resort's parking lot. In other words, this is Grand Central Station. Still, if you can ignore the crowds, it's an amiable and very convenient place to stay. The 55 guest rooms feature world-class decor, with queen-size beds covered with thick down linens, blond wood furnishings, and rich color schemes. Though they are slightly more pricey, the five specialty suites have luxurious amenities like Jacuzzi tubs, spacious kitchens, king-size beds, wet bars, big-screen TVs, and separate sitting areas. An outdoor heated pool and hot tubs are nice, but, not surprisingly, often too crowded for comfort … or romance.

SQUAW VALLEY LODGE, Squaw Valley
201 Squaw Peak Road
(916) 583-5500, (800) 922-9970
Moderate to Unbelievably Expensive
Minimum stay requirement on weekends

It was the whirlpool tubs that won us over—two of them, just off the exercise room, with a fireplace in the corner and a view of the snowy peaks outside. Or maybe it was the 100 spacious, contemporary Southwest-style rental condominiums equipped with full kitchens that make possible a late-night cup of cocoa or a no-hassle bathrobe breakfast. Then again, the location, adjacent to some of the best skiing and hiking in the Tahoe area, is a definite plus. If your toes get cold while you're outside, you can simply ski off the mountain and straight to your room.

As if skiing weren't enough exercise already, you can tone up on Nautilus equipment and Lifecycles in the gym, indulge in a sauna, dive into the outdoor heated pool, or melt in the hands of a masseuse. If you have any energy left, celebrate your health together in your room overlooking the mountains.

Romantic Alternative: THE RESORT AT SQUAW CREEK, 400 Squaw Creek Road, (916) 583-6300, (800) 327-3353 (Expensive to Unbelievably Expensive) is the newest and grandest addition to Squaw Valley's expanding village. The dramatic lobby alone is worth a peek, with its wall of cathedral-high windows framing the mountain face. Outside, the resort's own waterfall tumbles down past the skating rink to three whirlpools. A shopping arcade, spa and health center, restaurants, water slide, and plunge pool—every amenity of a modern resort is here. Surprisingly, the 405 guest rooms are merely standard, with a comfortable but comparatively unimaginative hotel feel.

Outdoor Kissing

OLYMPIC ICE PAVILION, Squaw Valley
1960 Squaw Valley Road
(916) 583-6985

$14 for the cable car, $7 skating with skate rental, $19 ($11 after 4 p.m.) for the cable car, skating, and skate rental combined

Look for the cable car building at the base of Squaw Valley Ski Resort. Take the Cable Car aerial tramway to the top of the mountain.

Having frequented Tahoe for many years, we thought we had seen the most magnificent views the area could afford—that is, until we rode the cable car to the Olympic Ice Pavilion. Riding the aerial tramway is an adventure in itself, as you soar above the eagles, over a pinnacle, then high to the zenith of the mountaintop. On the edge of the summit, almost like a gateway to heaven, especially in the rosy light of sunset, the outdoor skating rink overlooks the vast expanse of the valley far below. In the distance, Lake Tahoe winks on the horizon. After a kiss here you'll never be the same.

Romantic Note: Perched on the top of a mountain peak next to the Olympic Ice Pavilion, **THE TERRACE RESTAURANT**, (916) 583-6985, shares the same extraordinary panorama. Despite this magnificent setting and the pleasant ambience of the restaurant, lunch features basic American hamburgers, chili, and sandwiches served cafeteria-style at very reasonable prices. This may be the only cafeteria in the world that inspires kissing. Nearby, **ALEXANDER'S POOLSIDE CAFE AND BAR** looks out over a swimming pool (you can't be shy if you plan to swim here) and the peaks and valleys beyond.

Tahoe City

Like Tahoe Vista, Tahoe City is a bustling community filled with businesses, but fortunately they are a little more spread out. Go to the center of town for provisions and a great dinner, then head to the outskirts for tranquil lodgings.

Hotel/Bed and Breakfast Kissing

THE COTTAGE INN, Tahoe City
1690 West Lake Boulevard
(916) 581-4073, (800) 581-4073
Moderate to Very Expensive
Minimum stay requirement on weekends

You'll feel like pioneers in this little roadside village of rustic cabins by the lakeshore. Far from the glitz of the casinos and the sterility of high-rise hotels, the Cottage Inn embraces nature rather than trying to overwhelm it. Set in a circle, the 15 duplex cabin units are designed for privacy, with their own private entrances. Each cottage is decorated in a rustic theme, ranging from Western-style to alpine. (For the purposes of this book, we recommend the intimate alpine honeymoon suite, which has a natural rock Jacuzzi waterfall.) Each room has the luxury of a gas fireplace and TV with VCR. You can also warm yourself by the fire in the 1938 Pomin House, where wine and home-baked cookies are laid out in the evening and a full breakfast is served in the morning. After a day of hiking, indulge in an evening sauna or stroll to the nearby beach, where you can dig your toes into the cool sand and kiss to the lullaby of Lake Tahoe's quiet, lapping waters.

SUNNYSIDE LODGE, Tahoe City
1850 West Lake Boulevard
(916) 583-7200, (800) 822-2SKI
Inexpensive to Expensive
Minimum stay requirement on weekends

A true mountain lodge of wood and gables, Sunnyside takes full advantage of its perch on Lake Tahoe's forested western shore. In the warmer months, put a blush in your cheeks on its expansive, sun-soaked wooden deck. Boaters can pull up to the dock or, if the water is too low, use the restaurant's buoy shuttle. In winter, a blazing fire crackles in the large river-rock fireplace in the lounge. Sailors and skiers will appreciate the nautical and ski memorabilia that flows throughout the lodge and its pleasant waterfront restaurant (see Restaurant Kissing). Sunnyside's 23 guest rooms are sleek and airy, with high ceilings, modest wall coverings, chests for coffee tables, and boating or skiing prints decorating the walls. All of the rooms are oriented to the sparkling lake view. Some have fireplaces and balconies where you can stand together in the twilight, kiss, and imagine you're on the prow of your private yacht.

Restaurant Kissing

CHRISTY HILL RESTAURANT, Tahoe City
115 Grove Street
(916) 583-8551
Expensive
Dinner Tuesday-Sunday

Make your reservation for before the sun goes down—you don't want to miss a sunset here, even though Christy Hill's dining room is romantic at any time of day. Picture windows allow views of the lake; watercolor paintings accentuate the cushioned booths and tables covered in pink tablecloths. The menu here is the safest bet around. Favorites include the mixed organic greens with fresh peach, crispy pecans, and Gorgonzola cheese with champagne vinaigrette, and the fresh Canadian halibut baked with garlic bread crumbs, served over a sauce of golden tomato, garlic, ginger, sesame, soy, scallion, and fresh basil.

SUNNYSIDE RESTAURANT, Tahoe City
1850 West Lake Boulevard
(916) 583-7200
Moderate
Call for seasonal hours.

Paneled in mahogany, the nautically inspired Chris Craft dining room is so close to the lake that you might think it's floating. Enjoy a piping hot bowl of clam chowder with a seafood dish or grilled entrée, accompanied by a remarkable view of the glistening lake.

Romantic Suggestion: If you're interested in lingering a little bit longer over the view, consider checking out the Sunnyside's guest rooms (see Hotel/Bed and Breakfast Kissing).

WOLFDALE'S RESTAURANT, Tahoe City
640 North Lake Boulevard
(916) 583-5700
Moderate to Expensive
Dinner Wednesday-Monday

The unique cuisine at Wolfdale's is so good, it almost makes up for the lack of lake views. The two dining rooms, separated by shoji screens and punctuated with a collection of provocative modern art, are pleasant. We were especially partial to the first dining room, with its hardwood floors, white tablecloths, and potted flowers at each table. The Monterey salmon with a spicy crust and the grilled Columbia River sturgeon with baked black-eyed peas and a juniper berry vinaigrette are both delicious. Save room for peach kuchen with a lemon-blackberry mousse and berry coulis or autumn apple–mascarpone tart served with fresh cream and ginger-plum sauce.

Outdoor Kissing

MOUNTAIN HIGH BALLOONS
(916) 587-6922, (888) 462-2683
$85 per person for half-hour balloon ride,
$145 per person for an hour balloon ride

The main office is located in the town of Truckee, approximately fourteen miles north of Tahoe City. Call for directions and reservations.

If you're thinking that a hot-air balloon ride sounds like a frivolous, expensive, childish sort of excursion, you're right. If you also think it sounds like an unforgettable experience, you're right again. Both the enormous mass of billowing material overhead and the loud, blistering dragon fire that heats the air filling the balloon are astonishing. Once you're aloft, the wind guides your craft high above treetops and shimmering water, and the world seems more peaceful than you ever thought possible. From this perspective, Lake Tahoe glitters like a diamond and the shore appears to have brilliant emeralds scattered along the water's edge. This is a thoroughly transcendent experience, meant to be shared with someone you love.

Romantic Warning: Be forewarned that the burner that keeps the balloon full of hot air is terribly loud and hot on the top of your head. Don't let this hold you back though: the flame doesn't run constantly. It can just be startling if you aren't expecting it.

WEST SHORE

Homewood

Of the three developed shores of Lake Tahoe, the West Shore remains the most pristine. You won't find big hotels, flashy casinos, or shopping centers in tiny Homewood. What you will find are a few fine establishments set amidst towering pines.

Hotel/Bed and Breakfast Kissing

ROCKWOOD LODGE, Homewood
5295 West Lake Boulevard
(916) 525-5273, (800) 538-2463
Moderate to Expensive; No Credit Cards
Minimum stay requirement on weekends and holidays

You will immediately feel comfortable upon entering this stone "Old Tahoe"–style home, so take off your shoes (required) and relax a while. Honey-colored knotty pine walls, hand-hewn open beam ceilings, and soft cream carpets provide a warm, soothing ambience. If this atmosphere alone doesn't shake the chill off snow-kissed cheeks, then a snuggle by the roaring fire in the living room and some kisses from your beloved should do the trick.

Although the home's knotty pine interior suggests rusticity, the five guest rooms are quite stylish, decorated with antiques and country linens. Cozy down comforters adorn fluffy feather beds, and fresh flowers brighten the mood. Each room has its own private bath and warm, snuggly bathrobes.

Both the Secret Harbor and the Rubicon Bay rooms have excellent views of the lake, as well as tile tubs with dual shower heads. The Zephyr Cove Room surveys peaceful views of the surrounding forest.

An ample full breakfast is served in the backyard beneath tall pines or on the front patio in front of the outdoor stone fireplace, when the weather permits. Otherwise it is served at a large table in the dining room.

Romantic Suggestion: For spectacular views of the glistening lake while rushing down the slopes, try the nearby **HOMEWOOD SKI AREA**, (916) 525-2900.

Restaurant Kissing

SWISS LAKEWOOD RESTAURANT, Homewood
5055 West Lake Boulevard
(916) 525-5211
Moderate to Expensive
Call for seasonal hours.

Old Swiss photographs, cow bells, and other memorabilia fill the walls and corners of Swiss Lakewood's dining room, dominated by the color red. Sound a little garish? We thought so at first, but after we were greeted by a charming international staff and had a scrumptious meal, we decided this place was "tastefully cluttered." Authentic Swiss cuisine graces the menu year-round, but fondue—cheese or beef—is the specialty during winter. Feeding this tasty treat to each other is a fun way to warm hungry stomachs and playful hearts.

Outdoor Kissing

D.L. BLISS PARK
Highway 89

From Highway 89 south, follow signs to the park. It will be on your right, between Emerald Bay and Meeks Bay.

Bliss is a fitting name for this park which hugs the shore of brilliant Lake Tahoe, where the sand is visible through transparent water. Snowcapped Sierra peaks ascend in the distance. The best place to kiss in all of Tahoe is located here at **RUBICON POINT**, a quarter-mile hike from the last accessible parking lot. Views of the lake grow more magnificent at every turn as you traverse a well-worn path that weaves along the shore and winds higher and higher into the rock cliffs above. Though Rubicon Point is not well marked, you'll know when you've arrived—the already gorgeous view becomes almost spellbinding. Pine trees give way to a panoramic view of the lake, mountains, and neighboring inlet. Waves lap gently at the rocky shore below, and the sound of chattering birds and wind rustling in the trees provides background music for a long kiss.

SOUTH SHORE

South Lake Tahoe

If you want to elope, South Lake Tahoe is the place for you—as long as you don't mind pledging "I do" in a roadside chapel, surrounded by an endless sea of neon lights and casinos. Tahoe's south shore sits astride the California and Nevada state borders and is known for its economy hotels, gambling casinos, and wedding chapels. "No thanks," you say? Don't worry—there's something here for nature enthusiasts too. South Lake Tahoe's **HEAVENLY SKI RESORT**, (702) 586-7000, is America's largest, encompassing 20 square miles of terrain and dazzling panoramic views of Lake Tahoe.

Hotel/Bed and Breakfast Kissing

CHRISTIANIA INN, South Lake Tahoe
3819 Saddle Road
(916) 544-7337
http://www.christianiainn.com
Very Inexpensive to Expensive
Minimum stay requirement on weekends

Tucked beneath pine trees at the base of Heavenly Ski Resort, Christiania Inn is reminiscent of a European youth hostel. You can literally ski from the slopes (across the street) right to the door of this cozy lodge. Six guest rooms await, ranging from simple bedrooms to full two-story suites, all appointed with a blend of contemporary and antique furnishings. You can warm your toes together in front of a fireplace in four of the suites, enjoy a dry sauna in Suites 5 and 6 (Suite 6 also has a jetted bathtub), or share a steam bath in Suite 3. Suite 4 features a loft that overlooks the ski runs at Heavenly, which is just the word for the view. Revive your spirits after a day on the slopes with complimentary brandy provided in each room; in the morning, enjoy a complimentary continental breakfast served in the privacy of your own room.

Romantic Suggestion: You won't have to go far for dinner. We highly recommend Christiania Inn's fireside restaurant for a romantic repast (see Restaurant Kissing).

EMBASSY SUITES, South Lake Tahoe
4130 Lake Tahoe Boulevard
(916) 544-5400, (800) EMBASSY
http://www.embassy-suites.com
Moderate to Expensive
Recommended Wedding Site

Situated yards away from the Nevada state line, this recently built high-rise hotel surveys neon casino country. If casinos aren't your thing, neither is this hotel—its flashy neighbors are hard to ignore. On the other hand, if you're in the mood to try your luck at the slot machines, the Embassy Suites is the best (and most tasteful) option in the nearby area.

The Bavarian-motif hotel features a series of three soaring nine-story-tall atriums. In the first, water splashes over a paddle wheel and down a flume to a decorative pool surrounded by lush greenery. Umbrella-crowned cafe tables fill the patios of the other atriums, where complimentary breakfast and afternoon cocktails and hors d'oeuvres are served. A glass elevator lifts you to the 396 hotel-style two-room suites, the kind Embassy Suites is known for, set high above the city.

LAKELAND VILLAGE BEACH
AND SKI RESORT, South Lake Tahoe
3535 Highway 50
(916) 544-1685, (800) 822-5969
Moderate to Unbelievably Expensive
Minimum stay requirement on weekends

Recommending individually owned and decorated condominiums is tricky business because of their random design and care. Lakeland Village's 212 rental units are no exception: they run the gamut from shabby to luxurious, depending on your luck (and how much you're willing to pay). This sizable condominium complex is sandwiched between a busy highway and a sandy beach, so the closer your accommodations are to the water, the better. Most of Lakeland's units are unimpressive, although we can't resist mentioning the gorgeous lakeside condominiums, appointed with modern furnishings and enclosed in glass, showcasing views of tranquil Lake Tahoe. The price is steep, but the view is worth every penny.

TAHOE SEASONS RESORT, South Lake Tahoe
3901 Saddle Road, at Keller Road
(916) 541-6700, (800) 540-4874
Moderate to Very Expensive
Minimum stay requirement on weekends

Sheltered by woods and situated across the street from Heavenly Ski Resort, this modern resort has a knack for pleasing everybody: the nearby casinos are nowhere in sight, but only minutes away. Sleek in design, each of the 182 sumptuous mini-suites feature a beautifully appointed living room and bedroom, separated by an oversized whirlpool that is enclosed by shoji screens. A gas fire flickers in the hearth of nearly every room, while microwaves and refrigerators make inventive midnight snacks a romantic possibility. Request one of the newly renovated rooms when making your reservation; they are pleasantly decorated with contemporary furnishings accented by teal and mauve fabrics and wall coverings.

TAMARACK VACATION RENTALS, South Lake Tahoe
(916) 541-2595, (800) 854-2827
Inexpensive to Unbelievably Expensive

Country chalets, waterfront cabins, pioneer homes, mountainside condominiums ... take your pick—Tamarack Rentals really has them all. When making your reservation, be sure to specify your desired location, type of accommodation, and price range. If you're willing to get specific, Tamarack is sure to set you up with just what you're looking for.

Restaurant Kissing

CAFE FIORE, South Lake Tahoe
1169 Ski Run Boulevard, No. 5
(916) 541-2908
Moderate to Expensive
Dinner Daily

You don't have to worry about distractions at Cafe Fiori—there are only seven tables! It doesn't get more intimate than this. Candles glimmer at each of the windowside tables arranged in the cozy wood-paneled dining room. In the summer, tables are set up outside. Wherever you sit, be adventurous: the Italian menu features items such as blackened alligator fillet served with drawn garlic butter, among other unusual selections. Desserts are out-of-this-world, especially the homemade white chocolate ice cream, so deliciously thick it's hard to swallow. We were tempted to spend an extra day in South Lake Tahoe just to come back here. In summer tables are set up outside.

Romantic Alternative: Because Cafe Fiori has so few tables, reservations are hard to come by. Luckily, **NEPHELES**, 1169 Ski Run Boulevard, (916) 544-8130 (Moderate) is located next door and, though not as intimate as Fiori's, it has a romantic appeal of its own. A large stained glass window depicting a smiling sun sets the mood for tasty, creative California cuisine and adds a rustic touch to the otherwise Victorian-style dining rooms.

CHRISTIANIA INN RESTAURANT, South Lake Tahoe
3819 Saddle Road, at the Christiana Inn
(916) 544-7337
http://www.christianiainn.com
Very Inexpensive to Expensive
Dinner Daily

Low-slung couches invite you to relax in the sunken sitting area of the lounge in this old alpine-style inn, where a fire flickers in a brick hearth framed by boulders and antique skis. It's the perfect place to linger over a warm drink and chase away the cool of the evening before or after dinner. Lace curtains, beams decorated with tiny white lights, and intimate booths set the scene for heartwarming dishes such as lobster Napoleon, tender medallions of Maine lobster baked with a basil-and-lobster mousse, served between two layers of pastry with a chardonnay sauce. Or try the grilled beef tenderloin served with a roasted shallot demi-glace and a fresh artichoke sour cream. You'll have no trouble finding the right wine to go with your meal; the wine list offers more than 200 choices. For a romantic finale, share a dessert for two. We highly recommend the bananas flambé, cherries jubilee, or baked Alaska, all flamed tableside.

EVAN'S AMERICAN
GOURMET CAFE, South Lake Tahoe
536 Emerald Bay Road
(916) 542-1990
Moderate to Expensive
Dinner Monday–Saturday

The food at Evan's was so divine, it's hard for us to remember anything but the flavor of our grilled sea scallops tossed with sautéed spinach, fresh grated tomatoes, capers, and Greek olives, swimming in parsley brown butter. Normally we're eager to share our entrées, but not this time—we wanted to savor every last bite of this impeccably delicious meal. Not that the surroundings weren't lovely—they were. Floral window coverings, lovely watercolors, and fresh flowers at every table infuse the crisp cafe with color. But the food … simply unforgettable.

MONUMENT PEAK RESTAURANT, South Lake Tahoe
Heavenly Valley Ski Resort, at Top Of The Tram
(916) 542-5222
Moderate; $10.50 per person for tram
Call for seasonal hours.

It's no surprise that Mark Twain called the view from here "the fairest picture the whole earth affords." Witness the splendor with your own eyes from a large tram that climbs to a soaring 2,000 feet above Lake Tahoe. Once on top, forgo the cafeteria, which is perfect for heavy-booted skiers, and head to the Monument Peak Restaurant, which is a bit too posh for skiers. Linen cloths and fresh flowers add a touch of elegance to the three-tiered dining room, but the real draw is the wall of windows framing a heavenly view of crystal blue Lake Tahoe enfolded by jagged, often snowcapped, mountain peaks. If you come for dinner in the summer, be sure to arrive before sunset. The menu features standard American fare like steak, chicken, and shrimp scampi, which is usually quite good, but not nearly as impressive as the views. Though food prices are reasonable, keep in mind that the tram alone is $10.50.

Outdoor Kissing

BORGES CARRIAGE & SLEIGH RIDES, South Lake Tahoe
Lake Parkway and Highway 50
(702) 588-2953, (800) 726-RIDE
$15 per adult

Call ahead for reservations and directions.

"Dashing through the snow, in a one-horse open sleigh" are more than familiar words of a Christmas carol to the Borges family. They offer rides on a selection of sleighs, from six- to 20-passenger rigs pulled by two Belgian draft horses to two-person, one-horse cutters. It's wonderful to skim through a snowy meadow overlooking the sapphire lake. Plus, an intriguing history lesson gives you a new perspective on glitzy South Lake Tahoe.

Stateline, Nevada

Restaurant Kissing

THE SUMMIT RESTAURANT, Stateline
16th floor of Harrah's Hotel and Casino
(702) 588-6611, (800) HARRAHS
Very Expensive
Dinner Daily

A romantic restaurant in Harrah's? Are we kidding? (We thought the joke was on us when somebody first recommended the Summit for this book.) Luckily, this is not a joke. You would never guess this restaurant is situated on an upper floor of one of Nevada's best-known casinos; the lofty setting once served as Harrah's Star Suite, the secluded aerie reserved for visiting royalty and Hollywood VIPs.

A fire blazes in the hearth and candles flicker in a candelabra on the ebony piano, where a tuxedo-clad virtuoso plays. Each dining area is intimate and romantically lit, whether you sit by the fire or climb the stairs to a mezzanine with a smoked glass balustrade. Windowside tables look out at the city lights and the velvet expanse of Lake Tahoe far below. The cuisine is as heavenly as the ambience. Feast on appetizers like pumpkin fettuccine with Gorgonzola cream or smoked salmon cheesecake with lemon aioli; salads so beautiful they could double as centerpieces; and live Maine lobster thermidor or salmon with basil, ricotta cheese, and sun-dried tomatoes in phyllo. The Summit is a touch of heaven—possibly the only touch this side of the state border.

Gold Country

Highway 49 travels directly through most of the Gold Country towns. From San Francisco, take Interstate 80 east toward Sacramento. From Sacramento, continue on Interstate 80 to intersect with Highway 49 in Auburn, or take Interstate 50 to Highway 49 in Placerville.

When news spread in 1848 that gold had been discovered in the Sierra Nevada foothills, people from all walks of life rushed toward the promised land of California. Determined to find riches, this sudden flood of settlers made the Gold Country a ruthless, gun-toting region. Finding the mother lode was a prime objective, and the end, for many, often justified the means. Although many travelers still think of California as a desirable destination for the pursuit of fame and riches, gold fever is a thing of the past. However, the Sierras' Western heritage still reigns, and serious romancing can be your main objective today.

At the height of the gold rush, little Nevada City, at the northern tip of Gold Country, was as populous as Sacramento is today, and towns like Auburn, Coloma, Sutter Creek, Jackson, and Jamestown bustled with activity, tucked amidst rolling golden hills and valleys. As the gold supply began to dwindle, settlers deserted the area just as quickly as they had rushed in. Many of the original buildings remain, creating a ghost-town feeling in some of these now-quiet small towns. History buffs will want to stop and read the countless historical markers that dot the highway, and, who knows, you might even strike it rich … in the memories you bring home together.

Romantic Warning: Highway 49, which runs directly through most of the Gold Country towns, is a surprisingly busy two-lane road. Expect driving to be a hassle on weekends, especially in the summer. Also, unless the place you stay has soundproof windows or is far from the highway, it is hard to escape traffic noise.

Sacramento

Despite the fact that it is a four-county metropolis and one of the ten fastest-growing regions in the United States, the capital of the Golden State exudes an amiable, small-town charm. Year-round sunshine graces Sacramento's wide streets, which are lined with tall shade trees and renovated turn-of-the-century homes. Coffeehouses, antique stores, stylish restaurants, and a handful of elegant Victorian bed and breakfasts enrich Sacramento's friendly allure. But although Sacramento may *feel* like a small town, keep in mind that it is not. Traffic noise is a near constant, but you probably won't even notice—you'll be too busy kissing.

Hotel/Bed and Breakfast Kissing

AMBER HOUSE, Sacramento
1315 22nd Street
(916) 444-8085, (800) 755-6526
http://www.amberhouse.com
Moderate to Very Expensive

Poets and artists inspired the decor at Amber House, and now it's your turn to be inspired. Set on a quiet residential street in downtown Sacramento, two early-20th-century homes called the Poet's Refuge and the Artist's Retreat house nine guest rooms. Massive exposed beams, a dark brick hearth, and hardwood floors in the Poet's Refuge parlor are the perfect counterpoint to the parlor in the newer Artist's Retreat, which boasts rose walls, a white hearth, and overstuffed floral sofa.

Eight of the nine guest rooms have Jacuzzi tubs, and all are wonderfully elegant and romantic. In the Poet's quarters, we were especially taken with the Lord Byron Room, with its wrought-iron canopy bed draped with floral linens and white fabric, not to mention the circular two-person Jacuzzi tub in the sensuous marble bathroom. Surrounding windows fill the airy Emily Dickinson Room with sunlight, and the romantic mood is enhanced by a double-sided fireplace that faces the bedroom on one side and a double Jacuzzi tub in the bathroom on the other.

Bright colors give the accommodations in the neighboring Artist's Retreat a cheerful disposition. A stunning, bright yellow bedroom opens to a solarium bathroom with a double Jacuzzi tub and a glass-enclosed shower in the lovely Van Gogh Room. Rose-patterned linens drape a king-size wrought iron canopy in the Renoir Room, which also has a double whirlpool. All of the rooms in this building feature reproductions of masterpieces by the respective artists after whom they're named.

A full, delicious breakfast is served at one large table in the elegant dining room in the Poet's Refuge, or, when the weather permits, out on the semiquiet front porch. Don't worry if you have trouble resisting temptation and overeat: bicycles are on hand so you can burn off the extra calories as you pedal through Sacramento's lovely old-fashioned neighborhoods.

AUNT ABIGAIL'S, Sacramento
2120 G Street
(916) 441-5007, (800) 858-1568
Moderate to Very Inexpensive

Guests are taken back in time and embraced by old-world elegance in the grand foyer of this 1912 Colonial Revival mansion, nestled in a busy residential neighborhood. A fire crackles in the antique-filled parlor, and the hardwood floors are accented with Oriental rugs. You may want to spend the evening tucked away in your room sipping herb tea and nibbling on scrumptious home-baked cookies (available at all hours) or, better yet, soaking in the whirlpool set outside in the slightly overgrown garden.

A stay in the Solarium, surrounded by windows on three sides, is almost like sleeping in a tree house, only much more comfortable, with a canopied feather bed appointed with scintillating white fabric and a private door that leads to a private deck. Thick robes make the trek to the bathroom just down the hall feel like less of an inconvenience. (This is the only room with a detached bath.) Margaret's Room is lovely, with soft tones, an immense vanity with a hand-painted sink, and a claw-foot tub. Green vines and sheer white fabric entwine around the top of a wrought-iron canopy bed covered with an old-fashioned wedding ring quilt. Uncle Albert's Room is decidedly more stalwart, with maroon and gray paisleys and stripes.

In the morning, guests head to the sunny dining room and sit at one table to enjoy a hearty breakfast that may include warm applesauce, vegetable and cheese strata, fresh fruit, cinnamon muffins, and an assortment of teas and coffee. On the third Sunday of each month, Aunt Abigail's invites guests and nonguests to afternoon tea, which costs $15 per person.

HARTLEY HOUSE INN, Sacramento
700 22nd Street
(916) 447-7829, (800) 831-5806
http://www.hartleyhouse.com
Moderate to Expensive

A certain straightforward simplicity dominates this smaller turn-of-the-century Italianate Victorian, situated on a corner in a busy residential neighborhood. Hartley House's dark-stained woodwork, hardwood floors, distinctive Oriental carpets, leaded and stained glass windows, and the stately ticktocking of its old clocks will appeal to many guests as a fresh alternative to the frilly accoutrements of other bed and breakfasts. Although Hartley House caters to executives during the week, weekends are prime time for romantic getaways. Five small guest rooms are handsomely outfitted with lush feather beds, antique wardrobes, claw-foot and antique tubs, and dusky paisley bedcoverings. Brighton is the brightest room in the inn: daylight streams in through a dozen lace-trimmed windows in this former sunporch. In the morning, a full breakfast of stuffed French toast or blueberry-raspberry pancakes is served in the dining room at private two-person tables.

STERLING HOTEL, Sacramento
1300 H Street
(916) 448-1300, (800) 365-6770
Moderate to Expensive

Don't let the word "hotel" mislead you. This baronial Victorian set in the heart of downtown Sacramento has the personality of a bed and breakfast—without the breakfast. (Actually, breakfast in bed *is* available via room service; it's just not included with your stay.) Because of its location and amenities, business executives flock here on weekdays, but on weekends the Sterling caters primarily to couples in search of relaxation. Simple yet sophisticated, the common area's contemporary decor is accented by black marble fireplaces, Oriental carpets, and a recently added refreshment bar. Each of the 16 handsome though sparsely appointed guest rooms has a marble-tiled double Jacuzzi tub (several of which are architectural wonders), intriguing artwork, fireplaces, and a four-poster or canopy bed with floral linens.

VIZCAYA, Sacramento
2019 21st Street
(916) 455-5243, (800) 456-2019
Inexpensive to Very Expensive
Recommended Wedding Site

Still one of the capital's more formal inns, the two stately Colonial Revival structures that comprise Vizcaya crown a grassy knoll in the heart of downtown. The inn's spacious parlor is furnished with turn-of-the-century antiques and an elegant grand piano. Amenities in four of the nine guest rooms include marble-tiled fireplaces, and five rooms feature Jacuzzi tubs. Maintenance of the rooms seems to be slipping, however, and the eclectic combination of modern and antique furnishings in many rooms seems out of place in such elegant surroundings. The three Carriage House rooms in back are preferable because they are farthest from the adjacent busy street, but unfortunately these are the rooms with the most carpet stains and smoke damage on the walls and ceiling.

Weddings are the specialty at Vizcaya, but unless the rooms are given some immediate attention, that will be the only reason to come and kiss here. Many couples do exchange vows here, and Vizcaya has perfected the art of producing wedding ceremonies with all of the frills. We hope that the management will spend some time, energy, and money upgrading the rooms so newlyweds aren't disappointed with the overnight accommodations.

Restaurant Kissing

CHANTERELLE, Sacramento
1300 H Street, at the Sterling Hotel
(916) 448-1300, (800) 365-7660
Moderate to Expensive
Lunch Monday-Friday; Dinner Daily; Sunday Brunch

Set in the heart of downtown Sacramento in the popular Sterling Hotel, Chanterelle is housed in a daylight basement fronted by a brick terrace appointed with patio furniture. Sunlight sifts through its leaded glass windows and streams into two separate dining rooms adorned with provocative modern paintings. A single tall candle flickers at every white-clothed table, infusing the otherwise subdued atmosphere with warmth. Dishes such as a smoked salmon salad topped with goat cheese croutons, or the seafood lasagne with shrimp, scallops, and lobster, are sure to satisfy. Finish in style with a slice of chocolate decadence cake resting on a bed of raspberry sauce.

CITY TREASURE RESTAURANT, Sacramento
1730 L Street
(916) 447-7380
Moderate to Expensive
Lunch Monday-Friday; Dinner Daily; Sunday Brunch

We can't think of a better name for this newly opened urban jewel, tucked in a side street in the heart of Sacramento. Floor-to-ceiling windows look out to a small outdoor terrace and the street beyond. Triangular lamps suspended from exposed ceiling pipes give the small dining room a modern flair, although exotic flower arrangements, miniature white lights, and watercolor paintings soften the effect. The closely arranged brass-topped tables are all adorned with a single fresh flower and a flickering candle. Casual but elegant, in typical California fashion, City Treasure features a large, enticing menu. From angel hair pasta with eggplant to cioppino chock-full of every imaginable fruit of the sea, you're in for a treat. Desserts here tend toward the unusual; the colorfully decorated cheesecake we sampled was covered with candy sprinkles and unlike anything we've ever seen *or* tasted before.

Romantic Alternative: BIBA, 2801 Capitol Avenue, (916) 455-BIBA (Moderate to Expensive) serves lunch on weekdays and dinner Monday through Saturday, and is another romantic dining possibility in downtown Sacramento. Reservations are a must at this extremely busy art deco Italian eatery highlighted by square white pillars, arched windows, surrounding mirrors, and modern artwork. Fresh flowers add a dash of color to this animated atmosphere, where cozy linen-draped tables are much too close together. Among the pasta specialties are spinach lasagne, filled with meat, tomatoes, and béchamel sauce, and penne with smoked salmon and red onion in a light cream sauce. Service is pleasant, but, due to the restaurant's popularity, can be a little too slow.

Outdoor Kissing

ADVENTURE LIMOUSINE SERVICE
(916) 878-8212
From $325 per day
Call for information about pickup and drop-off details.

Although we never recommend splurging capriciously, we would be remiss if we didn't tell you how much fun it can be to tour the Gold Country wineries in the backseat of your own private limo. Your driver will take you almost anywhere your heart, or your sweetheart, desires. Your itinerary can begin with a continental breakfast en route to a stop at the **SOBON** and **SHENANDOAH WINERIES** to check out their tours, tastings, and on-site museums (see Outdoor Kissing in Shenandoah Valley for recommended wineries.) Continue your tour through the heart of Gold Country by exploring the historic and picturesque towns of Amador City, Sutter Creek, Jackson, and Ione. Return home via antique stores, photo shops, or more wineries, and share one last chauffeur-driven kiss.

Romantic Note: Adventure Limousine also will arrange tours of the Napa Valley's wineries, including lunch for two at one of the valley's fine restaurants.

Old Sacramento

The restored Western-style facades lining Old Sacramento's narrow streets are just authentic enough to make you feel as though you've stepped into a John Wayne movie. Unfortunately, this is as nostalgic as it gets (and if you're not a John Wayne fan, you might be less than amused). The drone of neighboring highways tarnishes the cowboy character of this little village, and the horse-drawn buggies seem sadly out of place. Nevertheless, you can browse in quaint boutiques (more than 100 shops and restaurants line the busy blocks), stroll along the placid Sacramento River, indulge in old-fashioned chocolate fudge, or investigate the **WELLS FARGO MUSEUM** in the B.F. Hastings Building, Second and Jay Streets, (916) 440-4263, where you can sit across the room from each other and telegraph endearments to your partner.

Restaurant Kissing

THE DELTA KING, Old Sacramento
1000 Front Street
(916) 444-KING, (800) 825-KING
Moderate to Expensive
Lunch and Dinner Daily; Sunday Brunch
Recommended Wedding Site

Take a dockside voyage into the past on a restored stern-wheel paddleboat, the kind so often connected with the Mississippi. The *Delta King* plied the river between Sacramento and San Francisco from 1927 to 1940. It was a floating pleasure palace for flappers when Prohibition outlawed drinking in landlocked lounges. Today, it looks much the same inside as it did in its heyday. A broad staircase sweeps up to the refined saloon, aglow with lovingly rubbed mahogany and teak, where two-person tables are arranged beneath windows that overlook the river's swirling waters on one side and the vintage Western-style facades of Old Sacramento on the other. An oak-paneled restaurant on the lower floor is similar in appearance, brimming with small tables covered with white linens and illuminated by softly lit wall sconces. Because of the river views and vintage setting, the restaurant rates high on romantic ambience; unfortunately, the cuisine is noted for its mediocrity.

THE FIREHOUSE, Old Sacramento
1112 Second Street
(916) 442-4772
http://fireno3.aol
Moderate to Expensive
Lunch Monday-Friday; Dinner Tuesday-Saturday

Venture into the Firehouse and you will feel like gold miners who have finally struck it rich. This unexpected find is well hidden among the store-fronts of Old Sacramento. In spite of its name, the Firehouse revels in its gold-rush history both subtly and graciously. Unusually high cathedral ceilings offset by beautiful red brick walls and a wrought-iron spiral staircase winding down through the lobby are the only visible traces of the restaurant's past as an actual firehouse. Teardrop chandeliers illuminate a handful of tables, massive floral arrangements are set around the dining room, and over-sized oil paintings with elaborate gold frames adorn the walls, lending a European air.

The quaint European feel continues in the brick courtyard, where large trees provide ample shade to wrought-iron tables and chairs. This is a thoroughly engaging lunch spot, but tiny white lights set the trees aglow after dark. Day or night, a burbling fountain drowns out any street noise that might otherwise be an annoyance. Service is good, and the menu offers a variety of classic American dishes, such as New York steak and roasted duck breast. A starter of asparagus and wild mushroom risotto with fresh basil and Reggiano cheese provides the luscious beginning of an exquisite dining experience, culminating in a selection of ambrosial desserts. Savor the food and the atmosphere—it's not every day you strike gold.

Lodi

The trick to finding Lodi and having a nice outing along the way is to enter from the west side of town via Turner Road, so you drive past farmland and acres of vineyards before hitting the main part of town. Lodi is a rich agricultural area, not a tourist town or a romantic destination. However, one establishment there specializes in matters of the heart. If you're headed to **WINE AND ROSES COUNTRY INN** (see Hotel/Bed and Breakfast Kissing), you won't be disappointed.

Hotel/Bed and Breakfast Kissing

WINE AND ROSES COUNTRY INN, Lodi
2505 West Turner Road
(209) 334-6988
Moderate to Expensive
Lunch Tuesday-Friday; Dinner Wednesday-Saturday; Sunday Brunch
Recommended Wedding Site

The name of this five-acre country estate is well-suited, but falls short in its description. The grounds are replete with flowers of every imaginable color and kind: azaleas, impatiens, violets, daisies, and, of course, roses. Flowers are not the only thing blossoming here. Diamond engagement rings are frequently presented over filet mignon or rosemary lamb chops in the intimate pink dining room warmed by a fireplace. Proposals are a specialty at Wine and Roses Country Inn, as are the garden weddings that follow.

The Victorian farmhouse inn has been beautifully renovated and radiates a fresh country charm in all ten guest rooms. Moonlight and Roses is one of the more romantic rooms, with deep burgundy carpet, a white brass bed, a sitting area surrounded by windows, and a claw-foot tub. White Lace and Promises is a lovely two-room honeymoon attic suite exulting in garden views from its own private terrace. The televisions in each room, a necessity for the midweek business clientele, can be removed on request so as not to distract you from more affectionate activities.

Romantic Warning: Heavily trafficked West Turner Road runs adjacent to the inn. Although Wine and Roses is wonderfully sheltered by tall trees that hide views of the road, the whiz of cars during rush hour invades the otherwise tranquil country setting.

Nevada City

You might expect a place named Nevada City to be full of flashing lights, casinos, nondescript motels, and oversized hotels, but instead, it is one of the most picturesque towns in Gold Country, abounding with quality accommodations. Nevada City has been compared to a rural New England community, and on crisp fall afternoons, after the leaves have turned myriad shades of red, orange, gold, and purple (yes, purple!), you'll see why. Many of the area's earliest settlers were from New England, and some brought along their favorite trees as they journeyed west more than a hundred years ago.

Romantic Suggestion: Give yourselves at least a day to behold the grand display of fall colors, then visit the shops and restaurants of the downtown streets. The annual blaze of autumn glory usually begins early in October and lasts about six weeks. For more information and a walking map of the town, contact the **NEVADA CITY CHAMBER OF COMMERCE**, (916) 265-2692, (800) 655-NJOY.

Hotel/Bed and Breakfast Kissing

DEER CREEK INN, Nevada City
116 Nevada Street
(916) 265-0363, (800) 655-0363
Inexpensive to Expensive
Minimum stay requirement on weekends
Recommended Wedding Site

Countless establishments are named after lakes or rivers, even if they are not remotely near the picturesque site, but Deer Creek Inn is another story. This venerable blue Queen Anne Victorian is beautifully placed at the edge of Deer Creek, just as the name implies. A grassy front yard dotted with lawn furniture and hammocks for lounging is all that separates the house from the rushing stream.

The five rooms all feature private marble baths, canopied or four-poster beds, down comforters, private verandas, air-conditioning, and antique furnishings. Elaine's Room has been dubbed the honeymoon suite because of its private entrance, wrought-iron canopied bed, garden patio facing the grassy yard and creek, and Roman tub and shower for two. Winifred's Room, dressed in violets, is also extremely popular with romantics who like the claw-foot tub at the foot of the bed and the excellent creek view from the patio. Each room is decorated differently, but comfortable elegance is a constant.

Wine and appetizers are served by the creek each summer afternoon, and the hospitable innkeeper's fresh baked goods will keep your sweet tooth satisfied. A delicious full breakfast that may include orange-pecan French toast, warm banana bread, and fresh fruit salad is served on the deck overlooking the creek, or by candlelight in the formal dining room on cooler mornings.

DOWNEY HOUSE, Nevada City
517 West Broad Street
(916) 265-2815, (800) 258-2815
Inexpensive to Moderate
Minimum stay requirement on weekends seasonally

Downey House is living proof that you should never judge a book by its cover. From the outside, this elegant, cream-colored Eastlake Victorian oozes opulence and refinement. Any passerby would assume that this is a frilly, antique-filled bed and breakfast. Inside, though, the innkeepers have taken a totally different approach to decorating. Contemporary pastels and Southwest accents fill this historic home. Although the style seems a bit out of place at first, it is a refreshing change of pace from Victorian decor that starts to look the same after a while. Each of the six soundproofed guest rooms is wonderfully comfortable, with down comforters, central air-conditioning, and private baths. Two rooms have only full-size beds, but the others are queen-size. Small aquariums placed on every bedside table are unusual, but nice.

Breakfast is casually served buffet-style in the main-floor parlor (the only room with antiques). After filling up your plates, you may want to take them to the garden-trimmed backyard or head up to the sunny second-floor sitting area, where white wicker chairs are placed beside expansive windows that overlook the town and treetops below.

EMMA NEVADA HOUSE, Nevada City
528 East Broad Street
(916) 265-4415, (800) 916-EMMA
Moderate to Expensive
Minimum stay requirement seasonally
Recommended Wedding Site

Built in 1856, this picturesque beige Victorian set in the heart of charming downtown Nevada City was home to 19th-century opera singer Emma Nevada. Today, impressive renovations have made her home one of the more appealing historic properties to stay in when visiting Gold Country. Red roses hem the white picket fence that encloses this architectural beauty. Inside, tall ceilings and generous windows give the home an unusually spacious feeling.

Of the six guest rooms, we preferred the three on the main floor, with their higher ceilings and added space. In Nightingale's Bower, luxurious Italian bedding drapes a queen-size bed and bay windows look out to the front veranda. (If you've got serious romancing in mind, we recommend shutting the drapes for privacy.) An oval Jacuzzi tub is the highlight of the small bathroom. Red velvet chairs and a beautifully restored armoire are elegant and bring to life the historic sense of the home.

Touted as the honeymoon suite, the Empress's Chamber features a hand-carved queen-size bed covered with pristine white linens; a Jacuzzi tub for two awaits in the lovely bathroom. The Mignon Boudoir, also on the main floor, has a decidedly French country feeling, with floral linens, hardwood floors, and a pretty bathroom with a claw-foot tub. The remaining three bedrooms, tucked upstairs under the gables, are slightly smaller. Though they are snug, plush down comforters and private baths with claw-foot tubs make them comfortable places to stay.

With its peaked cathedral ceiling and circular wall of windows, the airy sunroom is a delightful place for a filling breakfast of Belgian waffles, onion-caraway quiche, and sometimes a fruit cobbler. You can also enjoy the year-round sunshine on the adjacent veranda, which overlooks trees and a burbling creek. After breakfast, follow the stairs down to the secluded creekside, where the owners have placed secluded benches with one purpose in mind: kissing, of course.

GRANDMERE'S, Nevada City
449 Broad Street
(916) 265-4660
Moderate to Expensive
http://www.virtualcities.com
Minimum stay requirement on weekends and holidays seasonally
Recommended Wedding Site

Grandmere's has been called the grand dame of local bed and breakfasts, and rightly so. A wrought-iron fence encloses this stately white Colonial and its expansive, beautifully landscaped, flower-filled grounds dotted with park benches. Daylight fills the comfortable parlor, which is appointed with a cozy cushioned window seat and a mixture of modern and antique furnishings. The seven commodious guest rooms here have been beautifully decorated with simple but endearing country-style furnishings, including antique pine pieces, hand-worked patchwork quilts, and baskets. Dawn's Room has a private sunporch; Gertie's Room has a private garden entrance and an oversized tub. A private porch entrance leads to the Master Suite, which is worth every penny of its higher rate. The large room features hardwood floors, a beautiful four-poster king-size bed covered with white linens, delightful country knickknacks on a bookshelf in the corner, and French doors that open into a room filled with antique dolls. A claw-foot tub awaits in the pretty, countrified private bath.

A full country breakfast is served in the dining room, but we suggest that you take your trays to a secluded spot in the Victorian garden, a wonderful place to spend some affectionate time together planning the rest of the day.

RED CASTLE INN HISTORIC LODGINGS, Nevada City
109 Prospect Street
(916) 265-5135, (800) 761-4766
http://www.virtualcities.com
Moderate to Expensive
Minimum stay requirement on weekends seasonally

Tucked into a forested hillside above Nevada City, this imposing four-story brick mansion with wraparound verandas and intricate white trim seems oddly out of place. Maybe that's because it is one of only two genuine Gothic Revival brick houses on the West Coast, so it is not something you see every day. Lace curtains, rich colors, and elegant chandeliers set the mood as you enter the tall front door. Of the eight guest rooms, the more spacious ones on the entry level and top floor are recommended. All three entry-level rooms have queen-size beds, private in-suite baths, and high ceilings. Vintage antiques and wallpapers, chandeliers, French doors, and four-poster or canopied beds provide Victorian charm at every turn. On the top floor, the two-bedroom Garret Suite is designed for four people, but it is also great for just one couple seeking seclusion. A private little veranda affords an incredible view of the town below through the treetops, and a comfortable antique-filled sitting area separates the two bedrooms. The only drawback of this fourth-floor suite (besides having to carry your luggage up the steep stairs) is that the sleigh beds in each room are just double-size, and the detached bathroom, though reserved only for this suite, is down a short flight of stairs.

As for the other rooms, the middle level was originally built as the children's floor, so the ceiling is only seven feet high. The ground-level Forest View Room is commonly called the most romantic because of its private entrance, secluded setting, and massive canopied mahogany bed, but we did not care for the closet-turned-bathroom setup where the toilet and shower share the share the same space. While we understand that the historic integrity of the house could not be marred, this has to be the strangest renovation we have seen.

A generous full breakfast is served buffet-style on the main floor, but you are welcome to savor it privately in your room or on the veranda, or to find a secluded spot near a fountain. With half an acre of lovely terraced gardens here, finding an intimate site shouldn't be difficult.

Romantic Suggestion: On this hillside, you are far enough away to escape the rush of busy little Nevada City. But if you are in the mood to explore the town or simply want to enjoy an afternoon stroll together, a winding pathway leads through trees and greenery to the town below. It is only about a five-minute walk, and since the path is well lit at night you may even want to walk to dinner.

Restaurant Kissing

THE COUNTRY ROSE CAFE, Nevada City
300 Commercial Street
(916) 265-6248
Moderate to Expensive
Breakfast, Lunch, and Dinner Daily

Historic brick buildings abound in these little gold-rush towns, and one of them houses the very charming Country Rose Cafe. High ceilings, exposed brick walls, floral table linens, and carved oak chairs create a casual, countrified setting; high-backed booths along one wall provide a small amount of privacy. On a summer day, try to secure a table on the shady deck. Lunch consists of soups, sandwiches, and salads, while dinner offers a hearty variety of pasta, seafood, chicken, and beef dishes. Service is friendly but rushed at times due to the cafe's popularity.

KIRBY'S CREEKSIDE RESTAURANT
AND BAR, Nevada City
101 Broad Street
(916) 265-3445
Moderate
Lunch Monday-Saturday; Dinner Daily; Sunday Brunch

As you pass the bar area and check out the posters lining the stairwell that leads down to Kirby's, it becomes clear that this is a very casual establishment. The clamorous staff confirms this assumption. When you sit down on the pleasant creekside patio, however, you will probably forgive all the informality and just enjoy the setting. Leafy oaks and pretty greenery trim the deck, and the sound of rushing water is all around. Indoors, there are booths along the walls and little brass lamps at every table. A variety of pasta and seafood dishes are available, portions are generous, the food is satisfactory, and service is prompt.

POTAGER, Nevada City
320 Broad Street
(916) 265-5697
http://www.potager.com
Moderate to Expensive
Dinner Tuesday-Saturday

Potager (pronounced "po-ta-JAY") is a French word meaning kitchen garden. The creative kitchen uses fresh, local ingredients and classic European techniques to create scrumptious dishes like freshly made ravioli, sautéed halibut with an almond crust and cashew sauce, and rack of lamb roasted with a thyme-honey mustard crust and served in a port wine barbecue sauce.

While the food alone merits a visit, the atmosphere is absolutely charming. Country-style decor in the front dining room accents white table linens, lace curtains, and chandeliers, but the most romantic tables are in the back dining room, affectionately called the Diggin's because it resembles a mine shaft and is warmly lit by lamplight. Gold-rush artifacts hang from the walls and rafters, soft melodies float through the air, and fresh flowers sit at every table. Desserts are all homemade, even the ice cream, and you will easily find an intimate nook or cranny where sharing this treat becomes a treat in itself.

Romantic Option: If you are only passing through Nevada City at lunchtime, consider stopping at the **POTAGER DELI CAFE**, 110 York Street, (916) 265-0558 (Inexpensive), located behind the restaurant. This deli cafe specializes in gourmet lunches and is open from 11 A.M. until 3 P.M., Monday through Friday. The small cafe has a casual group of tables, but we suggest you order takeout and find a shady spot for a picnic.

Outdoor Kissing

INDEPENDENCE TRAIL, Nevada City

In this dry and dusty region, you may find yourselves searching for water, and not just for drinking purposes. Independence Trail leads to waterfalls and pools that will quench your desire to be near refreshing clear blue water. This wheelchair-accessible trail is paved and extremely well maintained. Depending on your pace, the walk takes about an hour round-trip.

Grass Valley

Grass Valley was the most heavily mined area in the northern section of Gold Country, but, like most gold-rush communities, when the gold ran out so did the locals. Today it retains some of that rundown, almost ghost-town feel, but there are some charming little shops and a few good restaurants, and the folks who do live here will make you feel welcome and comfortable.

Hotel/Bed and Breakfast Kissing

MURPHY'S INN, Grass Valley
318 Neal Street
(916) 273-6873, (800) 895-2488
Inexpensive to Expensive
Minimum stay requirement on holidays

Manicured ivy and lovely gardens trim this opulent estate built by one of Gold Country's most successful mine owners as a wedding present for his wife in 1866. A hammock swings lazily in the breeze between two trees on the lovely grounds, near a gently trickling water fountain. Brightly colored modern carpeting and visible televisions contrast sharply with the otherwise old-fashioned Victorian mood of the six guest rooms in the main house. White lace curtains, floral wallpapers, and canopy or four-poster beds are authentic, though somewhat mismatched. Two rooms have the added luxury of fireplaces, but if they happen to be booked when you are here, you can seek out the two fireside sitting rooms on the main floor. Wherever you decide to relax, there are enough common areas to keep you from feeling crowded by other guests. A full breakfast is served at one large dining table in the breakfast room.

Romantic Note: A separate house across the street has two rooms, each with a king-size bed, fireplace, and a private bath. Families with children are encouraged to stay here, so unless you have to bring the kids on your romantic getaway, ask for a room in the main house.

Restaurant Kissing

THE HOLBROOKE HOTEL RESTAURANT, Grass Valley
212 West Main Street
(916) 273-1353, (800) 933-7077
Moderate
Lunch and Dinner Daily; Sunday Brunch

Step off the dusty trail and into this vintage hotel that looks and feels much as it did in the late 1850s, rowdy saloon and all. Tucked down the hall and just past the front desk, this old-fashioned restaurant is an elegant surprise. A globe chandelier hangs from the high ceiling, antique wall fixtures subtly light each of the tables, and brick walls and archways make cozy alcoves for intimate dining. Seasonal menu offerings focus on American regional cuisine and might showcase sea bass baked with an herbed sundried tomato bread crust in a lime-cilantro jus, or grilled filet mignon with stir-fried vegetables and sherry-soy sauce. The fine food is sure to delight, but try to save room for the "Grand Dessert." We suggest you share this one, because you don't get just a dollop of a few of the scrumptious desserts—you get what looks like a full serving of each. Awesome!

Romantic Option: The historic **HOLBROOKE HOTEL** has a variety of antiquated and time-worn rooms upstairs, but we don't recommend them for a romantic encounter. Legendary individuals such as Mark Twain and Ulysses S. Grant have supposedly stayed here, but if their rooms were anywhere near the noisy saloon on the main floor they certainly didn't sleep well.

Coloma

Ensconced in the wooded section of the American River canyon, the tiny town of Coloma is actually comprised of a 300-acre park formally known as **MARSHALL GOLD DISCOVERY STATE HISTORIC PARK**. With a population of 175, Coloma hasn't changed much since its prime as a goldrush town in the 1850s. You can find the local tinsmith and blacksmith hard at work in their workshops, or hopeful visitors panning for gold in the south fork of the American River. While the dry, rural scenery here is spectacular and hosts an abundance of outdoor adventure opportunities, keep in mind that the town of Coloma tends to gear itself toward tour groups, which are (needless to say) *never* romantic. To avoid getting swept away by the crowds during your visit here, we recommend checking into the **COLOMA COUNTRY INN** (see Hotel/Bed and Breakfast Kissing).

Hotel/Bed and Breakfast Kissing

COLOMA COUNTRY INN, Coloma
345 High Street
(916) 622-6919
Inexpensive to Very Expensive
Minimum stay requirement on holidays

Five acres of quiet country surround this enchanting gray and white home and carriage house, hemmed in by flower gardens and a white picket fence. Domestic chickens run freely through the yard, and a rope swing suspended from a high bough swings right out over a small duck pond.

Hands-on service is a focal point here. In the afternoon, fresh lemonade and iced tea are served in the gazebo, and baskets can be provided for guests who want to hand-pick and enjoy local berries. In the morning a generous gourmet breakfast is served in the formal dining room or, on especially warm days, outside under the pergola overlooking the pond.

Though all seven guest rooms are comfortable places to call home for an evening or two, the two Carriage House suites are most conducive to romance. Set back from the main house and enveloped by gardens, the 1898 Carriage House has a storybook appearance, with window boxes and an antique weather vane. Couples traveling together will appreciate the Carriage House's Cottage Suite, which features two bedrooms and a sitting room. The Geranium Suite is better designed for couples, with a private kitchenette and French doors that open onto a charming garden. Both are beautifully appointed with French country antiques, floral fabrics and linens, and abundant charm. In the main farmhouse, handmade quilts, folk art, and American antiques lend a homespun flavor to most of the rooms.

Romantic Note: Though many are drawn to the Coloma Country Inn because of its picturesque, serene setting, many more arrive looking for adventures. Hot-air balloon rides, white-water rafting trips, hikes, and, of course, gold-panning expeditions can be incorporated into your stay. Specify which adventures interest you most when you book your reservation.

Plymouth

Plymouth is best known for the Shenandoah Valley: wine country paradise. Acres upon acres of well-tended vineyards grace the sloping Sierra Nevada foothills, creating a wondrous setting for bed and breakfasts, award-winning wineries, not to mention kissing.

Hotel/Bed and Breakfast Kissing

INDIAN CREEK BED AND BREAKFAST, Plymouth
21950 Highway 49
(209) 245-4648
Inexpensive to Expensive
Recommended Wedding Site

In Gold Country, things can start to look alike. After you've passed through several small gold-rush towns sporting Western-style facades and Victorian inns, it becomes difficult to distinguish one place from the next. Indian Creek Bed and Breakfast is a welcome change. Built in 1932 by a Hollywood producer, this refined two-story log house is sequestered on the edge of ten acres of woodland. Endowed with a wonderful bucolic elegance, the home's interior has been masterfully crafted, with pine walls and Douglas fir floors. A floor-to-ceiling fireplace made of quartz warms the large living room, where Hollywood's select were entertained in the '30s and '40s. Today, leather couches, Southwestern fabrics, and Native American artwork and relics give the home an intriguing lodge-style flavor. A hallway leads to the back of the house, where swinging doors open into an authentic "cowboy bar" with saddle bar-stools and decorator ropes, halters, and boots. "It's never too late to become a cowboy," claim the owners. Apparently not.

A wooden staircase climbs to a manzanita-wood balcony overlooking the living room, and to four upstairs guest rooms. A hand-painted wood floor and a mural of birch trees decorate the Margaret Breen Room, which also features a four-poster pine bed, a fireplace, and French doors that open to a private wraparound deck. Horseshoes and a saddle embellish the wrought-iron bed, draped with a denim duvet, in the Way Out West Room. Though it is the smallest and least expensive, the Southwestern Room is still attractive, with sponge-painted walls and a wrought-iron demi-canopied bed. The Dances with Wolves Room features wolf pictures and horse-patterned linens. However, the rust-colored carpeting in this room could use some updating.

A gourmet breakfast and generous afternoon appetizers are included with your stay and served in the wood-paneled dining room. During the day, guests can lounge in the outdoor pool and Jacuzzi tub, sway in the creekside hammock, or walk alongside the seasonal creek that (nine months out of the year) purls through Indian Creek's ten wooded acres, past serene meadows, to the goldfish pond. Flashlights are provided for guests who wish to explore the property by moonlight.

Outdoor Kissing

SHENANDOAH VALLEY

For a closer look at the beautiful Shenandoah Valley, take a day or two and tour the host of wineries here, set in the gently sloping Sierra foothills. Many of the wineries offer sublime views of the countryside in addition to tastes of the superb, award-winning local wines. Although most of the wineries are worth stopping at, the list below reflects our particular favorites.

AMADOR FOOTHILL WINERY, 12500 Steiner Road, Plymouth, (209) 245-6307; open noon to 5 P.M. weekends and holidays. Perched high on a hillside, the Amador Foothill Winery offers exquisite views of the orchards, vineyards, and shimmering lakes in the valley below; this entire scene is encircled by the Sierras, which are snowcapped in the winter. Sit at one of the umbrella-shaded picnic tables, where you can survey the pastoral scenery and sample an award-winning zinfandel or fume blanc.

KARLY, 11076 Bell Road, Plymouth, (209) 245-3922; open noon to 4 P.M. daily. A long, winding, and dusty drive past sprawling oaks and rows of grapevines brings you to Karly's beautifully landscaped winery. Views of the surrounding country are almost as delicious as Karly's wines.

SHENANDOAH VINEYARDS, 12300 Steiner Road, Plymouth, (209) 245-4455; open 10 A.M. to 5 P.M. daily. An enormous Newfoundland greets guests (don't worry, he's friendly!) at this small family estate nestled among vineyards. Partake of classic vintages while you browse in the contemporary art and ceramics gallery or admire views of the vineyards from a cozy picnic table outside.

STORY WINERY, 10525 Bell Road, Plymouth, (209) 245-6208; open 12 P.M. to 4 P.M. on weekdays, and 11 A.M. to 5 P.M. on weekends. The Story Winery is more like a fairy tale. Far off the beaten path, this family-operated winery takes pride in its 50-year-old vineyards that still produce extraordinary vintages. Sip wine to your hearts' content as you bask in the visual splendor of the gorgeous Cosumnes River canyon.

Amador City

Restaurant Kissing

IMPERIAL HOTEL RESTAURANT, Amador City
14202 Highway 49
(209) 267-9172, (800) 242-5594
Moderate to Expensive
Dinner Daily

Though you can't elude the past anywhere in Gold Country, the Imperial Hotel is one of the few places that encourages you to feel at home in the present. The brick interior of this gold rush–era mercantile-turned-hotel lends warmth to the airy dining room, which is enhanced by high ceilings and elaborate artwork. The linen-covered tables are embellished with fresh flowers, and sunflowers adorn the hanging lamps. If you enjoy fresh-air dining, sit outside under Japanese lanterns on a charming patio made of native stone, surrounded by plants, more flowers, and a murmuring fountain.

Ambience isn't the only thing the Imperial does right—the food here is heavenly. The menu changes seasonally, so everything is as fresh as possible. Grilled molasses salmon served on mixed greens with black mustard dressing is one succulent choice; grilled pork loin with sour cherry–zinfandel sauce is another. Indulging in a dessert such as pecan caramel tart with créme fraîche or Grand Marnier crème brûlée is a wonderfully decadent way to complete your meal.

Romantic Note: The Imperial Hotel's dining room has more to offer than the upstairs guest rooms, simply because the hotel sits adjacent to Highway 49 and traffic noise can be invasive. What a shame. The beautifully restored rooms have brick interiors, hardwood floors, Oriental carpets, colorful art pieces, and an eclectic mix of furnishings. All six rooms here do have private baths, air-conditioning, and they all fall in the Inexpensive category, even on weekends and holidays, so they're worth knowing about if you're traveling on a budget and don't mind dealing with a little road noise.

Sutter Creek

Set in the brown velvet folds of the surrounding hills, the former gold-rush town of Sutter Creek has retained its whitewashed overhanging balconies, balustrades, and Western-style storefronts. Boardwalks hemmed with antique shops, gift boutiques, and casual cafes invite a relaxing stroll together.

Hotel/Bed and Breakfast Kissing

THE FOXES IN SUTTER CREEK, Sutter Creek
77 Main Street (Highway 49)
(209) 267-5882
Moderate to Expensive
Minimum stay requirement on weekends and holidays

This beautifully restored 1857 Victorian is one of the better finds in Gold Country. The Victorian furnishings throughout the inn are elegant but not at all pretentious. Polished silver tea services gleam in the large country kitchen, hinting at the lovely gourmet breakfasts delivered to your room each morning. Unlike other bed and breakfasts, meals here are cooked to order, so you will have several dishes to choose from.

Walk through a garden to the private entrance of the spacious Honeymoon Suite, which features an antique claw-foot tub and a half-canopied bed warmed by a wood-burning fireplace with a brick hearth. (A fire also crackles in the hearths of two other rooms, including the cozy private library in the Fox Den guest suite.) Sleep like royalty in the Victorian Suite's bed, graced with a magnificently carved nine-foot-tall headboard. Decor varies in each of the seven rooms, but they share touches such as silk flowers, a mix of antiques, leather chairs, and a comfortable, homey feel.

GOLD QUARTZ INN, Sutter Creek
15 Bryson Drive
(209) 267-9155, (800) 752-8738
Inexpensive to Expensive

If you love the style of the Victorian era but historic bed and breakfasts aren't your cup of tea, check into the Gold Quartz Inn. This relatively new, white-gabled hotel boasts a Queen Anne motif, but provides the appointments and amenities of today. A spacious parlor and several sitting areas are filled with graceful wing chairs and plush sofas, accented with floral needle-point pillows and beautifully framed artwork. Past the lobby, a sunny breakfast room overlooks the inn's lawns and gardens. A full breakfast buffet is set up here each morning, there is afternoon tea service, and home-baked goodies are always available.

In all but one of the 24 country Victorian rooms, lace-curtained French doors open onto the wraparound veranda. Each spacious guest room features pastel color schemes, telephones, and armoires concealing a television with VCR. Most of the rooms are set up to accommodate more than two people, with daybeds or two king-size beds. Obviously, the rooms designed just for two are the most romantic, particularly the two special-occasion suites, which are furnished with a four-poster king-size bed, antique claw-foot tub, and polished antique furnishings. Whatever the Gold Quartz Inn lacks in authentic architecture, it makes up for with comfort and privacy.

GREY GABLES INN, Sutter Creek
161 Hanford Street (Highway 49)
(209) 267-1039, (800) 473-9422
Moderate to Expensive
Minimum stay requirement on weekends

A dash of the English countryside has been transplanted to Gold Country with the opening of the Grey Gables Inn. This sprawling gray and white Victorian sits at the side of the road just outside Sutter Creek's town center. Flowering gardens encircle the house, and eight delightful rooms, each named after an English poet, await inside. Comforts such as private baths, air-conditioning, and gas log fireplaces are found in every one. The very elegant Byron Room has mauve walls, hunter green appointments, and rich mahogany furnishings. Country Victorian antiques beautify the Browning

Room, with its brass bed, lace curtains, and claw-foot tub. Tucked away on the inn's top floor is the pretty Victorian Suite, with arched ceilings, pink walls, lace curtains, and a claw-foot tub. Windows in all of these picture-perfect rooms are quite soundproof, so road noise should not be a problem despite the proximity to the main road.

In proper English tradition, afternoon tea is presented daily, and drinks and hors d'oeuvres are served in the evening. At breakfast, fine china and complete silver service enhance a satisfying meal. Four tables are set up in the dining room, so you may be able to secure a table for two, but if you want to ensure privacy you can request that breakfast be delivered to your room. It is options like these that make an establishment truly kissable.

THE HANFORD HOUSE, Sutter Creek
61 Hanford Street, Highway 49
(209) 267-0747, (800) 871-5839
http://www.hanfordhouse.com
Inexpensive to Expensive
Minimum stay requirement for suites on weekends

The Hanford House's new owners have made an effort to clear out the 200-plus teddy bears that once inhabited every corner of this inn that sits just off the highway in the charming town of Sutter Creek. In fact, they might have gone too far in the opposite direction: the inn's ten exceedingly austere guest suites could use a few more warm, fuzzy touches. Early pine furnishings, whitewashed walls, and high ceilings lend an air of clean spaciousness to each sparingly decorated room. Our two favorite rooms are also the most expensive (but still reasonable): the Roof Top Suite and the Gold Country Escape. A gorgeous wrought-iron canopy bed bedecked with white drapes and floral embroidered linens welcomes you in the Roof Top Suite, which also has a fireplace and access to a rooftop deck. Romantics will appreciate the Jacuzzi tub and private sundeck in the Gold Country Escape. Even if you opt for one of the lower-end rooms, you'll find plenty of space for outdoor kissing on the sunny redwood deck above Sutter Creek's pleasant jumble of rooftops or on the sun-dappled patio on the west side of the inn. A continental breakfast buffet is served in the cheerful breakfast room, where guests have left their names and appreciative comments on every inch of the walls and ceiling. (Definitely different, but guests seem to think it's a fun touch.)

Restaurant Kissing

SUSAN'S PLACE WINE BAR AND EATERY, Sutter Creek
15 Eureka Street

(209) 267-0945
Inexpensive to Moderate
Lunch Wednesday-Sunday; Dinner Wednesday-Saturday

Casual yet charming, this bistro is nestled in the back of the lively Eureka Street outdoor courtyard, adjoining several other restaurants and gift shops. Enjoy the open air at one of a handful of picnic tables with purple umbrellas and gingham tablecloths or, if you prefer more privacy, eat inside where wine bottles surround you and the scent of freshly baked goods wafts through the country-style dining room. Consider a wine and cheese board, which includes samples of wine, cheese, pâtés, and meats, served with an array of vegetables. Come with a hearty appetite and a taste for variety—they're more than happy to oblige you here.

ZINFANDELS AT SUTTER CREEK, Sutter Creek
51 Hanford Street, at Highway 49
(209) 267-5008
Moderate
Dinner Wednesday-Monday

Looking somewhat out of place on the edge of Highway 49, this blue and white country farmhouse really belongs out in the country amidst trees and lush foliage. Surprisingly, the traffic hasn't affected the newly-opened Zinfandels reputation in the slightest, and once you've eaten here you'll know why. The house's original living areas serve as intimate dining rooms, where wax-covered empty Zindandel bottles serve as candle holders and clusters of grapes and grape leaves accent the tablecloths and curtains. The adept kitchen rarely disappoints and has won regular patrons over with the grilled polenta appetizer topped with assorted mushrooms, roasted sweet red peppers, and fresh herbs and cream. (They actually call to request this dish when they make their reservations!) Fresh bread is baked daily and tantalizing desserts change weekly.

Ione

Many of the Gold Country's historic towns are little more than tumbledown testaments to days gone by. Sad to say, Ione is no exception, although we understand that efforts are under way to revitalize some of the oldest structures on the town's main street. Even if renovations don't happen, once you've passed beyond the crumbling storefronts of this small two-block town, you will be spellbound by the golden beauty of the surrounding countryside.

Hotel/Bed and Breakfast Kissing

THE HEIRLOOM, Ione
214 Shakeley Lane
(209) 274-4468
Inexpensive
Minimum stay requirement on weekends
Recommended Wedding Site

Built by a transplanted Virginian in 1863, this bed and breakfast is a world apart from anything else in Gold Country. Although it is located in a residential area, it is set back from the road and encircled by lawns bordered with thickly leafed trees. The brick two-story inn feels completely secluded—a sanctuary for romance. Many of the extraordinary antiques that crowd the spacious parlor are family heirlooms and others are regional antiques, including a square rosewood piano that once belonged to the famous gold rush–era entertainer Lola Montez. You could settle by the wood-burning fireplace in this old manor home and spend an entire evening nibbling on appetizers and admiring antiques.

As you might expect, more antiques fill the four cozy upstairs guest rooms. The Winter and Summer rooms each have a private bath, but the other two share facilities. Winter, warmed by a fire, is the most elegant room, with a four-poster Colonial-style bed with blue and white linens and matching wallpaper. Summer has a more grandmotherly feel, with a pink handmade quilt and Eastlake furnishings. Away from the main house, an authentic rammed-earth adobe harbors the last two units. These graciously rustic rooms are warmed by woodstoves and feature homey appointments, oversized tile showers, and a blend of cedar, redwood, and pine paneling.

Breakfast, a full array of homemade specialties, can be delivered to your room or to one of the second-floor balconies, or it can be served in the lovely garden—the choice is yours.

Outdoor Kissing

GREENSTONE WINERY, Ione
(209) 274-2238

On Highway 88, across from Jackson Valley Road.

The setting of this majestic winery is as beguiling as its award-winning vintages. A long drive rambles over vineyard-laden hills, past a duck pond, to a stately stone structure that looks like a French country manor. In the modern tasting room, sunlight pours through multipaned windows set high near the cathedral ceiling, casting a golden glow over the wood paneling. Outside, picnic tables set in natural greenstone outcroppings and shaded by old oaks overlook Eden-like fields and Bacchus Pond, and beyond them a stretch of Miwok Indian land. Complete this dreamy vision with a picnic lunch and a bottle of Greenstone's finest.

SUTTER CREEK-IONE ROAD

From Ione's Main Street, turn right onto Preston, then right again onto Highway 24. Watch for signs to Sutter Creek-Ione Road.

Those interested in exploring Ione's enchanting countryside can veer off the highway and take the road less traveled. This backcountry road winds for ten miles through velvety rolling hills and valleys speckled with venerable oaks and grazing cattle. Every season imparts a beauty of its own: autumn leaves heighten the already bronzed landscape; winter brings rain (when there isn't a drought) and turns the hillsides a delicious green; and wildflowers dab color everywhere in the spring and summer.

Jackson

As the Amador County seat in the heart of Gold Country, Jackson is home to most of the businesses in the area. It's not exactly a prime romantic destination; rather, it is where folks from surrounding towns do their shopping: great for provisions, but definitely not for maximizing moments together.

Hotel/Bed and Breakfast Kissing

THE COURT STREET INN, Jackson
215 Court Street
(209) 223-0416, (800) 200-0416
Inexpensive to Expensive
Minimum stay requirement on holiday weekends

Nestled on a quiet residential hillside in downtown Jackson, this sprightly yellow Victorian with white trim is fronted by a large veranda appointed with white wicker furniture. The interior, brimming with antiques, radiates an old-fashioned ambience. The five cozy guest rooms are decorated with floral wallpapers and linens and a plethora of time-worn antiques. Hardwood floors, Oriental rugs, and a king-size four-poster bed give the Angel Court Room an elegant turn, while a tiny private deck and skylights are cherished attributes of the homey Garden Court Room. A whirlpool tub and seductive glass-enclosed shower provide romantic inspiration in the Crystal Court Room, which is decorated with crystal lamps, hardwood floors, and more vintage antiques. A porch swing made for two and spa tub set outside behind a latticed fence are additional affectionate features.

A hearty full breakfast is served at large tables surrounded by antique cash registers and, you guessed it, more antiques. Some will find this bed and breakfast cozy, but believers in the "less is more" theory of decorating will feel cramped by the overflowing abundance of turn-of-the-century heirlooms.

We should mention that additional rooms are located in the 1857 Victorian home next door and the rustic Carriage House in the back, although they are much too homey and eclectic to be considered romantic. However, because this inn was under brand-new ownership when we saw it last, the romantic potential of the entire property could dramatically improve.

GATE HOUSE INN, Jackson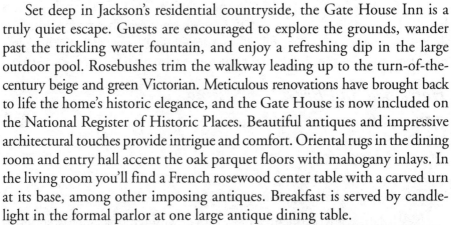
1330 Jackson Gate Road
(209) 223-3500, (800) 841-1072
http://www.gatehouseinn.com
Moderate to Expensive
Minimum stay requirement on holidays
Recommended Wedding Site

Set deep in Jackson's residential countryside, the Gate House Inn is a truly quiet escape. Guests are encouraged to explore the grounds, wander past the trickling water fountain, and enjoy a refreshing dip in the large outdoor pool. Rosebushes trim the walkway leading up to the turn-of-the-century beige and green Victorian. Meticulous renovations have brought back to life the home's historic elegance, and the Gate House is now included on the National Register of Historic Places. Beautiful antiques and impressive architectural touches provide intrigue and comfort. Oriental rugs in the dining room and entry hall accent the oak parquet floors with mahogany inlays. In the living room you'll find a French rosewood center table with a carved urn at its base, among other imposing antiques. Breakfast is served by candle-light in the formal parlor at one large antique dining table.

You're guaranteed to sleep well here—the owners have a penchant for angels and claim the inn is protected by them. A seven-foot angel ornaments the chimney's exterior, and guests who share the owners' passion can browse through the angel gift shop, which features angel items handmade by local artists. Surprising as it may sound, the angel theme is not obvious through-out the inn's five guest rooms. Some of the rooms are plainer than others, but all of them are comfortable, with private baths and an interesting blend of antiques. The French Room is probably the most impressive, with its commanding views of the north garden, and a Louis XIV bedroom set trimmed with gold. Secluded in the backyard, a renovated woodshed has been turned into the charming, self-contained Summerhouse. Rustic and cozy, the cottage features knotty cedar walls, a wood-burning stove, and a two-person Jacuzzi tub. It's a perfect spot to spend some quality time together.

THE WEDGEWOOD INN, Jackson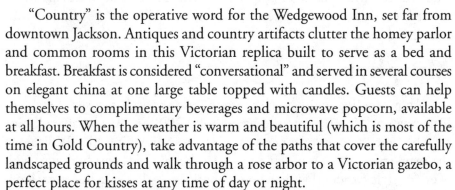
11941 Narcissus Road
(209) 296-4300, (800) WEDGEWD
http://www.wedgewoodinn.com
Inexpensive to Expensive
Two night minimum on holiday weekends

"Country" is the operative word for the Wedgewood Inn, set far from downtown Jackson. Antiques and country artifacts clutter the homey parlor and common rooms in this Victorian replica built to serve as a bed and breakfast. Breakfast is considered "conversational" and served in several courses on elegant china at one large table topped with candles. Guests can help themselves to complimentary beverages and microwave popcorn, available at all hours. When the weather is warm and beautiful (which is most of the time in Gold Country), take advantage of the paths that cover the carefully landscaped grounds and walk through a rose arbor to a Victorian gazebo, a perfect place for kisses at any time of day or night.

The six comfortable and spacious guest rooms, all of which have private baths, continue the country theme. Interesting antiques, black and white photographs, and family heirlooms abound. In the Wedgewood Cameo Room, a family wedding dress is on display and a white embroidered bed-spread dresses up a hand-carved bed. At the top of the house, Granny's Room lives up to its name with cozy peaked ceilings, a brick hearth, and a hand-made patchwork quilt. The self-contained two-room Carriage House Suite next door to the inn offers the most space and seclusion, with its own private entrance, enclosed patio, and sitting room. Here, cathedral ceilings enhance a sense of space, floral-patterned embroidered linens drape a wooden bed, and a pink-tiled two-person whirlpool tub is embraced by a bright window alcove.

Restaurant Kissing

UPSTAIRS RESTAURANT, Jackson
164 Main Street
(209) 223-3342
Moderate to Expensive
Dinner Daily

Hidden above a storefront in the heart of downtown Jackson, the Upstairs Restaurant is small but appealing. French doors at the front end of the restaurant open onto a small deck that overlooks the vintage Gold Country storefronts below. White and blue tablecloths topped with fresh flowers and oil lanterns cover a handful of tables inside, and local artwork dresses up the white brick walls (and can be purchased if something particularly strikes your fancy). Everything is made from scratch here, using the freshest ingredients. Appetizers range from baked Brie with roasted garlic to a more unusual black bean and goat cheese torta with ancho chile sauce and avocado. Entrées are slightly less eclectic, including shrimp scampi, pasta puttanesca, and fresh trout sautéed with lemon and capers. The chef takes pride in serving fresh-roasted, exotic blends of coffee and espresso, which can be enjoyed with tantalizing desserts.

Murphys

"Above the fog and below the snow," as the locals say, sits the quaint little town of Murphys, at an elevation of 2,200 feet. As you ascend, pine trees become more prevalent and the air grows a tiny bit cooler. Walk along the main street of town on raised wooden boardwalks, past buildings with Western-style facades that now house boutiques, galleries, a historic saloon, several restaurants, and an ice cream shop. You'll feel like you've stepped back in time.

Romantic Suggestion: Ascend farther up Highway 4 to reach **BIG TREES STATE PARK**, where you can picnic or hike among giant sequoias.

Romantic Warning: Events are scheduled in Murphys almost every summer weekend, overloading this tiny community. As charming as it is, on a busy weekend you might feel more like getting out of town.

Hotel/Bed and Breakfast Kissing

DUNBAR HOUSE, 1880, Murphys
271 Jones Street
(209) 728-2897, (800) 692-6006
Moderate to Expensive
Minimum stay requirement on weekends
Recommended Wedding Site

Touted as the crown jewel of Gold Country, this 1880 Italianate Victorian is a sight to behold. A white picket fence and lovingly tended flower gardens envelop the home's expansive grassy yard, where hummingbirds flit above a water fountain and a large hammock swings beneath the trees. From the moment you cross the threshold of this country refuge, you will be indulged with old-fashioned hospitality and romance. Chocolate macadamia nut cookies, along with coffee, tea, and cocoa, are served in the dining room every afternoon. Breakfast is an affair to remember, served beside a woodstove in the dining room (or in your room or on the lovely garden patio if you prefer).

Each of the four beautiful, countrified guest suites has a wood-burning stove, so you can warm yourselves as you toast each other with the complimentary bottle of wine affectionately provided by the innkeepers. Chocolates are left on your pillows at turndown service, and a welcome plate of appetizers awaits guests in every room upon arrival. Antiques, hardwood floors graced with Oriental carpets, and queen-size beds covered with lush down comforters add to the romantic climate. In the Sequoia Room, settle into a bubble bath in the claw-foot tub, decorated with hand-painted flowers and set next to the woodstove. In the spacious Cedar Suite, commonly reserved by couples looking for a special romantic getaway, you can cuddle on the white brass bed in front of a warm woodstove, relax on your private sunporch in the late afternoon, or pamper yourselves in the two-person whirlpool bathtub. No matter which room is yours, you'll feel rejuvenated and romantically charged after spending time at this inn of inns.

REDBUD INN, Murphys
402 Main Street
(209) 728-8533, (800) 827-8533
http://www.redbudinn.com
Inexpensive to Expensive
Minimum stay requirement on holidays

Recently built, the Redbud Inn provides romantic refuge in the heart of Murphys. This self-enclosed cedar-shake inn with stone chimneys houses 12 rooms, each decorated in slightly different fashion but all wonderfully private and attractive. Some rooms hold folk-art pieces, others have antique furnishings, and some are done in more contemporary style. Goldfields, one of the smallest, least expensive rooms, has an intimate French country atmosphere with warm saffron walls, hardwood floors, colorful bedspread, and claw-foot tub. Snug Skyview, another small unit, offers hardwood floors, a four-poster bed appointed with a plush featherbed, and a small patio that faces a neighboring building (hence the name Skyview, since the only view from here is if you look up). The top-of-the-line Anniversary Suite, done in shades of peach, is equipped with a huge two-person spa tub, double-sided wood-burning fireplace, and a wet bar. Several other rooms have fireplaces, and two others have whirlpool tubs for two. Wine and hors d'oeuvres are served in the early evening, and a full breakfast is also included with your stay.

Overall, the Redbud Inn is a great value. When an inn offers rooms priced under $100 that are decorated just as nicely as the best suites, even if they don't have all of the fancy amenities, we must congratulate the management. Check out the Redbud for yourselves.

Restaurant Kissing

GROUNDS, Murphys
402 Main Street
(209) 728-8663
Inexpensive
Lunch Wednesday-Monday; Dinner Thursday-Monday

Although Grounds is an extremely casual little restaurant, we found it quite charming. Pale hardwood floors with Turkish rugs, bare birch tables and chairs, and black and white photographs give this otherwise unadorned dining room an open and airy feeling. There is a walk-up counter at the front of the restaurant if you are just stopping in for espresso, or you may choose to sit in the back dining room or on the outside patio. Lunches are fresh and healthy, pastries are rich and delicious, and the Monday-night Mexican dinner menu offers a variety of spicy dishes. On other nights, the menu is primarily pastas, seafood, and steak.

Outdoor Kissing

WINE TOURING IN CALAVERAS COUNTY

Approximately seven wineries operate in the Murphys vicinity. For additional information, contact the **CALAVERAS WINE ASSOCIATION**, P.O. Box 2492, Murphys, CA 95247, (800) 225-3764.

Welcome to a wine-growing region where getting to the winery is half the fun. If you have been to the Napa or Sonoma valleys and were most impressed with wineries located off the beaten path, you will love the Calaveras wine country. Although this is one of the oldest wine-growing regions in California, wineries here are ensconced in rural seclusion. These small establishments have a down-home warmth, but the vintners take a serious approach to wine-making. The following are some of our favorite wineries, where sipping and kissing make a wonderful combination.

CHATOM VINEYARDS, 1969 Highway 4, Douglas Flat, (209) 736-6500; open 11 A.M. to 4:30 P.M. daily. Lovely gardens and vineyards surround the Chatom Vineyards' unusual rammed-earth builiding. Picnic grounds allow you to soak in the beauty while you taste the flavors of the region.

KAUTZ IRONSTONE VINEYARDS, 1894 Six Mile Road, Murphys, (209) 728-1251; open 11 A.M. to 5:00 P.M. daily. Colorful gardens lead to massive iron doors that open to the tasting room and gift shop of this impressive family-run facility. A massive stone fireplace marks the center of the room, and a cathedral ceiling caps the grand interior. A full gourmet deli off to one side offers an impressive variety of salads, sandwiches, desserts, and fresh breads. Two-person picnics that include wine are affordably priced under $20.

STEVENOT WINERY, 2690 San Domingo Road, Murphys, (209) 728-3436; open 11 A.M. to 5:00 P.M. daily. Stevenot Winery is a place to discover together. In the rustic, sod-roofed tasting room, you can sample wines, specialty mustards, scrumptious chocolate sauce, and delectable kiwi jam, then choose one of each, add Brie and bread, and enjoy your repast at one of the picnic tables beneath the lush arbor. Except for the winery buildings themselves, all you'll see around you are acres of idyllic vineyards and forested rolling hills.

Romantic Suggestion: If nobody wants to assume the role of designated driver, a safe and reliable option is to call **VAN GO WINERY TOURS**, (209) 728-3762. This small tour company specializes in custom tours of Calaveras County wineries (meaning you can combine whatever activities you have in mind, say, sightseeing, shopping, winery hopping, or all three). A picnic lunch and midday morsels are included, and the tour concludes with dessert and coffee. The cost for a four-hour tour is $50 per person and the maximum number of people on the tour is seven, so even if you aren't alone the group will be relatively small. Tours for two can also be arranged; call for details.

Angels Camp

Restaurant Kissing

CAMPS RESTAURANT, Angels Camp
676 McCauley Ranch Road
(209) 736-8181
Moderate to Expensive
Breakfast Friday-Saturday; Lunch Monday-Saturday;
Dinner Wednesday-Sunday; Sunday Brunch

Everybody was talking about this newly opened country-club restaurant, so we couldn't resist trying it for ourselves. Country clubs are typically the last place we recommend for kissing, but Camps strives to facilitate romantic agendas. While it does tend to draw a genteel, country-club crowd, the dining room's serene views of an expansive golf course and rolling hills dotted with oak trees will appeal to everyone. (Window tables enjoy the best views.)

Modern glass chandeliers hang from open rafters in the dining room's cathedral ceilings, giving the room a spartan, almost industrial look, but candle lanterns at every table and the lulling melodies of a player piano are appealing romantic touches. Service is efficient and the gourmet menu is small but interesting, with a focus on meat and seafood. While the chicken was far too dry, we did enjoy the salmon and sea scallops, lightly enhanced with fresh thyme and cilantro. Given some time, we hope the kitchen's quality will live up to its reputation.

Columbia

As you walk along Columbia's narrow streets, hemmed with Old West storefronts and overhanging balconies, you escape from the cares of today and enter the nostalgia of yesterday. **COLUMBIA STATE HISTORIC PARK**, the best-restored and most unusual of Gold Country's portals to the past, includes approximately one block of old-fashioned shops. Vehicles are not allowed inside the park, with the exception of the Wells Fargo stage coach and assorted ponies. Shopkeepers and wait staffs in period costume greet visitors at the antique stores and old-fashioned restaurants. Fiddlers and banjo players enliven the street with foot-stomping tunes, and children clamber onto the stagecoach and pan for gold in seeded wooden troughs. Tourist attractions might not be very intimate, but this one certainly is entertaining.

Both the **CITY HOTEL**, Main Street, (209) 532-1479, (800) 532-1479 (Very Inexpensive to Inexpensive) and the **FALLON HOTEL**, Main Street, (209) 532-1470 (Very Inexpensive to Inexpensive) rent rooms to overnight visitors. Although the collection of impressive antiques is awesome, the rooms themselves feel too much like public museums, as tourists come up to explore the vintage settings during the day. Also, the shared shower situation doesn't lend itself to privacy or romance.

Restaurant Kissing

CITY HOTEL DINING ROOM, Columbia
Main Street
(209) 532-1479
Expensive
Dinner Tuesday-Sunday; Sunday Brunch

With its high-backed leather chairs, burgundy velvet draperies, brass chandeliers with etched tulip glass, classical music, and elegant cuisine, the City Hotel Dining Room is a relatively refined departure from rough-and-ready Columbia. Established in 1856, this is where the wealthy celebrated their fortunes, away from the dusty trails. Today it is a training kitchen for hotel management students from nearby Columbia College. Eager beginning chefs create such unusual entrées as rack of lamb with curry crust, minted carrot jus, and potato-eggplant croquettes, or grilled tenderloins with sun-dried tomato and black olive butter and roasted garlic–potato gratin. Meals aren't always perfect, but they are always interesting.

Sonora

Sonora is a shock to the senses if you've spent time in the rest of Gold Country, because it is significantly larger and more populated than most of the other gold-rush towns. Sonora, too, flaunts its history with vintage old-fashioned storefronts and inns, but the development here is a glaring reminder of what century you're really in. In some ways, though, Sonora's size is its primary advantage: your kissing options are increased significantly.

Hotel/Bed and Breakfast Kissing

BARRETTA GARDENS INN, Sonora
700 South Barretta Street
(209) 532-6039, (800) 206-3333
Inexpensive to Moderate

"Gardens" is an appropriate middle name for this modest, recently refurbished turn-of-the-century Victorian set on a residential hillside. A wrap-around veranda overlooks compact terraced gardens, while a back balcony faces sunsets over rolling hills. The owners work hard to give their guests as much kissing room as possible and have designed the inn with ample common space. Wander through the gardens or seek out the bright sunporch filled with lush greenery and wicker furnishings. A wood-burning fireplace glows in the comfortable antique-embellished parlor.

The common areas aren't the only reason to come here. The five guest rooms are also lip-worthy, highlighted with details such as the original crystal chandelier and the ornate 18th-century Italian antiques in the Christy Room, or the hand-carved antique walnut bed set, hardwood floors, and Battenberg lace duvet in the Gennylee Room. While mementos from the past set the mood, sparkling new baths ensure modern comfort (although baths for two of the rooms are detached). The very sunny Krystal Room is the only one without antiques. The furnishings seem out of place in a historic home, but a large whirlpool tub promises relaxing soaks in this room.

After a full breakfast in the sun-filled breakfast room, you may want to walk to the town center. Downtown is about a mile away, but be prepared for an uphill trek coming back to the inn.

RYAN HOUSE, 1855, Sonora
153 South Shepherd Street
(209) 533-3445, (800) 831-4897
Inexpensive to Expensive
Minimum stay requirement on holiday weekends

If you stop to smell the roses at the Ryan House, your senses will be more than satiated by the time you reach the front door. A long garden walkway lined with blooming bushes summons you into this small 1850s Victorian. Pretty in its homespun simplicity, the interior decor is clean and uncluttered, with soft lavenders and blues accented in patchwork quilts and dried flower wreaths. The upstairs suite, endowed with a spacious private parlor and a large two-person soaking tub, offers the most privacy and is really the reason to stay here. The inn's emphasis is on old-fashioned comfort, from ultra-cozy beds to the warm aromas of baking—cookies for the afternoon sherry break or fresh scones for breakfast. In the evening you can share a favorite book on the love seat by the woodstove in the library downstairs or venture out for a stroll beneath the branches of the hawthorn tree.

SERENITY, Sonora
15305 Bear Cub Drive
(209) 533-1441, (800) 426-1441
Moderate

An American flag ripples in the wind on the wraparound porch of this brand-new white Colonial-style home, setting the stage for a Gold Country retreat with East Coast flair. Aptly named, the inn is sheltered on six acres of woodland and exudes quiet country elegance at every turn. Unwind with a glass of fresh local apple cider on the breezy veranda or in front of the woodburning stove in the parlor. The four guest rooms are modestly pleasant and feature private baths, lace-trimmed linens, modern-looking antique furnishings, and bright color schemes (sometimes a little too bright). Gas fireplaces in the two upstairs bedrooms can actually be turned on via remote control from bed. A queen-size sleigh bed makes the fireside Lilac Thyme room especially inviting, while a garden scene complete with life-size sunflowers in the Host of Daffodils room is enticing. Peruse the floor-to-ceiling bookshelves lining the walls of the library, where sunlight spills through a tall arched window. Breakfast is the clincher. As you relish carved pineapple boats or eggs Florentine, remember to save room for dessert: strawberry shortcake, apple cake, or, if you're lucky, warm gingerbread with homemade whipped cream.

Restaurant Kissing

BANNY'S CAFE, Sonora
83 South Stewart Street, Suite 100
(209) 533-4709
Inexpensive to Moderate
Lunch and Dinner Monday-Saturday

While the setting in a two-story office building is hardly picturesque, Banny's Cafe serves up fresh, light meals in an entirely unpretentious atmosphere. The dining room holds a number of pastel-covered tables; those along the window seem to be the best, but the street view is less than thrilling. Still, if friendly service, relaxed ambience, and great pasta sound good to you, Banny's is a nice place to have lunch or a reasonably priced dinner.

GOOD HEAVENS, A FOOD CONCERN, Sonora
49 North Washington Street (Highway 49)
(209) 532-3663
Inexpensive to Moderate; No Credit Cards
Lunch Tuesday-Sunday; Sunday Brunch

This unassuming eatery is a favorite lunch spot for locals. Exposed brick lines one wall, and windows peek out to Sonora's small-town main street along another. In between, cafe tables topped with country-style blue and pink floral cloths and linen napkins fanned in wine goblets invite diners to enjoy hearty brunch specials, quiches, and sandwiches. No frozen waffles here: the crêpes Normandie are filled with sautéed apples, onions, garlic, capers with a hint of ginger, and country sausage; topped with rum raisin sauce; and served with mixed veggies in a Parmesan flan. With this, you have your choice of four homemade salads and soups. Rumor has it that Good Heavens' famous orange crunch cake was sought after by *Bon Appetit*, but the recipe remains secret.

HEMINGWAY'S CAFE RESTAURANT, Sonora
362 South Stewart Street
(209) 532-4900

Moderate to Expensive
Call for seasonal hours.

The unusual combination of dinner and live entertainment at this contemporary bistro can be a lot of fun, but you have to be in the mood for it. The chef plays piano while your food cooks, and the waitresses sing Broadway tunes between taking orders. Dark green tablecloths are covered by white paper, and crayons are provided if you wish to write love notes by candlelight. The only problem is that the tableside performances can easily distract you from one another. Also, one wonders if the food quality is compromised by how long a song lasts. Nevertheless, this is a fun place to spend an evening if you like music—all it takes is the right mindset.

Generally, musical performances occur only on weekends and holidays. Other nights are more subdued, but the menu every night consists of a variety of pasta and seafood dishes.

Yosemite

Oakhurst

If you've ever been to Oakhurst, you might wonder why we bother to include this nondescript town as a romantic destination. Most people pass through without blinking an eye (or wanting to stop) on their way to Yosemite National Park. Well, no longer. **CHATEAU DU SUREAU** (see Hotel/ Bed and Breakfast Kissing) and **ERNA'S ELDERBERRY HOUSE** (see Restaurant Kissing) have become nationally known attractions, making Oakhurst a four-lip location.

Hotel/Bed and Breakfast Kissing

CHATEAU DU SUREAU, Oakhurst   😘😘😘😘
48688 Victoria Lane at Highway 41
(209) 683-6860
http://www.integra.fr/relaischateaux/sureau
Unbelievably Expensive
Minimum stay requirement on weekends and holidays
Recommended Wedding Site

A four-lip rating system fails us when we run across properties like Chateau du Sureau, which warrants at least ten lips (if not more). In fact, we were tempted to demote all of the other four-lip places in our book to three lips, because nothing we've seen compares to the luxurious grandeur of this authentic French Provincial country estate. There aren't enough words (or lips) to describe what makes this place so extraordinary—you have to see it for yourselves to believe it.

Wrought-iron gates swing open to reveal a luminous white stucco castle with a stone turret and red tiled roof, ensconced on seven acres of wooded hillside. Stone walkways meander past a murmuring fountain, a stream-fed swimming pool, lovely gardens, and even a life-size chessboard.

Inside the manor walls you are greeted like royalty and ushered past common areas brimming with luxurious appointments to the palatial comfort of your room. Soon after, a plate of delicious appetizers arrives at your door, the first of many pampering touches. Chandeliers add elegance to each of the nine guest rooms, which are appointed with fine European antiques, richly colored linens, fresh flowers, and French doors that open onto private balconies or patios. CD players are tucked discreetly in antique cabinets, a fire crackles in the stone hearth in colder months, and every light switch has a dimmer to set the right romantic mood. Nearly as large as bedrooms themselves, the beautiful spacious bathrooms feature hand-painted tilework and soaking tubs. Rooms located on the second floor have more expansive views and enhanced privacy.

Extraordinary doesn't begin to describe the service here, which caters to your every desire and whim (almost to the point of being overdone). Long-stemmed roses and decadent chocolates appear on your pillows after turndown service. You can even ask to have your bags unpacked and your pajamas laid out. For a slight fee a picnic lunch can be prepared for you to enjoy on a day hike; upon your return the staff will be happy to oblige you with some "magic to pamper tired feet"—a foot massage. (Gratuities are added to your bill to save you the trouble of tipping along the way.) In the morning, poached apples with cinnamon, vegetarian quiche with pesto sauce, homemade chicken sausage, gourmet cheeses, and homemade bread, among other delicacies, await guests in the sunny terra-cotta-tiled breakfast room or outdoor breakfast patio.

Once you've played king and queen of the castle for a day or two, you'll find that returning to reality is almost too much to bear.

THE HOMESTEAD, Oakhurst
41110 Road 600
(209) 683-0495
http://sierranet.net/~homestead
Moderate to Expensive
Minimum stay requirement on weekends and holidays
Closed January

One hundred and sixty acres of dry, wooded ranch country dotted with sprawling oak trees enfold The Homestead's five sophisticated adobe, stone, and cedar cottages. While the setting appeals primarily to naturalists who are looking to escape the city, the cabins are beautifully appointed and have all the modern comforts: wood-burning fireplaces, TVs with VCRs, and private full baths. Knotty pine walls, cathedral ceilings, and terra-cotta-tiled floors lend rural style (cowboy hats, lariats, and other memorabilia give the Ranch Cottage a particularly Western look), and floral linens drape a four-poster or canopy bed in the separate bedrooms. A basket of baked goods and fresh fruit awaits in the fully equipped kitchen—once you arrive you're on your own and your privacy is ensured.

Set on the second floor of the owners' storage quarters, the Star Gazing Loft is the least expensive accommodation here. Though slightly smaller than the cabins, it offers similar amenities: a cozy full kitchen, TV with VCR, handcrafted pine furniture, and views of the countryside (and the stars in the evening) through a large picture window.

Restaurant Kissing

ERNA'S ELDERBERRY HOUSE, Oakhurst
48688 Victoria Lane, at Chateau du Sureau
(209) 683-6800
http://www.integra.fr/relaischateaux/sureau
Unbelievably Expensive
Lunch Wednesday-Friday; Dinner Daily; Sunday Brunch
Recommended Wedding Site

People drive for hours just to have dinner at Erna's Elderberry House. You might wonder why a restaurant in such an obscure location merits so much time in a car, but once you've spent a blissful evening dining at this luxurious French restaurant nestled among elderberry trees, you'll undoubtedly be willing to drive for hours too. Chandeliers with glowing candles softly illuminate two country dining rooms appointed with rich burgundy walls, cathedral ceilings, an impressive collection of European antiques, and cozy tables adorned with French fabrics. Surrounding windows showcase views of the chateau, the gardens, and the sun setting behind the ponderosa pines.

Erna's exquisitely presented six-course prix-fixe dinners change daily and are served by an exceedingly formal and gracious wait staff. We savored a champagne and elderberry nectar aperitif, followed by sautéed scallops with red pepper timbale, polenta, and spicy pepper sauce; minted pea soup; compote and sorbet of pears and plums; broiled medallions of beef fillet; assorted garden lettuces with fruit vinaigrette; and mocha cloud torte. Utter perfection.

Bass Lake

Located just 14 miles outside Yosemite National Park, Bass Lake is a sizable freshwater lake surrounded by evergreens and Sierra Nevada peaks. Although much of the lakeshore has been inundated by residences and lodges, one side remains free from development, adding to its romantic allure and beauty.

Hotel/Bed and Breakfast Kissing

DUCEY'S ON THE LAKE, Bass Lake
39255 Marina Drive
(209) 642-3121, (800) 350-7463
http://www.basslake.com
Moderate to Unbelievably Expensive
Minimum stay requirement on weekends

Reminiscent of a ski lodge, Ducey's on the Lake features 20 suites, most with lake and marina views. Though the decor is fairly standard, with pine armoires, green carpeting, and floral bedspreads, newer furnishings, private balconies, wood-burning fireplaces, and two-person Jacuzzi tubs in some of the rooms are sure to assuage weary outdoor enthusiasts. Those who aren't so weary can take advantage of the resort's tennis courts, sauna and hot tub, outdoor swimming pool, and lake recreation (boating, skiing, fishing, and swimming), not to mention Yosemite National Park—a mere 14 miles away.

As for evening entertainment, dinner at the on-site restaurant (see Restaurant Kissing) is one option; jazz concerts performed on the lakeside deck every Friday night in the summer are another. Continental breakfast is delivered to your door each morning.

Romantic Note: Located on the same property, the Pines Chalets have older, somewhat dated furnishings and are geared mostly toward families. We recommend only the Ducey's suites.

Restaurant Kissing

DUCEY'S RESTAURANT, Bass Lake
39255 Marina Drive
(209) 642-3131, (800) 350-7463
Moderate to Very Expensive
Bar and Grill: Lunch and Dinner Daily
Restaurant: Dinner Daily

Knotty pine walls adorned with antique skis and snowshoes lend rustic warmth to this dining room overlooking Pines Marina on Bass Lake. Shiny wood tables and cozy booths create a casual but comfortable atmosphere for enjoying sandwiches, burgers, or seafood. Ducey's is a perfect stopover on your way to or from Yosemite. Although the atmosphere does not begin to compare with the grandeur of the famous Ahwahnee Restaurant, in the heart of Yosemite, the service and food here are far superior.

Fish Camp

Hotel/Bed and Breakfast Kissing

TENAYA LODGE, Fish Camp
1122 Highway 41
(209) 683-6555, (800) 635-5807
http://www.placestostay.com
Moderate to Expensive

The fact that awe-inspiring Yosemite National Park is minutes from Tenaya Lodge might be incentive enough to trek here. Set just off the highway, Tenaya commands views of a luscious valley hemmed by trees rising in succession to the horizon. This view would be heavenly if it weren't for the parking lot that surrounds the hotel. Still, there are advantages to staying here. You might not have uninterrupted views of Yosemite's splendor, but at least you get what you pay for in terms of accommodations, service, and amenities, which is more than we can say for the hotels farther inside the park.

Chandeliers trimmed with candles hang from cathedral ceilings in the large, slightly dated hotel lobby, where a fire crackles in an immense stone fireplace. The relaxed Southwestern theme in the 244 guest rooms adds a colorful flair to the otherwise conservative, hotel-style decor. For slightly higher but still relatively reasonable prices, the Luxury Suites and Honeymoon Suites offer hand-carved four-poster beds, private balconies with wonderful views, soaking tubs, and beautiful Native American artwork. An indoor pool, fitness center, sauna, Jacuzzi tub, and rental bicycles are available for guests who still have energy after breathtaking tours of Yosemite.

Yosemite National Park

To say that Yosemite National Park is paradise on earth is not an exaggeration. We could use every adjective in the thesaurus and still not begin to describe Yosemite in its full glory. No matter which entrance you take to get into the park, your first view of Yosemite will literally take your breath away. Myriad waterfalls cascade over towering rock formations that rise thousands of feet above lush valleys and meadows, surrounding you with sublime splendor.

A visit to this extraordinary park could easily change your life, giving you a newfound respect for nature. Although 89 percent of Yosemite's 1,170 square miles is designated wilderness, the millions of tourists who visit each year are taking a toll on park resources. The National Park Service is striving to preserve Yosemite's renowned beauty and hopes to eventually eliminate private vehicles in the park altogether. In the meantime, visitors are asked to tread lightly and disturb the land and the wildlife as little as possible.

Romantic Note: For hiking information, contact the **WILDERNESS OFFICE** at P.O. Box 577, Yosemite, CA 95389; for campground information, contact the **CAMPGROUND OFFICE** at (209) 372-0200.

Hotel/Bed and Breakfast Kissing

THE AHWAHNEE HOTEL, Yosemite Valley
Yosemite Valley
(209) 252-4848
Very Expensive

Even if you've never been to Yosemite, you're probably familiar with pictures of the legendary Ahwahnee Hotel. Built in 1927, this landmark six-story hotel, made of native granite and concrete stained to look like redwood, is an architectural masterpiece set beneath Yosemite's majestic Royal Arches. Walk-in fireplaces warm a colossal lounge where wrought-iron chandeliers hang from cathedral ceilings and floor-to-ceiling windows capture wondrous views of Yosemite's sheer rock walls.

Native American mosaics, rugs, and artwork adorn the Ahwahnee's public areas, but the guest rooms are much more modestly adorned. A slight Native American influence is evident, but overall the rooms have a standard hotel feeling. Location, not ambience, is what you are paying for here—and while the prices are very high, we must say that the location is incredible.

Romantic Warning: The Ahwahnee attracts an overabundance of tourists year-round. Reservations are hard to get, and the hotel staff is often overtired and sometimes downright rude. At these prices you should receive first-class service, but unfortunately you're a captive audience and the Ahwahnee takes full advantage of this fact.

Romantic Suggestion: If an overnight stay at the Ahwahnee isn't in your romantic budget, at least visit the magnificent lobby. Even though the lodge can get very busy, and even though the lobby is huge, the two of you can find a cozy and serene spot to relax by the fire and quietly visit.

YOSEMITE LODGE, Yosemite Valley
Yosemite Valley
(209) 252-4848
Very Inexpensive

This isn't the lap of luxury by any stretch of the imagination, but at least the price is right. Located near the base of Yosemite Falls, Yosemite Lodge has 495 rooms that range from better than standard to less than standard, in addition to rustic cabins both with and without private baths. (This may sound like faint praise, but lodging options in the heart of the valley are limited.) Compared to the Ahwahnee this is roughing it, but Yosemite Lodge is a much less costly alternative. If you plan to spend most of your time outdoors anyhow, this may be an option for you.

Restaurant Kissing

AHWAHNEE DINING ROOM, Yosemite Valley
Yosemite Valley, at the Ahwahnee Hotel
(209) 372-1489
Very Expensive
Breakfast, Lunch, and Dinner Daily; Sunday Brunch

Given the poor service at the **AHWAHNEE HOTEL** (see Hotel/Bed and Breakfast Kissing), it's not surprising that our dinner there was straight out of a Laurel and Hardy movie. (If we hadn't been so hungry we might have found it humorous.) The mismanaged wait staff tripped and stumbled over themselves as they forgot our drinks, then forgot to refill our drinks, and took an eternity to take our orders and bring our food. When our food finally did arrive, it was disappointingly mediocre, not to mention cold.

After all that, why do we bother to mention this place at all? Because the ambience is unquestionably romantic and its gorgeous surroundings nearly compensate for the appalling service. Grand sugar-pine trestles and granite pillars endow the enormous room with rustic elegance. During the day, full-length windows let in ample sunshine, as well as views of Glacier Point and Yosemite Falls. In the evening, chandeliers hanging from the high cathedral ceiling and slim candles in wrought-iron holders provide soft light for the cozy tables. To thoroughly enjoy this setting, consider limiting yourselves to drinks or just dessert—it will be easier on your patience, as well as your stomachs.

Romantic Alternative: The **MOUNTAIN ROOM BROILER**, Yosemite Lodge, (209) 372-1281 (Moderate) serves breakfast and dinner daily, and is the only other dining option in Yosemite Valley. Surrounded by murals depicting Yosemite scenes, the dining room is attractive, though somewhat dated. The menu is limited, but the food is quite good (how can you go wrong with pasta or chicken burgers?), prices are more than reasonable, and the service is actually attentive (imagine that!).

Outdoor Kissing

GLACIER POINT, Yosemite National Park

From Yosemite Valley follow signs to Glacier Point Road, which leads to Glacier Point.

No matter where you go, Yosemite abounds with spectacular views, but Glacier Point beats them all. The one-hour drive (closed in winter) winds through fertile meadows and dense forest, setting the mood for the visual ecstasy that awaits you. Perched 3,200 feet above Yosemite Valley, Glacier Point commands mesmerizing panoramic views of the valley below, as well as Nevada Falls, Vernal Falls, the Merced River, and the Sierras rising in the distance. Yosemite's near-constant tourist traffic deters much of the wildlife from wandering here, but red-tailed hawks often soar effortlessly overhead, and coyotes or deer sometimes emerge from the forest.

Romantic Note: An abundance of hiking trails originate at Glacier Point. Follow signs to these trails or get more information at the **VISITORS CENTER**, (209) 372-0200, located in Yosemite Valley.

MARIPOSA GROVE, Yosemite National Park

From the park's south entrance, follow signs to the Mariposa Grove on your immediate right.

This awesome grove of giant sequoias is right out of a storybook—you almost expect the trees to talk. What better place to pucker up than under the shade of the Grizzly Giant? (It takes 27 fifth-graders to reach around the trunk of this monstrous tree.) Cars are not allowed here (except for shuttle buses), so wander on foot through the hushed forest to your hearts' content.

TIOGA ROAD, Yosemite National Park

From Yosemite Valley, follow Big Oak Flat Road to Tioga Road and turn right.

Thirty-nine miles of scenic roadway might sound like a lot of driving, but Tioga Road boasts a multitude of spectacular turnouts, vistas, and natural attractions to keep you occupied. This long and winding road climbs high into the Sierras, past forested hillsides, luxuriant meadows, and steep granite slopes. Be sure to stop at **TENAYA LAKE**, where mammoth granite mountains plummet right into a clear blue lake fringed with evergreens and rocky rubble. Farther on you'll discover **TOULUMNE MEADOWS**, a peaceful roadside glen framed by mountains. If you continue into the eastern side of the Sierra Nevada, you'll find **MONO LAKE**, one of the oldest and most beautiful lakes in North America. Because of its high concentrations of salt and alkali, this crystal blue lake is outlined by white salt deposits that have been sculpted over time to resemble artistic sand castles.

Groveland

Set midway between Gold Country and Yosemite National Park, Groveland is a sleepy little community of about 450 people. While the once-bustling gold-rush town isn't exactly a destination spot on its own, its location just 23 miles west of Yosemite does make it a smart stopping point for park visitors.

Hotel/Bed and Breakfast Kissing

THE GROVELAND HOTEL, Groveland
18767 Main Street
(209) 962-4000, (800) 273-3314
http://www.groveland.com
Inexpensive to Very Expensive

There may not be much gold left in California's Gold Country, but one precious gem does remain: The Groveland Hotel. Set alongside Highway 120, the original adobe section of this historic inn was built in the 1850s. The other half of the inn, a neoclassical wood frame building, was added around the turn of the century. Today, after being saved from demolition and undergoing a massive restoration, this crisp pastel yellow hotel with an expansive front veranda boasts 17 guest rooms and an excellent restaurant (see Restaurant Kissing).

Four modest guest rooms are located on the second floor of the original house; the other 13 are in the building next door. Country-style Victorian florals and 19th-century furnishings grace every room, while couches, down comforters. and carpeting from the current era ensure comfort. Some rooms have the cozy charm of grandma's house and others have elegant appointments. The three suites with spa tubs and gas log fireplaces are especially popular with romantic travelers. Another frequently requested unit is Lyle's Room, said to be the dwelling place of the resident ghost. (Apparently this friendly spirit has preferences regarding where items are placed in his room, and he sneaks mints from guests' pillows from time to time. Ask anyone at the hotel about Lyle: he's the talk of the inn.)

After a good night's rest (if you weren't too spooked to sleep), a light continental breakfast is served in the main building's dining room. After this, you will be ready for a day of exploring the magnificent park; the entrance is only about an hour away.

Restaurant Kissing

THE GROVELAND HOTEL DINING ROOM, Groveland
18767 Main Street
(209) 962-4000
http://www.groveland.com
Moderate to Expensive
Dinner Daily

The Groveland Hotel is the only fine dining establishment in these parts, and it is definitely worth your romantic and gastronomical consideration. Set on the main floor of a historic gold-rush hostelry, this casually elegant Country Victorian restaurant is subtly lit by brass chandeliers. The cuisine is mostly American-style, but cooked with gourmet finesse. A Southern influence is apparent in the appetizer of grilled prawns with Cajun remoulade, while local flavors are shown off in the wild mushroom and leek strudel. Entrée selections include rib-eye steak, grilled pork loin, and poached salmon, to name a few. Warm hospitality and swift service make dinner here a happy experience.

South Coast

Traveling the coastline of California is the visual experience of a lifetime. For literally hundreds of miles the fury of the coast and the majestic scenery are nothing less than scintillating. Despite this seemingly unending spectacle, there are distinct differences between the coastal areas south and north of San Francisco.

While the North Coast's seaside villages are more rural, with laid-back personalities, the communities scattered along the South Coast are chic, urbane, and densely populated. Carmel, Monterey, and Pebble Beach are far more upscale and cosmopolitan than any of the little towns found up north, or, for that matter, in most other regions of Northern California. If you and your beloved like to shop in stylish boutiques, eat at choice restaurants, and relax in quality lodgings, the South Coast will more than live up to your dreams. And so will the area's numerous accessible beaches and incredible, dramatic views of the mighty Pacific.

Pacifica

Restaurant Kissing

MOONRAKER RESTAURANT, Pacifica
105 Rockaway Beach Avenue
(415) 359-0303
Moderate to Expensive
Dinner Daily; Sunday Brunch

Floor-to-ceiling windows in the Moonraker's series of softly lit dining rooms showcase views of the crashing ocean surf, which practically laps at the foot of the property. These are the best views in town, at least from the vantage point of a restaurant. Actually, it looks more like a lounge than a dining room. Deep, black leather booths encourage intimacy and face the ocean, taking full advantage of the spectacular display. Red lanterns perched atop wood posts and tiny white lights strewn across the ceiling to create the effect of a star-filled sky are peculiar touches. Fortunately, the food is as reliable as the views. The menu's fresh seafood and delicious pasta never disappoint, and the luscious desserts are a must.

Moss Beach

Unlike its neighbors, Moss Beach has been spared from overdevelopment, and its small neighborhood setting remains intact. Tourists travel from far and wide to visit Moss Bay's **FITZGERALD MARINE RESERVE**, where they can trek along oceanfront trails and observe tide pools teeming with aquatic life. This rocky intertidal habitat is sheltered from the crashing surf by a series of offshore terraces. Visitors are encouraged to tread lightly and respectfully when exploring the 30 acres of reef exposed during low tide. After a day of discovery, seek out nearby diminutive **MOSS BEACH**, a picture-perfect spot to observe the sun's nightly glissade into the ocean.

Hotel/Bed and Breakfast Kissing

SEAL COVE INN, Moss Beach
221 Cypress Avenue
(415) 728-7325, (800) 995-9987
Expensive to Very Expensive

The owner of this distinctive property is a well-known travel writer, so it's not at all surprising that the Seal Cove Inn is so beautifully rendered. All the nuances for an enamored escape from city life are here, a mere 30 minutes south of San Francisco. Surrounded by flower gardens, the expansive adobe-colored stucco inn enjoys narrow glimpses of the ocean beyond a dense stand of lofty cypress trees. Guests can walk through the property to rugged oceanside bluffs and spend hours exploring the neighboring marine reserve and tide pool beaches.

Although the inn's conference room and somewhat austere guest rooms attract executives and corporate retreats, many couples find the absence of frills and fuzzy teddy bears to be a welcome change of pace. Accented with plaid, paisley, or floral linens, the inn's ten spacious guest rooms feature an abundance of romantic amenities. Wood-burning fireplaces enhance cozy sitting areas, and TVs with VCRs are tastefully tucked away in armoires. Each room has a private bath and a deck or terrace that overlooks the property's resplendent herb and flower gardens. Vaulted ceilings lend an added feeling of spaciousness to the upstairs rooms, and Jacuzzi tubs in the Cypress and Fitzgerald suites are well worth the extra expense. If privacy is your priority, continental breakfast can be served to your room; otherwise, you can start your day with hot entrées like Grand Marnier French toast or blueberry pancakes in the formal sun-filled dining room with other guests.

Princeton

Hotel/Bed and Breakfast Kissing

PILLAR POINT INN, Princeton
380 Capistrano Road
(415) 728-7377, (800) 400-8281
Expensive
Minimum stay requirement on weekends

Escape to Cape Cod for the weekend without leaving the West Coast. How? By staying at this comfortably modern seaside inn that looks as if it were transplanted from a New England fishing village. Despite its location on a well-traveled street, the soundproof windows and sprawling architectural design make each room a haven unto itself.

Ten of the 11 rooms have bay windows with spectacular views of the ocean. Sit back and watch the graceful rise and fall of the fishing boats as they enter the harbor. The only room that does not face the ocean overlooks a lonely meadow and a well-kept, hedged garden. Each room has a beautifully tiled fireplace, a downy European feather bed, and the usual hotel-like amenities, such as a telephone, refrigerator, and concealed TV; some have walk-in steam baths with redwood seats. Vaulted ceilings in several of the upstairs rooms add a light, airy touch.

The glowing fireplace of the breakfast room is sure to warm your heart. Large windows allow you to bask in the morning sunshine as you enjoy delicious homemade granola, fresh muffins, coffee cake, waffles, quiches, and egg dishes. Stroll into the parlor for a fireside glass of sherry (available at all hours), but don't be surprised if you run into a business executive; the inn has a conference room on the main floor.

Romantic Note: For a momentary change of pace from the solitude of Pillar Point Inn, be sure to stop next door at **THE SHORE BIRD RESTAURANT**, 390 Capistrano Road, (415) 728-5541 (Moderate). The rustic furnishings and low ceilings create a friendly, easygoing environment in which to enjoy locally caught fresh fish. If you're willing to sacrifice a view of the sea, dining in the outdoor flower garden is also an option. Romance may not be the primary reason to visit the Shore Bird, but the food and relaxed pace are certainly worth a stop. Make sure to call ahead, as the hours change seasonally.

Half Moon Bay

When the rest of the world is heading north of San Francisco to Stinson Beach and other points along the exquisite northern coastline, you can wind your way south to Half Moon Bay. A mere 25 miles from San Francisco, this quaint little hamlet by the water feels worlds away from big-city life.

Half Moon Bay hugs the seaside along the rocky Pacific Coast Highway. Surrounded by epic scenery, it is difficult to find a place that isn't suitable for hugging and kissing. Replete with miles of sandy beaches, this area also has an abundance of equestrian trails and bicycle paths. Adventurers can arrange fishing charters, sailing sessions, and whale-watching expeditions. Local wineries, charming little lunch spots, and plenty of parks will help round out your day. At night, visit one of the restaurants serving up an eclectic assortment of cuisines, or a club featuring classical and jazz music. Both can keep you busy well into the wee hours of morning—unless, of course, you can find something better to do.

Hotel/Bed and Breakfast Kissing

CYPRESS INN ON MIRAMAR BEACH, Half Moon Bay 💋💋💋💋
407 Mirada Road
(415) 726-6002, (800) 83-BEACH (in California)
http://www.cypressinn.com
Expensive to Very Expensive

Highlighting nature's elegance is the Cypress Inn's specialty, and your first clue is the inn's winding, wooden porch, built around a lone cypress to accommodate its growth. The two contemporary beach houses that comprise the inn sit directly across the street from the ocean, so the melodic rhythm of crashing waves resounds throughout. Designed in celebration of nature and folk art, the inn's original building showcases a colorful collection of hand-carved Mexican sculptures and artwork. The eight smallish rooms in this building survey breathtaking ocean views and incorporate the elements with names like *La Luna* (moon), *Las Nubes* (clouds), and *El Cielo* (sky). Vividly colored stucco walls, terra-cotta tile floors, and native folk art lend the rooms simple distinction. Luxurious snow white linens accent the fluffy feather beds, and a gas fireplace glows in every room. Although the spacious Penthouse Suite is the only room with a Jacuzzi tub (built for two), all of the rooms have private bathrooms and private balconies where you can sit and listen to the raging Pacific perform its eternal symphony.

Four new luxury suites occupy the second beach house, set directly behind the original inn. Located a little farther from the ocean, these rooms overflow with sumptuous details and romantic amenities such as gas fireplaces, extra-deep soaking tubs, elegant bathrooms, expansive decks in some of the rooms, and striking contemporary color schemes. Bushels of pillows, yards of fabric, and luxurious down comforters drape the king-size beds. TVs and VCRs emerge magically from a cabinet at the push of a button. Seals, sea otters, and strands of kelp float gracefully in a beautifully painted seascape mural that runs the length of the entry hall; the same elements reappear on the walls in several of the rooms.

In the morning, share sweet kisses during a bountiful breakfast brought directly to your room or served family-style in the inn's cheery dining room. Choices might include peaches-and-cream French toast, salmon roulade, or a stuffed zucchini chock-full of vegetables. Wine and hors d'oeuvres are served in the early evening.

MILL ROSE INN, Half Moon Bay　　　　　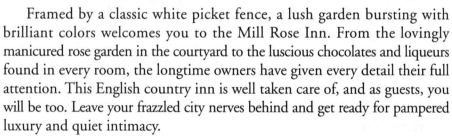
615 Mill Street
(415) 726-9794, (800) 900-7673
http://www.millroseinn.com
Expensive to Very Expensive
Minimum stay requirement on weekends
Recommended Wedding Site

Framed by a classic white picket fence, a lush garden bursting with brilliant colors welcomes you to the Mill Rose Inn. From the lovingly manicured rose garden in the courtyard to the luscious chocolates and liqueurs found in every room, the longtime owners have given every detail their full attention. This English country inn is well taken care of, and as guests, you will be too. Leave your frazzled city nerves behind and get ready for pampered luxury and quiet intimacy.

Antiques fill the cozy common areas, where guests can take in the ambience of bygone days while sampling wine, cheese, and decadent desserts served in the early evening. In the six intimate suites, choice linens adorn unbelievably plush European feather beds, and extravagant bouquets of silk and fresh-cut flowers brighten every room. Ornate wallpaper, claw-foot tubs, beautiful antiques, and hand-painted tile fireplaces (one room lacks the latter) recreate authentic turn-of-the-century elegance. Modern conveniences like TVs, VCRs, and stereos are hidden in armoires, and each suite has its own private garden entrance. Cushioned window seats provide the perfect spot to cozy up and read, snuggle, or play board games. An ample whirlpool tub (large enough for two) highlights the Bordeaux Rose Suite, but all guests have access to a flower-shielded gazebo that encloses a Jacuzzi spa enhanced by lush greenery, more flowers, and a bubbling fountain. Don't worry about finding a crowd in the spa—you can reserve time here for a private, hot steamy soak of your own.

After a good night's sleep, enjoy a champagne breakfast at your own private table in the dining room or, better yet, have it delivered to your room or to a table in the peaceful rose garden. Mill Rose Inn also prides itself on offering special, affectionate services, such as preparing snacks and towels for a picnic on the beach or helping arrange a candlelight dinner in your room.

OLD THYME INN, Half Moon Bay
779 Main Street
(415) 726-1616
http://www.virtualcities.com
Inexpensive to Very Expensive

Sometimes frills can encourage even the most skeptical among us to expose our amorous, snuggly side; at other times they can do just the opposite. The Old Thyme Inn has been careful to avoid being trite or corny with its warmhearted touches, including stuffed bears in every room. Built in 1899, this handsomely renovated Victorian home retains a sense of history. Vintage photographs, old-fashioned wallpapers, patchwork quilts, claw-foot tubs, and stained glass windows take you back to the turn of the century. The effect is a little like staying at grandma's house, although modern touches like private baths, fireplaces, and whirlpool tubs can be found in four of the seven guest rooms. By far the most romantic and spacious room is the Garden Suite, with its own private entrance off the herb garden, a double Jacuzzi tub set under a large skylight, and vaulted ceilings. Guests in this suite also have the indulgent option of having breakfast in bed delivered at their leisure.

In the evening, wine and sherry are served around a wood-burning stove in the parlor. Breakfast is always a plentiful offering of fresh scones, fruit and nut breads, quiches, and fresh fruits. Garnishes come from the inn's own overproductive herb garden, which contains more than 80 aromatic varieties, all available for tasting by inquisitive guests.

Restaurant Kissing

MIRAMAR BEACH RESTAURANT, Half Moon Bay
131 Mirada Road
(415) 726-9053

Inexpensive to Expensive
Lunch and Dinner Daily; Sunday Brunch

Known more for its location than its ambience, the Mirimar Beach Restaurant delights in glorious views of the azure Pacific, directly across the street. Many of the wooden tables scattered around the small, casual dining room are positioned next to windows, offering unhindered views of spectacular sunsets and crashing waves. Table lamps and wall sconces soften the effect of dark wood accents, and fresh flowers at every table dress up the otherwise uninspired mood. All of the seafood on the menu is delicious, especially the "fresh catch of the day," delivered by local fisherman.

PASTA MOON, Half Moon Bay
315 Main Street
(415) 726-5125
Moderate
Lunch and Dinner Daily

It seems fitting to find a restaurant called Pasta Moon in the town of Half Moon Bay. Set among the small boutiques that line Main Street, this restaurant offers tantalizing Italian dishes in a refined cafe atmosphere. Glowing candles, white tablecloths, and soft Mediterranean music conspire to create an affectionate ambience, although true romantics may find the tables a bit too close for private communication. For a slightly more intimate setting, request one of two tables set near the large picture windows, where noise from the open kitchen is less audible. Savor the sun-dried tomato pâté as you gaze at the stars in each other's eyes. We found the shellfish linguine to be simply heavenly, although the sautéed jumbo prawns with saffron capellini were a bit overpowering. You're guaranteed to find something tempting among the selection of salads, seafood, and pasta dishes. Be sure to save room for dessert, because the tiramisu is definitely out of this world. As for the service, the friendly wait staff would gladly bring you the moon if they could.

SAN BENITO HOUSE, Half Moon Bay
356 Main Street
(415) 726-3425
Inexpensive to Moderate
Dinner Thursday-Sunday

The wafting aroma of freshly baked bread caught our attention as we happened past the San Benito House Restaurant one extremely lazy, sun-drenched summer afternoon. Unfortunately, it was not open for lunch.

As the day progressed, that tempting fragrance lingered in our memories and we couldn't resist returning for dinner.

Adorned with a fanciful blend of dried and fresh flowers, wicker baskets, and original oil paintings, the French country dining room radiates charming sophistication. Tables draped in floral linens are strategically arranged throughout the restaurant to allow for quiet conversation and a few discreet kisses. French doors open to a wooden deck where guests can dine under the stars in the warmer months. As for the food, you simply can't go wrong. The creative menu changes constantly to incorporate fresh fish brought in by local fishermen and fresh produce grown by regional farmers. Our homemade ravioli with acorn squash, hazelnuts, and ricotta served over red chard with sage cream was divine, and the homemade bread tasted even better than we'd anticipated.

Romantic Warning: Don't let the adjoining saloon dissuade you from dining at the San Benito House; the saloon's patrons are respectful and unobtrusive. Also, while the inn attached to San Benito House is not as expensive as some of the other places to stay in Half Moon Bay, be forewarned: it is nowhere near as nice, either.

Santa Cruz

In the spring and summer, hordes of tourists flock to Santa Cruz to stroll the commercialized (and sometimes seedy) oceanfront boardwalk, eat cotton candy and caramel corn, and ride the roller coaster. Locals spike volleyballs over nets scattered across a long stretch of sandy beach, and crowds of sunbathers bake in rows as far as the eye can see. But even though its beachfront and boardwalk are what Santa Cruz is best known for, there is much more to this crowded oceanfront town than is first apparent.

More than 30 wineries dot the nearby Santa Cruz Mountains, boasting award-winning wines and pastoral vistas. If being enveloped by nature is your idea of romantic, the options in this area are limitless. Travel north along winding, narrow Highway 9 to **HENRY COWELL REDWOOD STATE PARK**, where dense groves of towering redwoods extend for miles. Here, hiking paths meander through lush meadows and deep forests, and California sunshine spills through the canopy, illuminating the trails.

The **UNIVERSITY OF SANTA CRUZ ARBORETUM** offers slightly tamer views of Mother Nature, and in the summer hosts a popular Shakespeare festival. Book tickets for an early show, then, after an inspiring production, wander past fragrant flower and herb gardens to a vine-covered trellis set at the edge of a hillside and kiss the night away.

For the adventurous at heart, yacht charters, scenic cruises, and sailing lessons are available from **O'NEILL YACHT CENTER**, 2222 East Cliff Drive, (408) 476-5200, and **PACIFIC YACHTING**, 790 Mariner Park Way, (408) 476-2370. Hot-air balloon rides are available from **BALLOONS BY-THE-SEA**, (800) 464-6420, (408) 424-0111, (408) 476-2370. Kayak rentals are the newest craze. Call **KAYAKING ADVENTURE SPORTS**, (408) 458-3648; **KAYAKING CONNECTION**, (408) 479-1121; or **ADVENTURE QUEST**, (408) 425-8445. The **BICYCLE RENTAL CENTER**, on the corner of Pacific Avenue and Front Street, (408) 426-8687, provides mountain and cruising bikes for self-guided tours of the area. If you're after the ultimate California experience, **RICHARD SCHMIDT'S**, (408) 423-0928, provides surfing lessons to people of all ages and athletic abilities.

Hotel/Bed and Breakfast Kissing

BABBLING BROOK INN, Santa Cruz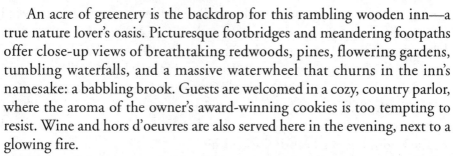
1025 Laurel Street
(408) 427-2437, (800) 866-1131
http://www.innaccess.com
Moderate
Minimum stay requirement on weekends
Recommended Wedding Site

An acre of greenery is the backdrop for this rambling wooden inn—a true nature lover's oasis. Picturesque footbridges and meandering footpaths offer close-up views of breathtaking redwoods, pines, flowering gardens, tumbling waterfalls, and a massive waterwheel that churns in the inn's namesake: a babbling brook. Guests are welcomed in a cozy, country parlor, where the aroma of the owner's award-winning cookies is too tempting to resist. Wine and hors d'oeuvres are also served here in the evening, next to a glowing fire.

Eight of the property's 12 guest rooms and cottages are named after famous French painters. Beautifully framed reproductions of paintings by Cezanne, van Gogh, Monet, Renoir, and Toulouse-Lautrec (among others) establish the theme in these rooms. Special romantic touches add character to the winsome French country decor. A ten-foot-tall white wrought-iron bed from the University of California at Santa Cruz's production of *Romeo and Juliet* is the highlight of the Degas Room. A private deck in the Honeymoon Suite boasts mesmerizing views of a small cascading waterfall, and the king-size canopy bed is draped with enticing ivory and blue Laura Ashley linens. Private entrances, private decks, and wood-burning stoves in every room help to keep the fire burning (so to speak), and the two-person whirlpool tubs in two of the rooms are romantic bonuses.

Take advantage of the fact that the boardwalk, beach, and sparkling Pacific Ocean are a mere five-minute stroll from the inn. In the morning, a generous country repast served buffet-style in the parlor will give you plenty of energy to battle the crowds and build sand castles at the nearby beach to your hearts' content.

Romantic Note: Although the Babbling Brook Inn fronts a very busy street, traffic noise is noticeable only in the Countess Room (which is closest to the street). While the traffic is more audible outside on the property's grounds, you'll be so enchanted by the murmur of the babbling brook and the turning waterwheel that you'll scarcely notice.

Restaurant Kissing

CASABLANCA RESTAURANT, Santa Cruz
101 Main Street
(408) 426-9063
Moderate to Expensive
Dinner Daily; Sunday Brunch

If you're looking for a restaurant with a water view, you need look no further. This renovated 1918 mansion sits directly across the street from the beach, and the dining room's tall, stately windows overlook the crowded boardwalk and crashing ocean surf. Candle lanterns at every nicely spaced table illuminate the small dining room, which is decorated with leafy palm trees and crisp white linens. Fried Brie served with jalapeño jelly and toast rounds is an unusual prelude to classic continental and seafood dishes. After an enjoyable dinner, or a wonderful Sunday brunch, don't be surprised if the one you're with reaches for your hand and says something like, "This could be the beginning of a beautiful friendship."

Romantic Warning: There is nothing romantic about the **CASA BLANCA INN**, attached to the restaurant; it's your basic clean motel—and that's putting it nicely.

THE LIBRARY, Santa Cruz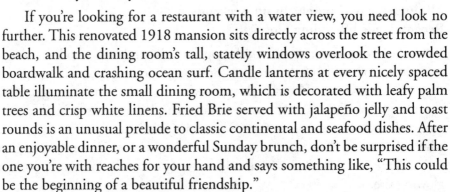
One Chaminade Lane, at Chaminade at Santa Cruz
(408) 475-5600, (800) 283-6569
Moderate to Very Expensive
Dinner Daily; Lunch Monday-Saturday

True to its name, The Library features floor-to-ceiling bookshelves stocked with an interesting assortment of novels and biographies. But before you reach for a book you'll both enjoy and settle down for a good read, we recommend scouting out the best table, picking up a menu, and deciding what you're going to have for dinner. Designed around breathtaking views of the surrounding hillside, forest, and vistas beyond, nearly every table in The Library's small dining room (yes, this is a restaurant!) has a glimpse of the all-encompassing scenery. In the warmer months, a handful of tables on the outdoor patio have especially spectacular vantage points. Modern artwork and brightly patterned linens adorn the candlelit dining room, creating a crisp but romantic atmosphere for enjoying creative California cuisine. The menu offers three- and four-course prix fixe dinners (which are pricey), as well as less expensive à la carte entrées and delicious nightly specials. Choices might include grilled vegetable lasagne with tomato-basil coulis, seared Moroccan sea bass served over canellini beans and pernod broth, or herb and artichoke canneloni. Save room: the desserts are almost as delicious as the views. After you've eaten your fill, stroll along one of the property's nature trails and explore the enticing terrain between moonlight kisses.

Romantic Note: Accommodations at **CHAMINADE AT SANTA CRUZ** cater primarily to business travelers and conference attendees. The 152 standard hotel-style rooms in this sprawling Mediterranean-style complex offer just enough amenities to keep you comfortable, but not enough to inspire any serious kissing.

Outdoor Kissing

NATURAL BRIDGES STATE PARK, Santa Cruz
West Cliff Drive
(408) 423-4609
$6 per car per day plus 50 cents per guide map

From the Santa Cruz boardwalk, follow West Cliff Drive north along the shore to the park entrance.

Once upon a time, a beautiful orange-and-black monarch butterfly came to court its mate in a wooded canyon near the seashore. Before long, other wooing butterflies discovered this lover's lure. Today, hundreds of thousands of monarchs return to this spot each winter, creating a kaleidoscope of color among the sweet-scented eucalyptus. Stroll hand-in-hand into this storybook setting along a wooden walkway that leads down into the woods to a platform nested in the monarchs' winter home. Once there, you can simply lie on the platform and watch them flutter above you like colorful stars. Sixty-five acres of forest, beach, and tide pools nearby invite additional kissing as you wander toward the ocean.

Romantic Note: The best time to visit is midday in late November to early February. Migration times vary, but you can always call ahead to make sure the colorful creatures have arrived. Also, be aware that this site is popular with elementary and junior high school science classes during the school year, which can be a noisy distraction.

Aptos, Soquel, and Capitola

Capitola has been described as "what Carmel was like 30 years ago." This quaint seaside village has just enough handicraft stores and clothing boutiques to make it interesting, but not enough to detract from the melodic Pacific surf. Though it is farther north than its affluent seaside neighbor, Carmel, Capitola has a decidedly Southern California feel. Brightly clad surfers skim through the waves, students from the nearby college play beach games, and couples picnic on the sand. A promenade stretches along the shore, and the view stretches even farther north and south along the coastline. Benches face the ocean, so you can sit, embrace, and daydream.

Nearby and inland, Aptos and Soquel also have a certain amount of charm. Although they don't share Capitola's ocean drama, they offer quiet seclusion and country appeal. Spectacular sunsets are a daily treat at our two favorite nearby beaches, **MANRESA STATE BEACH** and **SUNSET STATE BEACH**, where you can wander for miles at the water's edge.

Hotel/Bed and Breakfast Kissing

THE BAYVIEW HOTEL, Aptos
8041 Soquel Drive
(408) 688-8654, (800) 429-8439
Moderate to Expensive
Minimum stay requirement seasonally

Recent renovations by new owners have revived much of this grand Italianate Victorian's historic charm. Situated in a busy section of town, the Bayview Hotel is the oldest operating hotel in the Monterey Bay area (it was built in 1878) and offers surprisingly good old-fashioned quiet and comfort. The hotel's 11 guest rooms have high ceilings, but are otherwise on the small side. Plush feather beds covered with beautiful linens are complemented by rich floral wallpaper accents and fabrics. Although some of the decorative touches are a little dated (like the carpet and artwork), ongoing renovations should improve this with time. Two of the most romance-oriented rooms have soaking tubs in their spacious tiled bathrooms, and one has a gas-burning fireplace. In the morning, a delicious hot breakfast is served on the sunny glass-enclosed veranda that overlooks the parking lot and bustling street beyond.

BLUE SPRUCE INN, Soquel
2815 South Main Street
(408) 464-1137, (800)559-1137
http://BlueSpruce.com
Inexpensive to Moderate
Minimum stay requirement on weekends

With the nearby Pacific as inspiration, it's no wonder that the Blue Spruce Inn indulges its guests with unpretentious elegance. Enclosed by a white picket fence, the beautifully renovated 120-year-old farmhouse, carriage house, and barn are fresh and endearing. Colorful Amish quilts drape luxurious feather beds in the six guest rooms. Local artists were commissioned by the innkeepers to echo the colors and motifs of the quilts in paintings that adorn the walls. Although the guest rooms are quite small, most offer private entrances and patios. Romantic luxuries in some of the rooms also help to compensate: Jacuzzi tubs built for two, a four-jetted massage shower (dubbed "The Human Car Wash"), gas fireplaces, skylights, and an outdoor hot tub that all guests are welcome to use. Seascape, decorated in ocean blues and greens, features wicker chairs, an inviting feather bed, gas stove, bow-shaped double Jacuzzi tub, and a private entrance. Two Hearts is a cozy hideaway with a deep red heart-patterned quilt, touches of white eyelet, dormer ceilings, and a full-body shower. In the Carriage House, skylights just above the headboard of the raised bed invite kissing beneath the stars. A generous full breakfast is presented to guests in the cheery dining room in the morning.

INN AT DEPOT HILL, Capitola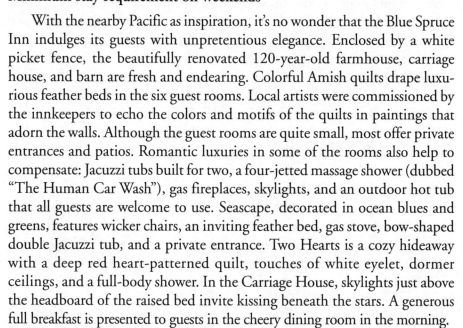
250 Monterey Avenue
(408) 462-3376, (800) 572-2632
Very Expensive to Unbelievably Expensive
Recommended Wedding Site

If ever an inn deserved to enter the annals of romance, this one does. If we could extend our kiss rating we would, because the Inn at Depot Hill deserves ten lips, possibly even more. Built in 1901, the opulent inn once served as a turn-of-the-century railroad depot. (In the dining room, a hand-painted mural that depicts a train window and a pastoral landscape beyond, recalls the past.) Hop on board and select one of the lavishly decorated rooms that evoke the world's most romantic destinations. You can kiss in a Parisian pied-à-terre, a Mediterranean retreat on the Cote d'Azur, an English cottage in Stratford-on-Avon, or an Italian coastal villa in Portofino. Each guest room truly reflects the essence of these locales.

No matter which "destination" you choose, prepare yourselves for luxury and pampering. The spectacularly decorated rooms are magazine material, with architectural touches such as domed ceilings, whitewashed columns, and two-sided fireplaces. Sumptuous fabrics drape unbelievably plush canopied feather beds, and magnificent antique furnishings enhance the foreign flair in every room. A blue-and-white Dutch tiled hearth warms the Delft Room, where a cushioned window seat overlooks a private garden. Frescoed walls in the Portofino Room, create the impression of a coastal Italian villa. Decorated in royal red, the Railroad Baron's Room is adorned with handcrafted furniture covered with silk. Spacious marble bathrooms have all the amenities you could ever need (and many more): hair dryer, fabric steamer, small television, telephone, and coffeemaker, to name a few. Each room also has a wood-burning fireplace, an irresistible two-person shower, stereo system, television with VCR (concealed unobtrusively in a cabinet), and fresh flowers to match the decor.

We could fill a book with each room description, and we haven't even begun to tell you about the private red brick patios with their own gazebos. Five rooms have private outdoor Jacuzzi tubs; guests in the three that don't can reserve time in the communal soaking tub set outside behind a latticed fence in the garden courtyard. Full breakfasts, afternoon wine with appetizers, and evening desserts ensure energy for continuous kissing, because if you can't kiss here, you can't kiss anywhere.

MANGELS HOUSE, Aptos
570 Aptos Creek Road
(408) 688-7982, (800) 320-7401
Expensive
Minimum stay requirement weekends and holidays

During the Victorian heyday, the elite vacationed far from the cares of the city, in fabulous country homes equipped with every imaginable luxury. Built in the 1880s by California's sugar beet king, Mangels House is one of the most secluded and best restored of these homes. Set at the edge of a 10,000-acre state park and encompassed by four acres of lush gardens, the whitewashed Italianate mansion with green trim is a sight to behold. Guests are ushered into a stunning ballroom-size parlor, where the grand piano seems dwarfed. Hardwood floors gleam under Oriental carpets and comfortable overstuffed sofas are clustered around a massive stone fireplace, where a fire blazes in the cooler months.

Fresh, contemporary color schemes and a vast collection of local pottery, sculptures, and paintings brighten the six immensely spacious upstairs guest rooms. Decorated in a variety of styles, these room have their own eclectic flair and delightfully romantic touches. Murmurs from the fountain in the English garden are audible in the Guest Room, which has its own private porch with lovely views of the garden and gazebo. A fire crackles in the hearth of the Mauve Room, set overlooking the lawn and trees. The African Room is quite different (and may be a bit jarring for some tastes), with African artifacts, dark walls, shiny white furnishings, and bold geometric prints.

A full breakfast is served to guests at one large table in the elegant, formal dining room. The limitless array of freshly baked scones, muffins, coffee cake, apple pancakes, and sometimes even English lemon curd makes breakfast an affair to remember. You don't have to feel guilty about gorging yourselves, either; 10,000 acres of hikeable wilderness are right outside the front door.

MARVISTA, Aptos
212 Martin Drive
(408) 684-9311, (800) 559-1137
Expensive to Very Expensive
Minimum stay requirement on weekends

Harbored in the residential town of Aptos, the yellow stucco exterior of this two-story home gives no indication that a stylish bed and breakfast awaits inside. The two guest rooms here are decorated in a comfortable, contemporary fashion with down comforters, wicker chairs, new beige carpeting, and Pottery Barn–style furnishings. The spacious Palo Alto Room has a gas stove, a four-poster king-size bed with a neutral-toned floral duvet, and a bathroom with a tiled Jacuzzi tub and a two-headed shower. Manresa, the smaller room, with a detached bath across the hall, has blue and white linens, a skylight, and a gas stove. Amenities in both rooms include televisions, telephones, small refrigerators, and little balconies that face the ocean beyond the rooftops of other homes.

If the glow from the gas stove in your room does not provide the effect you are looking for, there is a wood-burning fireplace in the cozy common living room. Full breakfasts are served each morning in the casual dining room.

SEASCAPE RESORT, Aptos
One Seascape Resort Drive
(408) 688-6800, (800) 929-7727
Expensive to Unbelievably Expensive

First impressions count for a lot, but they're not everything. This is especially true at Seascape Resort. At first glance, there is nothing remotely romantic about the resort's two (soon to be three) looming, light-brown cement buildings. But you can't argue with the prime location, atop a series of ocean-front bluffs. Enjoy spectacular views of the lovely natural setting from a cushioned fireside window seat in the hotel's expansive, elegant lobby. Although the water is partially hidden behind a dense grove of cypress trees, a footpath winds through a tree-laden ravine right to the ocean and mile after mile of soft sandy beaches. While most of the resort's 110 guest rooms are typical of a standard hotel, they all have unexpected touches of romance, with fireplaces, private balconies, fully equipped kitchens, upscale linens, and blonde bamboo furniture. Rooms in the north wing are particularly enticing because of their wonderful views of the water beyond the trees.

Romantic Suggestion: SANDERLINGS (Inexpensive to Moderate), the property's restaurant, serves breakfast, lunch, and dinner daily. Distant water views are the main attraction at this contemporary restaurant, which is decorated with tall green plants, white linens, and fresh flowers. Casual outdoor patio seating is available during warm weather. The kitchen serves up better-than-average but still fairly standard fare.

Restaurant Kissing

BALZAC BISTRO, Capitola
112 Capitola Avenue
(408) 476-5035
Inexpensive to Moderate
Lunch and Dinner Daily; Sunday Brunch

With a name like Balzac Bistro, you might expect an ultra-casual cabaret complete with bar, live music, and an expansive window overlooking the street. Your expectations would prove correct, at least for the lower half of this establishment, but upstairs you'll find a simple, handsomely furnished dining area that offers fresh salads, homemade soups, pastas, steaks, and a variety of other European dishes. Tiny wooden tables draped with burgundy tablecloths are arrayed along the edges of the room. The green and white pinstriped wallpaper adds a touch of informality to the softly lit, intimate setting. Live guitar music from downstairs filters upward to mix with the sound of laughter and pleasant conversation. For those seeking casual dining in downtown Capitola, Balzac Bistro is definitely worth a visit.

BITTERSWEET BISTRO, Aptos
787 Rio Del Mar Boulevard
(408) 662-9799
Moderate
Dinner Tuesday-Sunday

Chocoholics flock here in droves to sample Bittersweet Bistro's food and delectable desserts. A flower garden fronts the entrace to this sophisticated restaurant, designed with romance in mind. Choose from several different dining areas, appointed with warm Mediterranean decor. Wrought-iron wall sconces adorn the walls and flowers and candles appoint linen-cloaked tables. You can watch Chef Vinolus work wonders in the chef's room where tables offer unhindered views of the open kitchen, or opt for more privacy in the fireplace room where a fire crackles in the hearth. When the weather is warm, the outdoor patio is a quiet and pleasant spot to dine. The menu lists a variety of pasta, seafood, and meat dishes; we recommend starting with the mushrooms stuffed with polenta, followed by the herbed salmon or the lasagne primavera (a vegetarian delight). The evening's finale includes elegant desserts presented on enormous plates lightly dusted with powdered sugar. Although you might not want to bite into sweets this artistic (people have been known to take pictures of them), the fruity sorbets are consistently wonderful, and the pumpkin brûlée with gingerbread cookie is a rich and spicy treat. Although the restaurant's ambience will not spark romance, true connoisseurs are bound to fall in love at Bittersweet Bistro.

CAFE SPARROW, Aptos
8042 Soquel Drive
(408) 688-6238
Inexpensive to Moderate
Lunch and Dinner Daily; Sunday Brunch

Treat yourselves to a taste of the French countryside at Cafe Sparrow. Food this good is usually found in a more refined setting, but the casual provincial ambience is a breath of fresh air for most city folks. Bright and airy, the main dining room is warmed by sunlight streaming through an ample window that overlooks Soquel Drive. Blue and white sponge-painted walls, floral tablecloths, and a worn wood floor give the restaurant its quaint, rustic feel. Charming hand-painted knickknacks fill each nook and cranny, while dried flower wreaths and strands of garlic adorn the walls. At center

stage hangs a large painting of sparrows dressed in formal attire sipping tea—
a nod to the restaurant's namesake, no doubt. The front dining room is
slightly more formal, with a peaked ceiling, cushioned booths, and candles
at every table; however, the proximity of the open kitchen makes this area
less desirable.

Open for both lunch and dinner, Cafe Sparrow offers a variety of savory
French dishes. With its delicate blend of cheddar, Gruyere, and Brie, the
fromage baguette is a cheese lover's dream come true! As for the albacore
cheese puff, tuna just doesn't get any better than this. Dinner entrées include
filet mignon and rack of lamb. For dessert, indulge yourselves with the
profiteroles, light pastries filled with your choice of ice cream or pastry cream
and sprinkled with Ghiradelli chocolate. If you're an early bird, be sure to
catch breakfast here, served Sundays only; we recommend the omelet with
sautéed chicken livers, smoked bacon, apples, and crème fraîche.

Our only hesitation about Cafe Sparrow is that the casual atmosphere
seems to have rubbed off on the wait staff; the service may be a little too
leisurely for fast-paced city dwellers.

CAFFE LIDO, Capitola
110 Monterey Avenue
(408) 475-6544
Moderate
Call for seasonal hours.

This contemporary Italian cafe, with its hardwood floors, beamed ceiling, and dark wood tables, provides a *perfetto* combination of fun, romance,
and good food in a casual setting. Italian opera and Mediterranean guitar set
the mood for lighthearted romance, while watercolor prints and dried
flowers add splashes of color to the rather dim interior.

Decidedly deli-style, Caffe Lido has a small pastry case along the far wall
and an espresso bar where you can get special liqueur-laced coffees. Rumor
has it that the food is rather inconsistent, but you'll have to decide for yourselves. Menu items include pasta with seafood, grilled Mediterranean chicken
dishes, and hearty coppa or prosciutto sandwiches with cheese. As the California sun streams through the windows, you can gaze out over the beach to
watch couples strolling by, monarch butterflies flitting on bushes, and surfers
seeking the perfect wave. Be prepared to spend an entire afternoon beach watching, however, because the service at Caffe Lido leaves much to be desired.

Romantic Suggestion: If you're planning a picnic or a romantic outing of some sort, stop by **GAYLE'S BAKERY AND ROSTICCERIA**, 504
Bay Avenue, Capitola, (408) 462-1200 (Inexpensive to Moderate). Before

choosing your meal, you'll want to wade through the bustling crowd to peruse the pastry cases spanning the entire length of the cafe. The outstanding spit-roasted chicken, gourmet salads and pastas, and sinful desserts are some of the best deals in town.

CAFFE MICHELANGELO, Capitola
911 Capitola Avenue
(408) 477-9244
Moderate
Call for seasonal hours.

If you think Michelangelo's Sistine Chapel is a masterpiece, just wait until you see the creative entrées this restaurant has to offer. Culinary craftsmen dish up authentic Italian cuisine that will awe the most exacting critic. Notable works of art include the ravioli with goat cheese and porcini mushrooms, and the rotina with chicken breast and pesto. Seafood dishes and fresh salads dressed with homemade vinaigrette also deserve honorary mentions.

The restaurant's location at the rear of the Carriage House Center shelters it from potential traffic noise. Enter your own private Italy through the garden courtyard, where you can sit outside in warm weather. Enthralling opera music draws you into this quaint home, where you will discover genuine Mediterranean hospitality at its finest. The interior features knotty pine floors, French doors, peach walls, and white linens while fresh flowers and elegant bottles of mineral water adorn the intimate tables. In the bar area, an amazing replica of Michelangelo's *Creation of Man*, painted by a local high-school student, will capture your attention. Subtle and refined, Caffe Michelangelo is an attractive composition of sights, sounds, and smells that will inspire any artist's "palate."

CHEZ RENÉE, Aptos
9051 Soquel Drive
(408) 688-5566
Moderate to Expensive
Lunch Wednesday-Friday; Dinner Wednesday-Sunday

Embedded in a small business complex, the exterior of this simple but elegant French restaurant resembles a dentist's office. Fortunately, there's nothing office-like about its cozy interior. Lengths of leaf-patterned fabric adorn the barrel ceilings in the restaurant's four intimate but unpretentious dining rooms. A blazing fire spreads warmth throughout the restaurant, and a handful of cozy tables draped in white linen and topped with flickering candles encourage quiet conversation (and a few discerning pecks). When weather permits, you can choose to dine on an outdoor patio. The award-winning California cuisine is spiced with French and Italian accents, among others. Standouts include the halibut "picot" coated with Caribbean-style spices and the pan-grilled salmon served with a tomato-lime-butter salsa. Desserts are equally tantalizing.

COUNTRY COURT TEA ROOM, Capitola
911B Capitola Avenue
(408) 462-2498
Inexpensive; No Credit Cards
Call for seasonal hours.

Small but brimming with charm, this authentic tea house specializes in fireside breakfasts, lunches, and genuine English-style high teas. Set beside a busy residential street, the cozy, countrified dining room is warmed by a fireplace and holds just a handful of tables. Trailing ivy is painted on the walls, and adorable figurines and knickknacks are tucked in every corner. No matter what time of day you dine, the homemade soups, breads, and pastries are always a treat. Loyal fans flock here weekly for an abundant Sunday-afternoon high tea. We don't think the English ever had it this good!

SHADOWBROOK, Capitola
(408) 475-1511
Moderate
Dinner Daily; Sunday Brunch

Located on the banks of Soquel Creek, this unique and exceedingly popular restaurant is reached via a steep, winding footpath surrounded by greenery. (You can also hop on board a little red cable car that creaks over its tracks to drop you at the restaurant's front door.) Nearly swallowed by dense, lush foliage, the Swiss-style chalet has an enchanting storybook appearance. Multilevel dining rooms scattered throughout the dimly lit restaurant offer a variety of views and surroundings in which to enjoy a romantic repast. Heavy wrought-iron chandeliers illuminate tables set next to a floor-to-ceiling rock fireplace in one dining room. Another handful of tables are arranged in a solarium with lovely views of the chattering creek just beyond. More tables are set in a renovated wine cellar where bottles of wine line the walls, a large brick hearth warms the interior, and a beautiful tapestry depicts an old-fashioned wine press.

Our favorite table of all is a two-person table set off by itself, cozied in the stairwell near the front of the restaurant. Here you can wine and dine to your hearts' content in relative seclusion. The traditional California-style cuisine and fresh seafood is usually quite good, especially if you order what's fresh.

THEO'S, Soquel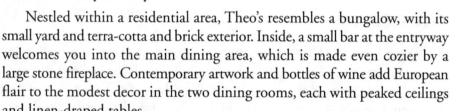
3101 North Main Street
(408) 462-3657
http://www.infopoint.com/dining/theos
Moderate
Dinner Tuesday-Sunday

Nestled within a residential area, Theo's resembles a bungalow, with its small yard and terra-cotta and brick exterior. Inside, a small bar at the entryway welcomes you into the main dining area, which is made even cozier by a large stone fireplace. Contemporary artwork and bottles of wine add European flair to the modest decor in the two dining rooms, each with peaked ceilings and linen-draped tables.

French doors open to a rock patio that wraps around to the back of the house. Guests are encouraged to retreat there, wineglass in hand, to enjoy the cool evening breeze or explore the expansive herb garden, which contributes fresh flavors to the chef's inspired creations.

Fresh California halibut, grilled lamb chops, and sautéed duck are just a few of the consistently well-prepared main courses. Desserts are equally toothsome; the blueberry soup will pique both your curiousity and your taste buds (it's a purée of Maine blueberries and ice cream, with crème fraîche and raspberry coulis).

Outdoor Kissing

THE FOREST OF NISENE MARKS STATE PARK, Aptos
(408) 763-7062

From southbound Highway 1, take the Seacliff Beach exit and turn left over the freeway to the first light. Turn right onto Soquel Drive. In about one-half mile, turn left onto Trout Gulch Road and follow it to the entrance of the park.

Named after a Danish woman who became a successful farmer in the Salinas Valley, the Forest of Nisene Marks State Park is a wonderful place to sample nature's splendor. Patches of sunlight stream through breaks in the leafy canopy above, dappling the dense tangle of trees and bushes below. Nature-loving romantics will discover a number of picnic areas, and several residential areas, scattered throughout the park. More than 30 miles of hiking trails, open to the public, offer suitable challenges for both casual walkers and hard-core hikers.

Even if you're not the outdoor type, you can experience the park's natural beauty from the comfort of your car. We recommend putting in a tape of classical music, reaching for your loved one's hand (hopefully your car has an automatic transmission), and driving through the tunnel of arching trees that lines the main road. Just make sure you keep your windows closed, because other touring vehicles stir up a tremendous amount of dust.

No matter how you choose to experience this incredible refuge, an afternoon in the solitude of Nisene Park is bound to nurture your appreciation for the earth as well as for each other.

Monterey

Rising from the blue-green waters of Monterey Bay and an adjoining marine sanctuary, the sound of barking seals resounds throughout this well-known seaside town. Pelicans and otters also frolic in the gentle surf and year-round sunshine bathes the rocky beaches and picturesque residential streets in golden warmth. Once a part of Mexico, Monterey has a rich heritage that is reflected in its venerable adobe homes and meticulously maintained waterfront parks bursting with flowers. In December many of these historic sites are decorated for the holidays and opened to the public for fascinating self-guided tours.

Of course, **FISHERMAN'S WHARF** and the **MONTEREY BAY AQUARIUM** are prime tourist attractions, and they draw year-round crowds. And speaking of popular destinations, **CANNERY ROW** is a bustling re-minder that the more things change, the more they stay the same. This build-ing complex once thrived on the business of catching and canning sardines. Now it is the site of a series of shops and restaurants in the business of catching tourists (who are often packed tight like sardines). Why would you want to kiss here? Well, you probably wouldn't. Instead, take the opportunity to explore Cannery Row's endless array of boutiques, art galleries, and gift stores. And while browsing isn't exactly romantic, it can be enjoyable, and that's a good prelude to just about anything—including kissing.

Hotel/Bed and Breakfast Kissing

HOTEL PACIFIC, Monterey
300 Pacific Street
(408) 373-5700, (800) 554-5542
Expensive to Unbelievably Expensive
Minimum stay requirement on weekends

With so many bed and breakfasts and charming inns to choose from on the Monterey Peninsula, it's hard to believe anyone would want to stay at a big hotel. Hard to believe, that is, until you see some of the very chic, exceedingly lavish hotels that have been developed in this area. Hotel Pacific is one of them, and it seems more like a romantic retreat than a traditional hotel. A circular fountain fronts the entrance to this Mediterranean-inspired escape, ring-necked doves serenade guests in the lobby, and dense flowering vines line the pathways that meander through two Spanish-style brick courtyards.

Terra-cotta tiles and Santa Fe-style fabrics accent the 105 guest rooms, where you'll also find wood-burning fireplaces, cushy feather beds, separate living areas with hardwood floors, and a private patio or balcony facing an inner courtyard. Top-floor rooms are particularly appealing, with high beamed ceilings and curtained, canopied beds made from sand-blasted pine logs. Although the hotel is close to Monterey's interesting sights and sounds, don't be surprised if you're tempted to spend the duration of your visit in the comfortable confines of your suite.

A complimentary continental breakfast is served buffet-style in a small plush lobby filled with overstuffed couches and chairs. There aren't enough seats in this room, but even if there were, it is far too cramped to accommodate so many guests. We took our pastries and fruit out to the garden-trimmed courtyard, sat at the fountain's edge, and planned our day in peace and quiet.

THE JABBERWOCK, Monterey
598 Laine Street
(408) 372-4777, http://www.innaccess.com/jwi/
Moderate to Expensive
Minimum stay requirement on weekends

At first glance, the Jabberwock looks like any other Victorian-style bed and breakfast, complete with hedges and lovely gardens. But once you venture "through the looking glass" and into the Jabberwock, you'll find yourselves in the topsy-turvy world of *Alice in Wonderland*. Don't be surprised to discover clocks that run backwards, a "burbling" room for private conversation, and other surprises.

This bed and breakfast has heaps of character and a charming lived-in ambience that can feel friendly to some and frumpy to others. Although four of the seven rooms share baths, romantic touches add a sense of enchantment to the otherwise modestly furnished accommodations. The rooms are all named appropriately, and you're likely to forget this home was previously a convent once you see Toves' eight-foot carved walnut bed or Borogrove's fireplace and spacious sitting area. A wraparound sundeck in back overlooks the delightful lawn and gardens.

Each morning, enjoy sweet and savory gourmet breakfasts with dishes like "snarkelberry flumptuous" or "fantasmagona." You can "jabbertalk" with others in the dining room or have breakfast delivered to your room. The only thing missing in such a wonderland is the Cheshire cat, but you will see plenty of smiles.

MONTEREY PLAZA HOTEL, Monterey
400 Cannery Row
(408) 646-1700, (800) 631-1339
http://mry.infohut.com/MontereyPlazaHotel
Expensive to Very Expensive
Minimum stay requirement seasonally

The Monterey Plaza Hotel is so large it hugs *both* sides of Cannery Row; a skywalk connects buildings on opposite sides of the street. Wrought-iron balconies with potted plants add a quaint touch to the white stucco exterior, but inside polished elegance reigns. The expansive lobby harbors marble floors, cherry-wood columns, candle-style sconces, and a grand piano; the outdoor terrace juts out over the water as if it were part of the jagged coastline. It's the perfect place to admire a horizon full of blue sea as you sip drinks under the warm California sun.

Although the guest rooms have a standard hotel-like feel, they are tastefully decorated in green and burgundy, with dark wood furnishings and small marble bathrooms. When making a reservation, be sure to request a room with a water view; only half of the rooms afford such vistas, but to tell the truth (and we *always* tell the truth), the ocean panorama is the primary attraction at the Monterey Plaza Hotel. Corner rooms in Building A offer the best views of the bay because they have extra windows and wraparound decks. Listen as distant fog horns and the high-pitched cries of sea gulls mix with the sound of crashing waves below.

Romantic Note: After a day of sea-gazing, head downstairs to dine at **THE DUCK CLUB RESTAURANT**, (408) 646-1701 (Expensive), where well-spaced tables with heavy cushioned chairs are surrounded by cherry-wood paneling, green plants, bird statues, and large drawings of ducks in their natural habitat. The open kitchen serves up a standard but tasty array of pasta, seafood, and meat dishes. If you're lucky enough to get a seat near the windows, you can watch the shimmering moon dance across the bay as the lights of the city sparkle in the distance.

Romantic Alternative: Just up the street from the Monterey Plaza, at the entrance to Cannery Row, is the **MONTEREY BAY INN**, 242 Cannery Row, (408) 373-6242, (800) 424-6242 (Moderate to Unbelievably Expensive).

Fronted by an emerald green lawn, this nondescript white stucco building enjoys splendid views of the ocean, harbor, and marine sanctuary. This is the property's only real romantic draw, however. Unless you reserve a room with full-on ocean views, the obtrusive cement decks, standard bathrooms, and upscale hotel-style furnishings are not particularly impressive.

OLD MONTEREY INN, Monterey
500 Martin Street
(408) 375-8284, (800) 350-2344
http://www.innaccess.com/omi/
Expensive to Very Expensive
Minimum stay requirement on weekends

Nestled on a quiet hillside far from the bustle of town, the Old Monterey Inn is the kind of place you fall in love with the moment you enter the garden gate. Terra-cotta pots filled with flowers hang like jewels from the gnarled branches of old trees in the front yard, while meandering paths lead to lovingly tended gardens and secluded niches where you can kiss to your hearts' content. Attention to affectionate details is equally evident inside the 1929 English Tudor inn. An antique book of poetry placed upon a shawl sets the mood for old-fashioned cuddling in each of the ten rooms, eight of which have fireplaces. Billowing floral draperies, English-style antiques, and plush feather beds with down comforters make this an enviable place to stay. Even the Dovecote, despite its dormer ceilings, feels bright and spacious, with a skylight overhead and a wood-burning fireplace. We were especially drawn to the Garden Cottage, which has its own private entrance, a linen-and-lace crown canopy above the bed, and a tiled fireplace that warms the white wicker-furnished sitting room.

Hot beverages and freshly baked cookies are available at all hours, and a lavish spread of wine and cheese is served every afternoon in the homey fireside parlor. In the morning, a delicious hot breakfast is served on hand-painted china in the adjacent formal dining room overlooking the gardens; breakfast in bed can be a memorable alternative. In the warmer months, breakfast is served outdoors on a brick patio surrounded by a profusion of pink and white impatiens, roses, wisteria, and boxwood hedges. There can be no question that this is a real slice of paradise.

SPINDRIFT INN, Monterey
652 Cannery Row
(408) 646-8900, (800) 841-1879
Expensive to Unbelievably Expensive
Minimum stay requirement on weekends

Standing at the water's edge in the middle of Cannery Row, the Spindrift Inn is ultra-chic and architecturally impressive. The tang of saltwater wafting through the air and the sound of waves roaring up against the rocks of its foundation enhance the mood. Window seats and binoculars in the oceanside rooms allow you to watch seals, otters, pelicans, and other marine animals at play in the waves. Behind you, a wood-burning fireplace casts an amber glow on the hardwood floors, Oriental carpets, and sumptuous fabrics. The 41 rooms here also feature down comforters and feather beds (some with canopies), TVs and VCRs, and spacious marble bathrooms with brass accents and fixtures. If it's a warm evening, only one option could possibly tempt you away from all this newfound comfort: a stroll along the silvery moonlit beach. In the morning, a continental breakfast awaits at your door on a silver tray with a long-stemmed rose. High tea is served every afternoon on the inn's rooftop garden, where you can enjoy a magnificent view of Monterey Bay.

VICTORIAN INN, Monterey
487 Foam Street, at McClellan
(408) 373-8000, (800) 232-4141
http://www.bestwestern.com
Expensive to Unbelievably Expensive
Minimum stay requirement seasonally

Although the name may lead you to envision a charming little bed and breakfast, the Victorian Inn is more like a hotel than a traditional inn. Located on busy Foam Street near Cannery Row, the property resembles a cross between a small park and a motel, with a stone walking path leading across the grounds to the main building. The lobby is certainly Victorian in style; the antique furniture, high ceilings, banister staircase, and sunny window seat exhibit classic elegance. Once you leave the tiny lobby to find your room, however, you may be disappointed by the plain, hotel-like interiors.

Clearly, efforts have been made. The guest rooms do have handsome rust-colored carpeting and marble-edged fireplaces. Unimpressive floral bedspreads with ordinary cherry-wood headboards are balanced by endearing touches such as the heart-shaped baskets and flower wreaths on the walls. Many rooms have bay windows that bring in extra doses of sunshine, and rooms on the top floor have vaulted open-beamed ceilings. Private patios or balconies are also available with some rooms.

Continental breakfast is served in the lovely parlor just off the lobby. Here a grandfather clock stands guard among marble busts, ornate mirrors, pretty chandeliers, and classic settees. Several cozy tables provide a relaxing place to begin your day over fresh fruit and croissants.

Restaurant Kissing

CAFE FINA, Monterey
47 Fisherman's Wharf
(408) 372-5200, (800) 843-3462
Moderate
Lunch and Dinner Daily

Although Cafe Fina doesn't look very promising from the outside—its yellow facade blends in with the other seafood vendors on the pier—you'll be surprised by how handsome the restaurant is inside. Leaping silver fish accentuate purple sponge-painted walls in both the upstairs and downstairs dining areas. Vintage photographs of hardworking fishermen add charm to the simple decor. Burgundy cloth napkins bring a splash of color to the tables, which are draped in white tablecloths and coupled with either black lacquered chairs or cushioned booths.

Seating along the windows provides spectacular views of the harbor. Occasionally you'll glimpse sea lions sunning themselves on the rocks along the water's edge while anchored ships bob in the background. For an extra-special rendezvous, request table #26, an intimate table for two in the upstairs corner with the best views in the house.

Cafe Fina uses a wood-burning oven for its lamb and pizza entrées. If it's seafood you're fishing for, try the sautéed mussels or the deep-fried Monterey calamari. Fish can be blackened Cajun-style or broiled over mesquite charcoal if so desired. Cafe Fina also offers favorite Italian classics, including ricotta and spinach ravioli in marinara sauce. Whatever you decide to feast upon, the magnificent views and friendly service will surely bring you back for more.

CIBO, Monterey
301 Alvarado Street, at Del Monte
(408) 649-8151
Inexpensive to Moderate
Dinner Daily

Cibo may merely mean "food" in Italian, but *Cibo* in this case means elegance, romance, jazz, and wonderful Sicilian cuisine. Italian-owned and -operated, Cibo offers a variety of meat, poultry, and seafood dishes garnished with locally grown herbs and vegetables. Creative interpretations of traditional Sicilian recipes are prepared in the open kitchen that spans the entire back wall of the restaurant.

Cibo's decor handsomely blends neoclassic, urban, and rustic elements. Painted a fiery burnt sienna, the plaster walls are adorned with classical architectural drawings. Niches in the wall hold fresh flowers, ivy vines trail from pots near the entryway, and exotic plant arrangements decorate the archways. The lighting is stark and dark wood tables, some a little too close for comfort, fill the dining areas. Snuggle close in the cushioned booths while you enjoy live jazz Tuesday through Sunday evenings.

FRESH CREAM, Monterey
100-C Heritage Harbor, at the corner of Scott and Pacific Streets
(408) 375-9798
http://www.montereybay.com/fresh/
Expensive
Dinner Daily

Fresh Cream has a long-standing reputation as the *crème de la crème* of French dining in Monterey. Spectacular views of the harbor create a romantic backdrop in the two dining rooms with floor-to-ceiling windows. (There is a third dining area, but the view rooms are the most romantic.) Subtle gray and blue tablecloths accentuate the blond wood of the chairs and walls. Well-spaced tables, fresh flowers, and gentle lighting are more than conducive to amorous conversation. Although its simple architectural design gives the restaurant an almost sterile feel, the service definitely makes up for it; Fresh Cream has one of the most gracious and refined wait staffs we've encountered.

Hearty portions of classic French dishes with California accents are artistically presented and so delicately scrumptious that you will savor every bite. We recommended the artichoke purée or crab ravioli appetizers, and the fresh salad with enoki mushrooms and tarragon dressing. As for dinner, you certainly won't be disappointed by the vegetable plate, which consists of artichoke heart, whipped potatoes, polenta, and baked goat cheese in phyllo dough. Madeira and white wine sauces enhance the wonderful veal sausage en croûte; the rack of lamb Dijonnaise, however, is inconsistent. If you still have room after such a feast, try the dessert taster, which lets you sample four different sweets—perfect for those who can't make up their mind when it comes to chocolate.

MONTRIO, AN AMERICAN BISTRO, Monterey
414 Calle Principal
(408) 648-8880
Moderate to Expensive
Lunch and Dinner Daily; Sunday Brunch

Locals throng to Montrio's upbeat, tightly packed dining room, where tables are jammed almost on top of each other. Though the crowds present an obvious distraction, Montrio's unusual interior and enticing, artistically presented seafood entrées and desserts are its saving grace. Billowing white clouds hover beneath the sky blue ceiling, and modernistic sculptures and artwork are tucked into alcoves and corners. Black track lights dangle from exposed ceiling pipes, illuminating closely spaced tables covered with white linens, brightly colored crayons, and blank paper that beckons to your creative senses. (When was the last time you composed a passionate sonnet for your beloved?) A second dining room upstairs is slightly less funky but equally noisy due to crowded tables and an adjacent open bar. Fortunately, the service is gracious and the food is reliably superb.

SARDINE FACTORY RESTAURANT, Monterey
701 Wave Street
(408) 373-3775
Expensive
Dinner Daily

Popularity with tourists has made the Sardine Factory one of the more sought-after dining spots in Monterey. Eager out-of-towners flock nightly to this historic site to enjoy the fresh seafood and elegant turn-of-the-century ambience. Due to consistent crowds the noise level can become distracting, but the restaurant's five intriguing dining rooms still provide many of the essentials for an amorous rendezvous.

A stunning 120-year-old hand-carved wooden bar is the centerpiece of the lounge, where patrons wait to be seated. (Be warned that even when you have reservations, a wait is sometimes necessary.) A fire crackles in the hearths of large stone fireplaces in two dining rooms, vintage photographs ornament the walls, and lanterns cast dim light down onto the nicely spaced candlelit tables. Encased by an immense glass dome and surrounded by a flourishing garden, the dining room in the Conservatory is a prime, refined setting for soft conversation. We were thoroughly impressed with the gracious, efficient service, but less impressed with the kitchen's fare. Our recommendation: try to time your meal when you're least likely to encounter crowds and stick with basic seafood dishes.

TRATTORIA PARADISO, Monterey
654 Cannery Row
(408) 375-4155
Moderate to Expensive
Lunch and Dinner Daily

The fresh, tantalizing antipasti displayed in the front window draw patrons into this Mediterranean-style trattoria, but it's the spectacular waterfront setting that convinces them to stay. An abundance of two-person tables are placed next to oversized windows that capture views of otters and pelicans diving for fish in Monterey Bay. Ceramic fruit sculptures, peach-colored linens, and tropical flower arrangements give the oceanfront dining room an exotic, artsy flair. Delicious fresh seafood and Italian specialties, including polenta vegetable towers and Mediterranean cioppino are available noon and night. Sunset is definitely the most romantic time to dine (at least as far as the views are concerned), although this is also when you're likely to encounter the most competition for a window table.

TRIPLES, Monterey
220 Olivier Street
(408) 372-4744
Moderate to Expensive
Dinner Tuesday-Sunday

Who would guess that this charming restaurant has a history dating back to the mid-19th century? From ship chandlery to grocery store, from art gallery to coffeehouse, this Victorian-style home has evolved over the years to become a quaint dining spot known as Triples.

Enter the restaurant through the back via a garden patio. A handful of tables are situated near heaters and a brick fireplace to allow for alfresco dining all year round. The inside of the restaurant still resembles a Victorian home, with its hardwood floors, 18-foot cedar ceilings, and candle-adorned chandelier. The walls are bare except for vintage photographs of the Duarte family, the original owners of the building. Both of the small dining rooms are decorated in shades of pale pink, with tableside views of the courtyard. You'll find oil candles and floral-cushioned chairs with bamboo backs at every table. A small open bar near the entrance adds a slight bistro feel, although the subtle lighting, sweet music, and wonderful food are bound to sway you toward romance.

Triples serves California cuisine that earns top grades for presentation and taste. Excellent choices include the capellini pasta and the creamy hot risotto with goat cheese and oyster mushrooms. And the homemade ice cream is a must. With a name like Triples and its exemplary cuisine, how could we resist giving this place a three-lip rating?

Outdoor Kissing

ADVENTURES BY THE SEA, Monterey
299 Cannery Row
(408) 372-1807
http://mry.infohut.com/adventuresbythesea
Call for rental prices for kayaks, bikes, and in-line skates

Between Reeside and Drake on Cannery Row, across from the Monterey Plaza Hotel.

Kayaking side by side on the gentle waters of the Monterey Bay is a special experience you'll remember long after you return home. Pelicans skim the water's surface. Seals sun themselves on rocky islands. Playful otters loop in and out of the kelp, sometimes even plopping coquettishly on the front of your kayak. Beneath you, dazzling colors and textures flow by, punctuated with bright orange and gold starfish. These stable boats are made for laid-back drifting, interspersed with unhurried paddling. Far from the crowds of Cannery Row, you can hold hands and, perhaps, steal an adventurous kiss. You'll even stay nice and dry, with special coveralls that pull over your clothes. If you pack a picnic before heading out, you can pull up onto a beach or share it right on the water.

Romantic Note: Landlubbers can rent bikes or in-line skates and admire the views from the safety of the shore.

FISHERMAN'S WHARF, Monterey

At the intersection of Scott and Oliver Streets.

Due to its oceanfront location, Fisherman's Wharf is definitely worth visiting for an hour or two on a sunny afternoon. As you and your loved one amble down the boardwalk, your senses will be tickled by the smell and taste of the salty ocean breezes. Stop and watch as pelicans and sea gulls soar overhead, while boats rock gently in the nearby harbor. The wharf is home to the usual souvenir shops, stands selling OK-to-mediocre seafood, and many restaurants boasting views of the bay. If the smell of the sea arouses your hunger, stop by **CAFE FINA** (see Restaurant Kissing), about two-thirds of the way down the wharf, port side.

JACKS PEAK COUNTY PARK, Monterey
(408) 755-4899
$2-$3 daily vehicle charge

Head north from Monterey on Highway 68 and watch for signs that direct you to the park.

Just outside Monterey is a delightful park known as Jacks Peak. Explore the eight and a half miles of riding and hiking trails (each trail is roughly a mile long) or simply share your midday meal at one of the many picnic areas. Nature lovers can befriend Steller's jays and gray squirrels beneath sheltering pines. Ridgetop views overlooking the Monterey Peninsula are found throughout the 525-acre park; for an extraordinary vista, however, follow the Skyline Self-Guided Nature Trail to the summit of Jacks Peak. The park is open most days between 10:30 A.M. and 5:30 P.M.

MONTEREY BAY AQUARIUM, Monterey
886 Cannery Row
(408) 648-4888
$13.75 admission fee

At the end of Cannery Row is another of the city's tourist attractions, but this one presents a not-to-be-missed opportunity to view the marine life that abounds below the water's surface. Housed in an unbelievably realistic underwater setting, the Monterey Bay Aquarium is one of the world's largest and best.

RENT-A-ROADSTER, Monterey
229 Cannery Row
(408) 647-1929
$30 per hour

We never knew driving could be so much fun. With a toot of the "ah-ooga" horn, we were off to tour the coastline in our reproduction of a 1929 Model A roadster. The top was down, the sun was shining, waves were crashing, and people waved to us as we trundled by. This unusual company offers five Model As and one two-door deluxe phaeton for rent, all very easy to drive, with modern engines capable of doing 55 miles per hour (but why hurry?). Be sure to allow enough time to stop by the seashore along **LOVERS POINT** near Pacific Grove, which is only a few minutes away from Rent-A-Roadster. Or plan on doing the **17-MILE DRIVE** in style (see Outdoor Kissing in Pacific Grove). If you know another romantically inclined couple, they can join the fun in the Model A's rumble seat.

Romantic Alternative: Another playful way to tool around Monterey is to rent a pedal surrey or a bicycle built for two at **BAY BIKES**, 640 Wave Street, (408) 646-9090. The surreys have two sets of pedals and a brightly striped, fringed roof, but you can pedal them only on Monterey's bike path along Cannery Row: the surreys aren't allowed on streets. Athletic romantics can pedal their bicycle built for two along the 17-Mile Drive or all the way to Carmel (about 14 miles).

Pacific Grove

Unlike neighboring Monterey and Carmel, which are often crowded to the point of overflowing, you can still find a measure of peace and solitude in the enchanting oceanfront town of Pacific Grove. Picturesque Victorian mansions line Ocean View Boulevard, where the tide laps at the endless stretch of sandy shoreline. Not only is Pacific Grove's quiet charm a welcome change of pace, its bevy of bed and breakfasts and restaurants are some of the most impressive properties we've encountered.

Hotel/Bed and Breakfast Kissing

THE CENTRELLA, Pacific Grove
612 Central Avenue
(408) 372-3372, (800) 233-3372
Moderate to Very Expensive
Minimum stay requirement on weekends

Harbored in a residential neighborhood, this renovated turn-of-the-century home specializes in friendly hospitality. Every afternoon, freshly baked cookies and a carafe of cream sherry sit on an old oak table in the bright parlor, where the sun beams in through a wall of beveled glass windows. Here you can relax by the fire after a long, unhurried afternoon of meandering through the streets of Pacific Grove. In the morning, the scent of freshly brewed coffee and homemade breakfast goodies provide (almost) all the incentive you'll need to get out of bed.

Down comforters, old-fashioned wallpaper, and antique furniture create an authentic Victorian mood in the 21 rooms found in the main house. Although we felt the rooms on the first and second floor were rather small and somewhat confining (especially those with shared baths), your romantic options here are still plentiful. Two spacious attic suites tucked under skylights on the third floor offer considerably more space and privacy. Outside, a brick walkway bordered by camellias and gardenias leads to five additional cottage suites with private entrances, fireplaces, and cozy sitting areas. Unfortunately these bungalows lack much of the Victorian charm found in the main house.

Last but certainly not least is the Centrella's newest addition: the appropriately named Honeymoon Hideaway. This self-contained suite was still under construction when we visited, but it promises to be the most inspiring room of all. A private entrance ensures seclusion in this spacious room, replete with a wood-burning fireplace, beautiful Ralph Lauren linens, and a two-person Jacuzzi tub in the black and white tiled bathroom.

THE GATEHOUSE INN, Pacific Grove
225 Central Avenue
(408) 649-1881, (800) 753-1881
http://mry.infohut.com
Moderate to Expensive

Built as a seaside "cottage" in 1884, this cheerfully restored Victorian flaunts trappings and amenities its original builders would envy. Elaborate, custom-designed, hand-silkscreened wallpapers adorn the walls and ceilings in the homey parlor and snug, antique-filled guest rooms. You'll want to lie in bed together just to admire the intricate Middle East-inspired patterns above you. In the Langford Suite, a lacy canopy hangs like a billowy cloud above the bed and a gas fire glows in the sparkling white cast-iron stove. The Sunroom, which features a white wrought-iron bed and a view of the nearby ocean, feels almost like an indoor garden. Wine-colored curtains cast a rosy glow over the sexy Victorian Room's sumptuous burgundy linens and claw-foot tub. For those who want additional privacy, five of the nine rooms have their own entrances and three adjoin secluded brick patios.

The owners do everything to make this feel like your home away from home. Fresh home-baked cookies, fresh fruit, and tea and coffee are available at all hours, and you can help yourself to the fully stocked refrigerator filled with juice, soda, milk, cheese, and yogurt. We also enjoyed the afternoon wine and appetizers, including delicious homemade cheeses. In the morning, a full breakfast buffet of specialties such as pumpkin-cornmeal pancakes or cheese strata provides the perfect start to a romantic day by the sea.

Romantic Suggestion: Somehow, not having to get dressed for breakfast makes a morning together that much more romantic. For $5 per person, you can have breakfast delivered to your room if you arrange it in advance.

GOSBY HOUSE INN, Pacific Grove
643 Lighthouse Avenue
(408) 375-1287, (800) 527-8828
Moderate to Expensive
Recommended Wedding Site

Since its early years as a boardinghouse, this yellow and white Victorian inn has undergone several renovations while retaining all of its charm. (The house's history is illustrated in a series of black-and-white photographs inside.) Of the 22 rooms here, 16 are in the main house; the other six are in the Carriage House, and they all have private entrances. The rooms are all quite large, with comfortable sitting areas and a light, airy ambience enhanced by floral wallpaper, antique wood furnishings, and white embroidered bedspreads. Several of the rooms have fireplaces, and some have marble sinks that stand apart from the bathroom. A private balcony with a porch swing is an added benefit for guests in the Trimmer Hill Room, and another room boasts a skylight. Rooms in the Carriage House are equipped with whirlpool tubs with separate showers. The pretty floral parlor is a beautiful setting in which to enjoy a delicious country breakfast or afternoon tea.

Every effort has been made to make your stay as comfortable as possible, right down to the teddy bears placed on each of the beds. If there is any hesitation at all in our enthusiasm about the Gosby House Inn, it is that the decor may be a bit too flowery for some tastes.

GRAND VIEW INN, Pacific Grove
557 Ocean View Boulevard
(408) 372-4341
Moderate to Very Expensive

If you're familiar with Pacific Grove's famous **SEVEN GABLES INN** (reviewed elsewhere in this section), you know what kind of luxury to expect from its recently opened sister property. Situated right next door, the Grand View Inn is managed by the same discriminating owners and shares Seven Gables' spectacular oceanfront setting. Not surprisingly, it also shares a well-deserved four-lip rating.

A small creek trickles through boulders and greenery in the beautifully landscaped yard that fronts this expansive blue and white Edwardian home. Notable for their simple elegance and sleek lines, the ten newly renovated guest rooms boast high ceilings, marble bathrooms, beautiful blond wood detailing, and ample space. Chandeliers cast a formal light on brass and canopied beds and other enticing period touches. A beautifully hand-crafted wood staircase spirals to the top of the house, where bay windows in the Rocky Shores Room showcase the best views on the property. Non-oceanside rooms overlook the Grand View's lovely rambling gardens.

Afternoon hors d'oeuvres and an all-you-can-eat breakfast of baked egg dishes, muffins, pastries, fruit, yogurt ,and much more are served at two large tables in the lovely oceanfront dining room. After filling up on a meal of this magnitude, you can easily go without lunch (and you probably should). Instead, take the time to explore this section of the wondrous California coast.

GREEN GABLES INN, Pacific Grove
104 Fifth Street
(408) 375-2095, (800) 722-1774
Moderate to Expensive

From the moment you step inside this Queen Anne-style mansion, you'll know you are in for an enchanting experience. The Green Gables Inn, as its name suggests, is a multigabled structure with leaded glass windows that overlook dreamy views of Monterey Bay. A collection of antiques decorates the parlor, where a brightly painted carousel horse sits behind a sofa, stained glass panels frame the fireplace, and freshly cut flowers are arranged about the room. Halfway up the stairway that leads to the guest rooms, a gang of teddy bears plan mischief on a small bookshelf.

Most of the 11 rooms are decorated in paisley and country floral prints. Some rooms have sloped ceilings, while others have bay windows, comfortable sitting areas, fireplaces, and scintillating views of the nearby ocean. One room with angled ceilings and a love-seat bench resembles a small chapel (which might or might not be romantic, depending on your religious views.) The Lacey Suite is the largest room at the inn; located adjacent to the parlor, it is beautifully appointed with hardwood floors, a four-poster canopy bed, tiled fireplace, and an antique claw-foot tub in the private marble bathroom. The five rooms in the Carriage House are all spacious, but the ocean view isn't as grand. These rooms have fireplaces and private baths, and one even sports a Jacuzzi tub.

Regardless of which corner is yours, you can indulge in a full country-style breakfast, served beside a fireplace and expansive windows that face the shimmering sea. Breakfast in bed is also available for an additional charge.

Romantic Warning: Except for the Lacey Suite and Jennifer Room, all of the rooms in the main house share bathrooms, which in our opinion is not conducive to uninterrupted kissing. Be sure to request a room with private facilities, unless your ability to partake in continual smooching here is contingent upon lower-priced accommodations.

LIGHTHOUSE LODGE SUITES, Pacific Grove
1249 Lighthouse Avenue
(408) 655-2111, (800) 858-1249
Very Expensive to Unbelievably Expensive
Minimum stay requirement on weekends

A large cypress shades the colorful manicured gardens that embrace this assembly of contemporary cedar-shingled cabins. If your budget can handle the surprisingly steep price tag for a suite here, all of the privacy and modern comforts you could ever want can be exclusively yours. A welcome change of pace from the all-too-familiar Victorian bed and breakfasts found along the South Coast, these 29 exceedingly modern suites are perfectly designed for romantic seclusion. Private entrances and decks ensure solitude, while vaulted ceilings, rich color schemes, and handsome furnishings guarantee stylish comfort. Everything you need is at your fingertips: a full kitchen and wet bar, gas fireplace, Jacuzzi tub set in a seductive marble bathroom, even a bedside dimmer switch to help set an amorous mood. Although there is no reason to leave this lap of luxury, don't forget that the ocean is a short drive from your front door.

Complimentary full breakfasts are served at private two-person tables in the nearby spacious common dining room, which has a fireplace at either end. In the afternoon, a hearty variety of complimentary appetizers and local wines invite quiet conversation after a busy day of touring together.

Romantic Warning: Too often, when properties are bought by large hotel chains, they lose their individuality and charm. Best Western purchased the Lighthouse Lodge several years ago, but fortunately the lodge suites haven't been altered. When making your reservations, be absolutely sure that you reserve a Lighthouse Lodge Suite rather than a unit in the separate Lighthouse Lodge hotel; otherwise you will end up with a below-standard, dark little room that isn't even remotely romantic.

SEVEN GABLES INN, Pacific Grove
555 Ocean View Boulevard
(408) 372-4341
Moderate to Very Expensive

Wildly popular bed and breakfasts are bound to experience some wear and tear, and the Seven Gables is no exception, but recent renovations were completed for just this reason. Truly a sight to behold, this immense yellow and white Victorian mansion holds court on a rocky promontory in Pacific Grove. Every plush, stately room offers dramatic views of the glistening ocean and rugged coastal mountains. Built in 1886, this celestial bed and breakfast has been painstakingly renovated, and an extensive collection of fine art and antiques sets it off to perfection. Tiffany glass windows, Persian carpets, 18th-century oil paintings, marble statues, and crystal chandeliers are just some of the collector's items crowded into the inn's common areas. Surprisingly, despite the formal polish, this is a place where you will feel at ease and comfortable.

The 14 guest rooms are inviting, cozy retreats with private baths and ocean views. Broad windows draped in lace and balloon valances make the rooms bright and sunny by day. At night, classic lighting fixtures shed a soft, warm glow. Oriental carpets, canopy beds, and classical artwork add to the historic flavor of every room. We especially liked the seven guest rooms housed in cottages behind the main house, which enjoy similar ocean views and enhanced privacy. On most weekends you will find at least one or two couples spending their wedding night here. And even if it's not your honeymoon, all that romance is sure to rub off!

Breakfast, served family-style, is a grand affair of freshly made muffins, croissants, and special egg dishes. A generous, proper high tea, also served in the exquisite dining room, features tortes, homemade fudge, and a large assortment of pastries, not to mention a stunning view of the water.

Restaurant Kissing

FANDANGO, Pacific Grove
223 17th Street
(408) 372-3456
Moderate to Expensive
Lunch and Dinner Daily; Sunday Brunch

Although the name of this restaurant may stir up images of the fast and furious gypsy dancing of southern Spain, you won't find any fancy footwork here. Instead, this is the kind of cafe where you can linger over a country meal and pleasant conversation. Fandango embraces the flavor of the Mediterranean countryside with strong influences from Spain, Italy, and France.

Most of the dining rooms in this historic adobe home offer the mellow cheer of a crackling fire. For an intimate dining experience, request seating in one of the three front rooms (the romantic appeal tends to decline as you go farther back in the restaurant). Tables are appointed with bottles of olive oil and white tablecloths, colorful checkered curtains frame the windows, dried flower arrangements abound, and the wood floors and brick hearth add a touch of Mediterranean warmth. For a more casual, slightly less amorous setting, step down a curving stone staircase to the rustic wine cellar. Here you'll find oak tables, red-curtained lampshades, and country decor accented by lively conversation. A more informal environment awaits you in the glass-domed terrace, where the open grill is sure to entice you with the scent of seafood and poultry being cooked over mesquite and fruitwood. We also recommend the sunny outside patio for a delightful lunch or Sunday brunch.

Explore the entire Mediterranean as you peruse the menu. For a taste of North Africa, try the couscous Algérois, made according to a century-old family recipe. France is represented by rack of lamb à la Provençale; Spain and Italy by wonderful paellas and pastas. Swordfish, salmon, and scallops are examples of the sea's bounty. These are but a handful of Fandango's creatively prepared dishes; you'll have to discover the rest on your own.

GERNOT'S VICTORIA HOUSE, Pacific Grove
649 Lighthouse Avenue
(408) 646-1477
Moderate
Dinner Tuesday-Sunday

No one remains in town for long without hearing word of Gernot's; in fact, its outstanding reputation speaks for itself. This stately Victorian mansion holds three circular dining rooms, each decorated with floral wallpaper, lace curtains, hardwood floors, and Oriental rugs. One room features a cozy fireplace tucked away near a handful of intimate tables. The warm glow of candlelight makes this a perfect place for a heartfelt rendezvous.

Intriguing specials, moderately priced, are offered every evening, including such delicacies as simple broiled salmon with angel-hair pasta, or breast of duck roasted with raspberry-brandy sauce. Share bites of poached salmon served on spinach with a dill sauce followed by chocolate cake covered with tart raspberry sauce. Dinners include soup and salad and the gracious service lives up to the food and the setting.

JOE ROMBI'S LA MIA CUCINA, Pacific Grove
208 17th Street
(408) 373-2416
Moderate
Dinner Wednesday-Sunday

In a minimalist approach to decorating, a handful of tables with white linens and black chairs are organized around the perimeter of Joe Rombi's lively restaurant. The dining area itself resembles a small box with large windows overlooking a quiet street. Illuminated by track lights, European advertising art posters from the late 1800s stand out as the only splashes of color against the stark white walls. Although the atmosphere is a little slick for romantic tastes, you won't be disappointed with the savory pasta specials, hearty pizzas, and succulent seafood entrées that highlight the menu.

OLD BATH HOUSE, Pacific Grove
620 Ocean View Boulevard
(408) 375-5196
Moderate to Expensive
Dinner Daily

The Old Bath House is a time-honored establishment cherished by locals and visitors alike. Set at the edge of Lovers Point Park, the restaurant is known for intimate oceanside dining and scrumptious desserts. Dark wood walls, dim track lighting, and gracious service create a private world where you can enjoy the view and each other's company. Cozy tables draped in burgundy face large picture windows; watch as otters play in the surf and lovers stroll along the beach arm in arm. When the sea finally swallows up the sun, distant city lights from the distant shore mingle with the flickering flames of candles alight all over the restaurant. Little can compete with the intimacy this place sparks, except the food, which is a blend of French and northern Italian cuisine. Desserts are created by the kitchen's own pastry chef and worth every sinfully rich calorie.

PASTA MIA, Pacific Grove
481 Lighthouse Avenue
(408) 375-7709
Moderate
Dinner Daily

Set in the heart of Pacific Grove, this renovated Victorian home looks more like a private residence than an Italian restaurant—at least from the outside. Inside, smooth hardwood floors and lace window treatments in the former dining and living areas are the only traces left of the home's historic past. Garlic cloves, chiles, and culinary knickknacks adorn the walls. Freshly cut red roses accent tables draped with white linens in the two casual dining rooms. For more privacy, request a table in the cozy window alcove that overlooks Pacific Grove's charming store-lined streets. Hearty homemade soups and pastas are the kitchen's specialties; try the half-moon pasta stuffed with pesto in a zesty lemon cream sauce or the prawns sautéed in a champagne cream sauce. For dessert, Pasta Mia serves up some of the best tiramisu in town.

THAI BISTRO II, Pacific Grove
159 Central Avenue
(408) 372-8700
Inexpensive to Moderate
Lunch and Dinner Daily

Located on busy Central Avenue, Thai Bistro II is a great place for a casual lunch, especially if you're seeking a respite from the all-too-familiar California cuisine. Thai soups, spicy salads, fried rice, and curry and noodle dishes are featured on the extensive menu. Modestly decorated, the restaurant has a small bar at the entryway and adobe walls adorned with landscape paintings. We found the tables a bit too close for comfort, but the striped cushions and pillows help create a cozy atmosphere. If you don't mind plastic chairs, take advantage of the outdoor patio seating available most sunny days.

Outdoor Kissing

PACIFIC GROVE SHORELINE

Take Highway 1 to westbound Highway 68. Highway 68 becomes Forest Avenue; take it all the way to the ocean.

Take time to saunter hand-in-hand along **OCEAN VIEW BOULEVARD**, where a whisper of saltwater gently sprays over you as waves thunder against the rocks at water's edge. Here you can watch sea otters splashing in kelp beds and pelicans perching in sunny spots. If the time of year is right, you might even catch sight of a whale or two swimming by as they migrate south for winter. If you expect your walk to take you to **LOVERS POINT PARK**, at the southern tip of Monterey Bay, consider packing a wine and cheese picnic to share in the shade of a tree or the warmth of a gloriously sunny day.

For more breathtaking ocean views and a look at Monterey County's past, be sure to visit the **POINT PINOS LIGHTHOUSE**, situated at the northernmost tip of the Monterey Peninsula. This National Historic Landmark was built in 1855 to guide mariners past the hazards of the rocky coast. Now the oldest operating lighthouse on the West Coast, it is fascinating to explore, and an ideal vantage point for savoring magnificent ocean vistas. If you crave isolation, be sure to traverse the glorious, windswept sands of nearby **ASILOMAR BEACH**.

17-MILE DRIVE
$6.50 entry fee

From Highway 1, take Highway 68 west to Sunset Drive, and go west again to the Pacific Grove entrance gate.

Plan on taking an entire day to tour the 17-Mile Drive. It is so awesome and resplendent that you will want to take much longer to travel this unspoiled terrain than its 17-mile length suggests. Stop along the way to observe the infinite variations as ocean and land converge along the Monterey Peninsula. White, foamy waves wash up on black rocks, sending a spray of sea into the crisp, clean air; sea gulls' cries pierce the misty air as unruffled pelicans glide near the water's surface.

As you round one spiral of road, you'll spy a crescent-shaped, sandy cove that provides a calm place to pause. Here, sunlight shimmers on the vast Pacific, and in the distance a sailing vessel slowly makes its way across the horizon. Other turns in the road reveal undulating sand dunes, violently frothing sea currents, and abundant marine life sanctuaries. Watch for the stark beauty of a lone cypress clinging to the side of a cliff, swaying in the wind, and be sure to stop at **SEAL AND BIRD ROCK** to witness a multitude of marine mammals and birds basking in the sun and frolicking in the water.

As you continue on your passage up a hill, turning to the east, you enter a deeply wooded area that shelters palatial homes and estates and the occasional world-class golf course. Unless watching the rich and famous is your idea of an intimate interlude, continue on and in a few more turns the natural beauty of the peninsula will be yours again. If you are hungry or would like to pause, you can visit one of the restaurants at the **INN AT SPANISH BAY** or **THE LODGE AT PEBBLE BEACH** (see Hotel/Bed and Breakfast Kissing in Pebble Beach). Some of these restaurants over-look the stunningly profound landscape below, and the food almost equals the views.

Don't let the weather dissuade you from traversing 17-Mile Drive. On stormy days the ocean and clouds create an even more dramatic visual tapestry and you're less likely to encounter swarms of tourists.

Pebble Beach

Elite Pebble Beach, securely established on 17-Mile Drive, is home to millionaires, deluxe accommodations, five-star restaurants, and the dramatic meeting of surf and shore. It is probably best known for its championship golf courses, which, on occasion, host the U.S. Open. Golf isn't typically a couples sport, although we know some couples who love golfing together. Even so, we don't recommend staying here because of the impressive courses. It's the sheer beauty of Pebble Beach's coastline that makes this a lip-worthy destination. Unfortunately, views of this caliber merit higher rates, so don't expect to find reasonably priced accommodations here.

Hotel/Bed and Breakfast Kissing   4-98

THE INN AT SPANISH BAY, Pebble Beach   3-99   ❤❤❤
2700 17-Mile Drive
(408) 647-7500, (800) 654-9300
http://www.pebble-beach.com
Unbelievably Expensive

Although the exclusive Inn at Spanish Bay looks like a condominium complex and feels like a country-club, your affectionate inclinations will not be repressed. Not only does this world-class resort cater to your every imaginable need, it also has breathtaking ocean views beyond a sloping, emerald green golf course dotted with cypress trees. Deer graze at their leisure in this serene setting and at dusk bagpipe melodies drift into earshot from the dune cliffs at the water's edge. In addition to spectacular views, the resort has a full-service fitness club, tennis courts, a premier golf course, several choice restaurants, and an exemplary staff that will spoil you rotten.

Guest rooms with ocean vistas are preferred, but they are also considerably more expensive. Many rooms command refreshing views of cypress forests instead and are much more reasonably priced (keep in mind that "reasonable" is a relative term here). No matter what kind of view your budget allows, you are sure to appreciate the modern artwork and elegant decor. The 270 rooms are equipped with fireplaces, deep soaking tubs with separate glass-enclosed showers, and all the amenities you'd expect from a luxury resort. Nintendos have even been included for "kids at heart," although we know better ways to spend romantic time together.

Romantic Suggestion: If you don't want to leave this prime locale to find a place to eat, fear not. The inn has two excellent dining options: **ROY'S** and **THE BAY CLUB** (see Restaurant Kissing).

THE LODGE AT PEBBLE BEACH, Pebble Beach
17-Mile Drive
(408) 624-3811, (800) 654-9300
http://www.pebble-beach.com
Unbelievably Expensive
Recommended Wedding Site

Upscale and refined, the Lodge at Pebble Beach is a luxury resort for romance-seekers with deep pockets and a desire for elegance. (Don't be fooled by the word "lodge"; you won't find any antlers on the walls here, just a plethora of golf-related mementos and photographs.) Built in 1919, this world-renowned piece of heaven has attracted golfers and lovers alike for decades. Although the service is a bit stuffy at times, that shouldn't distract you from enjoying the golf course, shopping square, fitness area, tennis club, and equestrian center.

The lobby is simply breathtaking. Two large marble fireplaces stand guard at opposite ends of the enormous sitting area. Plaster sculptures, leafy green plants, and original landscapes add splashes of color to the rich cream decor. Plush sofas and chairs are clustered around glass tables and a stately grand piano. Lining the entire far wall, immense floor-to-ceiling windows look out over a perfectly manicured golf course and beyond to the dramatic ocean surf. Step outside on the wrought-iron deck for a panoramic view of the grounds.

Although the property itself is too large to be considered intimate, the incredibly posh rooms more than make up for it. Each of the 161 luxury suites and guest rooms is appointed with polished, contemporary furnishings and all the right amenities to make your stay extremely comfortable. Forty-seven rooms offer fantastic ocean views with nothing standing between you and the sea. Sixty-five have what they call garden views, which really means they overlook the expansive main lawn and the award-winning 18-hole golf course. Rooms with scenic vistas have partial views of the ocean. After a day on the green, you and your loved one can retire to your suite and relax in the wonderful Jacuzzi tub or cuddle up in front of a wood-burning fireplace as the murmur of the Pacific Ocean lulls you to sleep.

One of the more choice buildings is the Sloat, where the rooms are decorated in soft browns and accented with rich maroon and hunter green linens. The antique-style overstuffed couches and chairs invite you to surround yourselves in comfort. Whatever your taste, from timeless antiques to fresh art deco, or somewhere in between, the Lodge at Pebble Beach will inspire many elegant ocean kisses.

Romantic Note: CLUB XIX, (408) 625-8519 (Moderate to Expensive), located on the lower level of the main building, doubles as a casual Parisian cafe by day and an intimate French restaurant by night. Whether you decide on lunch or dinner, you'll enjoy the view: Club XIX's windows face Carmel Bay and the 18th green. Each table is coupled with plush chairs and adorned with white and black linens, gold-rimmed china, and candles. Wine bottles are stored in the light wood walls, and a small open bar stands near the entryway. Try the herb-coated rack of lamb, served on grilled polenta and accompanied by spinach, goat cheese, and wild mushrooms.

For fresh regional seafood, we recommend **THE CYPRESS ROOM**, (408) 625-8524 (Moderate to Expensive) on the entrance level of the main building. Light wood furnishings, cream walls and pillars, and glass-encased chandeliers give the space an airy elegance while the contemporary decor complements spectacular views of the bay. White tablecloths and fresh flowers add the final touches. Specialties include Cajun-spiced sea bass and grilled swordfish. Lunch and dinner are served daily.

Restaurant Kissing

ROY'S, Pebble Beach
2700 17-Mile Drive, at the Inn at Spanish Bay
(408) 647-7423
Moderate to Expensive
Breakfast Lunch and Dinner Daily

Yes, this is Roy Yamaguchi's newest outpost, and to our delight the Eurasian cuisine here more than lives up to his far-reaching reputation. Watch the chef performing culinary wonders in an open kitchen that extends along one wall of this casual but classy contemporary dining room. Peaked copper ceilings and brightly patterned linens are fun accents, and service is laid-back and friendly but still efficient. The restaurant's popularity means quiet intimacy is hard to come by, but the splendid ocean scenery and faultless seafood will take your mind off the crowds. What to order? Now is the time to be adventurous—you simply can't go wrong at Roy's. We recommend the hibachi-style salmon, the spicy seared ono, or the ginger-seared mahimahi. For dessert, the special chocolate almond soufflé with vanilla ice cream, drowned in a sinfully decadent chocolate sauce, is an absolute must.

Romantic Alternative: Although the Inn at Spanish Bay's **BAY CLUB RESTAURANT**, (408) 647-7490 (Moderate to Expensive) lacks a nation-wide reputation, its hearty northern Italian cuisine is delicious. If your priority is quiet time together, the Bay Club's quiet atmosphere is a preferable alternative to upbeat Roy's. Sleek and sophisticated, the dining room is appointed with high-backed plush chairs, track lighting, and lavish flower arrangements. The long-stemmed rose at every linen-cloaked table is a decidedly romantic touch. Although some of the tables set against the walls are a little too close for comfort, tables next to the bay windows have inspiring ocean views and adequate privacy. Dinner is served nightly.

Carmel

Artists, poets, and playwrights congregated in this seaside hamlet at the turn-of-the-century, and even today Carmel retains much of its bohemian charm. Upscale boutiques, art galleries, quaint inns, and some of the finest restaurants in the state occupy the rows of storybook cottages cloistered in Carmel's one-square-mile city limits. There are no streetlights, and in the evenings lamps in storefronts and restaurants illuminate the town's narrow boulevards. Streetlights aren't the only big city amenities missing in Carmel—you won't find address numbers, billboards, parking meters, or neon signs either. There is actually a law on the books stating that it is illegal to wear high heels on the sidewalks, although you don't need to worry—it is not enforced!

Naturalists and romantics will appreciate Carmel's serene seaside setting. Beautiful white sandy beaches provide a more restful setting in which to while away the hours. Without question, you will find yourselves captivated by this town's charm and its flawless natural setting.

Romantic Note: Part of Carmel's appeal is its small size. As we mentioned, most establishments don't even have numbers on their doors. Consequently, most of the entries in this section use street junctions instead of formal addresses. Once you are in Carmel, this will be more than enough to help you find your destination.

Romantic Warning: Idyllic Carmel is the South Coast's most popular destination. Be forewarned that most weekends (year-round) are disturbingly crowded. During the summer the town is full to the point of bursting. We recommend timing your visit on a weekday or in the off-season.

Hotel/Bed and Breakfast Kissing

CARMEL GARDEN COURT INN, Carmel
Torres and Fourth
(408) 624-6926
Moderate to Very Expensive
Minimum stay requirement on weekends

Despite its location on a busy street, the Carmel Garden Court Inn is a delightful place to retreat from the world. Follow the brick pathway through a garden accented with wooden trestles, hanging pots of greenery, and bubbling fountains. Stroll among the oak trees or rest on a park bench surrounded by beautiful bougainvillea. At the end of the day, you can create your own secluded haven by simply closing the gate to your private flower-filled patio.

All nine rooms at the inn have wood-burning fireplaces, private entrances, and a few unexpected amenities, such as towel warmers, VCRs, and refrigerators, to make your stay as comfortable as possible. Although individually decorated, they share a simple country theme of knotty pine walls, wicker furnishings, floral prints, and homey knickknacks. The five mini-suites have large picture windows overlooking lovely secluded patios, as well as cozy eating nooks furnished with intimate tables for two. The four remaining rooms are attached to the main building and do not have private patios; however, the largest upstairs suite does offer a full kitchen and a lovely antique headboard. We hesitate to recommend the smaller Torre Street rooms only because they suffer from distracting traffic noise. Each morning a champagne buffet is served in the tiny lobby, or you can ask to have breakfast delivered to your room on a silver platter.

CARRIAGE HOUSE INN, Carmel
Junipero, between Seventh and Eighth
(408) 625-2585, (800) 433-4732
http://www.Webdzine.com/inns
Very Expensive
Minimum stay requirement on weekends

Although this wood-shingled country inn is nestled in the heart of picturesque Carmel, you'll feel worlds away from the bustling village once you've settled inside your room. All 13 comfortably appointed rooms are spacious retreats with wood-burning fireplaces, king-size beds, and down comforters. Lace curtains, old-fashioned wallpapers, and country antiques give each room upscale turn-of-the-century character. Upstairs rooms have open-beam cathedral ceilings and sunken or whirlpool bathtubs. In one of the two-room suites, touches of mauve accent a massive four-poster pine bed, an exposed beam ceiling towers overhead, and a fireplace crackles right by the bed. Another fireplace in the private sitting area is supplied with plenty of logs, ideal for fireside kissing.

An assortment of wines and cheeses is served every afternoon in the lobby. In the morning a generous continental breakfast is delivered to each room on an old-fashioned platter.

COBBLESTONE INN, Carmel
Junipero, between Seventh and Eighth
(408) 625-5222, (800) 833-8836
Moderate to Expensive

The Cobblestone has a reputation as Carmel's best-run bed-and-breakfast establishment (and that's saying a lot), so you'll be pleased to know that it also has some of the more reasonable prices in town. Teddy bears and country knickknacks accent the cheery living room, which fronts a cobblestone courtyard. In this comfortable setting, a lavish breakfast buffet and afternoon hors d'oeuvres are served next to a massive stone fireplace. (You can also have breakfast brought to your room if that is your kissing preference.)

White shutters ensure privacy in each of the 24 countrified guest rooms decorated with floral wallpapers, watercolor paintings, and plaid linens. Antique brass beds and river-rock fireplaces are the romantic highlights of every room. Although the lower-priced rooms are quite small, they are still charming and comfortable. In the larger rooms, couches are snuggled near the fireplaces in an additional sitting room. All of the rooms, regardless of price, have standard private baths, and the largest window in every room looks out toward the courtyard, which unfortunately also doubles as a parking lot, limiting your privacy when your shutters are open.

THE CYPRESS INN, Carmel
Lincoln and Seventh
(408) 624-3871, (800) 443-7443
Moderate to Expensive
Minimum stay requirement on weekends

With its Moorish Mediterranean architecture, the Cypress Inn is an attractive display of white stucco walls, red tile roof, and Spanish arches. This stately inn wraps around a lovely garden courtyard overflowing with flowers and greenery; wrought-iron tables take full advantage of the setting.

After enjoying a continental breakfast in the courtyard, relax in one of the two parlors. Part library and part lounge, the smaller sitting area features a full-service bar and dignified reading tables. Movie star Doris Day owns this inn, and posters from her stellar career adorn the walls. Elegantly decorated in shades of pale apricot, the main lobby is a great place to curl up in front of the white marble fireplace. Evenly spaced windows and a peaked wood-beamed ceiling give this room its spacious, sunny atmosphere.

If you're expecting the guest rooms to match the refined elegance of the lobby, you're bound to be disappointed. Most of the rooms are small, with peach walls and unimpressive linens. Fortunately, the rooms are currently undergoing renovations to include down comforters and attractive new window treatments. For now, the inn's redeeming features include glass showers and marble bathrooms, and one room boasts a Jacuzzi tub. Some rooms offer verandas with far-off glimpses of blue sea, and a few have fireplaces. Despite the rather ordinary guest rooms, the inn's charming design and engaging ambience can evoke the appropriate frame of mind for encounters of the heart.

LA PLAYA HOTEL, Carmel   😘😘😘
Camino Real and Eighth
(408) 624-6476, (800) 582-8900
http://mry.infohut.com
Moderate to Unbelievably Expensive
Minimum stay requirement on weekends
Recommended Wedding Site

At the grand La Playa Hotel, the Pacific Ocean peers at you through pine and cypress trees, and the sound of the dramatic surf echoes in the distance. In spite of its "hotel" appellation, this sprawling pink Mediterranean-style villa is the place to stay if you long for both a tranquil setting and all the luxury of a larger establishment.

La Playa's lobby is warmed by an enormous fireplace and decorated with hand-loomed area rugs and lovely antiques. A sweeping staircase winds upstairs to spartan guest rooms filled with hand-carved Spanish-style furnishings. Rooms in the main building are somewhat smaller, just right for couples who want to be closer than usual, and some offer fireplaces and breathtaking ocean views. Our favorites are situated on the lower floor, with private terraces that open onto the property's lush inner courtyard and two acres of formal gardens. Here, you'll also find a heated pool encircled by lavender poppies swaying on slender stems.

Five additional cottages are nestled in a nearby garden grove. Although these cabins offer all the privacy in the world, they are also the most expensive units at La Playa. Each has its own full kitchen or wet bar, terrace or garden patio, and wood-stocked fireplace. Bordering on rustic, the cottages' eclectic antiques and countrified interiors are not as upscale or elegant as La Playa's other accommodations.

Romantic Suggestion: Breakfast is not included with your stay, but is available at La Playa's semicasual **TERRACE GRILL RESTAURANT**, (408) 624-4010 (Moderate to Expensive), which is open for breakfast, lunch, and dinner. The eclectic menu includes standard items like sandwiches, pasta, steak, and seafood, but the views of the lovely inner courtyard and resplendent gardens are wonderful.

LINCOLN GREEN INN, Carmel
Carmelo, between 15th and 16th
(408) 624-1880, (800) 262-1262
Expensive
Minimum stay requirement on weekends

Lincoln Green Cottages would be a much more appropriate name for this modest inn. Far from Carmel's bustling town center, these four quaint English country cottages reside behind a white picket fence in a quiet neighborhood, mere blocks from Carmel's legendary beachfront. A white picket fence encloses the picturesque cottages, painted white with forest green trim and named Robin Hood, Little John, Friar Tuck, and Maid Marian. To our surprise and disappointment, their interiors lack much of the setting's exterior charm. Despite beamed cathedral ceilings and stone fireplaces, the dated kitchens and other amenities are purely utilitarian, lacking any sense of style or élan. (At these prices you definitely expect more.) What makes them worth your romantic consideration is the peaceful setting and nearby beaches. From this vantage point, you may never know that the summer crowds are only a mile down the street.

Romantic Note: Food provisions are your own responsibility here and breakfast is not included with your stay.

MISSION RANCH, Carmel
26270 Dolores Street
(408) 624-6436, (800) 538-8221

Moderate to Very Expensive
Minimum stay requirement on weekends

A short distance away from the often intense city of Carmel lies a down-home surprise. Worth visiting for its setting alone, the Mission Ranch looks as if it were dropped here straight from the ranchlands of Texas. (The six championship tennis courts, exercise room, putting green, and banquet facilities feel oddly out of place.) A renovated 1850s farmhouse and a handful of white cottages with green trim are scattered on this rambling property, surrounded by cypress trees, sheep pastures, and rolling hills that reach down to the fringes of the ocean. Owned by Clint Eastwood (this distinction may give it more prestige than it deserves), this friendly place encourages you to leave any notion of city life behind.

Mismatched antiques and old-fashioned colors and fabrics give some of the ranch's 31 guest rooms a somewhat dated, motel-style look. The queen- or king-size beds are draped with floral or country-style patchwork quilts, and picture windows survey enticing views of lush green meadows dotted with sea grass. Meadow View rooms and the Hay Loft Bedroom have gas fireplaces and one-person whirlpool tubs. The Bunkhouse cottage is equipped with a full kitchen in case you want to cook a lovers' feast and dine in together. Our favorite spots for some easygoing country togetherness are the six guest rooms in the picturesque farmhouse with hardwood floors, lovely antiques, and wide wraparound verandas with trailing bougainvillea.

Romantic Warning: The bar-and-grill-style **RESTAURANT AT MISSION RANCH**, (408) 625-9040 (Moderate) serves up standard steak and seafood and features checked tablecloths and an informal atmosphere. Look elsewhere for romantic, intimate dining.

VAGABOND'S HOUSE INN, Carmel
Fourth and Dolores
(408) 624-7738, (800) 262-1262
Inexpensive to Expensive

A large gnarled oak stands guard in the center of the Vagabond's small inner courtyard, where a waterfall spills over rocks, and potted camellias, rhododendrons, and ferns are caressed by the breeze. Many of the 11 modestly decorated guest rooms in this unpretentious English Tudor home face this quiet scene. Although some of the rooms are dim and have dated touches, special amenities include kitchenettes, wood-burning fireplaces, and a decanter of sherry beside each bed. Knotty pine walls lend rustic charm to several rooms. Our favorite room has a direct view of the massive oak, which is adorned with tiny white lights that could almost be mistaken for twinkling stars against the midnight sky. In the morning, an extended continental breakfast of freshly baked breads, fruit, and egg dishes can be served directly to your own room. Best of all, the price is right, making the Vagabond's House a relatively inexpensive place to call home for a few days of relaxing time together.

Restaurant Kissing

ANTON AND MICHEL, Carmel
Mission, between Ocean and Seventh
(408) 624-2406
Expensive
Lunch and Dinner Daily

Anton and Michel prides itself on having "just the right touch." True enough, almost everything about this luxurious restaurant is impressive and memorable. Decorative oil paintings embellish the pastel walls, sleek white columns separate the dining rooms from one another, and an entire wall of windows in one room looks out to a poolside courtyard with bronze statues and a cascading water fountain. Candle lanterns placed on the linen-draped tables cast a soft, romantic glow, inspiring intimate conversation—that is, until the food arrives. You can't help but be diverted by the aroma of Pacific salmon broiled with gazpacho beurre blanc or medallion of pepper-crusted ahi tuna. Once you've satiated your appetites and turned your attention back to each other, it is time for dessert. We highly recommend the bananas flambé or bananas Foster. However, don't expect much from the tiramisu—the night we ate here the mascarpone cheese was hardened and distasteful.

CALIFORNIA THAI, Carmel
Between San Carlos and Fourth
(408) 622-1160
Inexpensive to Moderate
Lunch Wednesday-Monday; Dinner Daily

From the black-and-white-checked floor to the sparsely decorated coral walls, it's obvious that this isn't your usual Thai eatery. Contemporary floral arrangements, white tablecloths, flickering candles, and high-backed chairs suggest European elegance rather than exotic Southeast Asia. A raised terrace hugs the perimeter of the room in the main dining area, while simple chandeliers hang overhead. Each table is draped with white paper and equipped with colorful pens for those moments of artistic adoration inspired by your sweetheart.

The menu is filled with traditional Thai favorites such as spring rolls, phad Thai, and cashew chicken among the many options. Vegetarians need not worry; California Thai offers an extensive list of vegetarian entrées made from organic produce, and many of the meat dishes can be adapted to vegetarian preferences as well.

CASANOVA, Carmel
On Fifth, between San Carlos and Mission
(408) 625-0501
Expensive
Breakfast, Lunch, and Dinner Daily

Tucked away on one of Carmel's quiet side streets, this charming restaurant resides in an adobe home once owned by Charlie Chaplin's cook (a footnote that is more interesting than significant). A small brick patio surrounded by shrubs gives no hint of the excellent French and Italian country-style cuisine served inside. Romantic repasts, accompanied by lively international music, can be had in any of the cozy dining rooms. Striped curtains adorn the windows, low hanging lamps add rural character, and pastoral odds and ends decorate the earthy clay walls. An inner courtyard offers dining beneath the stars, with heat lamps that will warm your hearts even in winter.

Entrées include cannelloni and filet mignon béarnaise. If you have a difficult time deciding between seafood and meat, compromise with the paella Catalane, full of chorizo and assorted shellfish, or the suprême de poulet, a chicken breast stuffed with prawns, basil, and sun-dried tomatoes. All dinners come with three courses, including antipasto and a variety of scrumptious appetizers. One can hardly help but hold hands across the table (and make romantic plans) while enjoying everything Casanova has to offer.

FLYING FISH GRILL, Carmel
On Mission, between Ocean and Seventh
(408) 625-1962
Moderate
Dinner Daily

Imagine a redwood den where flying fish soar overhead as you enjoy mouthwatering Japanese dishes. If this sounds inviting, make your way to the basement of Carmel Plaza to discover Kenny Fukumoto's Flying Fish Grill. Dark and intimate, the interior features a glowing fireplace and cozy booths. Blue linens make a splash on the bare wood tables, accented with a fan of chopsticks. The warm glow of candlelight illuminates a mobile of fish swimming under the open beams of the ceiling. You'll have difficulty deciding between the many tempting seafood dishes waiting to please your palate. We recommend the California rolls, tempura prawns, or scrumptious grilled salmon in a ginger-soy glaze. Vegetables prepared to perfection accompany most meals. If you're ready for a feast, try the seafood clay pot for two: a delicious medley of seafood, vegetables, tofu, rice noodles, sauces, and jasmine rice.

THE FRENCH POODLE, Carmel
Junipero, at Fifth
(408) 624-8643
Expensive
Dinner Monday-Saturday

Why would anyone name a restaurant The French Poodle and expect to be taken seriously? (In this case, the management actually may take itself a little *too* seriously; see the Romantic Warning.) Exquisite crystal chandeliers cast a soft, warm glow in the exceedingly small and intimate dining room, appointed with mauve walls and luxurious draperies. Candles flicker in oversized wineglasses placed atop every linen-draped table. As you would guess, the specialty is authentic French cuisine, from escargot to goose liver pâté. We highly recommend the tenderly grilled salmon with muscadet wine and shallots, or the savory giant prawns served over perfectly cooked angel-hair pasta. Desserts include traditional French *denouements* like cheese and fruit plates, in addition to not-so-traditional homemade sorbets and strawberries laced with Grand Marnier.

Romantic Warning: In spite of all this praise, we must warn you that even for a classic French restaurant, The French Poodle takes formality to an exceedingly high plane. Our waiter stood stiffly at attention several feet from our table and catered to our every need. When we slipped our jackets off, he asked if he could turn up the heater. When our glasses dwindled down to empty, he rushed to our table with refills without being asked. Although we were spoiled beyond belief, we found this level of service to be rather intrusive and distracting. We also got the distinct feeling that our waiter was listening to our entire conversation.

GIULIANO'S, Carmel
Mission and Fifth
(408) 622-0650
Moderate to Expensive
Dinner Daily

Flowers spill over the garden box that fronts Giuliano's tiny one-room restaurant, nestled on the first floor of a picturesque Tudor home in the heart of Carmel. Smiling pig figurines hold menus in the front window, lending winsome humor to the otherwise sleek and modern dining room. Oversized mirrors and racks of wine adorn the walls above snug red-cushioned booths that border the room. Dimly lit wall sconces and glowing candles at every table create a romantic climate ripe for kissing (although some of the tables are a little too close together for comfortable displays of affection). There is something here for all tastes, including Louisiana prawns, classic Italian pasta entrées, and mesquite-grilled seafood. The delicious menu and featured wines change daily.

MONDO'S TRATTORIA, Carmel
Delores Street, between Ocean and Seventh
(408) 624-8977
Inexpensive to Moderate
Lunch and Dinner Daily

This rustic Italian trattoria looks like it belongs in the rolling hills of Tuscany instead of downtown Carmel. A fire warms the bucolic dining room, with its brick floor and open-beamed ceiling bejeweled with wine bottles. A large wrought-iron chandelier illuminates a handful of dark wood tables topped with bottles of olive oil and dried flower arrangements. Although some of the tables are arranged too closely for our romantic preferences, cozy floral booths set against the wall allow for quiet moments. The kitchen serves up delicious northern and southern Italian fare ranging from savory bruschetta to linguine or penne pasta topped with vegetables and seafood, accented with fresh Parmesan and Romano cheese. And if you like tiramisu, you've come to the right place.

RAFFAELLO, Carmel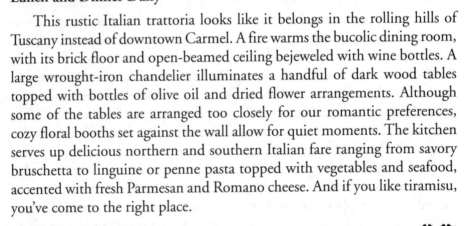
On Mission, between Ocean and Seventh
(408) 624-1541
Moderate
Dinner Wednesday-Monday

Raffaello claims to be the oldest singularly owned restaurant in Carmel; in fact, rumor has it that the 82-year-old owner still does the cooking! One bite of your delectable dinner, however, and you'll be glad such a legacy continues. The atmosphere is formal but simple, with only 12 tables enclosed by the pink stucco walls. Whisper sweet nothings across the table as candle-light dances before your eyes. Traditional Italian entrées from seafood to veal to free range chicken appear on the menu each night, along with a selection of pasta dishes that can be served à la carte. Homemade crêpes for dessert are an absolute delicious must.

SANS SOUCI, Carmel
Lincoln, between Fifth and Sixth
(408) 624-6220
Expensive
Dinner Thursday-Tuesday

Locals have been finding romance at Sans Souci for more than 30 years. Elegance and warmth are provide by the crystal chandeliers and a blazing fire in the hearth. Exotic flower displays are arranged on the mantel, and tall candles flicker on the linen-covered tables. The menu is classically French, with innovative treatments of local seasonal produce and seafood. Upon request, tuxedo-clad waiters will prepare certain dishes at your table, including chateaubriand and rack of lamb. Desserts made only for two are the perfect finale: we recommend the cherries jubilee or crêpes with ice cream and fresh fruit, both flamed tableside.

SIMPSON'S RESTAURANT, Carmel
San Carlos, at Fifth
(408) 624-5755
Moderate to Expensive
Dinner Monday-Saturday

If you've always wanted to travel to Wonderland with Alice and visit the Queen of Hearts, here's your chance. You'll also get to meet the Joker and the Knave, who are depicted in playful murals that decorate this unusual dining room. Strands of ivy wind around terra-cotta pillars and hanging lamps shed soft light on handfuls of cozy red booths set against the walls. White linens and fresh flowers give each table a fresh, formal appearance. Although the menu is small, this family-owned establishment specializes in continental cuisine and oak- and mesquite-grilled steaks and seafood. Simpson's is a happy alternative to the plethora of Italian and French restaurants in the area.

Outdoor Kissing

CARMEL BEACH

From Highway 1, turn west onto Ocean and follow it until it dead-ends at the beach.

Carmel Beach is an awesome stretch of surf and sand. Those lucky souls with houses that border this mile-long parcel of heaven are in an enviable position. The landscape is an inspiring combination of surging waves, rolling hills, and endless ocean. A sandy stroll in the morning (before the populace wakes up) or at sunset, when the sky is burnished with fire (and it doesn't matter who else is there), can renew the soul. All kinds of sparks can be kindled from this vantage point. Don't miss it.

POINT LOBOS STATE RESERVE, Carmel
(408) 624-4909
$6 per car day-use fee

Located on the ocean side of Highway 1, four miles south of Carmel.

It's been called "the greatest meeting of land and water in the world." Where better to share a lasting kiss? Almost as exhilarating as love itself, Point Lobos is one of our favorite spots in the Monterey area. At the Sea Lion Point parking lot, the first sound you'll hear are the sharp barks of these stalwart creatures. A short trail along a hillside blanketed with ice plants leads to the promontory, where you'll see them crowded on the water-washed rocks. Nearby are tide pools you can explore together, searching out scrambling crabs and purple sea urchins. If you wish, follow one of the less traveled trails that hug the cliffs of this rugged coastline. Seclusion and spectacular scenery are yours to share.

ROBINSON JEFFERS' TOR HOUSE, Carmel
26304 Ocean View Avenue
(408) 624-1813
http://www.torhouse.org
$5 for adults
Reservations Recommended
Open by guided tour only on Friday and Saturday,
from 10 A.M. to 3 P.M.

From Highway 1, turn onto Ocean Avenue and head toward downtown Carmel. Turn left onto Scenic, left onto Stewart, then left again onto Ocean View. Look for Tor House and its stone Hawk Tower on the left.

Even those who have never heard of the poet Robinson Jeffers will be inspired by his ocean-view homestead. A simple Tudor cottage built in 1918, Tor House ("tor" is an old Irish word for a craggy knoll) is where Jeffers wrote all of his major works and most of his poetry. More important, this is where he lived happily with his wife, Una, and their twin sons. Loving epigrams are carved into the timbers throughout the home. Jeffers built the Hawk Tower by hand, making "stone love stone," as a treasured retreat for Una and a magical playground for the children. In Una's room, at the very top of the tower, an epigram carved in the wooden mantel of the fireplace reads, "THEY MAKE THEIR DREAMS FOR THEMSELVES," truly reflecting Jeffers' lifestyle, and perhaps expressing the affections of others who come here.

Carmel Valley

Hotel/ Bed and Breakfast Kissing

CARMEL VALLEY RANCH RESORT, Carmel Valley
One Old Ranch Road
(408) 625-9500, (800) 422-7635
Unbelievably Expensive
Minimum stay required seasonally

Even if you're not a celebrity, you'll feel like one as you pass through the gated entrance of this exclusive estate. Upon arrival, you are greeted by name and chauffeured via golf cart to your secluded, luxurious suite (this is especially handy if you haven't mastered the art of packing light). Nestled in the undulating hills of the Carmel Valley, 1,200 acres of this 1,700-acre wooded property remain pristine and undeveloped. Deer are frequently seen grazing under the aged, sculpted oaks that shade the sprawling grounds.

A scattering of contemporary ranch-style guest buildings fits right into this sensational natural setting. Privacy is guaranteed in each of the 100 upscale two-room guest suites, which have private entrances, decks, and all the comforts of home. Cathedral ceilings soar above modern appointments, soft floral watercolors set the mood, and white shutters open to reveal stunning views of the valley. A gas fireplace radiates warmth in the stylish living room, and a second fireplace in the bedroom promises late-night romance. If you have the good fortune of reserving a spa suite (there are only 12), you can indulge in a romantic soak beneath the stars in a private hot tub on a wrap-around deck set high in the trees—a true nest for lovebirds.

Exclusive usually translates into expensive, and Carmel Valley Ranch is no exception. Fortunately, you get what you pay for here. Your comfort is the ranch's top priority, and the gracious staff is a phone call (and golf cart) away. Nightly turn-down service delivers freshly baked cookies to your room. Other amenities cater to the athletically inclined; choices include golfing on an 18-hole championship course, playing tennis, horseback riding, hiking, and swimming. You'll want for nothing during your stay here, except more time to relish the breathtaking scenery and quiet surroundings.

Romantic Note: Although Carmel is a relatively short drive (15 minutes) from the ranch, you won't even have to go that far for good food. Adjacent to the lobby, the lovely **OAKS RESTAURANT**, (408) 626-2533 (Moderate to Expensive) is open daily for breakfast, lunch, and dinner. Well-spaced tables covered with white linens look out to views of the oak-dotted valley. Relish a zesty Spanish omelet for breakfast. For dinner try the inspired cioppino with vine-ripened tomatoes, grilled sourdough, and Carmel Valley goat cheese. The home-baked whole wheat hazelnut bread is divine, and we savored every rich, earthy bite of the shiitake mushrooms with cream in phyllo. Last but never least, top off your meal with a decadent slice of chocolate marquise. Artfully presented and flawlessly served, these masterpieces are complemented by an award-winning wine list, a warm fire crackling in the stone hearth, and the clear tones of a grand piano that feels like it is being played just for you.

QUAIL LODGE RESORT AND GOLF CLUB, Carmel Valley
8205 Valley Greens Drive
(408) 624-1581, (800) 538-9516
Very Expensive to Unbelievably Expensive

As you would expect, the Quail Lodge Resort and Golf Club is a resort built around an 18-hole golf course. If the two of you don't fare well on a fairway, you can dine at **THE COVEY RESTAURANT** (see Restaurant Kissing) and head for home—unless you are tempted to utilize the resort's tennis facilities, swimming pools, or jogging and hiking trails. For golf lovers, however, this 600-acre resort makes a convenient place to stay while visiting Carmel Valley.

Quail Lodge's lobby is trying to be something, but it isn't exactly clear what. Orange and brown appointments frame the handsome atrium, where a small trickling fountain is surrounded by abundant plants. Dim lighting barely illuminates the dark wood walls, which are decorated with artificial-looking artifacts.

All 100 rooms are connected by foliage-lined walkways that meander throughout the resort. Although the rooms were recently remodeled, they remain outdated, with orange and green '70s-style decor. Unattractive linens and drab artwork make the rooms tacky at best. You may be wondering if this place has any romantic attractions at all. We wondered the same thing until we saw the gas fireplaces and beautifully tiled bathrooms with soaking tubs in the newly renovated rooms. Private decks and patios with views of the lakes, gardens, or golf course are agreeable, and, if your hearts so desire, you can close off the bedroom from the sitting area to enhance intimacy. It is a mixed blessing that the rooms feel very little like standard hotel rooms, and more like those in a condominium complex.

The Executive Villa consists of one- or two-bedroom suites, each with its own private garden, hardwood hot tub, and fireplace. Although you have the luxury of more space, don't expect the decor to be any better. Also, be aware that some of the bedrooms in the Villa share central sitting areas, which may be fine for families traveling together, but not for couples.

STONEPINE, Carmel Valley
150 East Carmel Valley Road
(408) 659-2245
Unbelievably Expensive
Minimum stay requirement on weekends
Recommended Wedding Site

Lined with gnarled oaks, a mile-long access road crosses a wooden bridge over a swiftly running creek and passes corrals full of energetic horses on the way to Stonepine. As the wrought-iron reception gate swings open, a formidable French country manor covered with ivy is revealed. This aristocratic yet amorous setting is uniquely intimate. Your first kiss here is just the beginning of a magnificent weekend.

Morning light floods through a gallery of windows in the spacious foyer and living room of the main house (dubbed Chateau Noel), enhancing the subtle elegance of the damask-covered sofas and love seats. A handwoven Chinese rug, threaded with rose tones, stretches across the hardwood floor, and golden flames crackle warmly in an oversized limestone hearth. In the evening, this room is often graced by the sounds of a string ensemble.

Eight of Stonepine's 13 fashionable rooms are located in the main house. Lavish draperies, carpets, and other appointments surround guests with old-world style and modern luxury. A sexy Roman marble bath with a Jacuzzi tub and his-and-her bathrooms are enticing features of the Taittinger Suite. Revive your spirits in the Don Quixote Room, which has a king-size bed, two bathrooms, and French doors that lead to a private garden and patio. Even the petite Dong Kingman Suite is captivating, with its peaches and cream color scheme. Fireplaces and canopied beds in many of the rooms are romantic grace notes. Next door in the ranch-style Paddock House, four more suites have Jacuzzi tubs and the use of a fully equipped country kitchen. The most secluded unit of all is the self-contained two-bedroom Briar Rose Cottage, with a rustic stone fireplace and its own porch overlooking a fragrant rose garden.

Stonepine prides itself on a gracious European-trained staff that cater to your every need and desire. No matter which room you choose, you and your beloved can count on being thoroughly indulged. Afternoon tea and a complimentary gourmet breakfast are served in the lovely formal dining room, which boasts burnished oak paneling, cathedral ceilings, and an immense fireplace. A superb five-course dinner is also served here to guests only, but is not included with your stay.

Romantic Suggestion: Stonepine also runs an equestrian center, where you can saddle up two horses and explore some of the 330 prodigious acres of forest, meadow, and bridle trails. Do keep in mind, however, that the center is not exclusively for guest use.

Restaurant Kissing

THE COVEY RESTAURANT, Carmel Valley   ❧ ❧ ❧
8205 Valley Greens Drive, at the Quail Lodge Resort and Golf Club
(408) 624-1581, (800) 538-9516
Expensive
Dinner Daily
Jackets and Reservations Required

We can't think of a name more appropriate for this restaurant than The Covey. Its handsome dark wood paneling displays flocks of partridges, ducks, and other game birds painted in deep colors. A peaked ceiling overhead features heavy, exposed beams and dim track lighting. Wine cabinets hold select vintages and exotic plant arrangements add visual punctuation. Along the far wall, large windows reveal a charming pond with an illuminated fountain and arched footbridge.

The Covey's main dining room is split into two levels. Booths with colorful contemporary designs complement the larger tables of the upper level. For better views and a more intimate setting, however, request a table on the lower level, closer to the windows. Several smaller, more secluded dining areas branch off from the main room, and one even has a fireplace. Although somewhat close together, the tables are beautifully appointed with white linens, fresh flowers, and silver place settings set aglow by soft candlelight.

The excellent European cuisine here is often garnished with flavorful artichokes that are grown locally. Santa Barbara abalone, Maine lobster, and tenderloin béarnaise are but a few of the scrumptious entrées from which to choose. Before or after your meal, stop by the small adjacent lounge for a drink. A tall brick hearth decorated with stone plates overshadows a handful of tiny tables, while the grand piano in the corner soothes with its romantic melodies. You can enjoy the same wonderful view from here, although you may be too busy gazing into your sweetheart's eyes to notice.

Carmel Highlands

Located four miles south of the town of Carmel, the Highlands are the gateway to celebrated Big Sur. This region's unparalleled views of the churning Pacific Ocean thundering against craggy bluffs almost merit the exorbitant price tags on the posh, elite properties found here. If you're tempted to splurge, you couldn't pick a better place to spend your hard-earned money. The Highland's ocean views provide a visual feast to last a lifetime. And you won't have any regrets—even after the bill arrives.

Hotel/Bed and Breakfast Kissing

HIGHLANDS INN, Carmel Highlands
4 miles south of Carmel on Highway 1
(408) 624-3801, (800) 682-4811
http://www.highlands-inn.com
Very Expensive to Unbelievably Expensive
Minimum stay required on weekends

You really need to see this location to appreciate what a rare romantic treat you are in for. Views of the coastline from the Highland Inn will literally take your breath away. The unparalleled panorama takes in windswept trees, white surf breaking over outcroppings of rocks, and an occasional pod of spouting whales in the distant horizon.

All of the 142 sleek rooms here share the same explosive view. You can even glimpse the ocean from the beautifully tiled Jacuzzi spas in the suites and townhouses, enclosed behind sliding glass doors that open to the bedroom and the views beyond. Fireplaces give every room a romantic glow, and upscale modern furnishings create a comfortable, relaxing atmosphere. The townhouse-style apartments have the added convenience of a full kitchen, and most of the rooms have televisions and VCRs. Outside, a sloping staircase winds past cypress trees and gardens to an outdoor heated pool surrounded by patio furniture and umbrella-shaded tables. From start to finish, everything here is very first-class, very California, and very romantic.

TICKLE PINK INN, Carmel Highlands
155 Highland Drive
(408) 624-1244, (800) 635-4774
Very Expensive to Unbelievably Expensive
Minimum stay requirement on weekends

With a name like Tickle Pink Inn, it's hard to envision that this could be anything more than a tacky pink eyesore. Forget the name—there is nothing tacky or pink in sight. Perched atop rugged shoreline cliffs, Tickle Pink (it's actually a light beige) overlooks endless miles of the Pacific coast. All but one of the 36 rooms share this colossal view. Although some of the lower-priced rooms have cheap-looking linens and appointments, you won't be disappointed with any of the newly renovated mini-suites. River-rock fireplaces and wrought-iron beds draped with twists of fabric are lovely romantic elements. Five rooms even have pretty green-tiled bathrooms with luxurious Jacuzzi tubs. Blonde wood furnishings, pretty floral bedspreads, and private decks are equally inspiring. A separate stone cottage ensconced lower on the hillside offers the most seclusion.

Complimentary fruit, wines, breads, and cheeses are served every evening on the glass-enclosed wood patio overlooking the crashing waves. When the winds are blowing, guests can congregate in the plush fireside lobby furnished with comfy, overstuffed sofas. Continental breakfast is also served here, unless you ask to have it delivered to your room.

Restaurant Kissing

PACIFIC'S EDGE, Carmel Highlands
Four miles south of Carmel on Highway 1
(408) 624-3801
Very Expensive
Lunch and Dinner Daily
Recommended Wedding Site

The glass-enclosed views of the untamed ocean from Pacific Edge's formal dining room alone are worth the price of dinner here. Every single table has a glimpse or more of the ocean through expansive floor-to-ceiling windows that front one side of the restaurant. Even if you opt for drinks alone, the contemporary fireside lobby is just as wonderful a place to watch the sunset, when the sky explodes in a riot of intoxicating, evocative colors.

Blonde wood and stone accents lend natural elegance to the airy, spacious dining room. The ever-changing menu is as irresistibly sensuous as the views and sure to inspire some passionate kisses. We enjoyed an appetizer of caramelized sea scallops with white corn and English peas, followed by Yukon gold potato and roasted garlic soup, with an outrageously delicious springroll of local field mushrooms with vegetable fricassee for a main course. It's doubtful you'll have much room for dessert, but can you really resist a chocolate tart with sautéed bananas in a crispy phyllo shell? Out of this world!

Big Sur

Big Sur is only about 30 miles or 45 minutes from the packed streets of Carmel, but it seems worlds apart. This coastal town spreads out over a portion of Highway 1 and has become well known for its New Age attitude, laid-back atmosphere, and, most recently, for the highly acclaimed, upscale establishments along its coastline. The dramatic cliffs, aquamarine waters, and breathtaking vistas of this area have inspired people to slow down and get in touch with the natural beauty around them—and such a setting demands a premium price.

Hotel/Bed and Breakfast Kissing

POST RANCH INN, Big Sur   💋 💋 💋 💋
Highway 1
(408) 667-2200, (800) 527-2200
Unbelievably Expensive
Minimum stay requirement on weekends

Environment-conscious design meets exclusive luxury at Post Ranch Inn, set high atop the coastal cliffs of Big Sur. The unusual glass-and-wood units discreetly blend into their spectacular surroundings: California redwoods and oaks, dramatic sea cliffs, crashing waves, and rolling mountains. Given this prime location, the upscale atmosphere, and the amenities of a full-service resort, it is not surprising that this relatively new inn has become a choice destination.

The inn's 30 rooms are spread across the cliffside acreage. Setting and layout vary, but like the exterior, the interiors are stylish but subtle, incorporating natural wood and stone. Huge picture windows allow the encompassing natural beauty to pour in from every angle, and each room has its own terrace, king-size bed with recycled denim duvet, cushioned wicker chairs, wood-burning fireplace, slate-tiled bathroom with large indoor spa tub, stereo system, and pull-out massage table for in-room treatments. A small refrigerator is stocked with complimentary healthy snacks and nonalcoholic beverages, and a lavish continental breakfast is presented in **SIERRA MAR**, the inn's restaurant (see Restaurant Kissing).

Ocean House units are built into the side of the ocean bluff and have curved- beam sod roofs where grass and wildflowers grow. Prices for these rooms go far beyond Unbelievably Expensive, but the ocean views from the bed, bath, window seat, and terrace are absolutely mesmerizing. Another place to savor the view is the heated cliffside pool, where water seems to overflow into the ocean below.

It will cost you to stay here, as the management makes very clear. A sign at the bottom of the driveway posts the Unbelievably Expensive rates and states that the restaurant is "by reservation only." This keeps out the general public, but if you aren't expecting such exclusivity, it could be interpreted as unwelcoming.

VENTANA, Big Sur
Highway 1
(408) 667-2331, (408) 624-4812, (800) 628-6500
Very Expensive to Unbelievably Expensive
Minimum stay requirement on weekends

The unspoiled Santa Lucia Mountains seem to tumble directly into the sea; these rocky slopes and jagged outcroppings abut Big Sur's astonishing coastline. Ventana, set on 253 acres of forested mountainside, has a ringside view of all this, and its amenities will satisfy every other need you might have for a sultry weekend away, far removed from anything that vaguely resembles the pressures of the real world. Stimulate or soothe your senses in two heated pools, Japanese hot baths, a sauna, and a Jacuzzi tub, then don a fluffy robe and retreat to your room for the rustic elegance Ventana has become famous for. All 62 guest rooms have roaring wood-burning fireplaces, vaulted ceilings, all-wood interiors, pine furnishings with pastel accents, and private patios facing either the forest and towering mountains or the endless ocean in the distance. Everything is designed to direct your interests to romantic interactions.

In the afternoon, wine and cheese are offered in the lobby. A continental breakfast buffet is also presented here in the morning, but late-risers will appreciate that breakfast can be delivered to their room for no additional charge. For extra diversion, consider treating yourselves to an in-room spa treatment or venturing to the clothing-optional sundeck. The feelings that will fill your souls during your stay in Big Sur may surpass every expectation.

Restaurant Kissing

GLEN OAKS RESTAURANT, Big Sur
Highway 1
(408) 667-2264
Moderate to Expensive
Dinner Wednesday-Monday

Glen Oaks Restaurant may not have Ventana's view, Nepenthe's star-studded past, or Sierra Mar's super-chic interior, but what it lacks in glamour it makes up for in charisma. Gourmet international cuisine, a charming cabin-style exterior, and an intimate candlelit interior resplendent with peach walls, modern artwork, and a corner fireplace, make Glen Oaks a location ripe for kissing. Gauze curtains shield any distractions from Highway 1, service is friendly, and the food hearty and delicious. Barbecued pork wrapped in rice paper and served with Thai dipping sauce is an appetizing starter. Our only complaint after the chicken Marsala was that we had no room left for dessert.

NEPENTHE, Big Sur
Highway 1
(408) 667-2345
Expensive
Dinner Daily

Nepenthe is hardly a secret—you may even call it a landmark or tourist attraction of sorts. Interesting Zen-inspired sculptures cover the expansive landscaped grounds, a gift shop sells an array of earth-friendly mementos, and wind chimes play a soft melody in the breeze. At the top of an outdoor staircase, a massive redwood carving of a phoenix marks the entry to the famous restaurant. A student of Frank Lloyd Wright designed the building, and the fact that this was the honeymoon cottage of Rita Hayworth and Orson Welles adds to the mystique. Inside, the atmosphere is very relaxed and earthy, the menu typical, the food all right, and service just OK. What makes it a suitable kissing location? How about its perch on a cliff 800 feet above the Big Sur shoreline? This feature alone is enough to make an otherwise ordinary meal here a rapturous adventure.

Sunset is the best time to visit Nepenthe for a snack or drinks. As the sun begins to settle into the ocean, its light penetrates the drifting clouds with a pale lavender-blue haze. Suddenly these dusky colors shift to an intense golden amber, culminating in a deep red that sets the sky afire. As night makes its entrance, the clouds fade to steel blue and the sky turns from cobalt to indigo. "Awesome" is the only possible word for this celestial transformation. Window seats are perfectly arranged to take advantage of the view, and outdoor seating is equally good. Weather permitting, this show is performed nightly along the coastline, and Nepenthe (a Greek word for a potion that eases or obliterates grief and pain) has some of the best seats in the house.

Romantic Note: If outside dining appeals to you, **CAFÉ KEVAH**, (408) 667-2344 (Inexpensive to Moderate), set one level lower than Nepenthe, is another option. Brunch is served at a walk-up order counter, and colorful umbrella-shaded tables are set on a spacious patio overlooking the Big Sur coast.

SIERRA MAR, Big Sur
Highway 1, at Post Ranch Inn
(408) 667-2200
Very Expensive to Unbelievably Expensive
Reservations Required
Dinner Daily

A long outdoor staircase leads to Sierra Mar, the restaurant at the exclusive Post Ranch Inn (see Hotel/Bed and Breakfast Kissing). If you arrive after dark the walk may be challenging, since the stars and moon above you are the only illumination augmenting the dim lighting on the stairs. But if you are careful, the walk could set an intriguing tone for the night ahead. On the other hand, if you come after dark you will miss a chance to watch sunset from what is possibly the best vantage point on the coast.

Perched on an ocean cliff with banks of floor-to-ceiling windows facing the Pacific, this avant-garde restaurant has a breathtaking view, ultra-stylish decor, and fantastic food. Stone floors, peeled log beams, and art deco chairs add to a sophisticated, modern atmosphere. Candles set in stones and exotic little floral arrangements are placed at every table, while suspended track lighting and sculpted torchieres impart a warm glow.

Elegantly prepared California cuisine with an Asian influence is served in a four-course, prix-fixe format, but à la carte items are also available. You might try a savory starter of grilled quail with tortilla salad and mango salsa, followed by curried split pea soup. Entrée choices range from hoisin barbecued wild boar to pan-roasted halibut or grilled swordfish with saffron couscous and black mussels. Desserts are also presented beautifully, from fruit gazpacho with assorted sorbets to almond-hazelnut parfait dunked in coffee sauce. If the sun is still above the horizon when you are done, linger over a cappuccino or an after-dinner drink—this is truly one of the most spectacular places to watch the sun dramatically sinking into the sea, and you do not want to miss it.

VENTANA RESTAURANT, Big Sur
Highway 1
(408) 667-2331, (800) 628-6500
Expensive to Very Expensive
Lunch and Dinner Daily

Overnight guests of Ventana (see Hotel/Bed and Breakfast Kissing) can stroll along a wilderness path that leads to the inn's elegantly rustic restaurant. The walk, accompanied by the sounds of singing birds and rustling leaves as you pass through rolling meadows and massive oak groves, is an engaging prelude to dinner. It takes only about ten minutes, but slow down and savor the quiet: Ventana inspires a sense of tranquility that truly can "nourish your spirit," as the brochure claims.

The natural materials found in the inn also adorn the restaurant, which features beautifully stained wood, from the high open-beamed ceiling down to the hardwood floor. A cozy bar area sits off to one side of the restaurant, and expansive windows face an outdoor terrace and the beauty of nature all around. White linens, single roses, and little candle lanterns at each table add romantic flair, but when the restaurant is full (a regular event on summer weekends), the tables are a little too close to one another for comfort. If the weather allows, less-crowded seating and spectacular Pacific Ocean views can be found on the fireside terrace fronting the restaurant. It doesn't get much better than this—in terms of both the view and the cuisine.

Fresh regional ingredients are featured on the international, French-Asian menu. Chestnut-crusted ahi tuna in a citrus-chile sauce, Petaluma chicken breast stuffed with garlic-herb croutons, and potato-wrapped Sonoma quail are just a few of the interesting main courses. Desserts such as toasted vanilla crème brûlée or a crêpe filled with poached pear and topped with Belgian chocolate sauce and whipped cream are as delectable and beautifully presented as one can imagine. Exemplary service enhances the flawless meal, and if you are a guest at the inn, the quiet walk back to your room on the well-lit path is an affectionate finale to the day.

Romantic Suggestion: If you have the time and the inclination, the wooded path to the restaurant is also open to dinner guests who park at the inn but are not necessarily spending the night there. Consider stopping at the front desk to ask for directions, and enjoy this little nature trek.

Outdoor Kissing

BIG SUR COASTLINE

Along Highway 1, about 150 miles south of San Francisco and approximately 30 miles south of Carmel.

The drive from Carmel to Big Sur provides unsurpassed scenery in which to lose yourselves in an afternoon together. The road along this rugged, arduous coastline offers some of the most glorious, breathtaking views you may ever see. We almost guarantee that once you've passed through Big Sur, its potent impact will be felt in your lives for years to come—it is that compelling. Take it slow through here: an experience of this magnitude should be approached with patient appreciation and reverent awe. Besides, there is no real destination to head for, because there isn't an actual town of

Big Sur. According to the signs, though, Big Sur stretches for about six miles along Highway 1 and then continues south for more of the same impeccable scenery.

What makes all this such a heartthrob? The road penetrates a precariously severe landscape, literally snaking its way along the unblemished shoreline. Beneath you, the relentless surf pounds the jagged outcroppings along the water's edge as nature continues to refine her sculpted masterpiece. Isolated beaches and secluded spots in the wilderness nearby provide momentary respite from the road for those who want to stop for private showcase views. Hard as it is to believe, each mile seems more remarkable and intoxicating than the one before. Every moment you share here will be as seductive and as passionate as the first.

Romantic Suggestion: Do not confuse **JULIA PFEIFFER BURNS STATE PARK** with Pfeiffer Big Sur State Park; Julia is 11 miles south of the other, but it offers what feels like 100 miles more privacy and landscape. Pfeiffer Big Sur State Park is exceedingly popular and disappointingly developed. Julia Pfeiffer Burns State Park, on the other hand, is 2,000 acres of prime hiking territory in nature's virgin wonderland. Enchanting waterfalls, sequestered beaches, and spellbinding views are scattered along the way.

In the same vicinity, **PFEIFFER BEACH** (just off Highway 1 on Sycamore Canyon Road) is an exhilarating seascape crowded with massive, eroded outcroppings and haystack rocks that are approachable during low tide. Watching the sunset from this vantage point could be a life-altering proposition (or could inspire one), it is that beautiful.

Index